DATE DUE

NOV 1 3 2001 KR		

RADS

RADS

The 1970 Bombing of the
Army Math Research Center
at the University of Wisconsin
and Its Aftermath

TOM BATES

HarperCollins*Publishers*

HarperCollins books may be purchased for educational, business, or sales promotional use. For information, please write: Special Markets Department, HarperCollins Publishers, Inc., 10 East 53rd Street, New York, NY 10022.

FIRST EDITION

Designed by Jessica Shatan
Map by Paul Pugliese

Library of Congress Cataloging-in-Publication Data
Bates, Tom.
    Rads: the 1970 bombing of the Army Math Research Center at the University of Wisconsin and its aftermath / Tom Bates.—1st ed.
        p.   cm.
    Includes index.
    ISBN 0-06-016754-8 (cloth)
    1. Bombings—Wisconsin—Madison—Case studies. 2. Vietnamese Conflict, 1961–1974—Protest Movements—Wisconsin—Madison. 3. Mathematics Research Center (United States Army). 4. Fassnacht, Robert, d1970. 5. Armstrong, Karleton Lewis. 6. University of Wisconsin—Madison—Students—Crimes against—Case studies. I. Title.
HV6432.B38   1992
364. 1'64—dc20   91-59935

---

92 93 94 95 96 ❖/HC 10 9 8 7 6 5 4 3 2 1

FOR ELOISE

WHO HELD MY HAND

IN THE STREETS OF MIFFLAND

IN MEMORY OF

ROBERT FASSNACHT

Contents

IV THE EVE OF DESTRUCTION

V OUTLAWS OF AMERIKA

VI JUSTICE

Illustrations follow page 264.

Acknowledgments

First, the Armstrongs—Karl, Dwight, Mira, and Lorene. Their honesty made this book possible. David Fine also told me much that was useful, as did Leo Burt's former crewmates Tim Mickelson and Phil Resch, his coach Randall Jablonic, and his friends Jane Adamson, George Bogdanich, and Gary Dretzka.

Among the dozens of former movement heavies who recounted their war stories for my benefit, I am especially grateful to Phil Ball for his marvelous anecdotes and to Mike Felner for permission to view the FBI reports on Madison activists obtained under the Freedom of Information Act and now in the Social Action Collection of the Wisconsin State Historical Society.

The *Daily Cardinal* alumni of the late sixties were very helpful, particularly Peter Greenberg, who encouraged me to undertake this project, and Patrick McGilligan, whose own research on the Army Math bombing helped me to get started and who was my harshest critic as the work progressed. David Newman, a former member of the Armstrong defense committee, shared his files and thoughts on the question of government foreknowledge.

Of the university administrators of the day, Fred Harvey Harrington was exceptionally forthcoming. Annetta Rosser, wife of AMRC director J. Barkley Rosser, Sr., provided helpful background on her late husband.

Among the lawmen who worked the protest scene from the other side, most now retired and able to review their careers with a modicum of detachment, I received valuable assistance from George Baxtrum, Tom McMillen, Joe Sullivan, George Croal, Herman Thomas, Tom Kretschman, Charles Lulling, and Frank Roberts, along with their former informants Mark Baganz and Julie Maynard.

Of Karl Armstrong's defenders, I owe special thanks to Toronto attorneys Bobby Kellerman and Paul Copeland; of his prosecutors, to Mike Zaleski.

Michael Bemis, law librarian for the Wisconsin Department of

Justice; Frank Cook, director of the University of Wisconsin Archives; Jerry Ham, former director of the State Historical Society; Laura Smail, director of the Wisconsin Oral History Project; Mickey Kienitz of the University of Wisconsin News Service; David Hartsell of the FOIA Section of the Federal Bureau of Investigation in Washington, D.C.; Glen Silber, producer of *The War at Home;* and the Weather Bureau of the U.S. Department of Commerce provided access to essential photographic, printed, and audio-visual sources. Jeff and Roberta Wilkes, Dennis Blumer, Walter Ezell, Patrick McGilligan, John Schweitzer, Sister Dorothy Schweitzer, David Kelly, William Boly, John Strawn, Aldo Marchini, and Mark Christensen provided helpful comment in the manuscript stage.

Thanks finally to my agent, Richard Pine, for getting me an advance; to HarperCollins and my editor, Rick Kot, for financial support, advice, and patience; to my former graduate school adviser, Professor Edward Gargan, for a sense of the human in history; to my father-in-law, Dr. Paul Schweitzer, for his unfailing enthusiasm and expert advice on English usage; to my research assistant, Tamara Mehuran; to my friends in the Portland writing community; and most of all to Eloise, Melody, Alex, and Johnny, who stayed with me at the bottom of the mineshaft for five difficult years.

Introduction

In the spring of 1987 I was having a drink with Peter Greenberg, a freelance writer and television producer, at a bar called the Redwood Room, a few blocks from Times Mirror Square in downtown Los Angeles. At the time, I was an editor at *Los Angeles Times Magazine,* and Greenberg had offered to sell the publication an interview with Imelda Marcos. We were talking shop when somehow the subject of Madison came up. As it turned out, we had both been students at the University of Wisconsin during the sixties and shared memories of that turbulent campus. Greenberg had worked for the student newspaper, the *Daily Cardinal,* during academic year 1969–70, when a group called the New Year's Gang had terrorized the city with repeated firebombings and threats and had, late in the summer, carried out the devastating bombing of the Army Mathematics Research Center. Greenberg added that he had been personally acquainted with David Fine and Leo Burt, two *Daily Cardinal* reporters named as co-conspirators in the Army Math plot.

Much of what Greenberg had to say about the New Year's Gang was new to me, because I had been in Rome researching a dissertation that year and, of stateside goings-on, knew only what I read in the *International Herald-Tribune.* When I got back to Madison in September 1970, it was immediately apparent that a terrible cataclysm had occurred. Much of the campus was boarded up, and students were calling it "Old Plywood U." A sign scrawled on the side of Sterling Hall, in which Army Math had been located, observed that "Chicken Little was right." The physical damage to the university was frightful, but even more sobering was the news that a brilliant young physicist who had nothing to do with the Pentagon-funded think tank had been killed in the explosion. For the Madison Left, with which I identified, it really was as though the sky had fallen.

Army Math was a turning point, I and my affable drinking companion agreed; the thing that amazed us was that no one had ever written a book about it. "Why don't you do it?" I said to Greenberg. He replied, "Why don't you?"

Five years have passed since my conversation with Peter Greenberg. It has taken me as long to write the story of Madison in the late sixties as it did to live it. While I was at work on the book, the historic era in which it is set came to an end. My eldest child earned a high school diploma and entered college. I entered decisively into middle age. With teenage sons of my own, with drug problems in the public schools, with AIDS raging across the planet, with property crime out of control, with living not nearly as easy as it once was for young Americans, it became impossible for me to view the historical data before me with the sanguinity I might have twenty years ago. The political utopianism, drug experimentation, and sexual license that I and my contemporaries had innocently associated with liberation looked completely different to me now that I could see it from the perspective of a parent, in the context of the wider community, and in full knowledge of consequences. Seen on yellowed pages of underground newspapers two decades old, the radical rhetoric that had fallen so easily from my own lips now seemed dangerously puerile. And so, because my heart remains with those who tried to stop the war in Vietnam, the book was very hard to write.

Many of the riotous events described in these pages are scenes personally witnessed, Dow Day, the Black Strike, and the Mifflin Street block party among them. As a graduate student in European history, I took courses from both Harvey Goldberg and George Mosse, and it is from firsthand knowledge that I write of the impact of their informal debate on Wisconsin students. As for myself, Goldberg was the greater influence at the time; I remember taking part in the standing, foot-stomping ovation for him when he concluded his lectures on Contemporary Societies with the cry, "The truth is radical!" Mosse, the great believer in reason, received only tepid applause when he summed up his course on European culture with the words, "Reality is a matter of degree."

For years I had no idea what Mosse was talking about. In fact, it was only as I sank deeper into the murky depths of Madison in the sixties, as I came face to face with the mutual ignorance and unreasoning hostility of the antagonists, as I got to know the sedition men and informants who had haunted the movement, as the self-defeating tactics of both militants and authorities became inescapably obvious, and as I saw beneath the defense committee's propaganda about the Armstrong family, that I began to appreciate the heuristic value of Professor Mosse's conclusion. To believe that the truth is radical is to presume an absolutely knowable reality. The bombers of Army Math believed they were in possession of such a truth. They were not. None of us was. We should have listened to Mosse.

Tom Bates
Portland, Oregon
1992

Cast of Characters

THE ARMSTRONGS
Karl: The eldest son and leader of the New Year's Gang
Dwight: Karl's younger brother and comrade-in-arms
Mira and Lorene: Respectively, Karl's older and younger sisters
Don and Ruth: Karl's parents
Paul: Karl's uncle in Minneapolis
Vance: Paul's son, a first cousin to Karl and Dwight
Alvah: Karl's grandfather
Ann Rector: Karl's great-grandmother

FAMILY FRIENDS AND ACQUAINTANCES
Scott Nelson: Karl's roommate at Phi Sigma Kappa
Lynn Schultz: Karl's girlfriend and sometime driver
Policronio De Venecia: Dwight's fraternity pal
Pastor Kenneth Hoffman: Lutheran minister and suicide interventionist
Reverend Sam Hunt: Mira's spiritual adviser
Max Sliter and Jeff Shearer: Housemates of Uncle Paul
Gino Gargano: Restaurateur who employs Karl
Field Morey: Airport operator who employs Dwight

THE YOUNG JOURNALISTS
Leo Burt: Daily Cardinal senior reporter recruited by the New Year's Gang
David Fine: Daily Cardinal freshman reporter; invited into the New Year's Gang by Leo Burt
Steve Reiner: Daily Cardinal editor and participant in Leo's drinking circle, the "Male Chauvinist Pigs"
Jim Rowen: Daily Cardinal reporter and antiwar activist who exposes classified work of Army Math
Rena Steinzor: Daily Cardinal news editor and a leader of the left-wing faction of the paper
Mark Knops: Editor of the underground newspaper *Madison Kaleidoscope* and a strong supporter of the New Year's Gang

THE COPS

Special Agent George Baxtrum: Madison FBI's top sedition man

Special Agent Tom McMillen: Baxtrum's understudy; handles New Left files

Inspector Joe Sullivan: Heads WISBOM investigation for FBI

Detective George Croal, aka "Chester White": Trains "counter-affinity squads" for Madison Police Department

Detective Charles Lulling: The MPD's senior homicide investigator

Sheriff Jack Leslie: Lulling associate and head of Dane County Sheriff's Department

Chief Ralph Hanson: Heads University Protection and Security

THE INFORMANTS

Mark Baganz, aka "Duroc": Infiltrates campus Left for MPD and FBI

Julie Maynard, aka "Fat Julie": Works for MPD, FBI, and CIA

Peter Obranovich, aka "Pete Bobo": Rock concert promoter; pursues fugitives in Canada for FBI

Sandy Nelson: Bobo's sidekick; befriends Karl Armstrong's ex, Lynn Schultz

THE PROSECUTORS

James Boll: Dane County District Attorney at time of Army Math bombing

Gerald "Buzz" Nichol: Dane County D.A. involved in extraditing Armstrong

H. J. Lynch: Dane County D.A. at time of Armstrong sentencing

David Mebane: Wisconsin Justice Department official who leads state effort to bring Armstrong to trial

Michael Zaleski and Douglas Haag: Wisconsin assistant attorney generals assigned to prosecute Karl Armstrong

Robert Warren: State Attorney General at time of bombings

John Olson: U.S. Attorney in Madison caught in professional rivalry with Warren

Guy Goodwin, Joe Tafe, and Robert Mardian: U.S. Justice Department officials working WISBOM case

Austin Cooper: Toronto attorney hired to represent the State of Wisconsin in extradition battle

THE JUDICIARY

Harry Waisberg: Toronto judge who presides over Karl Armstrong's extradition hearing

William Sachtjen: Wisconsin Circuit Court judge and former friend of Ruth Armstrong's called upon to pass sentence on her son

THE DEFENSE TEAM

Clayton Ruby, Paul Copeland, and Bobby Kellerman: Karl Armstrong's defenders in extradition battle

William Kunstler, Leonard Weinglass, and Melvin Greenberg: Attorneys representing Karl Armstrong in Madison

THE ACADEMICIANS

Fred Harvey Harrington: Diplomatic historian and president of the University of Wisconsin

Harvey Goldberg: Social historian and pied piper of the Madison Left

George Mosse: Cultural historian and defender of liberal values

William Appleman Williams: Harrington's prize student and a leading critic of the war in Vietnam

Edwin Young: Labor relations expert and chancellor of the University of Wisconsin

J. Barkley Rosser, Sr.: Director of the Army Mathematics Research Center and a pioneer of the computer revolution

Heinz Barschall: Nuclear physicist and Manhattan Project veteran whose life's work is wiped out in Sterling Hall blast

Robert Fassnacht: Low-temperature physicist killed in Sterling Hall bombing

Joe Dillinger: Fassnacht's faculty advisor

CANADIAN FRIENDS AND SUPPORTERS

Bernard Mergler: Montreal lawyer who finds housing for the Armstrongs

*Tom Lance: American Deserters Committee activist who supplies money to the Armstrongs in Montreal

Naomi Wall: Toronto antidraft activist who later marries Karl

*Jerardine McLoughlin: Canadian model and actress who hitches west with Dwight

Robert Rainbolt: Toronto expatriate who turns Karl in and collects reward

*Pseudonyms. The names Mahfood, Patrolman Dan, Teri Simon, Ann Mickola, Barry Friedman, Mrs. Connelly, Mark Conkle, Arden, Frank Slaughter, David Knauss, Diana Palafox, Cherri Lamkin, Saxum, Susan Baldie, Weinberg, Jolinda Orr, John Rancore, Jay Griss, Felix Detweiler, and Jane Adamson have also been changed.

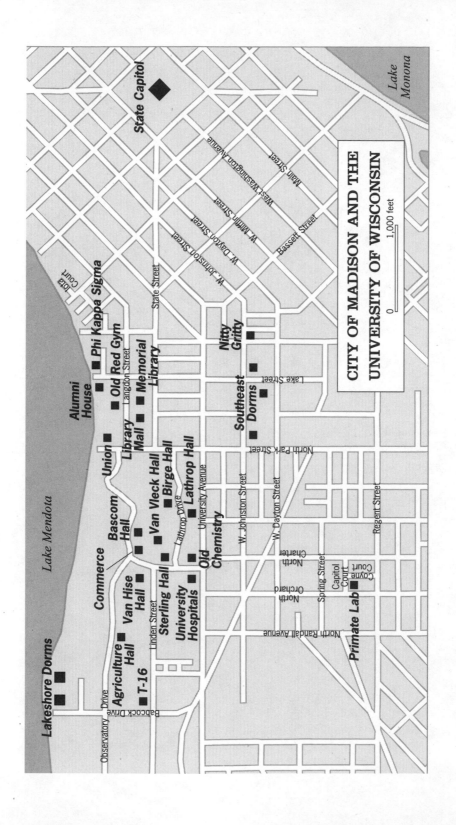

CITY OF MADISON AND THE UNIVERSITY OF WISCONSIN

0   1,000 feet

Lake Mendota

Lake Monona

State Capitol

Lakeshore Dorms

Observatory Drive

Babcock Drive

Agriculture Hall

Van Hise Hall

T-16

Linden Street

Commerce

Sterling Hall

University Hospitals

Bascom Hall

Union

Library Mall

Van Vleck Hall

Birge Hall

Lathrop Hall

Lathrop Drive

University Avenue

Old Chemistry

North Orchard

Spring Street

Capitol Court

Coyne Court

Primate Lab

North Charter

W. Dayton Street

W. Johnston Street

North Park Street

North Randall Avenue

Regent Street

Alumni House

Phi Kappa Sigma

Old Red Gym

Langdon Street

Memorial Library

Iota Court

State Street

Nitty Gritty

Southeast Dorms

Lake Street

W. Johnston Street

W. Dayton Street

W. Mifflin Street

West Washington Avenue

Main Street

Bassett Street

Bassett Street

We cannot believe that knowledge has reached its final goal, or that the present condition of society is perfect. In all lines of academic investigation it is of the utmost importance that the investigator should be absolutely free to follow the indications of truth wherever they may lead. We believe the great state University of Wisconsin should ever encourage that continual and fearless sifting and winnowing by which alone the truth can be found.

—UNIVERSITY OF WISCONSIN BOARD OF REGENTS, 1894

Part I

ALL FALL DOWN

1

Fassnacht

*There is no such thing as Army Math, any more than there is
Jewish Math or English Math or German Math.*

—R. CREIGHTON BUCK,
mathematician, for the prosecution

*The truth is, the AMRC did function as a deliberate and
planned intrusion of the military mentality into the life of the
University of Wisconsin.*

—HUGH ILTIS,
botanist, for the defense

On the day that he would die, Bob Fassnacht was working on the
secret of superconductivity, a fascinating subatomic phenomenon with immense practical possibilities. "Fass," as he was
known around the University of Wisconsin Physics Department, a
thirty-three-year-old postdoctoral researcher, was obsessed by
those possibilities. Once the technology was perfected, he imagined,
transmission lines between power plants and cities hundreds of
miles away could be made 100 percent efficient, with tremendous
energy savings. Pollution-free electromagnetic engines might power
a ship through the sea—or through space. High-speed trains, riding

on a cushion of magnetism, could shorten the travel time between cities. That superconductive properties existed in certain metals at temperatures near absolute zero had been known for decades, but no one had ever found a way to exploit them. The University of Chicago, with its large, well-funded low temperature research program, was the acknowledged leader in the field, but Fass had been making steady progress on his own. In fact, he had a surprise in store for his competitors.

It was Sunday, August 23, 1970. After ten years of repeated failures, of tinkering with his refrigeration system and refining his isotopes of aluminum and zinc, Fassnacht was close to a breakthrough, he thought. On Friday Lloyd Ochalla, a Physics Department machinist, had finished building the small part he needed for his supercooling apparatus, and on Saturday Fass had started bringing down the temperature in the dewer, a six-foot liquid nitrogen thermos buried in the concrete floor of his Sterling Hall laboratory. The process took forty-eight hours or so, and on Sunday he was in and out all day. The fact that it was a weekend and that school was out of session meant nothing to him. He was a scientist closing in on a discovery, fundamental knowledge that he believed could change the world for all time to come. His colleagues were excited about his progress; one asked Fass to write his results on a blackboard before he left that night. And so Bob Fassnacht wasn't pacing himself that weekend; he was going for it.

His wife Stephanie was understanding about his long hours. Like her husband, she came from a family of scientists, and until the children arrived, had been pursuing a career in physics herself. Now she was home much of the time with their three-year-old son Chris and twin daughters, Heidi and Karin, just a year old. She and Bob couldn't both be gone all night.

The University of Wisconsin is situated on the southern shore of Lake Mendota, the largest of several watery expanses, leftovers from the last Ice Age, that fall within the boundaries of Madison. At the heart of the campus is a low hill named for John Bascom, president of the university in the 1870s. A palatial building, constructed of the ocher-colored sandstone typical of the region, and also named for Bascom, stands at the top of the hill, set off by a broad expanse of lawn and steep, elm-lined esplanades. Other fine examples of nineteenth-century architecture grace the flanks of the

promontory. At the foot of the hill, on its east side, is the Library
Mall, and next to it, the Memorial Student Union, a tile-roofed Ital-
ianate building that commands the waterfront like a grand old Riviera hotel. Stone-walled dormitories follow the curving shore to
Picnic Point. It is one of the most beautiful campuses in the world.

Sterling Hall could not have been more centrally located on the
sprawling, Big Ten campus. A yellow brick building in the stately
High Renaissance style favored by turn-of-the-century architects, it
faces Charter Street on the back of the hill, crowded in upon by
other large buildings: Old Chemistry, Lathrop, Birge, Commerce,
Van Vleck, and Old McArdle, in which a wing of University Hospital was then housed. Catercorner, at the intersection of Charter and
Linden, stands Van Hise, a skyscraper with the offices of the president and Board of Regents on its upper floors. Even on a Sunday
night in the midst of the semester break, Sterling Hall was busy.
Graduate students and "postdocs," drones of the scientific revolution, tended their experiments, searching for the new theorem or
counterexample that would make their careers. Much of the activity was concentrated in the newer East Wing, built in the late 1950s
specifically to house the Army Mathematics Research Center
(AMRC), a Department of Defense plum that Wisconsin had won
in competition with forty-four other universities. "Army Math," as
everyone called it, had its offices on the second, third, and fourth
floors of the six-story addition. The Astronomy Department had
been given the fifth and sixth floors, with an observatory on the
roof. The basement and first floor had been consumed by the
expanding Physics Department.

Fassnacht's lab was at midcorridor on the basement level. At the
end of the hall was a vault housing an atom smasher. Except for
Thanksgiving, Christmas, and New Year's Day, the accelerator was
manned seven days a week, twenty-four hours a day, year round.

Army Math's offices were dark that evening, locked tight. On the
sixth floor, a Ph.D. candidate in astronomy, Michael Molnar, was
putting the finishing touches on a dissertation about star spectra.
He departed sometime after midnight, leaving the manuscript on
his desk.

By 3 A.M. only the most dedicated or driven remained. Paul
Quin, a postdoc in nuclear physics, was processing data in the computer room. David Schuster, a South African doctoral student, and
a technician named Roger Whitmer alternated between the polar-

ized ion lab and the vault, conducting a neutron-scattering experiment. Another graduate student, William Evans, pursued his research in the basement of the old wing.

Until recently, Fassnacht had enjoyed Sterling Hall at night. There was more camaraderie than one experienced in the daytime. But for the past several months, he had been worried about security. Certain revelations about military research at AMRC had made the building the focal point of antiwar protests, and the demonstrators often seemed unaware that Army Math was only one of Sterling's several tenants. Fassnacht's windows had been broken several times that spring. He had stood tables on end to shield his equipment from rocks and eventually had the window glass replaced with Lexan, an unbreakable plastic. Someone in the department had put up a sign outside: THIS IS PHYSICS. AMRC IS UPSTAIRS. J. Barkley Rosser, Sr., director of the AMRC, had insisted that the sign be taken down.

Norbert Sutter was a man who knew how to do a route, and he didn't mind saying so. The stocky, stolid security guard had been making his nightly rounds for twenty-three years, lugging his big key chain from door to door, shining his flashlight into dark recesses, listening for unfamiliar noises, sniffing the air. He took pride in the uniform and in the badge of his employer, University Protection and Security (UP & S). He carried no weapon, but when the department had issued him a two-way radio some years earlier, he felt like he had been given a partner on his route. Now he checked in every hour or so with the dispatcher on the security channel.

"Sutter here, all clear, over and out," was all he had to say, usually.

A wave of arson that hit the campus at the beginning of the year had only made the job more interesting, as far as Sutter was concerned. It was he who had reported the fire in the Old Red Gym, where ROTC was headquartered, in early January. "I saved that building from burning down," he told his wife.

Sutter had a big route that Sunday evening—Birge, Bascom, North Hall, Commerce, Old Chemistry, and the Music Hall, along with Sterling. He'd already completed two circuits and was on his third swing through Sterling, around 3:40 A.M., when he saw the light on in Fassnacht's lab. The door was open, and Sutter walked in. Fassnacht was at his desk making notes.

"Be sure to close off the lights and equipment when you leave, Doctor Fassnacht," the watchman said.

"Yeah, I'll do it," Fass answered absentmindedly.

Sutter continued to the end of the hall, punched the call button on the elevator, and waited. Everything seemed normal; he hadn't noticed the white van parked on the loading ramp outside Fassnacht's window.

A moment later, Fassnacht suddenly rose from his desk and stepped into the hall. Had he seen the van? A delivery to the Physics Department that late at night would have been unusual, and he may have been going to ask Sutter to check it out.

He didn't get the chance.

The East Wing of Sterling Hall fronts on Lathrop Drive, a narrow blacktop lane snaking around the south side of Bascom Hill. The loading ramp in question sloped below the level of the drive to a large service door in the vault. A concrete retaining wall, reaching a height of twelve feet or so, bordered the ramp on the outside, next to the roadbed. It was there, halfway down, that the white van was parked, its side and rear windows blacked out. Jack Schwichtenberg had cruised Lathrop Drive in his unmarked squad car around 3:35 A.M., alert as always for any sign of trouble. The van may have been below his level of vision, concealed by the retaining wall; in any case, he didn't notice it. He continued east, two long blocks to Lake Street, where he parked across from Burgerville, his car pointed at University Avenue, the main drag through campus. The thirty-year-old cop was employed by the protection side of UP & S; he was the senior man on the night shift. The action on the shift was usually over by 2 A.M., but that night there had been none. Schwichtenberg rolled down his window and inhaled the dank night air. The campus was quiet. A muffled screech of tires in the vicinity of the YMCA a few blocks west failed to catch his attention. In a university town like Madison, the sound of a car peeling out was of no special interest.

It was 3:41 A.M. when his dispatcher called to inform him of a bomb threat against the AMRC. Word from the Madison Police Department, which had received the warning, was that the device was set to go off in five minutes. Schwichtenberg grabbed his flashing red light, stuck it on the roof of the car, and headed back toward Sterling on University Avenue. He didn't speed; bomb threats against Army Math had been routine that year, and they usually turned out to be pranks.

He was nearing the intersection of University and Charter, separated from Sterling by the bulk of Old Chemistry, when the bomb went off with strobelike flash and a deafening noise. Struggling to keep his vehicle on the road, he glimpsed a Toyota that had pulled over to get out of his way hurtling through the air, coming to rest in the bus lane. Schwichtenberg veered right onto Charter and found himself staring into a holocaust. The air was full of flying glass, and Sterling Hall appeared to be engulfed in flames. An orange column of fire rose hundreds of feet over the building, with a mushroom cloud of swirling objects at its top. Schwichtenberg had served in the marines and had seen a lot of ordnance expended in Vietnam; nonetheless, he was stupefied. *It's like an atomic bomb!* he thought.

The fireball exploded, raining bricks on his car. Schwichtenberg stopped and cautiously backed into Lathrop Drive. A few yards in, he found the way blocked by an uprooted, flaming tree. Over the roar of the fire he could hear sirens wailing all over the city, and somewhere in the miasma of smoke and dust, someone was screaming. He got out of the car, and a moment later William Evans stumbled toward him, holding his head, semihysterical.

"There's someone else inside!" Evans yelled. Schwichtenberg examined the cut on the student's forehead. It didn't look too serious, so he let Evans lead him into the building through the old wing, fronting on Charter Street, which, contrary to his first impression, did not seem to be on fire. Arriving at the stairwell where the two wings were joined, they found Norbert Sutter propped against the wall next to the elevator, which had not arrived in time to remove him from harm's way. Schwichtenberg hardly recognized his colleague. The watchman was covered with soot, his uniform was tattered and smoking, and his face was so swollen that it looked to Schwichtenberg as though Sutter had two heads. He was moaning, fading in and out of consciousness, barely hanging on.

Other campus cops arriving on the scene rushed the two victims across the street to University Hospital, which was also in panic, all its windows having been shattered. As soon as his wounds were bandaged, Evans phoned Bob Fassnacht's home. Fass was somebody he had leaned on for help with his experiments; he'd promised to stop by his lab for a cup of coffee later that night.

The Fassnacht home, several miles away on the East Side of

Madison, was protected from the blast wave by Bascom Hill; even so, a low thud, like a thunderclap, had rattled the bedroom windows. Stephanie answered uneasily. Bob did not often call her in the middle of the night.

"Is Bob there?" Evans asked.

"No," came the reply.

"Is he at Sterling Hall?"

"Yes."

Stephanie had been packing all day for a trip to San Diego, where her parents lived, and a much-needed vacation. It wasn't unusual for Bob to work so late, she reflected. His stamina, his ability to stay up without sleep had always amazed her. He was probably on his way home right then.

Charter Street was a parking lot of emergency vehicles. With the help of several other cops, Schwichtenberg had roped off the area. He was taken aback to see Evans again, still screaming his head off, only this time about someone named Fassnacht. "Okay, lead me to him," he said. They approached Sterling as before, but on entering the East Wing, the officer was overcome by fumes. "We can't go any farther," he told Evans. Swichtenberg returned to his car, dragging the student with him, and radioed for gas masks.

At that moment, Paul Quin came stumbling around the corner from the far side of the wing, where his office was located. He'd been knocked around like a pinball, but his injuries were slight. The researcher led a couple of firemen back in by a rear exit to look for Whitmer and Schuster. Whitmer had last been seen sitting in the accelerator operating room strumming his guitar. They found him still sitting there, totally dazed, his life saved by the thick, reinforced concrete walls of the vault. Schuster was nowhere to be found.

Fred Harvey Harrington, the president of the University of Wisconsin, lived in a twenty-room house in University Heights, about a mile west of Bascom Hill. At 3:42 A.M., a vibration passed through the mansion like the rumble of a subway, rattling his wife Nancy's crystal collection. Reconnoitering later in the morning, Mrs. Harrington found that nothing had fallen. Nonetheless, she had to call the physical plant and request a repairman; the hearthstone in the reception hall had cracked.

The explosion had awakened the entire sleeping city of 150,000; in fact, country dwellers thirty miles away heard the strangely tinny, hollow whump of the blast. People who lived within a few blocks of Bascom Hill reported being blown out of bed. Because of all the shaking, many thought they had experienced an earthquake or the explosion of a gas main; others assumed it was thunder (Madison being known for its summer storms). But among the city's constabulary, as well as in the countercultural segment of the community, there was an instant shared reaction: *Army Math.* Lawmen lay in their beds wide awake, waiting for the calls they knew would come. The young pulled on their denims and drifted through the predawn darkness toward Bascom Hill, suspecting that a "revolutionary action" had occurred.

Edwin Young, chancellor of the Madison campus, was one of those who had little doubt what had awakened him. From his home in University Heights, he could see a red glow in the sky over Bascom Hill. He picked up Fred Harrington, and they drove into campus together. Together, the two men always reminded people of Mutt and Jeff. Harrington was six feet six, broad shouldered and patrician in bearing, but with expressive hands that belied a nervous and impatient temperament. He could deliver a perfectly organized speech or lecture at the drop of a hat, and even his faculty colleagues considered him brilliant. A man of liberal inclinations, he was well disposed toward the common man, but lacked the common touch. He had held on to his position as long as he had (eight years), in part by delegating the problem of student unrest to his subordinates, the chancellors of the several state campuses over which he presided. In Madison, where the protests were at their worst, he'd gone through five in the past four years. But current chancellor Ed Young had been no more successful than his predecessors in containing campus revolutionaries, and Harrington had been forced to resign in May, like so many other campus administrators a domestic casualty of the Vietnam War. The lame-duck president had spent the summer tidying up, hoping for a graceful exit in the fall.

As they pulled up to the intersection of University and Charter, Harrington was rocked by what he saw. Even in the predawn gloom, it was apparent that many buildings on the south and west sides of Bascom Hill had been damaged—their windows were gone. A gaping hole had opened in the East Wing of Sterling Hall, a conduit was hanging out like so much spaghetti, and in the middle of the loading ramp was a smoking heap of debris. The service door to the accelerator vault, which had been reinforced that spring with three-inch aluminum channels, had been blown in. Investigators from half a dozen agencies were already picking through the rubble looking for clues to the cause of the explosion. As for the mysterious white van that had been sitting outside Fassnacht's office, there was not a trace.

Ralph Hanson, the campus police chief, ushered the two administrators inside the cordoned-off area. Hanson and Young were both from Maine and had a certain Yankee rapport. Of the two, Hanson was the more politically skilled. Nice looking, even tempered, and witty, he was so genial that even students found it hard not to like him. In his five years with UP & S, he'd earned a reputation for restraint, but that morning, every past policy, restraint included, seemed called into question. Three people had already been taken out of the building; two more were unaccounted for, he informed his boss. Young couldn't help noticing the crowd of young people watching from beyond the police boundaries. They were laughing, joking, apparently pleased by the destruction. The chancellor could not get over it. It made his hair stand on end.

Harrington and Young had been there only a few minutes when they saw the austere, slightly forbidding profile of the nuclear physicist Heinz Barschall, who was rushing pell-mell through the crowd, trying to get to the blown-out door in the now-darkened vault. This behavior was uncharacteristic of the distinguished scientist, a veteran of the Manhattan Project, who was usually so timid that he wouldn't set foot on campus on days when demonstrations had been announced. Young was understanding about Barschall's timidity; Barschall was a refugee from Nazi Germany and had a phobia about mobs. But when the physicist had written to him a year earlier, begging him to move Army Math out of the building, the chancellor had demurred. That would have been giving in, he'd replied, and besides, J. Barkley Rosser wouldn't hear of it.

A fireman now blocked Barschall's path. "No one's left in the building," he declared.

"I want to go in," Barschall insisted in his heavy German accent. He knew that the accelerator, a small but cleverly modified Van De Graaff, had to be attended at all times, and he correctly surmised that his South African student, David Schuster, was still inside.

"No sir, I can't allow that," the fireman said. "There's smoke. Stuff is falling. There's water on the ground and live wires sparking. We can't let anybody in."

"I am going in!" Barschall shouted hoarsely. He pushed past the fireman and began to grope his way down the ramp, but at this point Ed Young caught up with him and grasped him firmly by the shoulder.

"Why don't you let the firemen go in and take another look, Heinz?" he suggested reasonably. The firemen agreed and went back in to look for the South African. A feeble cry led them to a door to a small office. Schuster was lying in the doorway under a pile of debris, his eardrums blown out and suffering from internal injuries, but alive. He was carried across the street to the hospital.

Young escorted Barschall to a phone in the chancellor's office in Bascom Hall, so he could inform the Atomic Energy Commission, which owned the Van De Graaff, that its six-million-volt tandem linear accelerator had been damaged—to what extent was still unknown—by a mysterious and immense explosion. Word of the call passed among the authorities gathering in Young's office: the city police chief, the county sheriff, the state attorney general, the state fire inspector, the district attorney, the mayor. They all knew what it meant: Damage to federal property would automatically bring in the FBI.

Back at Sterling Hall, William Evans was joined by another young physicist, John Lynch, who had raced over from his Regent Street apartment after learning from a distraught Stephanie Fassnacht that Bob was not home. Approaching from the rear of the building, the pair led another search party into the shattered wing. Rubble was waist high in the basement corridor, water dripped from the upper stories, and severed electrical wires hung from the ceiling. However, they could now breathe without gas masks.

A hundred feet in, they stopped. Where Fassnacht's lab had been, their flashlights illuminated nothing but charred and twisted ruins. The outer wall of the lab was gone, the hallway itself collapsed. Fass was nowhere to be seen. Momentarily, the searchers experienced a glimmer of hope; maybe Fassnacht had been elsewhere in the building. But as they turned to leave, they stumbled upon the body; Lynch recognized his friend's curly red hair at once. They had walked right over him when they entered the lab.

It appeared as though a tremendous force had walloped Robert Fassnacht from behind. The physicist had landed face down, his backside shredded by flying particles. Debris had buried his legs; water covered his head. The coroner would find no evidence of drowning, however; Fassnacht's internal organs had been shattered. He must have been dead before he hit the floor. Madison's afternoon daily, the *Capital Times,* would herald Lynch's grisly story in two-inch type: "I FOUND BOB UNDER A FOOT OF WATER."

Jack Schwichtenberg had seen members of his platoon die in the mayhem of jungle warfare, which was why he couldn't change his mind about Vietnam; it would dishonor the memory of those who'd perished under his command. But after all the corpses he'd carried away from fire zones, this one got to him, as it did the other lawmen gripping the stretcher on which the distressing remains of Robert Fassnacht were laid out. When he'd left the marines in 1967, Schwichtenberg had been eagerly recruited by several police forces that were faced with civil unrest. He'd chosen UP & S because the job would allow him to take courses on the cheap at the university. In the next three years, the neophyte cop experienced more hand-to-hand combat than he had in Vietnam. *It's really escalated now,* he thought, angling toward a waiting ambulance. He was puzzled by the five-minute warning that had been called in. To him, it hadn't seemed anything like five minutes before the bomb went off; if he'd arrived ten seconds sooner, he would have been dead. A nasty thought crossed his mind: *They must have wanted to get themselves a couple of pigs.*

As onlookers saw what was on the stretcher, the joking stopped, the crowd fell silent. Schwichtenberg took note of the stunned looks, and a more hopeful thought crossed his mind: *Maybe this will be the end of it.*

It was about 4:30 A.M., still dark, when the ambulance carried Fassnacht's body to its appointment with the coroner. Joe Dillinger, Fassnacht's faculty supervisor, arrived at Sterling Hall shortly afterward. A short, paunchy, balding man in his middle years, he was regarded by his peers in the department as a tired scientist who had long since run out of steam on low-temperature research. Bob Fassnacht had been his best student and probably his only hope of salvaging his career. One glance at the ruptured, blackened building and Dillinger knew that his lab was gone, along with equipment and samples that were unique and irreplaceable. On hearing the news about Fassnacht, he sank to the ground, weeping not only for the loss of a friend, but also for his vanished dream of solving the riddle of superconductivity. Firemen had to get him out of the way.

A slender woman with delicate features and porcelain skin, Stephanie Fassnacht was considered the most beautiful woman in the Physics Department. Her marriage to Fassnacht had thrown her admirers into despair. What did Fass have that they didn't? He was not among the celebrities in the department, his research interests were obscure, and in looks he was average. But Stephanie had loved the things that often go unnoticed in a man: his low-key sense of humor, his considerateness, his quiet passion for music and nature. He had been equally fond of rock climbing and of singing in the local philharmonic chorus. With her help, he had recently built a harpsichord of cherrywood with rosewood trim, so he could play the Baroque masterpieces that he loved.

The funeral took place on Wednesday the twenty-sixth at Fitch Lawrence Funeral Home, a University Avenue establishment sandwiched between the Green Lantern, a meal cooperative going back to the forties, and a hip clothing store called No Hassel. Relatives came in from Indiana and San Diego: parents, aunts and uncles, siblings, many of them scientists of one sort or another. Fred Harrington and Ed Young attended, as did Joe Dillinger and Heinz Barschall and other members of the Physics Department, including William Evans and Paul Quin, who had recovered from their injuries. David Schuster was still in the hospital.

Though neither the deceased nor his widow was religiously active, Stephanie was of Jewish background, and Rabbi Manfred Swarsensky of Temple Beth-El was called in to give the eulogy. "He who destroys a single human life is like one who has destroyed an entire world," the rabbi intoned. His words rang true to the scientists present, who were mourning not only Fassnacht but the years of research they had lost.

Ironically, Army Math had been the least affected of Sterling Hall's tenants. Upstairs in the Astronomy Department, Michael Molnar's completed thesis had been 90 percent destroyed, and a three-year accumulation of data on nova had disappeared without a trace. In the basement, the superconductivity project was a total loss; Dillinger was doubtful about resuming it. The accelerator would be down for months. Twenty Ph.D. candidates in nuclear physics had lost their thesis research, but they at least were young enough to start over. Not so Heinz Barschall. The notes and samples he had collected over the decades had been wiped out. He and another, similarly affected senior colleague soon bowed out of nuclear physics altogether. At the pharmaceutical labs in Old Chemistry, a major cancer research project had been obliterated. All told, no fewer than twenty-six campus buildings had been damaged. It was going to take 38,000 square feet of plywood just to cover the broken windows. For several blocks along University Avenue, businesses, churches, and residence halls had also lost windows. Even the funeral home was boarded up.

Joe Dillinger had composed Fassnacht's obituary for the science journals. Fass had been the most outstanding young scientist to come out of Indiana in the mid-1950s, recognized in a national talent search when he was only a freshman in high school. In 1958 he won a Woodrow Wilson Fellowship to Wisconsin, where he earned his Ph.D. and made himself indispensable to the low-temperature research program. And there his *curriculum vitae* ended. As Dillinger well knew, a scientist is a prospector who has to believe that the gold is under the next shovelful of dirt; otherwise he would not continue. His notebook is filled with what does not work; only the last page, if he is lucky, contains what does. Dillinger would never know what Fass wrote in his that night.

Physics, the hardest hit, had, in fact, been the most dovish of the university's hard science departments. All but a few of its students and faculty were outspoken opponents of the war. Many of them had protested the AMRC's presence in their building and had even questioned its place in the university. The injured student Paul Quin was one of those; Bob Fassnacht had been another.

Stephanie didn't cry at her husband's funeral. For years afterward, her friends wondered about her behavior; it wasn't like Stephanie. One theory, advanced by a former suitor, was that her emotions were "frozen." Her in-laws had insisted on a closed-casket ceremony, and she didn't get to see the body before it was cremated—she never really got to say good-bye.

But Stephanie Fassnacht had another reason to hold back her tears. For three days the national news media had been rife with denunciations of the "senseless act" that had killed a researcher, injured innocent men, and so on. "Vicious and cowardly," "insane," "an intolerable act of anarchism," "political murder" were the typical pejoratives. The Board of Regents had condemned the bombing as an attempt to "cause the ultimate breakdown of our form of government." The evil against which the bombing seemed to have been directed, the ongoing slaughter in Southeast Asia, was forgotten. Most news accounts did not even mention the fact that the Mathematics Research Center, as the center had called itself in recent months, worked for the U.S. Army.

Stephanie Fassnacht was not a radical, but the political furor frightened her. The final straw was the presence in the funeral parlor of network news crews looking for the grief-stricken widow. The cameras being pushed in her face and the exploitation of her husband's death for political ends she didn't share incensed her. And so she held back her tears. Though it had made her a widow, the bombing hadn't changed the way she felt about the Vietnam War.

2

WISBOM

How do you tell a three-year-old boy and year-and-a-half-old twin girls that their dad's never going to be home again because some maniac blew him up?

—MICHAEL ZALESKI,
Wisconsin Assistant Attorney General
for the prosecution

Judge Sachtjen, how are you going to tell millions of little children in Southeast Asia that their fathers, brothers, sisters, mothers, uncles, grandparents, friends, and neighbors won't be home because some maniacs blew up their country?

—ATTORNEY WILLIAM KUNSTLER,
for the defense

Madison had always been a nice town. In 1948 *Life* had dubbed it "America's best place to live." It had the university, the state capital, stable industries, good public schools, safe streets, and clean air, and with five lakes within the city limits, recreational opportunities abounded. The two largest lakes, Mendota and Monona, were separated by a narrow strand less than a mile across. The Capitol stood on a hill at the east end of this isthmus. It was all white, with a dome like the one on the Capitol in Washington. The colonnaded facade of Bascom Hall faced it to the west. State Street, a mile-long strip of bratwurst dispensaries, bookstores, and bars,

connected the two. The gentle Winnebago, original inhabitants of
the isthmus, had been driven off long ago, leaving nothing but a few
burial mounds to serve as archeological curiosities for the Teutonic
and Scandinavian tribes that succeeded them.

There is a saying in Wisconsin that the climate tempers a man.
After freezing all winter, you are plunged into a steam bath with
hardly a pause for spring. Oldtimers say it can make a man as hard
as nails. Detective Charles Lulling was such a man. In the company
of lawmen like himself, Madison's balding senior homicide investigator was congenial enough, an avid duck hunter with a well-
stocked refrigerator in his trailer on the Wisconsin River. But if you
were a citizen of "the People's Republic of Miffland," Madison's
student ghetto, you knew a different Charlie Lulling, a hard cop
who liked to stare you down from the open window of his prowling
squad car. Lulling carried a small arsenal on his person, including a
matched set of pearl-handled revolvers and a snub-nosed .38 he
kept strapped to his ankle. Students called him "Quick Draw." The
wisdom at Madison Police Department headquarters was to keep
Lulling out of the sun, lest he blow up.

At 7 A.M. the morning of the bombing, Lulling was sipping a cup
of weak coffee at a secretary's desk in the vestibule of the chancellor's office in Bascom Hall. Through the cottage-pane windows he
could see straight up State Street to the Capitol, the big dome still
in shadow, and just outside his window, the seated figure of Lincoln
with the famous "sifting and winnowing" quote on its bronze back.
For the past three hours, he and his colleagues had been sifting and
winnowing what was left of Sterling Hall, sorting out the scraps and
piling them on squares of wire mesh.

All Lulling could think about that morning was Christine. She
had been a slender, beautiful woman, a treasure to her parents, the
Rothschilds of Chicago. Almost two years earlier, in May 1968, he
had found her naked corpse stretched out on a stone abutment in
front of Sterling Hall, hidden from the street only by a row of bushes. By Lulling's count, she had been killed three ways. Her assailant
had first struck her on the jaw and slammed her against the wall so
hard that it had left the decorative pattern in the concrete imprint-
ed on her flesh. Then he had ripped the lining from her coat and
stuffed it into her mouth, suffocating her. Finally he had stabbed
her seventeen times in the chest and throat with a stiletto. For
weeks afterward, Lulling had paraded a policewoman in a miniskirt

along Charter Street in the hope of luring the killer into the open. It had not worked.

There was no obvious similarity between the Rothschild murder and the bombing, but Lulling, who had so badly wanted a conviction for Christine's parents, was intrigued by the geographic coincidence. *Here we have this murder a couple of years ago, and now we go with this bombing,* he thought. Maybe there was a connection. Maybe Christine Rothschild's killer was back in town.

A little after seven, a student was brought in for Lulling to interview. His name was Michael McLaurin. According to the intelligence report Lulling had been handed, McLaurin had worked for Army Intelligence, first at Notre Dame and later in South Korea, before going over to the other side. An Army Intelligence agent had spotted McLaurin taking pictures at Sterling Hall only minutes after the bombing.

Lulling offered McLaurin a Camel straight. "How did you know to bring the camera?" he asked.

McLaurin had the build and features of a truck driver and a nasty wound in his upper arm, visible just below the sleeve of his T-shirt. He had been shot during an altercation with biker security guards at a rock festival in Iola, Wisconsin, earlier in the summer. According to witnesses, the bikers had been raping the college girls they were supposed to protect. "I had gone to bed about 3:30 A.M.," he answered smoothly. "The explosion woke me up. I ran outside to see what had happened. Someone told me that Army Math had been blown up. So I grabbed my camera and came right over."

Lulling studied the intelligence report. "Then why were you at Sterling Hall earlier today talking like you knew what was going to happen?"

"Like, I wanted you to know that I knew the building was going to be blown up," came the sardonic reply.

Lulling gave the suspect a watery smile. "Let's stay in touch," he said. In his write-up of the interview, he would note that McLaurin "admitted he would not give any information he might have, even considering an innocent person had been killed." Very suspicious, it seemed to Charlie Lulling.

Meanwhile, George Baxtrum and Tom McMillen had entered the vestibule. Baxtrum was the FBI's senior agent in Madison and a specialist in internal security investigations. Special Agent

McMillen worked closely with him. With the recent terrorist wave, they were busy men. Since the first of the year, the so-called New Year's Gang had firebombed ROTC classrooms and Selective Service offices, bombarded a nearby munitions plant from the air, and threatened to blow up the Capitol. As Mayor William Dyke told one reporter that day, Sterling Hall was merely the climax of "nine months of guerrilla warfare."

Baxtrum was in many ways the perfect gumshoe—compact, polite, businesslike, and self-effacing. He would have faded right into the walls except for the fresh bandages that often marred his face, the result of frequent operations for skin cancer. Too much sun in the navy, he explained. He had arrived in Madison in 1966 after years on the Trotskyist beat in New York. He was a Wisconsin native, and the transfer had been a reward for twenty years in the trenches of the Cold War. Even so, the timing of his arrival suggested to some another reason.

In 1966 the New Left was becoming a force to be reckoned with nationally, and Madison was one of the trouble spots on the FBI's map. The University of Wisconsin had a sizable contingent of Red Diaper Babies, children of present or former members of the Communist and Socialist Worker parties, who were determined to control the New Left. Their own front organizations, the DuBois Club and the Young Socialist Alliance, were small, but they had taken over the local Committee to End the War in Vietnam and had founded the first national antiwar organization, the National Coordinating Committee to End the War in Vietnam. Students for a Democratic Society had also gained a following in Madison. On the student grapevine, the isthmus was beginning to be known as the "Third Coast," a hotbed of activism.

Since Baxtrum's arrival, leftists had gained control of the student government and the student newspaper and had organized teaching assistants into a militant, confrontational union. In the fall of 1967, Baxtrum had witnessed the first use of tear gas on an American campus, and a year later the first use of military force against students. In the past three years, National Guardsmen had spent more time in Madison than in any college town in the United States. And so, although Baxtrum always insisted that he had come to Wisconsin expecting a holiday, the reality had been anything but.

In his twenty-four years in domestic intelligence, Baxtrum had handled about a thousand cases, including many people whose "propensity to violence" might be evinced only by membership in organizations based on Marxist or anarchist principles. None of those cases had led to indictments, but in the past three years the specter of violent revolution had begun to take on a certain reality. There had been bombings all over the country, most of them aimed at institutions linked to the war. Madison, a city of only 150,000, had experienced a disproportionate share. And so Baxtrum and his small staff had real crimes to investigate for a change, not just political heresies as defined by the Smith Act and J. Edgar Hoover, but serious breaches of the United States Code.

To the former naval officer, it looked as though the East Wing of Sterling Hall had been hit by a battleship salvo. The question was, Had federal property been damaged? By itself, the murder of Robert Fassnacht did not necessarily make the bombing a federal case. Heinz Barschall, the nuclear physicist, gave Baxtrum the answer he was looking for. The vacuum seal had broken on the atom smasher, and it was full of dust. It would be down for months, Barschall said. In addition, a drum-storage unit on the AMRC's in-house computer had collapsed. In other words, both the Atomic Energy Commission and the U.S. Army were affected. Baxtrum immediately called Edward Hayes, the regional special agent in charge in Milwaukee, and passed the information on. "It looks like it's our case," he said. "It's going to take more men, lots of men."

"George," Hayes said, "you're the senior agent on the scene. It's your ticket."

The chancellor's conference room was unusually well ventilated that morning, thanks to missing panes in the south-facing windows. The expression on the face of former university president John Bascom, preserved in oil on canvas at one end of the room, seemed gloomier than ever. The local officials present—campus, city, and county cops; criminal investigators from the state Department of Justice; Mayor Dyke; and Chancellor Young—were people with whom Baxtrum was already well acquainted. They had been meeting since the first of the year, trying to figure out who was behind the epidemic of incendiarism. So far they had solved only one incident, the trashing of an air force recruiting center on South Park Street in January. High school students had done it, kids not even old enough to have their names printed in the newspaper when they committed a crime.

Relations between the FBI and local investigators had become strained as a result of their collective failure to catch the New Year's Gang. Deputy Fire Marshal Frank Roberts had openly accused the FBI of withholding information, and so it was with some diffidence that Baxtrum made his announcement. Federal laws had been broken, he said. He had been instructed to take charge of the investigation on behalf of the federal government. FBI agents would henceforth be in control of the crime scene. Evidence already gathered was to be turned over to the FBI. Temporarily at least, Bascom Hall would serve as the command center; investigators would meet once a day. The bureau would share reports, he promised.

There were no arguments. For once, Baxtrum noted with satisfaction, they all seemed glad to have the FBI in charge.

Special Agent McMillen found President Harrington in a borrowed office next door, where Harrington was going over the preliminary damage report with his aides. McMillen was from Spokane, Washington, handsome, and, like Baxtrum, exceptionally polite. A glitter in his pale blue eyes was the only hint of his zealotry. Baxtrum might have the ticket on the case, but McMillen knew that he would be the "brick agent"—the one to whom all the others would have to turn for background—because under his control were the files for the New Left in Madison. Baxtrum had the files on the Old Left, the Red Diaper Babies, and the Soviet Bloc visitors, but those were relatively conservative types. McMillen's data, in contrast, covered SDS, the Yippies, the White Panthers, and so forth, groups that were much more likely in his view to be involved in a bombing.

In this connection he had approached Harrington before, asking for access to student records. Harrington had always turned him down. It was Harrington who was the problem with the university, McMillen thought; it was his "do your own thing" mentality that had led to the bombing. But McMillen was only thirty, none too sure of himself, and in the presence of the towering patrician he became tongue-tied. Did the university have any information on file that might help identify suspects? he mumbled.

Harrington gave him a frosty look. He had kept the FBI out of the student files for eight years, but that morning everything had changed. He handed McMillen a copy of the press statement he had written only a few hours earlier. "We are cooperating fully with all law enforcement agencies involved to see that the persons responsible for this unspeakable crime are apprehended and brought to justice," it stated.

"Cooperating fully?" McMillen repeated. He left feeling that nothing was changed, but on the following day UP & S made all of its files on student dissidents available to the FBI.

It would go down in the FBI annals as "WISBOM," for Wisconsin Bombing. All day Monday, FBI agents descended on Madison from every local office in the Midwest. Fred Smith, top man in the crime lab, flew in from Washington and took over the collection of evidence. By Tuesday Baxtrum had seventy-five men at his disposal, but by then he had effectively lost control of the investigation. FBI Director J. Edgar Hoover had deemed WISBOM a major case and had ordered Ed Hayes to Madison to give it his personal attention. Joe Sullivan, the bureau's legendary major case inspector, was also said to be on his way. George Menzel, case supervisor in Washington, advised Madison that the White House was following the case closely. With that kind of pressure, Baxtrum did not mind stepping back. He had always been more comfortable operating behind the scenes.

Madison's Resident Agency was next door to a dental suite on the second floor of a University Avenue minimall a few blocks west of campus. There was a shoe store downstairs, and the gumshoes had adopted its name—the "Stassi Shoe Store"—for their own headquarters. Of the eight-man staff, three were occupied full time by sedition work, with another two carrying the spillover. Even at that strength, they could not keep up with it.

For months the desk jockeys at FBI headquarters in Washington had been peppering Madison with teletypes, known in the field as "greenies" because of the color of the paper they were printed on, full of advice about what leads to follow in the earlier bombings. To Baxtrum's annoyance, the Stassi Shoe Store's limited resources had been diverted to the monitoring of gadfly journalists like Jim Rowen, an antiwar activist who happened to be married to U.S. Senator George McGovern's daughter Susan. Monday, August 24, brought a new flurry of greenies. "Identify all persons who have been previously connected with protest activity against the Army

Mathematics Research Center" advised the "URGENT" teletype. Baxtrum had to laugh. How many names did Washington want? Ten thousand?

Joe Sullivan flew into Madison late Tuesday with nothing more than his rumpled brown business suit, his luggage having gone to New York. He had been on his way home from a north woods vacation when Chicago agents pulled him off his plane at O'Hare Airport and turned him around. He took charge of WISBOM as soon as he arrived in Madison, giving the assembled force a pep talk and imposing the methodical style for which he was famed. Sectors, teams, daily oral and written reports, always be aware of what your men are doing, leave no unknowns—that was Joe Sullivan. And no leaks. That was Joe Sullivan, too.

In his thirty years with the FBI, Joseph A. Sullivan had managed to keep himself out of the limelight, even though he had been instrumental in solving some of the bureau's most famous cases. A widower with no children, he had for years been Hoover's traveling man, the one the director could count on to go anywhere at a moment's notice. Since December 1963, when Hoover appointed him major case inspector, his caseload read like a social history of the decade: the bombings of the Florida East Coast Railroad and of the Birmingham Baptist Church; the murders of Viola Liuzzo in Selma, Alabama and of Andrew Goodman, James Chaney, and Michael Schwerner in Philadelphia, Mississippi; the assassination of Martin Luther King, Jr.; the ghetto uprisings in Watts, Detroit, and Newark; the killing for hire of United Mine Workers reformer Jock Yablonsky; the slaying of four students by National Guardsmen at Kent State University; and now Sterling Hall, the most violent act of a violent decade.

Big and burly, with a crewcut gone gray at the sides and a precise, thoughtful manner, Sullivan had a knack for creating calm in the midst of crisis. Like George Baxtrum, he had grown up in the big snow country of northern Wisconsin and had a ruralite's natural repose. He also happened to be a University of Wisconsin alumnus, having received his law degree from the university in 1940. But that was a long time ago, and Sullivan felt no more sentiment that it was his alma mater that had been bombed than he did about the possibly exalted political motives of the perpetrators.

But walking the crime scene with lab man Fred Smith shook him a little. A big I-beam had been used to prop up the wall next to the loading ramp. Cleared of debris, the concrete ramp revealed a crater ten feet across and three feet deep. Smith told him a drive shaft had been found buried two feet below that. Other fragments of a vehicle had been discovered embedded in nearby walls and on rooftops blocks away. Across the alley, the Old Chemistry building had been moved eight inches off its foundation. The sheer size of the explosion struck Sullivan as out of the ordinary. A witness told him that the smoke plume had resembled the Hiroshima column. Another anomaly was the placement of the bomb. The perpetrators did not have to have done such enormous environmental damage to have taken out the AMRC. Both size and placement smacked of unskilled persons with access to dangerous materials. Students, probably.

Hurley, Sullivan's hometown, was in the Iron Belt near Lake Superior. Sullivan had worked in the mines to pay his way through college, and he knew something about explosives. The black-carbon smudges on the side of the East Wing looked vaguely familiar. When Smith mentioned agricultural fertilizer, it clicked. Every farmer in Wisconsin was familiar with ammonium nitrate. It could make things grow, but it could also be extremely dangerous. A shipload of it had leveled the port of Galveston, Texas, in 1953. Mixed with a small quantity of fuel oil, it became ANFO, an even more potent substance. Farmers used ANFO to blow stumps; quarrymen and miners employed it as a substitute for dynamite. You could buy the nitrate cheaply at any farm-supply house without a permit, and you could pick up fuel oil at any number of filling stations. As for putting it all together, Sullivan remembered a pamphlet his uncle, a professor in the School of Agriculture, had showed him, explaining how to use ANFO to create farm dams. Sullivan had not thought of it for thirty years.

Investigators had already identified the vehicle used in the bombing as a Ford Econoline van belonging to a computer scientist named Larry Travis. Travis had reported the van stolen four days earlier. The cargo bay of an Econoline could hold a lot of ANFO, Sullivan realized. So powerful an explosive in the hands of ignorant people would be a terrible thing.

George Baxtrum ran down the list of suspects. The van owner,

Larry Travis, had already been interviewed twice, and a background check had been completed. Travis was clean. Then there was Michael McLaurin. Detective Lulling thought McLaurin must know something; otherwise, why had he shown up with a camera? McLaurin did have a substantial FBI file. He was known to be in tight with the violence-prone Mother Jones Revolutionary League and was reportedly a fan of the mysterious local terrorist group known as the New Year's Gang. But Baxtrum did not share Lulling's suspicions of McLaurin. He could think of twenty people who were more likely to be involved. And finally, there were four students who had been stopped by Sauk County sheriff's deputies at Devil's Lake, forty miles north of Madison, only a few hours after the bombing. The students were driving a light yellow Corvair, and a Dane County patrol had reported a car of that description leaving the campus at high speed when the bomb went off. The boys had told the Sauk County officers that they were going camping, though they had no camping gear in the car. Interviewed separately, they had given conflicting accounts of where they had spent the night. But Sauk had nothing to hold them on. The four had broken no law in that county, and a new state law forbade the detention of suspects without a formal request from the jurisdiction in which they were wanted for questioning. The Sauk County Sheriff's Department had been unable to get a hold order from Madison, and after a couple of hours the suspects had been released. They were David Sylvan Fine, 18; Leo Frederick Burt, 22; Dwight Allan Armstrong, 18; and Karleton Lewes Armstrong, 23.

Sullivan immediately ordered five investigations, one of each of the four boys and a separate inquiry into the Devil's Lake episode. He assigned teams to survey local farm-supply houses and service stations for large purchases of ammonium nitrate and fuel oil and sent someone to the Agricultural Extension Library to see if anyone had checked out references on the use of ANFO. Meanwhile, in yet another sector, agents were to stay on the heels of Baxtrum's A-list of local subversives.

There was one more thing. Too much information was getting into the newspapers, in Sullivan's view. That always happened when the FBI shared reports with local agencies. Therefore, he insisted, Baxtrum and Hayes should be more selective about what was let out of house.

Sullivan had spent the early part of the summer at Kent State University in Ohio talking to students about the National Guard shootings. He had found them respectful and cooperative. Madison was a different story. After two days, the teams assigned to the student ghetto were getting nowhere. Residents of Mifflin Street would not even open their doors. Handbills had been posted along the street with warnings about dealing with the FBI: "Don't be duped by the nice guy approach. Don't philosophize with them. Under all that grooviness there is oinking."

Baxtrum thought that a reward would help if it was big enough. Sullivan agreed and dispatched Ed Hayes to campus late Wednesday morning to see about raising the money. "We want $100,000," Hayes told President Harrington flatly. "Nothing less will have an effect." Harrington offered no objection; it was actually gratifying to put the squeeze on the Board of Regents, the same crew of wealthy Republicans who had pressured him to resign. Wednesday afternoon, the *Capital Times* carried the announcement: $100,000 for information leading to the capture of Robert Fassnacht's killers.

The following morning, the underground newspaper the *Madison Kaleidoscope* was on the street with a special issue applauding the destruction of Sterling Hall and trumpeting an exclusive communiqué from the bombers, who identified themselves as the "Vanguard of the Revolution," the same group that the *Kaleidoscope* had been touting all year as the New Year's Gang. Apparently written in advance of the bombing, the message said nothing about Fassnacht. "As long as pig institutions like the Army Math Research Center exist in AMERIKA, the AMERIKAN government will be responsible for any deaths that occur when those institutions are attacked," the newspaper commented. However, the editor added an apologetic note: "The New Year's Gang regrets the death of Fassnacht."

The *Kaleidoscope*'s editor Mark Knops was a New Jersey boy who had belonged to SDS and studied under Harvey Goldberg, a radical historian on the university's faculty. The FBI had a file on him going back several years. How did Knops know the inner feelings of the conspirators with regard to the consequences of the bombing unless he had been in direct contact with them? the investigators wondered. Once again, as it had for the past nine months, the newspaper seemed to be in league with the saboteurs.

Baxtrum had a copy of the issue hand carried to Washington, along with a manifesto supporting the bombing, mysteriously signed "Life Above the Trees," that had appeared on the streets Monday morning. He also transmitted a digest of advice the newspaper had recently been giving to its readers, such as "Just sprinkle a can of gasoline over anything burnable, ignite, and take off through the nearest backyard," and "Remember, dynamite is easier to get in Wisconsin than firecrackers." The most damning was a headline that had appeared in the *Kaleidoscope* only a month earlier: "A.M.R.C.—blow it up."

Madison had been an unusually liberal community even when Joe Sullivan was a student, but this was something else. Sullivan had not seen such Johnny Rebel sentiments before outside the Deep South. He needed a grand jury investigation, and the sooner the better.

Meanwhile, the 302s had come in on the interviews with the parents of the Devil's Lake suspects. (The 302 was an informal report in which agents paraphrased the responses of the interviewees.) Baxtrum was upset by the report of the Armstrong interview. In the course of his questioning, Special Agent John Schroepfer had asked Donald Armstrong, father of two of the suspects, what he thought of President Nixon. Baxtrum ordered the agent back out to the Armstrong residence to apologize.

Sullivan read the reports carefully. Manuel and Anne Fine, parents of David, resided in Wilmington, Delaware. Manuel was a World War II veteran and a carpet salesman; Anne was a dental hygienist. They were Jewish and not Nixon supporters, but with no known subversive affiliations. An older married daughter, Marsha, attended Boston University. David was a straight-A student who had come to Wisconsin on a tuition scholarship and had completed his freshman year in journalism. He had returned to Madison on August 20 to attend the wedding of a friend, Eliot Silberberg, with whom he had worked at the *Daily Cardinal.* As far as his parents knew, he planned to remain in Madison that fall, residing at Silberberg's vacated apartment on Spaight Street. David had always been against the Vietnam War, Mrs. Fine told the agents, but he would never bomb anything.

Leo Burt was from a big Catholic family in Havertown, a suburb of Philadelphia. His father, Howard, was an engineer and a loyal American; his mother, May, a homemaker and very devout. His older brother was in the navy, his older sister in a convent. His uncle Donald was a member of the Augustinian order and chairman of the philosophy department at nearby Villanova University. Leo himself had attended Monsignor Bonner, an all-boys Catholic high school, where he had served in the altar society his senior year. Leo had never been political, according to his mother. His passion was rowing; he had been on the rowing team at both Monsignor Bonner and the university. He did write for the *Daily Cardinal,* but the Burts had never heard him mention David Fine. Nor were they familiar with the Armstrongs. They were quite sure that he was not involved in the bombing of Sterling Hall. In fact, they had just had a letter from him in New York announcing that he had completed his degree requirements and was looking for a job.

The Armstrongs sounded like a typical blue-collar family, the backbone of America. Donald was an air force veteran and a long-time employee of Gisholt Machine Works, one of Madison's largest manufacturers. He was an expert on the balancing of jet engines and had done considerable contract work for the military. His wife, Ruth, was employed as a nurse's aide at Central Colony, caring for the severely impaired. They owned a ranch house on Hintze Road, well out on Madison's East Side. There were two daughters, Mira and Lorene, both married with children of their own. Karleton seemed to be a perennial student. He had attended the university off and on since 1964, supporting himself with odd jobs, the latest with the railroad. Dwight, a high school dropout, had had a few run-ins with the law, but was beginning to straighten out, according to his parents. He had obtained a graduate equivalency diploma and had taken courses at the Wisconsin School of Electronics. Both boys were against the war, Mr. Armstrong told the agents, but then, so was he. Wasn't it a fact, he asked rhetorically, that half the country was against the war?

The name Leo Burt was familiar to Mr. and Mrs. Armstrong, but they had never met him. Ruth said she had met David Fine only once, on Monday morning of that week, when Karl returned the family Corvair. Karl told her they had been stopped by police at Devil's Lake and questioned about the bombing. The two boys had borrowed another car in town, returned to pick up some camping gear around 10 A.M., and departed for the lake. The Armstrongs had not heard from them since.

The FBI's files on the Madison Left were kept in Milwaukee. After the bombing, Special Agent Tom McMillen asked for pertinent files to be sent to Madison, and began going through them looking for the names of the four suspects. In the control files were thousands of names, including almost everyone who had ever been identified at a rally or meeting or arrested in a protest. The sedition men would highlight any names that looked suspicious with colored marker, and the secretaries would make up index cards on them. If an index card filled up, they might open a file.

McMillen found a card on Dwight Armstrong with several entries, but nothing on Karleton or on Leo Burt, though that name was familiar. David Fine had a file. It was small, about sixty pages, nothing compared to the local heavies, some of whom had files the size of Manhattan telephone directories. Wilmington had sent it out in the fall as a routine courtesy. It consisted mostly of news clippings showing David's antiwar and civil rights activities all through high school—but no crimes, nothing violent.

The first indication that the Devil's Lake suspects might be worth following up on came from Madison police detective George Croal. A former University of Wisconsin graduate student and the MPD's resident expert on the movement, Croal worked under Inspector Herman Thomas at police department headquarters in the City-County Building, but had a deal going with the FBI that included his own desk at the Stassi Shoe Store. Croal was a former university student who looked like a choirboy, and cops like Lulling considered him naive, but they all acknowledged that he did his homework. When Thomas handed him a sheet of paper with the names of the Devil's Lake suspects on it, Croal responded instantly. "David Fine is a radical," he said, handing the list back. "So what?"

Thomas was a big, hawk-nosed man of Manichaean outlook. The mere mention of radicals was enough to ire him. "These guys were stopped at Devil's Lake in a light-colored Corvair Monday morning. A light-colored Corvair was seen leaving the campus area right after the bombing. The feds are wondering what we got on 'em," he said.

Croal had been hearing about Fine off and on all year from one of his informants. He rang up the Stassi Shoe Store and spoke to McMillen. "You know this Fine character?"

"Yeah, the little guy, looks like he's about twelve years old, gets straight As without ever going to class," McMillen said.

"Duroc got close to Fine during the Groppi protest," Croal said, using the code name for his informant. "The kid talks a violent line."

McMillen was embarrassed. Because Fine belonged to SDS, he had been one of McMillen's files, but the agent had done practically nothing on it all year. Judging by his *Cardinal* pieces, Fine was more interested in music than in politics. "We closed our case on him six weeks ago," McMillen said.

For Joe Sullivan the clincher was the report from the Agricultural Extension Library. A few weeks earlier Leo Burt had checked out a how-to pamphlet on ANFO, published by the Wisconsin Fish and Game Department. It was called *Pothole Blasting for Wildlife.* And so, forty-eight hours after his arrival in Madison, Sullivan promoted the Devil's Lake four from suspects to subjects, making them targets of the FBI investigation. At the same time, he ordered strict secrecy as to the identities of the four until enough evidence was compiled to file a federal complaint.

When a big bombing occurred it was usually the FBI's Criminal Division that would recommend making it a major case and that would direct the investigation. Joe Sullivan noted with interest that, in the case of Army Math, Domestic Intelligence had taken charge, under the command of Hoover's top assistants, William Sullivan (no relation) and Charles Brennan, both alumni of Internal Security. Crazy Bill and Chick, as everyone called them, had made their reputations in what Joe Sullivan somewhat disdainfully referred to as the Paper Unit, a research section within Internal Security that produced position papers and studies. Why would ideologues like Crazy Bill and Chick be so excited about a bombing in Madison, Wisconsin? Maybe it was as Hoover said: If they didn't solve the WISBOM case quickly, it might inspire similar actions on other campuses that fall.

In this context, the four subjects under consideration did not look promising. The Armstrongs were virtual unknowns, and though Burt and Fine had both worked for the *Cardinal,* they could hardly be called leaders of the student movement. Were they really soloists, or was there a team behind them? Given the expressions of support in the underground press and the reluctance of witnesses to come forward even with a $100,000 reward on the table, Joe Sullivan had to consider the possibility of a wider conspiracy. It was time for a visit to Miffland.

A sweep was set for Saturday morning, August 29. Sixty agents would descend on the political houses with backup from the MPD. From central files, Washington compiled the names of suspects to be questioned, Priority I types, militants the bureau believed had the requisite propensity for violence. Baxtrum led the invasion force, with Sullivan monitoring by radio from the Stassi Shoe Store.

Miffland was Indian Territory. Centered in the intersection of Mifflin and Bassett streets, about a ten-minute walk from campus, it was an older neighborhood of mature trees and big, closely spaced tenements, divided into student apartments. Backed by the National Guard, the MPD had subdued the community with saturation gassing at the height of the Cambodia–Kent State uprising in May, but the police still hesitated to set foot there. In a nationally televised press conference following the Sterling Hall bombing, the president of the student body, a sophomore from Great Neck, New York, had told newsmen that students had stockpiled more than 1,000 guns in Madison anticipating a resumption of hostilities in the fall. Whether or not the figure was accurate, Baxtrum knew from his own sources that Mifflin Street was armed.

The plan was for two-man teams to approach the houses all at once in the hope of taking the occupants by surprise. It didn't quite work out that way, for reasons that would mystify the FBI for years to come. What Baxtrum did not know was that Miffland had prepared for an invasion, not of FBI agents, but of bikers. All summer, a local landlord named William Bandy had been trying to evict the tenants from several Mifflin Street rentals he had purchased from Patrick Lucey, a Democrat who was running for governor. The occupants, represented by an organization called the Madison Tenants Union, had declared a rent strike. The courts could not help Bandy because he did not know the names of the people living in his houses. Bandy tried to pay a call on the tenants, but found the floors covered with human excrement, apparently put there to deter his inspection. "Mine are the only houses in Madison in which you have to wipe your feet when you *leave*," he complained. The MPD declined to get involved. Judge William Sachtjen, called on to adjudicate the mess, threw up his hands. "If they were my houses," he told Bandy, "I would go in with a shotgun and give the little sons of bitches two minutes to clear out." Instead, Bandy brought in the C. C. Riders, a local motorcycle gang, to do the job for him.

Learning of the arrangement, the occupants of Bandy's houses and their Mifflin Street allies had prepared an ambush. Shotguns were loaded and stashed behind doors. A Kentucky drifter named Bobby Jo Burbridge, who had found his nesting place in the Madison counterculture, was assigned the role of Paul Revere. It was Burbridge whom Baxtrum unexpectedly encountered as he and his men advanced into the 500 block of Mifflin Street around 8 A.M.

It was shaping up to be a steam-bath day, and the heavily armed agents were already sweating under their bulletproof vests. Burbridge was keeping watch on a bicycle. "Heavy duty, man," he said when Baxtrum showed his badge. He spun around on his bike and took off down the street, blowing on a whistle. A minute later, the agents were face to face with hundreds of Mifflanders, not all of whom wore clothes, brandishing shotguns, baseball bats, and garden tools and waving the single-star blue-and-red flag of North Vietnam.

To Sullivan, following events on his two-way radio, it was clear that the element of surprise had been lost. "Cool it," he ordered Baxtrum over the radio. Baxtrum signaled a retreat, disgusted at the thought that someone in the MPD must have given away the plan. The search for the broader conspiracy was put on hold.

On Monday, August 31, the assignments Sullivan had made the week before began to produce results. An attendant at Owens Service Station in Middleton, a suburb on the west side of town, identified photos of the Armstrong brothers and Leo Burt as the three young men who had recently purchased a large quantity of fuel oil from him, storing it in several fifty-five-gallon drums that they were transporting in a U-Haul trailer. More positive IDs were obtained the next day at Forest Harbor Enco Station in Madison, where the U-Haul had been rented. Agents traced the ammonium nitrate purchase—over 1,700 pounds—to the Farmer's Union Co-op in Baraboo, a few miles north of Devil's Lake. The manager identified Karl Armstrong and Leo Burt from photos. Meanwhile, the FBI's Washington lab confirmed that a powdery residue found in one of the

Enco station's U-Hauls and on the floor mats of the Armstrong family's Corvair consisted of ammonium nitrate.

From the manager of the Iota Court apartment building where Leo Burt had lived that summer, agents learned that a certain Eliot Silberberg had arrived several days earlier to remove Leo Burt's belongings. Investigators recalled that David Fine had planned to take Silberberg's apartment for the fall. On Tuesday, September 1, two agents, searching Silberberg's vacated flat at 947 Spaight Street found a treasure trove of evidence, including personal items of both Fine and Burt, notebooks in which the conspirators had recorded nighttime observations of Sterling Hall and a diagram of the building with an X where the bomb was to be placed. They also found a letter and communiqué that Burt had mailed on Friday from New York, reportedly already opened and discarded on the ground beside the house. The hand-lettered communiqué was covered with Leo's prints. In it, he apologized for the death and injuries, but otherwise defended the bombing. The letter asked Silberberg to deliver the communiqué to the *Kaleidoscope,* warning him not to get his own fingerprints on it. Leo and David were in New York "with good contacts," it said, and were heading for Canada. The letter even included a phone number to pass along to Karl Armstrong in case he should call. Silberberg, with his bride and belongings, had already left for New York, however. He would later tell the FBI that he had not seen the letter and knew nothing about the bomb plot.

In Joe Sullivan's considered opinion, WISBOM was rolling nicely. He immediately called Buffalo and Philadelphia to get agents after Eliot Silberberg and Paul Bracken, the contact mentioned in Leo's letter. Late that afternoon, McMillen found a couple of teletypes in the backlog of incoming communications linking the Armstrongs to the New Year's bombings. The day after the bombing, a crime-stoppers program on Minneapolis radio station KSTO had received a letter regarding a certain "Carl and Dowain Armstrong," who the writer thought might be implicated in the bombing of the Federal Building in that city a week earlier. It identified the Armstrongs as nephews of a local underworld figure named Paul Armstrong. The station had passed the letter on to the FBI. Interviewed by Minneapolis agents on Saturday, August 29, Paul Armstrong had confirmed the information in the letter. He had just heard from his nephews, he said. They had called him separately

asking for money, and he had wired Karl fifty dollars. He said the
two had lived with him for a time that winter and had spoken of
their participation in a group called the New Year's Gang, which
was trying to stop the war in Vietnam. He directed the agents to a
friend named Malcolm (Max) Sliter, who was also acquainted with
the boys. After some urging, Sliter told a fascinating story about
Karl and Dwight stealing a plane and bombing a munitions plant on
New Year's Eve. According to Sliter, the boys had said they used a
"nitrate bomb." And, in fact, in checking out rumors of the nighttime attack in early January, a bomb squad found three undetonat-
ed containers of ANFO on the premises. That was good enough for
Joe Sullivan. It was time to draw up a complaint.

By now the *Milwaukee Journal* had the subjects' names and was
threatening to go public whether or not warrants had been issued.
And that was not the FBI's only reason for haste. In a move that
was apparently engineered by the state Department of Justice,
Mark Knops was subpoenaed by a Walworth County Grand Jury
investigating arson at Whitewater State University in southeastern
Wisconsin, on the theory that the Sterling Hall explosion might be
related to the burning of the Old Main Building there in February.
After refusing to answer questions about the communiqué published in the *Kaleidoscope,* Knops was charged with contempt of
court and placed in solitary confinement. John Olson, U.S. attorney
for the District of Western Wisconsin, had been planning to call
Knops before the federal grand jury that had been empaneled in
Madison on Monday, August 31. In Olson's view, Walworth County
had no jurisdiction in the matter; it was only a ploy by state investigators to get out in front of the FBI.

Joseph Tafe, an assistant attorney general in the Subversive
Activities Trial Section of the U.S. Department of Justice, had flown
in from Washington to help with the complaint. "Mr. Hoover would
like this to be a federal announcement," he reminded everyone.
The director did not want to be upstaged by ambitious locals.
Assisted by Baxtrum, Olson and Tafe worked furiously on the complaint throughout Wednesday, September 2. At midday word came
in from Buffalo that the Royal Canadian Mounted Police (RCMP)
had Burt and Fine under surveillance in a youth hostel in Peterborough, Ontario, east of Toronto. They would arrest the pair as soon
as warrants were available.

As the senior resident agent, Baxtrum signed the complaint and swore out the warrants. It was 5 P.M. The Federal Building, a somber monolith overlooking Lake Monona, was teeming with reporters begging for the story, but Baxtrum insisted that Olson delay the announcement until 6 P.M. That way, he could notify local investigators before they heard it on the news.

Everything was set. Hoover himself was going to make the announcement, adding the four to the FBI's "Ten Most Wanted" list. The director had given the *New York Times* a copy of the complaint. The full text, under Baxtrum's signature, would appear in its next edition. The RCMP was sitting on two of the suspects in Canada. Every patrolman in New York was on the lookout for the Armstrongs. One of the most impressive investigations in FBI history was coming to a triumphant close.

And then things began to go wrong. Hoover could not wait around for professional niceties to be observed in Madison. To make the evening news in New York, he had to issue his statement by 6:30 P.M. eastern time. It was an hour earlier in Madison, and so it was 5:30 P.M. local time when the announcement came over the airwaves. Baxtrum had not had time to reach everybody. Jack Leslie found out from a reporter who called him for a reaction. Sheriff Leslie was an ex-Marine with the temperament of a rhinoceros. Even cops were afraid of him because of his propensity for getting into fights at parties. Leslie drove straight to the Stassi Shoe Store and confronted Special Agent Tom McMillen. "The next time you need my help, don't even bother, McMillen, and that goes double for Baxtrum. As far as I'm concerned, you can both go fuck yourselves!"

Local editorialists denounced the affront to the city's dignity, asking why it was that the announcement had not been made in Madison. The feud spilled over into a meeting between Olson and Tafe and state officials the next morning in the old Lorraine Hotel on Capitol Square. The U.S. attorney had called the meeting to discuss what to do about Fine and Burt. Under Canada's extradition law, based on the nineteenth-century Webster-Ashburton Treaty, none of the federal crimes the fugitives was charged with—conspiracy, possession of an illegal explosive device, destruction of governmental property—was extraditable. That meant that the federal warrants issued the day before could not be executed in Peterborough. To satisfy the extradition law, common-law charges of murder and-or arson would have to be brought, and they could only be issued by local authorities. Baxtrum had provided Dane County District Attorney James Boll with a copy of the complaint, as well as the more substantial investigative report. Olson assumed that these documents would be adequate to support murder warrants.

But Boll was adamant in his refusal to cooperate, insisting, "It's not enough to go on. They'll be out of jail in two weeks."

Olson and Tafe were stunned. In their view, it was one of the most solid complaints ever. They had the four suspects stopped at Devil's Lake shortly after the bombing in a car seen leaving the scene of the crime. They had the Armstrong brothers' admissions to Max Sliter about the Badger Ordnance bombing, the positive IDs, the nitrate residues, the surveillance notebooks, and the second communiqué with Leo's fingerprints all over it. The conspirators themselves had volunteered a motive—the desire to make a political statement. And then there was the fact that all four suspects had disappeared—prima facie evidence of guilt. "We got a case," Olson insisted. "We *have* it!"

District Attorney Boll had made his reputation suppressing a campus production of *Peter Pan* that featured nude coeds dancing to Iron Butterfly's hallucinogenic "Inna gadda da vida." He had no sympathy for protesters and carried a blackjack whenever his duties took him on campus. Olson could think of no explanation for his reaction except spite.

"Look, you got the world's greatest investigative agency here," Joe Tafe blurted. "Anything not here will be here by the time they're caught."

Sheriff Leslie, MPD Chief Wilbur Emery, and the state justice people stared at Tafe, their resentment over being cut out of the investigation about to boil over.

"Have we ever heard of these guys?" Boll asked pointedly.

"Yeah, we matched a print on a pie tin used in a bomb attempt in February," Emery said. "It's Karl Armstrong's."

"Whoopee," Attorney General Warren commented acidly. "We knew something before they did."

Olson had considered Bob Warren a friend. Not any more. At the end of the day U.S. authorities had to tell the RCMP that murder warrants were stalled. Canada had no wish to be a haven for terrorists and sent immigration police to Peterborough the next morning to arrest the fugitives as illegal aliens. But Burt and Fine had slipped out during the night, leaving their baggage behind. That same evening, the Armstrong brothers had eluded a police dragnet along the border after being briefly detained in Little Falls, New York, on suspicion of car theft. It would be a while before any of them were seen again.

3

In the Ruins
of a Dream

*This analysis led to the conclusion that one should try and
raise the domestic cost, and it was a rational assumption, and
I think a correct assumption, that disruption and violence led
to consequences that were unwelcome to the decision-makers.*

—Noam Chomsky,
professor of linguistics, for the defense

*I'd ask the court to consider the statement of Gandhi: "Even
when violence appears to do good, it is only temporary. The
evil is permanent."*

—H. J. Lynch
Dane County District Attorney , for the prosecution

To its residents, Madison had always been two cities. The West
Side implied middle class—the university, professionals, insurance companies, and law offices, quiet winding streets lined by
stately mock-Tudor and Georgian-style homes with screened sun
porches and parklike backyards. The East Side, sprawling on the
level plain beyond the Yahara River, was a bustling center of industry, warehouses, railroad sidings, airports, and the Madison Gas &
Electric power plant, with its smokestacks pointed at the sky like a
row of Big Berthas. Although there were enclaves of affluence like
Maple Bluff along the eastern shore of Lake Mendota, the East

Side was predominantly blue collar. Most of Madison's cops were East Siders; so were the Armstrongs.

The Armstrongs had bought the Hintze Road house in 1960, at the dawn of the short-lived Kennedy era. It was one of the first houses in a new subdivision then on the outskirts of town, in a neighborhood bracketed by Mendota State Hospital for the Insane, Truax Air Force Base, and the Oscar Mayer meat-packing plant. Stray mental patients sometimes knocked at the front door, F-105s screamed overhead on preparedness drills, and the faintly sweet aroma of cooking hog parts wafted in on the breeze, but for Don and Ruth Armstrong, Hintze Road was the fulfillment of a dream. The ranch-style house had almost everything they wanted: four bedrooms; a roomy, eat-in kitchen; a picture window in the living room; a recreation room and workshop in the basement; and a two-car garage where Don could park his fishing boat and camper. Ruth would have liked a patio for backyard barbecues, but it was something she could live without. Hintze Road was a far cry from the cold garage she and Don had lived in when they were first married.

Don and Ruth were both from the Tomah area in Monroe County, about halfway between Madison and Eau Claire in central Wisconsin. Their paths had crossed many times while they were growing up—in Tunnel City, when they were small children; in Wyeville, where they had both attended elementary school; and at Tomah High. But it was not until they ran into each other in Madison in 1939 that they had become romantically involved. Ruth was working at Droster's General Store on the East Side; Don was on a Civilian Conservation Corps crew building a day lodge at Devil's Lake. He wore a bomber jacket, smoked Lucky Strikes, and drove an "Indian," a big motorcycle that made a deep-throated roar. It seemed that he had been everywhere and seen everything, and he was boss of his crew. Not only was he attractive to Ruth, but no one had ever been so attentive to her; she couldn't make a move without his being right there at her side.

Don had rugged features and a sadness in his eyes. When his crewcut got too long, he looked a little like an Apache warrior. He had never graduated from high school, but read such publications as *Popular Science* and the *Capital Times,* once the mouthpiece of the Progressive party, to keep up with current events. He had opinions on everything, liked to talk, and bristled like a hedgehog when provoked.

In some ways Ruth was the perfect mate for Don, a girl off the farm, short and rounded, with chestnut hair and light brown twinkly eyes, as good-natured and easygoing as Don was nervous and moody, as quiet as he was loud. She never spoke ill of anyone and shunned discussions of political or religious topics. When there was trouble, she tended to duck, let it wash right over her.

They were married in a civil ceremony after a brief courtship in which Don had somehow convinced Ruth that he liked to dance, when in fact he hated it. He was big and fast and physically aggressive, and what he really liked was football. He had played a little semipro ball when he was in his early twenties. Even now, watching the Green Bay Packers on TV was Don's version of Sunday religious observance.

Their first-born, Lorena, died in infancy. Mira came next, in 1941, followed by Karl in 1946, Lorene in 1948, and Dwight in 1951. They were healthy, good-looking children, smarter than average.

Gisholt Machine Works, where Don had been employed since the late 1940s, was a big industrial plant whose skylit yellow-brick buildings stretched along East Washington Avenue for blocks. Don was a master lathesman and shop steward in his local of the United Steelworkers. He had wanted to be a fighter pilot, but an injury to his knee during a base track meet had prematurely ended his air force career in 1946. The trauma of the injury had also triggered varicose veins, which made it painful for him to work on cement floors, such as those at Gisholt. At night he sometimes woke up with blood spurting from broken vessels in his legs. At one point his legs had turned so black that his doctor had recommended amputation. Don had ignored the advice and worked even harder, sometimes putting in seventy hours a week. Bad legs were something a man had to live with if he was ever going to have a place of his own.

But they could never have achieved their dreams on Don's income alone. During thirty years of marriage, Ruth had always held jobs outside the house, whether it was at Sears or Ray-O-Vac or just waitressing. Now she was an attendant at Central Colony Hospital, caring for people with serious physical handicaps, bathing and feeding them, changing their diapers and bed linen. Ruth considered herself lucky compared to her patients, some of whom were of adult size but had no more motor control than an infant. She was at work when the news came that was to shatter the world of material comforts that she and Don had built.

·

Ruth had been anxious those first several days after the bombing. She couldn't help wondering if her boys were mixed up in it. Karl hadn't been himself when he showed up Monday morning; he'd had no appetite. And she had never seen anyone as fidgety as his friend David. Sterling Hall was all her colleagues at work were talking about, leaving her with a tight feeling in her chest. It almost seemed inevitable when her supervisor rushed up looking frightened and said in a low voice, "Ruth, the FBI is here. They want to talk to you."

Ruth had quickly washed up and followed the woman down the corridor to the main office. Heads were sticking out of every office. She had lowered her eyes and tried not to cry. It was the longest walk she had ever taken.

Mira Armstrong Bakken, the oldest of the Armstrongs' four children, was Don's favorite. He had named her after a star, but usually called her "Mike" because he had been hoping for a boy. With her beautiful skin, doelike eyes, and good figure, she looked just like Ruth. Her husband, William Bakken, was a developer, doing quite well in the suburban building boom. They had two girls aged ten and eleven, and a big house farther out on the East Side.

Mira had just gotten a job as a teacher's aide at Lapham Elementary, where the Armstrong children had all gone to school. She was bending down, helping one of her kindergarten pupils, when the FBI agents entered the room and presented their badges. *What did I do?* she wondered. It had not occurred to her that Karl and Dwight might be involved in the bombing.

The FBI agents took her into a little room, sat her down, and launched into a standard Mutt and Jeff routine, one friendly and the other pushy, asking questions about her brothers. "I'm sure they didn't have anything to do with it," she insisted. Several days later, after the warrants were issued, another team showed up, this one from the Criminal Division of the state Department of Justice. "You'll be in trouble if you know where they are," one of them warned her.

Mira stared at them wide-eyed. "Even if I knew, how could I turn in my brothers?"

Mira had in fact seen Dwight only a few hours before the Sterling Hall bombing, and remembered how forlorn he had seemed, holding the family's gray cat and petting it and talking as though there was no tomorrow. She remembered Karl introducing her to a new friend named Leo whose cynicism frightened her. Mira had been praying for Karl and Dwight every Sunday at the Assembly of God Church. *If they are involved, it's because of Leo,* she now thought. A prayer ran through her head like a mantra: *God, don't let it be true!*

In the lives of the Armstrong, Burt, and Fine families, there had never been a bleaker morning than that of Thursday, September 3, 1970. Their children were on the Ten Most Wanted list, hunted by the police of two countries. They were besieged at home by reporters, FBI agents, and hecklers calling them on the phone. Nothing was yet proved, of course, and they were still in denial. "Lies, it's all a bunch of lies!" Mira tearfully told newsmen. They still hoped the charges would prove groundless.

Anne Fine could not believe that David was involved. David had always hated violence. He would cry when he saw the war footage Walter Cronkite presented on the "CBS Evening News." "Somebody must have given him LSD," she said later, when the fact could no longer be denied.

The Burts were just as puzzled. Leo had seemed his usual self over Christmas break. Like many young people he was against the war, but as an activist he did not compare to his cousin Joe Burt, who led the antiwar movement at Villanova. If Leo really was involved, it meant that almost every word of his recent letter from New York, signed "Leo the Graduate" and filled with hope and enthusiasm for life, was false. And that was hard for Howard and May Burt to imagine.

On Wednesday, September 2, a little before noon, Don had received a call from Karl in New York. The elder Armstrong had immediately reported the call to the FBI and that night he went on the "CBS Evening News" with an appeal to Karl and Dwight to turn themselves in. But in placing the fugitives on the FBI's Ten Most Wanted list, Hoover had described them as "armed and dangerous," and that worried Don: With a manhunt on, his boys could get hurt. "Karl wouldn't hurt anybody," he complained to George Baxtrum over the phone. Baxtrum tried to reassure Armstrong, and he dispatched Special Agent John Schroepfer, the one who had offended Donald by asking his opinion of Nixon, to Hintze Road to field threatening phone calls.

The Armstrong family's Labor Day gathering was to take place at the Bakkens' new house in Lakeview Heights. The Bakkens were

one of Madison's old German families, and Don, who was hyper-
sensitive in such matters, sensed that they looked down on the
Armstrongs. Mira's husband Bill voted Republican; Donald's hero
was Franklin Delano Roosevelt. At the dinner table, they got into
an argument over the boys, with Bill taking an "I told you so attitude" on the bombing. It ended with thc two of them going chin to
chin out in the driveway.

The women hunkered down with the dishes, trying not to hear
the shouts. Mira's thoughts were on Dwight, running for his life
somewhere in Canada. When Ruth had gone back to work after
Dwight was born, Mira had taken over, feeding and changing him
and toting him on her hip like a grown woman, though she was only
ten. She could still see him running away from home in his cowboy
outfit, telling neighbors he was on his way to Texas. *My baby, my
baby,* she thought. Then Ruth was crying, and they were two pairs
of trembling shoulders at the tile draining board, bravely rinsing the
plates and loading the automatic dishwasher and grieving for a
dream gone bad.

The crimes were very different, and yet to Joe Sullivan's way of
thinking, there were certain parallels. In both WISBOM and
MIBURN, the famous "Mississippi Burning" investigation of murdered civil rights workers, you had political motives, you had a conspiracy of silence, and you had recalcitrant local prosecutors. The
inspector could remember a meeting with the governor and attorney general of Mississippi in 1964. "We have a case," he informed
them, "but we recognize that the crimes you can charge them with
are more serious than ours, and we would defer to you if you want
to go first." "Mister Sullivan, you just go right ahead," they had
replied. And so Sullivan had, and it had been a most impressive
case, and the federal charges of conspiracy and civil rights violations had stuck. But Mississippi never had proceeded with its own
state charges, had never even asked to see his materials. The Nesho-
ba and Lauderdale county klansmen who were responsible for the
deaths of Chaney, Goodman, and Schwerner never had to pay the
price for cold-blooded murder.

Now he could not get state charges brought against the killers of
Robert Fassnacht even though the chances of apprehending the fugitives diminished with each passing day. From Ed Hayes he had
learned that state officials were upset because the suspects had been

announced in Washington rather than Madison. Tom McMillen was still shaking over his unpleasant encounter with Sheriff Leslie. Reportedly, MPD investigators had been leaving matchboxes on the Library Mall with money in them and messages to be delivered to the conspirators. Sullivan knew for a fact that Detective Lulling had been shadowing FBI investigators, reinterviewing everyone they talked to. It put a strain on Sullivan's usual equanimity. "I don't give a damn," he told Hayes in regard to all the bruised egos. "You can tell 'em I was responsible. It was an FBI investigation. We did it right."

But the fugitives were gone, and there was nothing to do but let the Mounties try to find them. Sullivan resumed the WISBOM investigation with a vengeance. One of his teams had been "doing a neighborhood," as FBI agents say, on eastern Sauk County, poking around in Devil's Lake State Park, inquiring at farmhouses, traveling dirt roads until their governmental sedans were gray with dust. On September 5, a team led by Hobart Lovett, an agent from LaCrosse, came upon a farmer named Curtis Hill, who remembered seeing some unusual activity as he was plowing at the Holland farm just north of Devil's Lake a few days before the bombing. Lovett followed Hill down nearby Newman Road to a point where an almost invisible track led off through the brush, a farm kids' lover's lane. A hundred yards in they discovered a grassy clearing, on the opposite side of which was the field Hill had been plowing. They found traces of ammonium nitrate and fuel oil everywhere in the chemically scorched grass and an oil drum with the mysterious words "Wes Hardner"—someone's name, they presumed— spray-painted on it. The surrounding brush yielded a gritty piece of plywood and an orange "Peterson for Governor" placard.

The plywood turned out to be from the Farmers Union Co-op in Baraboo; the manager remembered having had to use it to hold the doors shut on the fertilizer-loaded U-Haul. The barrel was traced to Cepek Construction, an East Side Madison firm, and had once contained cement hardener for use at the West Towne Mall project (hence the "Wes Hardner" notation). But it was the placard that convinced Sullivan that they had found the staging area. As Baxtrum explained to him, Don Peterson was a Democratic candidate for governor; Larry Travis, the man from whom the van had been stolen, was an avid Peterson supporter and had mentioned the placard in his interview. It was bright orange, he had said—made it himself.

Sullivan meanwhile had been spending a lot of time with the

files in Baxtrum's office, going over the material generated by the nine-month New Year's Gang investigation. "I want to see what turns up," he explained to Tom McMillen. McMillen would see him there scanning 302s when he left for home and again at 8:00 A.M. when he arrived for work. *When did Sullivan sleep?* he wondered.

Toward the end of his second week in Madison, Sullivan called McMillen into the office and handed him the report of an interview with a certain Lynn Marie Schultz, dated January 16, 1970, back in the early stages of the terrorism epidemic. McMillen recognized the words and the signature at the bottom of the page—they were his own. In the interview Schultz was accounting for her whereabouts the night of January 4, when the Wisconsin Primate Center had been mistakenly firebombed, instead of the State Selective Service headquarters, directly across the street. Madison police detective George Croal, who was on a stakeout that night, had gotten the license number of a Chevrolet Impala circling in the vicinity half an hour before he discovered the fire and passed the information to McMillen. McMillen had traced the car to a Mr. and Mrs. Schultz in Wisconsin Dells, a resort community about an hour north of Madison. Mr. Schultz, a plumber, said that his daughter Lynn Marie was the vehicle's primary user and that Lynn could be reached at the Ray-O-Vac Company, where she was employed as a clerk. A Ray-O-Vac secretary from the Dells did not fit McMillen's profile of a saboteur. Ten days elapsed before he got around to calling her, and she said nothing that might have fueled suspicion. McMillen had filed the following report:

During the early morning hours of January 4, 1970, at approximately 2:15 A.M., SCHULTZ, driving alone, drove in the vicinity of the State of Wisconsin Selective Service Headquarters situated on Capitol Court, Madison, to see a friend living on West Lawn Street, near the University of Wisconsin. The friend was not home. She then drove back through the Capitol Court area and proceeded on the main thoroughfares across town to pick up a boyfriend, KARL ARMSTRONG, who got off from work at 2:30 A.M.

SCHULTZ said that she did not return to the Capitol Court area after picking up her boyfriend, ARMSTRONG. She saw no suspicious individuals or automobiles when driving to or from the friend's house on West Lawn Street.

SCHULTZ is not in receipt of any information concerning the identities of the people or groups of people who may be responsible for the fire bombing incidents on the UW campus....

McMillen had not followed up with an in-person interview, nor had he attempted to check out Karl Armstrong. In retrospect it looked bad, and as he handed the document back to Sullivan, McMillen braced himself for a chewing out. But the inspector only grinned and waved him out of the office.

They found Lynn Schultz in Springfield Corners, twenty minutes north of the city, where she was staying with her boyfriend, Sandy Nelson, a partner in Golden Freek Enterprises. The Golden Freeks were in the business of promoting outdoor rock festivals, but they were not having a good year. They had gone broke on a festival in Poynette, Wisconsin, that spring, and since then, they had been hounded out of Iowa, Illinois, and Pennsylvania. Since a fatal stabbing incident at a Rolling Stones appearance in the hills of Altamont, California, in December 1969, authorities all over the United States had been discouraging outdoor rock festivals.

Lynn Schultz was nineteen, adopted, no siblings, no criminal record. She had quit her job at Ray-O-Vac in May to follow the Golden Freeks in their luckless interstate search for a new festival site. She spoke willingly to the FBI team, and like most people untutored in the art of deception, revealed much that was true among the lies—most important, that she had spent New Year's Eve with Karl Armstrong partying at the Nitty Gritty, a popular bar, and at Phi Sigma Kappa, the fraternity house where he was boarding at the time. Karl had borrowed her car and disappeared without explanation from 11 P.M. to 1 A.M., Schultz said—roughly the time frame of the Badger Ordnance bombing, as Baxtrum later informed Sullivan. Schultz also revealed that Dwight knew how to fly a plane. It was obvious that Lynn Schultz had a great deal of information, and she was promptly subpoenaed.

On September 9, under a grant of immunity worked out for her by Madison attorney Jack Van Metre, who was also counsel to Golden Freek Enterprises, Lynn Schultz testified at length to the federal grand jury, implicating Karl Armstrong in the December 28, 1969, firebombing of an ROTC classroom know as T-16; in the New Year's Eve raid on the Badger Ordnance Works; in the January 3 firebombing of the Old Red Gym (campus headquarters of the

ROTC); in the January 4 firebombing of the University of Wisconsin Primate Research Center; and in the February 22 attempt on the Wisconsin Power and Light substation at Prairie du Sac, supplier of electrical power to Badger Ordnance. As far as Lynn knew, Dwight had been involved only in the New Year's Eve mission, as the pilot. She had served as Karl's driver on that occasion and on at least two others. She had last seen Karl two weeks before the Sterling Hall bombing, when he stopped by to ask her if she would help him out with some "heavy revolutionary activity." He was driving a dilapidated Cadillac hearse.

One more piece of the puzzle fell into place when Scott Nelson turned up at an uncle's house in Gilroy in the heart of California's Salinas Valley. Nelson (no relation to Lynn's boyfriend Sandy Nelson), a good-looking northern Wisconsin boy, had been Karl Armstrong's roommate at Phi Sigma Kappa during the fall of 1969. After drawing a low number in the new draft lottery, he had dropped out of school, enlisted in the air force, and had recently completed his basic training. He was on leave, awaiting transfer to an air base in Spain, when the bombing took place. He had told his parents he was driving out West to climb Mount Rainier. That information had gotten Seattle agents a weekend in the great outdoors, but all to no avail: Scott had stopped at Glacier National Park instead.

Nelson was obviously reluctant to talk. However, the FBI had enough on him from Lynn Schultz to issue a subpoena and to threaten him with prosecution if he refused to cooperate. Nelson returned to Madison and testified on September 15, providing the government with one valuable detail: He had seen Burt, Fine, and the Armstrongs at Leo's apartment two days before the bombing.

That same day, federal agents found a rusted 1961 Plymouth with Wisconsin plates in the Tow Away Storage Facilities in New York City. The car had been towed on September 4 after standing in a restricted parking area for a week. Inside they found Leo Burt's checkbook with an uncashed check made out to David Fine; a keychain license plate facsimile with the Armstrong Corvair's number on it; a note from a certain "Bill" to someone named "Buzzy" regarding the parlous state of the car's tires; and road maps, newspapers, pop bottles, and an empty pack of Viceroys—Dwight's brand. Dwight's fingerprints were found on the rear-view mirror,

Karl's on the maps. Baxtrum, whose wife called him "Buddy," remembered that "Buzzy" was David Fine's nickname. "Bill" turned out to be William Limbach, a friend of Fine's from the campus YMCA, where David had resided during the fall semester. It was Limbach's car the boys had borrowed on the morning of their escape from Devil's Lake.

For the student movement, the rollback came fast and hard. After two editorials appeared in the *Daily Cardinal* supporting the conspirators, advertisers boycotted the paper, causing it to lose 75 percent of its news pages within a few weeks. The paper's outgoing editor, Steve Reiner, discovered that he could not get a newspaper job anywhere in the country, not even at the *Capital Times.* Even though the case against Burt, Fine, and the Armstrongs was already overwhelming, the FBI stayed on the attack, greeting returning student activists with unannounced visits and, in some cases, grand-jury subpoenas. Anyone who even knew a radical was interviewed, including the physician who had installed a pacemaker in the heart of John "Nekko" Nekkhorochef, a French anarchist residing in Miffland, and Rabbi Swarsensky, who had given Fassnacht's eulogy, because he had also presided at the wedding of the former *Cardinal* arts editor Eliot Silberberg. Silberberg himself, now teaching at Canisius College in Buffalo, New York and apparently ignorant of the bomb plot, nevertheless was interviewed repeatedly. Senator McGovern's son-in-law, Jim Rowen, was tracked down at a trailer court in Taos, New Mexico. The agents asked not only about the four suspects, but about SDS activities in Madison and the whereabouts of Weatherman fugitives Mark Rudd, Bernardine Dohrn, Jeff Jones, and Cathy Wilkerson. Many activists left town to avoid being subpoenaed, taking refuge in communes out West.

The role of revolutionary had suddenly become a lot more difficult to play. A local mime troupe performing a skit exculpating the bombers found itself chased off the Library Mall. Irate townspeople beat up hawkers of the *Kaleidoscope*'s "Bomb Extra" on Capitol Square. Addressing a group of Illinois legislators, Mayor Dyke defended such vigilantism. "This is a do-it-yourself age," he said, paraphrasing longshoreman-author Eric Hoffer, "and people must be induced to be their own policemen."

John Weaver, Fred Harrington's replacement, had elaborate electronic security systems installed in the president's mansion and in his office in Van Hise Hall. By pressing a button under her desk, his secretary could now instantly call both the building's elevators to the seventeenth floor and hold them there indefinitely. In the Wisconsin statehouse, conservatives introduced a bill to merge the Madison campus with those in Milwaukee, Green Bay, and Kenosha/Racine, threatening its proud independence. Former president Harrington had blocked such legislation in the past. Weaver, falling into step with the Board of Regents, announced that he would support the merger. Legislators also approved increased funds for campus security, taking the money from educational programs, and the MPD was granted permission, over the objections of UP & S chief Ralph Hanson, to patrol the campus.

The bombing yielded another unexpected dividend for law enforcement when Julie Maynard volunteered to work for the MPD as an informant. An East Side girl, Maynard suffered from extreme obesity as well as from the elongated jaw and crooked teeth that are symptomatic of Krohn's Disease. Around campus she was known as "Fat Julie." She had made herself indispensable to the movement by answering the all-night phone at Acid Rescue and managing the People's Office, a sort of hippie welfare agency. The death of Robert Fassnacht had so upset her that the next time she heard talk of violence, she called the MPD and was put through to Detective George Croal. Croal soon convinced her that she could save lives by working with the authorities. Maynard proved to have an ear for gossip, and in the next three years, she would become one of the most productive spies in the U.S, graduating from the MPD to the FBI and eventually serving the CIA in Beijing.

Mark Knops remained incarcerated in Walworth County Jail throughout the fall, spending much of the time in isolation with nothing to read but a Bible. No newspaper supported him in his stand for the right of journalists to protect their sources. The Wisconsin Supreme Court upheld the contempt ruling, citing the public's "overriding need to know" and arguing that the civil emergency created by the bombing justified infringing upon Knops's claim of journalistic immunity:

> In a disorderly society such as we are currently experiencing it may well be appropriate to curtail in a very minor way the free flow of information, if such curtailment will serve the purpose of restoring an atmosphere in which all our fundamental freedoms can flourish.

Nationally as well as locally, the bombing had changed the subject of conversation from the misdeeds of the Nixon administration to those of the activists and intellectuals. "It isn't just the radicals who set the bomb in a lighted, occupied building who are guilty," observed the *Wisconsin State Journal.* "The blood is on the hands of anyone who has encouraged them, anyone who has talked recklessly of 'revolution,' anyone who has chided with mild disparagement the violence of extremists while hinting that the cause is right all the same." In a September 16 speech at Kansas State University, President Nixon quoted the *Journal* editorial in the process of condemning the "cancerous disease" of terrorism:

> What corrodes a society even more deeply than violence itself is the acceptance of violence, the condoning of terror, the excusing of inhuman acts in a misguided effort to accommodate the community's standards to those of the violent few.

Nixon was determined to recapture the moral high ground lost as a result of the Kent State shootings. The text of his Kansas speech, widely quoted in the world press, presented the Madison bombing as Exhibit A:

> We saw it three weeks ago in the vicious bombing at the University of Wisconsin, in which one man lost his life, four were injured and years of painstaking research by a score of others destroyed.

The bombing also upset Melvin Laird, Nixon's secretary of defense. Laird was a Wisconsinite. His mother, a member of the university's Board of Regents, had helped obtain approval of the plan for the AMRC. Laird himself, while serving in the House of Representatives, had gained the defense committee's approval of funds to establish it. With a son involved in antiwar protests on the state campus at Eau Claire, Laird was probably the closest thing to a dove in the Nixon cabinet. In his first year in his post he had abolished the draft and replaced it with a lottery system that minimized class privilege in the method of recruitment. He had begun withdrawing U.S. troops and "Vietnamizing" the war. Having opposed the Administration in the matter of Cambodia, he was already on thin ice with Nixon, and now his influence slipped further. "The bombing hurt me," he said later. "It hurt my work to terminate the war."

Harvey Goldberg, the radical historian, had spent the 1969–70 academic year with his young partner Martin Jette in a rented flat on the rue Vaneau, across the street from an apartment Karl Marx had lived in on a visit to Paris 130 years earlier. "Madison is where I work; Paris is where I live," Goldberg liked to say. He was a sticklike little man of 47, with a shock of black hair that hung in his eyes, a long bony nose, an impish smile, and skin like the pages of an old paperback. His color was navy blue, whether the garment was a sweater, a cap, or one of his made-to-order suits from British American Imports in New York. Dark clothing and amber-tinted glasses gave him the forbidding look of a European intellectual. Incessant smoking and drinking had displaced the primary oral gratification of his youth, eating. (He had once weighed 200 pounds, but had lost the weight after an auto accident in West Virginia that had put him in a body cast for months.) In America his smoke was Pall Mall straights; a carton was good for two days. In France it was Gauloises Blu. He actually drank forty cups of coffee a day and rarely slept more than two or three hours.

Goldberg had grown up in the Oranges, New Jersey. He never talked about his father, who was a wastrel; it was his grandfather, a shtetl Jew from Russia and a Hassidic rabbi, to whom he looked up. Goldberg had long since abandoned Hassidism, but he still carried a picture of his grandfather, and his face lit up whenever he spoke of him. In his own way he carried on his grandfather's work.

Martin Jette was twenty years younger than Goldberg and looked suited to the part of a lieutenant in the Waffen SS, complete with a curving red scar on one cheek and cruel blue eyes. The two had been together since the day in 1965 when Jette, a beer-addled, sexually confused fraternity boy, had stumbled into Goldberg's office upset over a health problem of a sort that he could not discuss with his parents. He found Goldberg remarkably understanding and sympathetic. A five-hour coffee meeting followed at the National Motor Inn, followed by a jug of wine at Goldberg's Miffland apartment and a sampling of Goldberg's jazz and folk-music collection: Bud Powell, Odetta, Nina Simone, and a lot of smoky club music from the days of the Weimar Republic. Before long they were bumming around Europe together, taking the Whore's Walk in Genoa and exploring the Villa Floridiana in Naples. Harvey had a great sense of fun, it seemed to Jette, and he knew something about every street in Paris. In Paris Goldberg did not have to hide his homosexuality or soft-peddle his political views. He could write for the gay journals, participate in the Russell War Crimes Tribunal, and dine with Madame Binh and other members of the North Vietnamese delegation to the peace talks without giving it a second thought. He was happier in Paris, Jette observed, much happier.

But they had had a fight that summer after Jette broke up a political soiree at the swank rue Bonaparte apartment of Mariah Jolas, a prominent member of the international peace movement. The evening had been nothing more than a "group circle jerk for rich expatriates," in Jette's opinion, but Goldberg was furious at him. Goldberg could be especially unpleasant toward those to whom he was closest, and so Jette had been exiled to Madison early. He was sleeping in a friend's University Avenue apartment four blocks from Sterling Hall when the bomb went off, and the blast wave had knocked him out of bed. Goldberg arrived three weeks later, just in time for the start of classes.

Goldberg's reputation as an oracle of the New Left had only grown during his absence, and his followers eagerly awaited his resumption of teaching duties. That fall he was to present his famous course on European social history in the twentieth century, in which he covered Lenin, Trotsky, and the Bolshevik Revolution. When he arrived in late September for his first lecture at Agriculture Hall, the only building with an auditorium large enough to accommodate his classes, he faced an overflow crowd. What would Harvey say now that someone had blown up half the campus?

Goldberg lectured without notes, a technique he had learned from his mentor Fred Harvey Harrington in Harrington's teaching days. Harrington was brilliant, but Goldberg was a genius, his lectures carefully crafted one-act plays. In his seven years at the University of Wisconsin he had created a virtual cult. Thousands of students who, as a result of the Cold War, had reached college age knowing nothing of the socialist tradition had been introduced to that forbidden fruit by Harvey Goldberg. His classes had become like convenings of a revolutionary republic, with initiates at ground level, savants in the balcony, and the numerous teaching assistants functioning as sergeants at arms. Even more than his better-known colleague William Appleman Williams, it was Goldberg who had made America's "best place to live" a mecca for young radicals, who had turned Madison's isthmus into the Third Coast.

Now his followers were on the run, and Goldberg himself, appalled by the physical and political wreckage left by the bombing, could not bring himself to address the subject for several weeks. None of the accused was his student or even anyone he knew, yet he felt personally responsible for what had happened, he told friends. It was obvious from their communiqués that the bombers had believed in the revolution. The bombing had to be understood in its historical context, he said finally. It was a terrible tragedy, but it had to be seen in the light of seven years of failed efforts to stop the war by peaceful means. You had to consider the failure of the political machinery to respond to the cries of the people. Fassnacht's death and the injuries to innocents had to be set against the daily annihilation of Southeast Asians under American bombardment.

After issuing his analysis, Goldberg returned hastily to the past, to the romantic heyday of international socialism, where he was more at home. He had given the same set of lectures in the fall of 1966, arguing that *tout est possible* ("everything is possible") and that the only path to permanent peace was a revolution that would abolish class distinctions and national frontiers. But now, students ran a gauntlet of boarded-up buildings on their way to and from class, and a sign hung from a window in Sterling Hall deploring "the use of violence in the name of peace." Goldberg's one serious ideological rival, the cultural historian George Mosse, exploited his newfound advantage. "You were so respectable," Mosse told his students scathingly. "You thought you could make a revolution without consequences. Well, any revolution has to step over bodies, didn't you know?"

Goldberg's former student Mark Knops, the son of a hard-luck New Jersey bartender, was a pessimistic young man who, if it was snowing in the morning, was sure his car would go off the road, and if it did would say, "We'll never get it out." Yet he had convinced himself that, as Goldberg said, everything really was possible. In 1967 Knops thought he had seen a "window of opportunity" opening for that transformation of values that Goldberg had predicted. He had given up his promising academic career to pursue that vision, convinced that real change would be brought about by college students allied with street kids and dropouts. It was Knops who, as editor of the underground newspaper *Madison Kaleidoscope,* had given the New Year's Gang its name and had made folk heroes of the saboteurs, at least among student radicals.

It wasn't until January 1971 that Knops was released from jail. The temperature was five below zero. Phil Ball, a tenant-union activist, and several other friends picked him up in a beat-up station wagon. The floor was rusted, there was no heater, and they were all shivering under a blanket. Knops had to use a scraper to keep the ice off the inside of the windshield. On the way back to Madison they stopped at a farm in Ball's hometown of Mukwonago, where an elderly friend, curious about the notorious Mark Knops, asked him about his plans for the Madison campus. "I'd like to see a hundred bulldozers push the university into the lake," Knops replied. His friends could see that he meant it. It was as though he had given up on the world.

In Madison Knops found the streets quiet. Organizers could not make a move without the police being aware of it beforehand. (Knops did not know it, but the police had an informant, not Phil Ball, in the car that brought him home from jail.) The Mother Jones Revolutionary League had withered, and something called the Wisconsin Alliance, a reformist third-party movement, was on the ascendant. However, even liberal Democrats had a hard time winning a majority in local elections that fall. Patrick Quinn, a Trotskyist presenting himself as a prolabor candidate for the city council, had been heckled at every appearance by workers shouting "No more bombing!" The bombing had split the movement between the tough-minded few who condoned it and a much larger number who did not. Knops's own staff was divided, and one faction was planning to put out a more respectable publication to rival the *Kaleidoscope.*

Instead of inspiring copycat bombings, though, Army Math had been followed by a general retreat from violence, not only locally but all across the country. The biggest action of the fall in Madison had been a food fight in Gordon Commons, a cafeteria serving the Southeast Dorms. It was as if all the pent-up anger over the war had been vented in a single blast. To Mark Knops, the window of opportunity for revolution had been slammed shut while he was in jail. The sixties were over, not just chronologically, but spiritually. *That's just old pessimistic Mark; he'll snap out of it,* some of his friends thought. But Knops refused to resume his editorial responsibilities. He gradually withdrew from politics and eventually moved to Montana where he went to work as a surveyor.

By January 1971 Inspector Joe Sullivan and everyone else in the FBI were aware of a sea change in American society. It was especially noticeable to George Menzel on the Sabotage Desk in Washington: The level of political violence was subsiding nationwide. The WISBOM investigation seemed to have had the kind of sobering effect in the North that MIBURN had had all across the South.

The federal grand jury had brought down conspiracy indictments against the four fugitives at the end of September. Along with the AEC accelerator and computer that were damaged, the indictment specified Army Math as a target of the bombing and added a felony count for attempting to "injure, intimidate, and interfere with" center personnel "because of their participation in a program receiving federal financial assistance."

Joe Sullivan returned to New York. Before leaving Madison, he turned over an updated copy of his investigative report to U.S. Attorney John Olson, and Olson gave a copy to the Madison Police Department. In the opinion of both Sullivan and Olson, the report contained everything necessary to prosecute the four, but once again District Attorney Boll declined to issue murder warrants on the basis of the federal case.

The hunt for the fugitives continued in every corner of the North American continent. Sullivan no longer believed that Army Math was the target of a broader conspiracy. Karl Armstrong was such a blabbermouth that if higher-ups were involved, he surely would have told someone. No, it appeared that the largest homemade bomb in history had been set off by those four boys in the yellow Corvair, acting on their own. The two sons of a Madison factory hand, a former member of the university crew, and one of the smartest kids in the freshman class had somehow found each other and inadvertently brought down the house. What peculiar human chemistry had produced that immense and tragic blast? Looking at the 302s, Sullivan thought he recognized in Karl Armstrong a personality type he had encountered before, and not just in cases of left-wing activity. But not having met Karl, he couldn't be sure. Where had all that violence come from?

Part II

THE

SLEEPWALKER

4

An All-American Boy

It is not incorrect to state that the United States was lied into this war. And I think that acts of resistance are fully justified.

—ERNEST GRUENING,
former U.S. Senator, for the defense

Your honor, the inescapable conclusion of that kind of logic is anarchy.

—DOUGLAS HAAG,
Wisconsin Assistant Attorney General, for the prosecution

Donald Armstrong, the power in the Armstrong family and the shaping influence in Karl's life, had been abandoned by his parents when he was five and raised by a succession of relatives, most notably his paternal grandmother, Ann Rector Armstrong. A "hard-bitten, pie-eating Methodist," as he later described her, Ann Rector had communicated to Don a profound sense of his own unworthiness, treating him as a domestic slave and forcing him to wear girl's clothes to school. An arthritic, impoverished, and embittered old woman who walked with a cane, she never let Don forget that he was her punishment for Alvah, Don's wayward father, a bootlegger and career criminal.

Donald wanted his own children to know they were loved. At Christmas he would buy them expensive presents, things the family really could not afford. He taught them how to swim and fish and took them on camping trips all over the country, retracing the journeys he had undertaken after running away from home at seventeen. He had a well-equipped workshop and taught his boys carpentry. Dwight was not receptive to his father's overtures, so Don concentrated on Karl, getting him into the Madison Drum and Bugle Corps and the Madison Boys Choir, buying him patent-leather tap-dancing shoes, and paying for lessons at the Kales School of Dancing, opportunities such as Don had never had. Karl worked his way up through every level of scouting and, at Don's urging, joined DeMolay, the youth affiliate of the Masonic Lodge, of which Don was a member. He played Little League baseball and eventually went out for high school football, which made Don especially proud.

Ann Rector's Bible thumping had made Don an agnostic, but he did not discourage religious tendencies in his children. Mira would remember his holding her in his lap for hours as he went on about what heaven was like. Mira took to religion and occasionally succeeded in dragging the whole family to Sunday services, first at the Moravian Church and later at Lakeview Lutheran. The boys attended Bible school through the fifth grade.

For all his attentiveness, Donald was strict with the children. When Mira stole grapes from Carp's Grocery Store in the Greenbush, an old ethnic neighborhood where they resided for several years, he sent her back to pay for them and to say she was sorry. Any Armstrong child who was caught in a lie had to sit in the corner and say, "I will not tell a lie" 100 times. For a repeat offense it was 200 times.

On the rarer occasions that Ruth put her foot down, it could shake the house. However, neither she nor Donald tolerated anyone outside the family disciplining their children. Once Karl was set upon by Mrs. Connelly, the Irishwoman who lived next door to them in the Greenbush, a fine, old ethnic neighborhood destined to be "renewed" out of existence, for taking a radish from her garden. Mrs. Connelly was a formidable woman, especially when she'd been drinking, but no one could outtalk Donald when he was angry, and their shouting match drew the whole neighborhood. When Karl's sixth-grade teacher shoved him for taking an extra bowl of green jello salad in the cafeteria, Donald stormed into the school and shoved the teacher back, shouting, "Don't you ever touch my son again!"

At the dinner table Don would talk nonstop, usually about himself and the hardships he experienced growing up. Karl absorbed it all—the scavenging for cinders to feed the stove in Ann Rector's house, the dresses and high-heeled shoes he had to wear, riding the rails during the Great Depression, the building of Hoover Dam, the CCC project at Devil's Lake, the knee injury that ended his air force career. As an adult, Karl would remember his father's childhood better than his own.

Don also liked to expound on his admiration of FDR and the New Deal, his suspicion of Communists, and his loathing for Hitler. He would remind Karl that the day he was born—October 15, 1946—was the day the Nazi war criminals were hung. (Ten of them, in fact, were executed on October 16 of that year.) As Karl would testify years later, *We talked about Nuremberg, and my father couldn't understand why the German people didn't resist. He thought that just about any act of resistance would have been justified. And that left a lasting impression in my mind.*

The nurses at Madison General Hospital remembered Karl Armstrong as "the baby with the low cry." Karl's voice would always be that way, faint and high pitched; he made a good boy soprano. He seemed to take after Ruth more than Donald, gentle and accommodating, with a sly sense of humor. He was never disruptive in school, never got into playground fights, never complained, and was so quiet that his teachers sometimes forgot he was there. The only thing about him that worried Don and Ruth was his sleepwalking, a trait he shared with Mira. Once he came downstairs in his pajamas during a card party. "What are you doing out of bed, Karl?" Ruth asked. The question woke him up. In his dream he had been treading water in the ocean, dodging warships and shrapnel from barrage balloons and bursting antiaircraft shells. But all he said was, "Balloons!"

At his sentence mitigation hearing in 1973, Karl would talk about the Cold War and its effects on his development.

Somehow a very deep-rooted fear was indoctrinated into me about Communism. It was a very abstract idea, and yet the fear existed and

*I didn't know why it existed. Didn't know anything about Commu-
nism. I didn't even know it was a political system. It was just a word.
If you touched a Communist, that you would be brainwashed; you
would be duped.*

And then there was the atomic bomb. Karl would recall the civil
defense exercizes, the pictures he was shown of the damage to
Hiroshima and Nagasaki, Japanese cities destroyed by nuclear
weapons.

*We were in a constant state of terror. And I know that people in my
generation, I think that ... our major concern was to make sure that
there was peace in the world.*

One of Karl's teachers at Sunnyside Elementary School would
remember him standing up and lecturing his classmates on political
matters, probably repeating things he had heard Don say at home.
Only once is he known to have played a prank, and that was on a
substitute teacher, a certain Mrs. Harmon who had been his Sunday
School instructor at the Moravian Church. Karl was aware that she
was afraid of snakes and brought one in a coffee can for show-and-
tell, intending to give her a scare. She told him to put it in a cupboard. "It didn't work, did it?" he said sheepishly.

Karl always lived on the outskirts of town, at a distance from
school and isolated from classmates. It didn't matter much at Sunnyside, but when he began attending Sherman Middle School, he
got his first taste of cliquedom. Leah Sachtjen, the daughter of
Judge William Sachtjen, a former city manager and one of Madison's most prominent men, was a classmate. Leah had her father's
intelligence and good looks, as well as the Sachtjen drive, running
for student council president in the eighth grade and winning, after
a recount. Karl had heard Ruth talk about Bill Sachtjen, with
whom she had worked at Droster's General Store when Sachtjen
was still in law school. He admired Leah but did not know how to
approach her because she belonged to the "in" group at Sherman,
and he did not.

Mira had already graduated and gotten married by the time Karl
arrived at East High School in 1960. Lorene would follow him there
two years later, and eventually, so would Dwight. East High faced
East Washington Avenue, not far from the Gisholt plant. It was the
sort of stern, high-windowed, neoclassical building that seems
designed to intimidate the young. Its 1,500 students were a cross

section of Madison society, including not only children from blue-collar families like the Armstrongs, but students from the mansions of Maple Bluffs. Boys with souped-up cars and slicked-back hair gravitated to the Purgolder Cafe, a burger shack on Fifth Street across from the school. Schoep's Ice Cream Parlor, on East Washington, was for "nice" kids. Across the wide avenue from Schoep's, Tower Lunch drew the class-cutting delinquents.

Karl did not seem to fit in anywhere. His B average qualified him for the Schoep's set, but he felt inadequate around Maple Bluffs kids. He did not have a car. Greasers made him nervous. His only extracurricular activity was football, and though he played tackle on the reserve unit, he was splay-footed and unaggressive.

Karl seemed to be interested mainly in the outdoors. He liked to walk the heather-choked fields around Truax, flushing pheasant and quail. Until he acquired an aversion to killing, he would go bow hunting for rabbits or stab at carp in the swamps with his friends Ron and Randy Trachte. By Karl's standards, the Trachte brothers were rich kids. They lived in a house with a pier on Lake Mendota. Karl would arrive at their home with a bag of golf balls gleaned from the Maple Bluffs Country Club, and they would drive them off the dock. Robert Trachte, the boys' father, liked Karl and called him "Jack Armstrong, the All-American Boy" after a character in a national radio program. In winter he would take the boys for 80 miles-per-hour rides on his ice skimmer.

For Karl's fourteenth birthday, Don gave him a brand-new Remington .22 with a scope on it. Karl took it out and shot a gray squirrel with it. He brought the bloody carcass home and tried to get Lorene to cook it. When she refused, he cooked it himself and ate it at the dinner table. Karl never used the gun after that. He would cite the episode when he later gave up eating meat, and while incarcerated in Wunpun State Prison he would write a short story whose moral was that it is wrong to needlessly kill even a squirrel.

Scouting was the activity in which Karl continued to feel most at home. He stayed with it all through high school, taking part in boating and spelunking trips and snow-camping on the Wisconsin River. He would remember the campfire talks with his fellow scouts as being akin to a "religious experience." And along with everyone else he pledged to do his best "for God and my country," the Scout's honor.

In July 1960 Karl attended the National Jamboree in Colorado
Springs. It was the fiftieth anniversary of the founding of the Boy
Scouts, and scouts from all over the world attended—56,377 of
them, to be exact. The army built a tent city four miles square for
the event. Karl stayed with the Wisconsin delegation on Jamboree
Avenue, facing the archery range. President Eisenhower drove by,
waving from an open limousine, and James Arness of "Gunsmoke"
fame signed autographs. One night world friendship circles were
sponsored at which the boys were reminded that a "Scout is a
friend to all and a brother to every other Scout." Karl received a
Golden Rule marble to carry always.

On the last night, all 56,377 scouts lit candles on a dark hillside
and renewed their oath to God and country. They sang the famous
song that Katherine Lee Bates wrote one morning in 1893 after
watching a sunrise from the summit of Pike's Peak, and then it was
over, and the scouts went home.

In the next three years came a series of events that would change
forever the way Americans felt about their country: the election of
John Fitzgerald Kennedy, the Cuban Missile Crisis *(I recall listening
very intently to the radio because we had this president who was not
afraid of a nuclear confrontation),* the Bay of Pigs *(I put myself in
the shoes of the Cuban people),* the assassination of Kennedy and
the Johnson Administration's commitment of American troops to a
new land war in Asia *(I felt betrayed by the president of the United
States).* Before long, Karl Armstrong would ridicule his experience
at Colorado Springs, mocking the patriotic interpretation of American history. He would describe the feeling of oneness he had
enjoyed in scouting as bordering on "fascist."

But at the time, it was the only brotherhood he knew.

5

A University
for the People

*And because of the ferocious burning of Napalm B, the CS
gas is chemically changed and becomes hydrogen cyanide. It
is similar to the cyanide compounds that the Nazis used
against the Jews, and that's what we were using against the
Indochinese.*

—STEVEN HAWKINS,
Vietnam veteran, for the defense

We recognize that war is hell.

—DOUGLAS HAAG,
Wisconsin Assistant Attorney General, for the prosecution

Fred Harvey Harrington had seen the baby boom coming. As
early as 1958, when he was promoted to vice president of the
University of Wisconsin, he had begun to lobby for new dorms and
classrooms. Within a few short years, he predicted, the war babies
would be arriving at the gate, and what was the university going to
do, turn them away? Harrington did not go along with the Ivy
League snobs on the faculty who thought higher education should
be reserved for the elite; he wanted every child to have a chance.
But the committee that was responsible for new construction found
his numbers preposterous and simply revised them downward. It

wasn't until 1962, when President Conrad Elvehjem died unexpect-edly and Harrington was asked to replace him, that he was able to do something about it. And by then the flood had already begun.

The first several years of his administration were like an academ-ic version of the New Deal, with Harrington striding to the Capitol every day to free up the purse strings of state government. He expanded the Milwaukee campus and had new degree-granting campuses built in the industrial centers of Green Bay and Kenosha-Racine. In Madison he won approval for the Southeast Dorms, a Manhattan-like cluster of high rises that would give the city a new skyline; a new humanities complex at the foot of Bascom Hill; and a new journalism building and undergraduate library and cancer research center, among other projects.

Back in the early years of the century, when Governor Robert LaFollette, inspired by the "Wisconsin Idea," was calling upon the best minds of academia to help solve problems of state, Wisconsin was widely touted as the "greatest university in the world." Har-rington's ambition was no less than to return the school to that exalted status. One of his first presidential moves was to get WARF funds opened to the social sciences. The Wisconsin Alumni Research Foundation, whose endowment derived largely from a profitable rat poison that had been invented at the university, had hitherto reserved its largesse for the hard sciences. By the midsix-ties, with the help of more evenly distributed WARF funds, the uni-versity rose to the top ranks in a dozen fields and seemed to belong less in the Big Ten than in the Top Five, with Harvard, Stanford, Berkeley, and Yale. No university in the country held more govern-mental contracts.

Harrington could do nothing wrong; in his first year, even the football team was winning. The Board of Regents, dominated by liberals appointed by Governor Gaylord Nelson, was solidly behind him. No president since John Bascom had accomplished so much in so little time. But Harrington wasn't satisfied merely with institu-tional improvements. Like President Bascom, the father of progres-sivism, he was concerned with the moral content of education and its power to change the way we live. As a historian, Harrington had taken the ideas of two predecessors at Wisconsin, Frederick Jack-son Turner and Charles Beard, and fashioned them into a biting cri-tique of U.S. foreign policy, which he found to be the handmaiden of special interests. When he moved into administration, he had recruited his best student, William Appleman Williams, to fill his spot in the history department. Shortly afterward Williams published *The Tragedy of American Diplomacy,* instantly supplanting his mentor as the leading academic critic of the State Department. In 1959, students of Williams launched a new journal, *Studies on the Left,* which was to define the key historical issues of the sixties rebellion.

Harrington understood that an important ingredient in the Wisconsin success story all along had been the recruitment of Jewish scholars and students, who for many years had been barred from the Ivy League. He shocked the city fathers by quitting the Madison Club, a cliquish town-gown association, when it refused to admit a Jew. As chairman of the History Department, he had recruited the brilliant European cultural historian George Mosse, a refugee from Nazi Germany and the first Jew, as far as Harrington knew, to be appointed to that faculty. He continued to influence the department even after he entered the university administration by engineering the appointment of his friend and former student Harvey Goldberg, who had been teaching at Ohio State University.

Those three appointments—Mosse, Goldberg, and Williams—had not only helped place Wisconsin in the front ranks of history departments nationwide, but had created a powerful magnet to students who were interested in "relevance." Williams was an Iowa farm boy and former naval officer whose idea of the good society derived from the social teachings of the Bible. (In that he was at one with Harrington, who had so many books on Jesus Christ—over 100 volumes—in his private library that his maid suspected he was out to disprove the existence of God.) Goldberg was more devout than either of them, but his prophet was Karl Marx and his gospel, *The Communist Manifesto.* George Mosse belonged to a wealthy Jewish publishing family that Hitler had chased out of Germany. He was short and owlish in appearance, avuncular, his pronouncements delivered in a thick German accent and often with a sardonic grin. As a child he had been so frightened by the Brownshirts that he still saw danger in every form of irrationalism and crowd behavior. He was an entertaining albeit rather crusty lecturer, as anti-Marxist as he was anti-Nazi. Between his upper- and lower-division courses, he taught a thousand students a year, on a par with Williams and Goldberg. His teaching assistants reported back to him on what Goldberg was saying, and he would work subtle rejoinders into his own lectures. Many students took courses by Mosse and Goldberg at the same time to savor the cross fire. Mosse understood Goldberg's messianic appeal to the young in general and to Jews especially, and he would challenge them to become more self-aware. "For 19th century European Jewry, Marxism was a new religion," he warned. Then with a catty grin he would add, "But you're not really Marxists, you're Nietzscheans!"

Harrington was well pleased with his appointments and with the stimulating debate that he had brought about. It was just the thing for the war babies who were flooding the registration lines, he thought. Let the children of the working class learn to think critically, let them know the hard truths of human affairs, let them wake up from the intellectual torpor of the fifties.

When Karl Armstrong was accepted for admission to the University of Wisconsin in 1964, his father made a special point of warning him about the radicals at the campus. Although Donald was neither a John Bircher nor a McCarthyite, he certainly wasn't a Communist. In 1954 one of his best friends at work had been exposed as a card-carrying member of the Communist party, and it had greatly upset Don. "God damn it, why didn't you tell me, Arden?" he asked the man, who had lost his job as a result of the revelation. Don felt lucky not to be fired just for knowing him.

By 1964 the Wisconsin campus was already in ferment. Activists like Tom Hayden and Stokely Carmichael had been coming in and stirring things up, a Madison SDS chapter had been formed, and there were small but noisy demonstrations on the Library Mall, mostly over a little-known Southeast Asian country called Vietnam. An incident in the Gulf of Tonkin that summer had set things off.

Don had gotten to know the military fairly well during his air force consulting days. As he saw it, the air force had developed a lot of new hardware since Korea and had no good place to test it; they needed an out-of-the-way war. The protesters were probably in the right, he figured, but he cautioned Karl about getting mixed up with them: "Don't get involved in anything political because you won't get a job; you'll be put on blacklists; they'll find some way of destroying you."

Karl took the warning to heart. When he arrived at the university that fall, he shied away from the literature tables in front of Memorial Student Union and went straight to the Old Red Gym next door to register. With heavy brick walls and crenellated towers in the style of a Norman fortress, the Old Red Gym looked as though it had been designed to intimidate incoming freshmen. Dating from 1894, originally it had been called the Armory, and its huge spaces were reserved for the use of the ROTC, which was compulsory for all males until 1921 (obligatory participation was resumed in 1941). The ROTC offices were now hidden away in back, and most of the building was given over to intramural sports. The second floor was all basketball courts, three of them under one roof. The registration lines stretched from hoop to hoop.

Karl was anxious about getting the courses he wanted and nervous about the competition. Everyone around him looked smarter than he. Don had talked him into majoring in nuclear engineering. That's where the jobs were going to be, Don said, in harnessing the atom for peaceful purposes. With that in mind, Karl signed up for general chemistry, engineering, and calculus. And though ROTC was once again on a voluntary basis, he enrolled in air science and air force ROTC, all of this on top of first-year Russian and the required English 101. Not only would he someday manage a safe, clean, nuclear power plant, but he would serve his country as an air force pilot who was fluent in the language of the U.S.S.R. He would be everything his father had dreamed of being.

As he was leaving a big, burly man in a sweatsuit came up to him and introduced himself as Randall Jablonic, the freshman rowing coach. "You've got the build of an oarsman. You ought to come out for crew," Jablonic said.

Karl had often seen the long boats practicing on Lake Mendota, skimming over the surface like water spiders. It struck him as a boring activity, but not very difficult. "I'll give it a try," he told the coach, too flattered by the invitation to refuse.

Karl had spent the summer working as an oven man at Gardner's Bakery, where Ruth was employed on the donut line. He had saved enough for his tuition and fees but not for room and board, so he commuted to campus from Hintze Road on a motorbike, an old German-made NSU with a hole in the muffler. The motorbike made so much noise that Dwight could hear him coming all the way from Maple Bluffs.

Don used to take Karl to the ski-jump contests on Bascom Hill in the days when the ramp was still there, so Karl had some familiarity with the campus. Even in 1964 the university was a big place, stretching along the south shore of Lake Mendota for several miles, with a student body of over 20,000 and growing. Karl's class schedule took him from Bascom Hall to Van Vleck to Old Chemistry and farther west along University Avenue to Mechanical Engineering. ROTC classes were held in a quonset hut known as Temporary Building 16, "T-16," at the intersection of Linden and Babcock. After class he would jog across the street to Babcock Hall and buy an ice cream cone made with cream from the university's dairy barns. "Better than Schoep's," he declared.

Campus construction was going full tilt. Big holes pocked the ground all along West Johnson Avenue, where the Southeast Dorms were going up, and a two-block section at the foot of Bascom Hill was fenced off for the construction of the new humanities complex. Findorff Construction Company signs were posted on the fences, and jackhammers and pile drivers drowned out the carillon bells on Bascom Hill. Everywhere students turned, the dust of Harrington's empire building was blowing in their faces.

That fall President Lyndon Johnson announced draft call-ups in anticipation of ground actions in Vietnam, a decision supported by the Gulf of Tonkin Resolution in Congress. The news made little impression on Karl. *At that time Indochina was just, I don't know, a long ways away from the United States, and it didn't really impinge on my consciousness at all. I thought, you know, what possible interest could we have in Indochina?* Of greater interest to Madison students was the Free Speech Movement in Berkeley, sparked by the University of California's attempt to remove political literature tables from Sproul Plaza. Remembering what Don had told him, Karl steered clear of the rallies in support of the Berkeley protesters.

In late February 1965 Operation Rolling Thunder, the first sustained American bombing of North Vietnam, sparked a march of 10,000 from the Library Mall up State Street to the Capitol, a parade route that would eventually become so familiar to militants that they could walk it in their sleep. Karl was surprised that marching in the street would even be allowed. *And I said, "Man, they're really crazy. This isn't the kind of country you protest wars" And I was very afraid of having any contact with the protesters.*

Don congratulated him on his good sense. "Stay away from those people," he reiterated. "They just want to use you."

But Karl was isolated living at home and powerfully attracted by the action on campus. In March, as marine battalions took up defensive positions around Danang airfield, he often found himself cautiously looking on at protest rallies. Did he want to accept demonstrators as friends? Were they trustworthy? That winter he attended an antiwar meeting in the Memorial Student Union and even accepted a handout at the door, his "first political act" and a moment he would dwell on in court testimony. *And at first when I read these things I was really frightened by the violence of the rhetoric. And I thought that they really were Communists and that they were trying to subvert our government. But I got to talking with these people, and I found out that they were just like any other people except for one thing, that they were much more what I would call human beings than the rest of the people in society. And I wanted to know these people. Because they're very warm people and they weren't crazy.*

Rowing was more difficult than Karl had expected. After a long workout, varsity coach Norman Sonjiu would put all the boats through "just two more" 2,500-meter sprints and then demand yet another. No one was "cut" from crew; you stayed as long as you could take it. But after he crabbed an oar and threw everyone out of the boat one day, Karl gave up.

Karl's classes were taught in big, impersonal lecture halls, where he had little or no contact with his professors. He was taking too heavy a load, and he did not know that you could drop courses. He had done well in math at East, but in his freshman calculus course he found himself on the wrong end of the bell curve. Russian was especially difficult—a whole new alphabet. Even with Dwight quizzing him with vocabulary cards, he had a hard time remembering the cyrillic characters. In January he got his grades: Fs in Russian, chemistry, and physical education, and a D in calculus. He dropped out, but a few days later was readmitted on probation. Though he was not doing well in his studies, he was not ready to give up the student lifestyle.

In Madison that lifestyle centered around Memorial Student Union. Over the next five years, many of the important scenes in Karl's life would take place in its rooms: in the ornate Great Hall on the third floor, the television lounge and dining room on the second floor, the Rathskeller on the first floor, the phone bank in the stairwell, and the Terrace.

The "Rat" and the Terrace were what set Wisconsin's Student Union apart from those on other campuses. The oak-shaded terrace overlooked the lake, and in fair weather, with bratwursts cooking on the outdoor grill, it was heaven. The Rat was like a Bavarian beer hall, a big, barrel-vaulted room with heavy wooden booths, tables engraved with the love messages of generations, and a juke box selection heavy on British rock and Motown. When students gathered on Friday afternoons, the Rat became the scene of a nonstop party in which ideas flowed as freely as the weak (3.2 percent alcohol) beer served in the adjoining Stiftskeller. Karl longed to be recognized in the Rat, to feel himself part of that tribe.

The problem was his clothes. Walking into the Rat in his ROTC outfit, he looked as if he had stepped out of one of the nineteenth-century frescoes on the walls that showed military cadets saluting their officers with steins of beer. When heads had turned his way, he had thought that people were admiring him. He had dark eyes and a lean, well-shaped face, and at six feet four, he really did stand out. Ruth had told him he looked great in uniform. It made his skin crawl to realize that students were really looking at him with contempt.

One day in the spring of 1965 he showed up at the Rat in snug-fitting, faded denims and proudly announced to his acquaintances that he had quit ROTC. "What's the big deal?" they asked. "Why were you in ROTC to begin with?" Karl was too embarrassed to admit that the fifty-dollar-a-month stipend had been crucial income.

In April 1965 the first big Vietnam teach-in, inspired by a similar event at the University of Michigan in Ann Arbor, was held in Social Science, a relatively new building at the top of Observatory Drive, across the street from Commerce and Bascom. Student speakers took turns denouncing the U.S. war effort, but the main attraction was Harrington's protégé, Professor William Appleman Williams. Williams was so clean-cut that he could have been taken for an FBI agent, and his comments carried extra weight because he was a bonafide war hero, badly wounded in the Pacific islands during World War II. By April 1965 Operation Rolling Thunder was well under way and the first American combat battalions had landed at Da Nang airfield in South Vietnam. On April 7, President Johnson had offered the North Vietnamese leader Ho Chi Minh participation in a Southeast Asia development plan in exchange for peace. Ho Chi Minh had rejected the offer. But despite his uncompromising attitude, his alliance with the Soviet Union, and his Stalinist style of rule, Ho emerged as the hero of the teach-in, the popular leader of a nationalist war of liberation who had defeated the French only to find himself faced with a new imperialist threat from the United States. LBJ was the villain, meddling in a civil war that Ho's Communist forces, left alone, would have won long ago.

To Karl Armstrong, raptly following the discussion from the back row, it came as a shock to learn that had elections been held in Vietnam in 1955 as they were supposed to be under the Geneva accords formalizing the French defeat in Indochina, Ho Chi Minh would have won. Even more upsetting was the information—historically correct—that President Dwight Eisenhower himself had nixed the election. Karl would describe the impact of such teachings at his sentence mitigation hearing. *And the revelations that came out of Indochina made me question everything about this country. And I wondered how people, American people, could really accept that sort of thing. We're saying we want everything our way, and I don't think that those are the sort of principles this country was founded on.*

In May, ignoring Don's warnings, Karl attended the first "Anti-Military Ball," an event organized by anti-war activists to mock the annual gala held for military cadets. He was acquiring "political consciousness," as the saying went on campus. One night at home he volunteered the information that he now considered himself an atheist. Sometime later, exactly when he would not recall, he recorded his disillusionment in blood on the Humanities Building construction fence: "GOD IS DEAD."

Karl had done a little better academically in the spring semester, earning a C average, but was still a long way from winning any scholarships. To pay his tuition for the coming year, he took a summer job with a survey crew on a federal flood-control project near Bloomfield, Indiana. One of his crewmates was a college student from Michigan who had all the latest Beatles albums and who knew a pot plant when he saw one. They found marijuana growing wild along the White River, dried the leaves, and rolled their own cigarettes.

Karl hadn't forgotten the lessons of the teach-in. *I would get flashes of what was happening in Vietnam. And at a certain point I*

*really grasped what was going on there. And I wondered what had
happened to me, why I didn't feel that before.*

One day Karl announced that he was going on a hunger strike to
protest the war. When lunchtime came, he refused to eat with the
crew, sitting off to one side in a meditative pose. His Michigan
friend praised the gesture, but was not interested in missing lunch
himself. The others were Indianans with American flag decals on
their hard hats. They were uncomfortable eating in front of Karl.
"Have a candy bar," they would say, offering him items from their
lunch buckets. When he held firm, they began to badger him.
"What good is it going to do?" they teased.

"I have to do something," Karl explained. "It's the only thing I
can think of." He kept it up for three days.

Then there was Bev. Bev was the daughter of a middle-aged crew
member named Sam Hoffeditz, who had a small farm a few miles
outside the village of Linton, where Karl had rented a room. Karl
found Sam a congenial workmate and gladly accepted an invitation
to dinner. Bev was about five years older than Karl. She was a writer and like Karl somewhat withdrawn. They became close friends.
Later in the summer, he met Bev's cousin Sarah at church (the
Hoffeditzes were Baptists) and began an affair with the young
woman. There had been nothing romantic between Karl and Bev
until then, but when he started dating Sarah, Bev succumbed to
jealousy. Karl couldn't reconcile a romance with both—*I'll be a
traitor to one or the other,* he thought—so left town in the middle of
the night, two weeks before his summer job was to have ended.

In the fall of 1965 the Cultural Revolution, Chairman Mao
Zedong's bloody renewal of revolutionary fervor, was under way in
Communist China, arousing great enthusiasm among *gauchistes*
like Harvey Goldberg. U.S. troops were engaged in frontal combat
with North Vietnamese regulars in the Ia Drang Valley. Karl, who
had moved into a rooming house on Orchard Street, a block from
the university's physical plant, decorated his wall with a huge map
of Vietnam. He changed his major from nuclear to chemical engineering and was taking calculus and chemistry over again, along
with physics for engineers, which was taught in Sterling Hall. One
of his housemates was a disaffected ex-Peace Corps volunteer who
told him that the Kennedy administration's idealistic program was
now just another CIA front. Another housemate was a Peruvian

named Hugo Vega, an older student who would later room with Karl on the other side of campus. Vega worked for the Land Tenure Center, a program sponsored by the Agency for International Development that was devoted to the problems of agricultural reform in Latin America. Also living in the house was a tall, smart New Yorker named Jon Devereaux, whose father was a dean at Cornell University. Devereaux had a good friend named Mark Conkle, a medical student. The state legislature had recently lowered the drinking age in Wisconsin to eighteen, and almost every night, when they were through studying, Karl and his new friends would make the rounds of the student bars—Chesty's, the Kollege Klub, the Amber Grid.

Karl was in awe of Devereaux and Conkle, who were experimenting with drugs and exploiting the sexual revolution that had begun that year with the introduction of a miraculous pill that would prevent pregnancy if a girl took one every day. Karl's own sexual experience was limited to his summer fling with Beverly Hoffeditz's cousin. It literally had been his first time; he had never had an orgasm before.

Devereaux and Conkle had never met anyone as gullible as Karl Armstrong, and one of their favorite pastimes was putting him on. Once, when Karl said he wished he had some dope, Conkle offered him a handful of seeds, explaining that they were peyote buttons. Karl took one and got so "high" that he thought he saw Superman get out of a car and go into a house across the street. "Boy, this is a great trip," he told Hugo Vega, showing him the seeds. Vega knew apple seeds when he saw them, and also knew that the "Superman" Karl had seen was on his way to a masquerade party. "You got taken, man, but we won't tell Conkle you know. I'll tell him you freaked out on the peyote and went to the hospital and are now spilling your guts to the doctors." Devereaux and Conkle spent the next few days in a cold sweat, fully expecting to be expelled.

Karl would not forget Vega's loyalty. Several years later, when the Land Tenure Center came under fire from SDS, he would defend the institution, arguing in his communiqués that it could be "rehabilitated." It was the one institution targeted by the militants that he refused to attack.

By the end of 1965 the United States had 200,000 young men in Vietnam, and the Selective Service System was beginning to go after college students who were not in good standing. In May 1966, students occupied the Peterson Administration Building in an effort to persuade the university not to make grade-point averages (GPAs) and class rank available to draft boards on request. It was "condemning students to death" by cooperating, they charged.

Karl Armstrong, who had a 1.9 GPA, found himself very much in accord with the aims of the protest and spent several nights in the building. The atmosphere was festive. A student employed by Ella's, the famous State Street delicatessen, handed out candy bars from a seemingly bottomless bag while Robert Cohen and Evan Stark, U.W. graduate students as eloquent as Berkeley's Mario Savio, led all-night discussions of the war. *And, well, I was really amazed at ... the issues that were being raised about Selective Service. ... it was a real contradiction in the society that this institution should exist.* Toward the end, Professors Williams and Mosse made appearances urging the occupiers to go home and let the issue be decided by the faculty, which, at a meeting called to discuss the occupation, condemned the use of coercion in a place of learning. In the end, however, Chancellor Robben Fleming did agree not to provide draft boards with any more information than the university already did, thus protecting students who, like Karl Armstrong, were barely hanging on.

Summer was a letdown. Karl returned to Hintze Road and rejoined his mother at Gardner's Bakery. The job bored him, and he day-dreamed so much that his forearms were covered with oven burns. At home he clashed with his father. His failure to make crew, his poor grades, dropping out of ROTC, changing his major—it seemed that everything he did disappointed Don, and Don let him know it.

In the fall Karl returned to school, but dropped out after a few weeks. The way he now saw it, science just wasn't serving the people as it was supposed to. Instead he took a job at the Wisconsin Children's Treatment Center, caring for the mentally disturbed. In a notebook he kept while working there he wrote, "God, sometimes I feel crazier than the kids. If I want to help, I should get my own life in order."

He quit the treatment center in November and hitchhiked to Houston. With a ten-dollar grubstake, he rented a room; laid in a supply of bread, peanut butter, and milk; went to an employment agency; and got himself a job in a fast-food restaurant. With his first paycheck he bought a used ten-speed bike, visited the Houston space center, and began to hang out on the fringes of Rice University, making friends among the other drifters. His intuition told him that these experiences would be of value some day, though he had no idea how.

A few weeks before Christmas Dwight showed up and stayed for a day or two before moving on to New Orleans. Dwight wasn't doing any better than Karl. He was in the tenth grade at East High, but not on track to graduate with his class. He had let his hair grow long and was spending most of his time at Tower Lunch playing cards, chain-smoking Viceroy cigarettes, and listening to endless repetitions of the Mysterians's "96 Tears" on the jukebox. With his sad eyes and heavy brows, Dwight looked as though he had been drawn by Bruegel or Hals, but he wasn't stupid. He loved to tinker and turn knobs and always left a mess. When he was younger, it had been clocks; now that he was sixteen, it was the family camper. He would completely disassemble it on the front lawn and put it back together so that it ran better than before.

Don had never understood Dwight. He had been on the road consulting a lot when Dwight was young, and when the consulting had stopped and Don had tried to reassert his authority at home, Dwight had resisted. "What has this got to do with us?" he would say, interrupting Don's dinner table monologues. "We've heard this before." Dwight would not even address his father as "Dad."

Lorene, a real beauty with cover girl eyes and a foxy expression when she knitted her brows, had married that summer, right out of high school, and had moved to Illinois, leaving Dwight alone at home. Now he became more aware of the strains in his parents' marriage. He could see that they didn't love each other. It made him sick inside when Ruth showed him affection because he felt she was just using him to annoy Don. Nobody loved him for himself, Dwight believed.

At East High he didn't go out for sports or participate in school activities of any kind. The only course that interested him was literature. The teacher, a young woman, gave him books to read—contemporary American and European fiction and poetry—and sometimes talked to him in private. She complimented Dwight on his powers of observation and urged him to get his thoughts down on paper. But Dwight's Tower Lunch pals had meanwhile introduced him to the new hippie lifestyle of altered moods. He was a regular user of marijuana and LSD, along with caffeine, nicotine, and alcohol, so although he had a writer's watchfulness and a facility with words, he was never disciplined enough to keep a journal.

Mira was so concerned about Dwight "going hippie" that she insisted he accompany her to Lakeview Lutheran, where she introduced him to her pastor, the Reverend Kenneth Hoffman. Hoffman was an erudite man who knew Greek and Hebrew, but who had a down-to-earth manner. Like most Wisconsin Lutherans, he was conservative and patriotic in political outlook and had a devoted following among the town constables. He wore horn-rimmed glasses on a turned-up nose, kept his hair slicked back, and was quick with a smile and a quip. He had come to Madison from the hamlet of Rome, Wisconsin, in 1956, and had set up a suicide prevention program, the first the city had ever had. Troubled kids were his beat. He had had some close calls, but he had yet to lose one.

At Mira's urging Hoffman interceded when Dwight was arrested for vagrancy in New Orleans. Dwight refused to speak to anyone at home, but over the phone Hoffman talked him into getting on a plane to Chicago, where Don picked him up.

Karl, meanwhile, had returned to Madison from Houston and had taken a job on the graveyard shift at Gisholt, operating a turret lathe. His old friend Hugo Vega had given him a place to stay in his North Few Street apartment near Tenney Park, a few blocks east of the Capitol. Pastor Hoffman wanted the whole family to undergo counseling; in fact, he had promised as much to Dwight to urge him on the plane. But Don considered psychologists "guessers" who were partly to blame for what was happening to the nation's youth and backed out of the deal. Dwight ran away again. Hoffman found him at Karl's apartment, and Dwight was shocked when the good reverend walked in on him without so much as a knock.

Dwight was taking his cues from his peers now, and even Hoffman couldn't do much with him. In the summer of 1967, he brought home a new friend named Frank Slaughter, a delinquent his own age who looked up to Dwight as someone in the "high hippie class" of kids from good families. They toyed with the idea of going out for summer league baseball, but decided that it would be more fun to steal a car and drive to San Francisco, where hippies from all over the United States were gathering in Haight-Ashbury for something called a "Be In." On a parking ramp near Capitol Square they found a Wisconsin Telephone Company sedan complete with telephone and expense vouchers and keys in the ignition. They were in South Dakota, almost to the Badlands, when a service station attendant finally thought to question what two sixteen-year-olds were doing issuing phone-company vouchers for gas and reported them, and they were picked up by the state police. Slaughter, who had a previous car theft on his record, was sentenced to fifteen months in a reformatory. Dwight got probation, but as a condition of it, he had to submit to counseling. He was referred to Robert O'Connor, a West Side therapist, and started seeing him in October 1967.

O'Connor, a compassionate man with wide, placid features and a thick mane of silvering hair, had no trouble diagnosing Dwight. The boy had a problem with his father and was severely depressed. The psychologist's suspicions were confirmed by a lengthy letter he received from Pastor Hoffman, who offered the opinion that the entire family was disturbed. Hoffman was even more certain that Don's problems were the source of everyone else's. Don was antisocial, glowered, and would get up and leave in a huff when Hoffman tried to talk to him. But one night, Don had opened up and told him about the emotionally sterile environment he had grown up in. He talked about how he used to shoot lunch buckets out of the hands of his classmates when they teased him. He seemed to think that the men he worked with at Gisholt were dunderheads and led Hoffman to believe that he expected Ruth to be his mother.

Before he went to Houston, Karl left his dad a scathing letter berating his lack of love and true affection, according to Hoffman. The minister had also seen Karl's writeup of a boy at the children's treatment center, and it included many conclusions that he had repeated in his letter to Don. Hoffman discussed this with a psychiatrist at the treatment center. The doctor said he thought that Karl had serious psychological problems.

"Dwight cannot face up to a showdown, even minor; to him this means he must RUN," Hoffman added. He wished O'Connor luck with the Armstrongs.

I like them all, and Mr. is a lonesome soul. He doesn't like himself. He has never had a chance to get away from his negative background. He feels a lack of educational achievement and is mentally quite sharp, but that only handicaps him further, for he skillfully deflates suggestions that he needs to learn about things like human relations. One thing in your favor is that a number of crises and a current underlying tension persisting there have made them aware of a drastic need for action. They are ready; go for it.

But before Dr. O'Connor could begin his work, an incident took place on campus that was to change the lives of everyone in Madison.

6

Dow Day

Karl was a bust as a scholar. He was a bust as an athlete. He was a bust as an employee. I think he is a sick person crying out for recognition and, as such, he would have rallied to any cause.

—MICHAEL ZALESKI,
Wisconsin Assistant Attorney General, for the prosecution

It was a very tense scene, and all of a sudden, without any warning whatsoever, the police lined up shoulder to shoulder and started swinging their clubs to clear the hall. And the thing that's really etched in my mind is the sound of a club cracking a skull. It really seemed to reverberate through that room.

—TOM SIMON,
student, for the defense

In the beginning, the peace movement in Madison had been William Appleman Williams's kind of movement, broad based and nonviolent, with a significant component of experienced adults. These grown-up protesters included Gaylord Nelson, now a United States Senator from Wisconsin, Congressman William Kastenmeier, Federal Judge James Doyle and his wife Ruth; clergymen such as Father Arthur Doyle; Quakers such as Joe Elder and Betty Boardman, and members of Faculty for Peace. Those students who were involved made the rounds of Madison churches on Sundays, boldly but politely raising the moral issue of war. Williams held old-fashioned town meetings that brought students together with Establishment peaceniks and lined up speakers for an influential radio program called "Vietnam on the Air." Demonstrations were, by and large, peaceful and orderly, with silent vigils, appearances by SDS president Carl Oglesby and the Harvard scholar Staughton Lynd, and a forty-mile march to Baraboo to picket the munitions plant.

Fred Harvey Harrington, observing these developments from his new aerie on the seventeenth floor of Van Hise Hall, found himself agreeing with the demonstrators. The war was wrong. It made him glad things had not worked out for him with the Kennedy administration in 1961, when he had been in the final running for a high post at the State Department. If he had gone to Washington, he would now be defending a policy he despised. But what should he do as president of the University of Wisconsin? Williams was on his back to take a stand, even to speak to student groups on the issue. If he spoke out, it would place the university administration squarely on the students' side. He could be the Kingman Brewster of the Midwest.

But Wisconsin was not Yale, as Harrington was well aware. It was a public institution supported by tax revenues. And even though other public university administrators, such as Clark Kerr at UC-Berkeley, had spoken out, Harrington felt constrained by Wisconsin's charter, which dictated political neutrality. The University of Wisconsin also happened to be located in a state where the pro-Hitler German-American Bund had had a considerable following, not to mention Senator Joe McCarthy. Harrington was wary of the Right. He had been concerned when the House Un-American Activities Committee had called Bill Williams to testify in 1958. He felt vulnerable himself, especially now that he was president. A certain Captain Bollenbeck was engaged in an ongoing letter-writing campaign questioning his political loyalties. Moreover, the political makeup of the Board of Regents had changed since 1964, when Warren Knowles, a Republican, replaced Gaylord Nelson in the governor's office. As a practical matter, he could not achieve everything he wanted to at Wisconsin without the support of the regents; the governor; the legislature; and Congressman Melvin Laird, a prominent Republican who, even when Democrats were in power, had considerable influence on the flow of federal dollars to building projects in Wisconsin. Harrington was not going to risk that support over a brush war in Indochina.

Meanwhile, in the great historical debate between professors George Mosse and Harvey Goldberg, Vietnam had given the edge to Goldberg. In the fall of 1966, Goldberg electrified the campus with a series of lectures on efforts by the socialist parties of Europe to stop the outbreak of World War I and on the Bolshevik-inspired upheavals that followed. The only way to end war, he argued, was to replace the system of production for profit with one based on the satisfaction of human needs. Violent revolution was the surest path to lasting peace. *"Tout est possible!"* he cried, quoting the French bricklayer and communist Raymond Péricat.

And very soon students were acting as though, in Madison in 1966 as in Paris in 1919, everything really was possible. That fall, would-be revolutionaries heckled Senator Ted Kennedy during a speech at the Stock Pavilion and blockaded a new "wrong way" bus lane on University Avenue (in which a coed had been run over and lost a leg). The following spring they invaded the Engineering Building to protest job interviews by Dow Chemical Company and threatened to hold Chancellor Robben Fleming hostage in his own office. Lady Bird Johnson, wife of President Lyndon Johnson, canceled a visit to the Madison campus because the chancellor could not guarantee that she would be allowed to speak.

The Kennedy incident reminded Harrington of the late 1930s, when fraternity boys at the university would hoot down Communist speakers. Bill Williams, too, was alarmed. The new aggressiveness was a departure from the Gandhian principles that had worked so well for the civil rights movement in America, and it threatened to split the peace movement. Goldberg himself had been upset by the Kennedy fiasco, but except for advising the Young Socialist Alliance he remained aloof from the students' inept revolutionism. At heart Goldberg was a scholar, more comfortable in the archives than in the streets, and incapable of leading that which he had helped to set in motion.

Chancellor Fleming remained outwardly cheerful. After the Dow protest (soon to be known as "Dow I") he even put up bail money, a couple of thousand dollars, for those who were arrested. However, no one was too surprised when, at the end of the 1966–67 academic year, he announced that he had accepted the presidency of the University of Michigan. He never saw his bail money again.

During the March protest at the Engineering Building, a tall young man named Zwicker had carried a placard showing a close-up of napalm wounds into the office where a representative of Dow Chemical Company, maker of the jellied gasoline, was interviewing students for jobs. Zwicker was arrested, subsequently dropped out of school, and moved to Kathmandu. Many more lives were to be changed by the second Dow demonstration, the one that would go down in local history as Dow Day.

The new chancellor, William Sewell, was a highly respected sociologist with college-age children of his own. In fact, a son of his had been arrested in an antiwar demonstration at the University of California at Berkeley. Dr. Sewell had been in the faculty minority that had voted against a continuation of job interviews on campus that spring. He believed that the university had no obligation to run a placement agency. As far as he was concerned, Dow and General Electric and the CIA could rent hotel suites when they came to Madison, as they did when they recruited in the big cities. Now that he was chancellor, however, it was his duty to uphold the policies of the university, including Faculty Document 122, approved by the Faculty Senate after the Kennedy incident, authorizing the use of force against students who disrupted the campus. In a speech on October 2, 1967, Sewell let it be known to the faculty that unless they changed the guidelines, he would follow them. On the tenth he asked the Dean of Students, Joseph Kauffman, to issue a statement warning that disruptions of job interviewers would be met with university reprisals, whether or not those involved were arrested. Kauffman did so. It was not the companies whose rights the university was protecting, Kauffman believed, but the students who had requested interviews with those companies.

A number of job-placement interviews were scheduled for October 17 and 18, which happened to coincide with Vietnam Week. Antiwar rallies were planned from coast to coast, to culminate in a demonstration in Washington, D.C. There were now half a million GIs fighting in Vietnam. Casualties were running into the hundreds every week. Peaceful protests seemed to be having little effect. In Oakland, California, an extremist group called the Black Panthers had established a new standard of militancy by invading the state capitol in Sacramento sporting guns and jaunty Che Guevara berets and shouting slogans, such as Power to the People! and Off the Pig! White radicals wanted to appear no less militant.

Madison's two most visible anti-war spokesmen, Robert Cohen and Evan Stark, who drew crowds to spontaneous debates in the halls of the Memorial Student Union, were both graduate students at the university. Cohen affected a Lenin style of dress, hat, and beard. He would sit in Dean Kauffman's office and bum smokes and complain about how bad things were going on the Left, soliciting the dean's support and sympathy, only to return a week later to inform Kauffman that he would be the first to be hanged come the revolution. Short, pudgy and with a permanent snarl on his face, Stark looked more like a harried short-order cook than a prophet, but, like Cohen, he knew how to move a crowd.

On the evening of October 16, at the end of a lengthy SDS "mass meeting" in the Great Hall on the third floor of the Union, Stark, Cohen, and a handful of other militants pushed through a "compromise" calling for obstruction on the second day, ridiculing the Young Socialists and other voices of caution for acting like the "vanguard of the middle class," and insisting that it was time for Madison students to "join the world revolutionary struggle." The militants drafted a leaflet to be passed out the next day:

> We must move from protest to resistance. Before we talked. Now we must act. We must stop what we oppose.
> We must enter the arena of action to make the kind of history we want.
> We will enter a building in which Dow is recruiting and stop them.

October 18, 1967, was a fine, bright autumn day in Madison. The campus's famous Dutch elms and live oaks were at their most spectacular, the air crisp but not too chilly. There was a breeze off the lake, and a fair number of students had chosen to spend the morning sailing. The first day of the Dow protest had passed without incident, and until that morning, only about three dozen students had indicated a willingness to risk arrest by obstructing the job interviews. Though they might abhor the use of napalm on Asian villagers, most students were as yet unaccustomed to the idea of civil disobedience, and only a few volunteered to "witness" the sit-in.

But on the evening of the seventeenth, the San Francisco Mime

Troupe had concluded a performance in the Union Theater by announcing that it would be at the next day's protest. And so it was that troupe members in white face and playing pan pipes led several hundred students up Bascom Hill that morning. UP & S Chief Ralph Hanson walked beside the demonstrators, trying to figure out where they were going. Dow interviews were scheduled in three different buildings, and the precise location of the sit-in had not been revealed. At the top of the hill, the column swung left around Bascom Hall, crossed the Van Vleck plaza to the squat, yellow-brick facade of Commerce Hall, filed through a side door into the main hallway, and sat down. Hanson had his answer.

Before moving to Madison Ralph Hanson had been a Maine state trooper, but he displayed none of the roughness for which that particular agency was known. He had expected Madison to be a cream-puff job, nothing more serious to contend with than the ruffled dignity of a professor with a parking ticket, and in fact he had found that his dry Yankee wit could get him through most situations. But that morning, for the first time, he had a sense of foreboding. Intelligence had come in from a new MPD undercover cop named George Croal claiming that the hard core was spoiling for a fight. And so Hanson had taken the unusual precaution of hiring twenty off-duty Madison policemen to supplement his small squad of campus cops.

Hanson knew the prejudices of the MPD rank and file: They were East Siders, working men with families to support, and to them the campus was a place of enviable privilege, sexual license, and political heresy. So he had taken care earlier that morning to instruct his combined squad on the procedures they were to follow, reading to them from the protocol he had drafted for the occasion:

> When the decision to arrest, detain or remove a person has been made, every effort will be made first to identify the person, and if later in attempting to implement the arrest or removal, significant physical efforts of other students thwart the attempt, the police action will terminate to preclude further physical violence.

Hanson ordered the men to remove the bullets from their sidearms and to leave their billy clubs behind. They were not to try to "clear the building," he said. It would be sufficient to maintain a path through the crowd so that students could get to and from their interviews.

That fall Karl Armstrong had been readmitted to the university "on strict probation." He had signed up for first-year Spanish and introductory courses in psychology, English literature, and anthropology. He had given up on becoming a scientist or engineer and was heading in the direction of liberal arts. He was still sharing space with Hugo Vega on North Few Street and working nights at Gisholt. The metal workers at Gisholt had all been talking about the impending showdown over Dow, and most thought the cops should just go in and "kick ass." Don had argued with Karl about it the day before. "Why, with the frame of mind that's going around this community, you're going to get yourself hurt, and you're going to get yourself hurt bad!" he had said.

"Yah, but Dad, you're never going to accomplish anything if you're going to worry only about yourself," Karl had replied.

Hearing the radio reports of the impending confrontation on Bascom Hill, Karl caught a bus into campus. Arriving at the Student Union, he raced up Observatory Drive on foot, reminded as always of the time his bike went out from under him on the steep curve and he almost lost his life under a bus. What he was about to witness would leave no less indelible an impression.

For once personal diplomacy had failed Ralph Hanson. It was hard to breathe in the hot, smoke-filled corridor, and the students had become irritable. A student trying to get through to an interview with the Dow recruiter in Room 104 found himself in a choke hold applied not by police but by demonstrators. Hanson told three protesters who were blocking the door that they were under arrest. The three locked arms with people around them and refused to budge. Hanson backed off. He then asked for leaders to step forward to discuss the situation. This request met with cries of, "The leaders have resigned; there's no one to talk to!"

Moments later Hanson found himself trapped, along with the Dow recruiter, in the Business School office. "You are part of the society that this movement is going to negate," a student yelled when the chief asked to be let out. "If you want to leave, you can jump out the window!"

At 11:30 A.M. Hanson called Chancellor Sewell from the Business Office and informed him that the situation was out of his control and that if he was going to enforce Faculty Document 122, he would need outside help. Sewell told him to call MPD. Hanson did, urging Chief Wilbur Emery to "send every available man."

By 1 P.M. a paddy wagon and about two dozen MPD regulars had assembled in the parking area between Bascom and Commerce. Hanson, who had managed to get out of the building with the help of a ladder, was startled to see that the reinforcements were equipped with helmets and riot sticks. "Are those really necessary?" he asked the officer in charge, Lieutenant Baggot.

"They're only for defensive purposes," Baggot answered. "You can put your own men in front if you want."

Reassured, Hanson led a contingent of police into the foyer to begin clearing a path to the Business Office, where the Dow recruiter was still trapped. Suddenly the advance stopped, there was a hubbub, and Hanson emerged with Evan Stark and several other students. They all walked over to Bascom Hall, the crowd waiting while Stark conducted a last-ditch negotiation with Chancellor Sewell. A few minutes later they returned, grim faced. Hanson walked into the building alone and with his bullhorn told the demonstrators they had to get out of the hallway or they would be arrested. By this time, the coeds had been moved to the rear and instructed to remove their jewelry and to protect their heads with their jackets, and the front of the hallway was occupied by young men. "We're going to have a fight!" said one. "If they come, take off your belt and wrap it around your fist."

Hanson felt that Stark had played him for a fool, suggesting a compromise and then, when they got to Sewell's office, simply reiterating the militants' hard line. Hanson had begged Sewell to call the interviews off, postpone them, anything to buy time. Sewell was unmoved. He had to enforce Faculty Document 122. And so Hanson formed the two squads into a wedge formation with his own men in front and led them back into the foyer. He would remove the protesters one by one. There would be no violence. He, Ralph Hanson, was in control.

The building was about half-cleared when Karl reached the top of the hill. It was 1:30 P.M. For Karl, the next few minutes took on a dreamlike, slow-motion quality. Over the heads of those in front of him, he could see clubs rising and falling with a furious rhythm, the smooth, polished wooden surfaces reflecting the angular light. There was a zealousness about the work; the police went in and drove people out, and then went back in for more. There was blood on the faces of demonstrators emerging from the building. A slight, blond boy grabbed a club that had been aimed at his head and held on until his fingers were smashed by other clubs. The girls were all screaming.

Something stirred in Karl's reservoir of emotion. His fist shot up in a mock salute, and he joined in a guttural chant arising spontaneously from the witnessing crowd: *Sieg heil! Sieg heil! Sieg heil!*

A few students fought back. One MPD officer was hit in the face by a brick; another fell and was kicked and stomped. It was then that the gassing started. The students were at first so curious that they ran toward, rather than away from, the wispy clouds. Soon they were crying and coughing and covering their faces with handkerchiefs.

Noticing students watching from the roof of Bascom Hall, Karl climbed its four flights of stairs and joined the gawkers at the balustrade. Below, gas drifted across campus like an autumn haze. The crowd surged this way and that in search of fresh air. He saw a policeman dragging one of the mime artists by her hair, a radical professor named Maurice Zeitlin pushed roughly aside, and Karl's former housemate Jon Devereaux throwing up in the bushes beside Commerce.

An hour passed, and more people came up on the roof. Suddenly, there were staccato explosions behind the spectators. Karl could not see what was happening. A gaunt youth with barn-owl eyes and scraggly blond hair was kneeling at the base of the flagpole on a raised portion of the roof, a pair of wirecutters lying next to him. In one hand he held a box of kitchen matches, with which he had ignited a string of firecrackers. In the other was the severed end of the metal cable holding up the American and Wisconsin state flags, which were still flapping in the breeze high overhead. With a sorrowful expression the young man let go of the cable, and the flags came fluttering down.

The onlookers stared in amazement as the flag cutter picked up his tool, slipped it into the big side pocket of his army fatigue jacket, and stood up. "Hey, get him!" someone shouted. The student jumped to the main level and ran to the stairwell, pursued by several older men, probably members of the faculty or administrators, shouting "Stop! Get him!" But the long-legged youth took the stairs like a deer and disappeared into Bascom Hall's labyrinthine basement.

Dow Day, as it came to be known, resulted in injuries to about seventy-five people, most of them students. However, the most seriously injured were the police, one of whom lost his trachea. In the inquests that followed, a common theme among the police who were interviewed was the deep alarm stirred in them by members of the San Francisco Mime Troupe who pranced in front of them in whiteface like clowns at a bullfight. To the cops they seemed "vicious" and multiplied "like demons" until there were "thousands" of them pressing in. As for who was responsible for starting the riot, the most banal explanation is probably the truth. As Chief Hanson and his squad forged into the packed hall, they compressed the crowd like a spring until it rebounded. Hanson and the other unarmed men in front were carried clear out of the building by the surge, leaving the club-wielding MPD force inside, unaware of the restrictions that Hanson had imposed on his own men. And at that point some (but not all) of the MPD officers began hitting everybody in sight.

The media in Wisconsin and elsewhere portrayed the event as a student riot. The only state official to question this interpretation—to assert that perhaps it had been more of a police riot—was Assistant Attorney General Bronson LaFollette, grandson of Fighting Bob, and he was forced to recant. Seventeen students arrested at the scene were summarily suspended. Robert Cohen was relieved of his teaching assistantship in philosophy and expelled from the university. Evan Stark fled to Minneapolis. The Bascom Hall flag cutter was identified by Special Agent George Baxtrum from FBI photo files as Jonathan Stielstra, a good student and son of the vice president for student affairs at Stevens Point State University. Young Stielstra was sentenced to thirty days in jail.

For the thousands who witnessed the beatings and gassings on Bascom Hill, the first on an American campus, Dow Day was a scarring experience. "This is your university," a spokesman for the San Francisco Mime Troupe told a sold-out house at the Union Theater that night. "If you don't like it, change it. If you can't change it, destroy it." The same evening, a fire was set at the door to Joseph Kauffman's office in Bascom Hall, and someone smashed the glass protecting the oil portrait of John Bascom. After the faculty voted to support Chancellor Sewell's handling of the incident, students formed a gauntlet two blocks long and stared in stony silence as the teachers filed out. The teaching assistants went on strike, staying out for a week.

Harvey Goldberg broke with Harrington with typical drama and finality. "And to think that this man was the reason I came to Wisconsin in the first place!" he told an emergency all-faculty meeting at the Union Theater. Bill Williams reacted more moderately. The kind of society Wisconsin's student radicals seemed bent on creating was one "an orangutang wouldn't want to live in," he told the *New York Times.* (That statement got him an armload of bananas from his students.) But in a lengthy and impassioned letter to Harrington, he reserved his most stinging criticism for the university administration. Beginning with the construction of the beehive-like Southeast Dorms on the wrong side of busy University Avenue with no provision for students to cross safely, Williams ticked off the administrative mistakes that had generated "disgust for the simple incompetence of those who run the system." Williams urged Harrington to boot upcoming CIA job interviews off campus. "Here is a chance to break free of the embattled psychology that is now so apparent at all levels of the university," he wrote. Harrington responded with a perfunctory note, and the CIA resolved the pressing matter by announcing that it would conduct interviews downtown.

That weekend, several busloads of Dow Day combatants traveled to Washington for the Vietnam Week finale at the Washington Monument, some with their heads still in bandages. The Abraham Lincoln Brigade, aging veterans of the Spanish Civil War, dipped their flags as they marched by, convincing many in the Madison contingent that they too were now "living in history."

The psychic wounds of Dow Day would fester long after the students' scalp abrasions had healed. Karl's old friend Jon Devereaux dropped out and retreated to a communal farm in the countryside, where he would remain for ten years. Others, like Senator McGovern's son-in-law Jim Rowen, would despair of changing America through the system. "Don't throw the baby out with the bathwater!" cautioned Professor Mosse, who had had a tear-gas canister go off in his face as he was walking up the hill. But it was too late. Dow had "knocked the scales off our eyes," Rowen said. Another activist summed it up this way: "Dow showed people that civil rights movement tactics were totally useless."

One of those who shared the new cynicism was Karl Armstrong. "I examined the institutions of Nazi Germany," he later testified, "and I thought that around the year 1967 the institutions in America were taking on the same character." Thus did the civil war in Madison begin.

7

Chicago

And the sense of having been betrayed is universal around the Vietnam War.

—ROBERT JAY LIFTON,
psychiatrist, for the defense

His behavior pattern was one of a kind of drifting.

—H. J. LYNCH,
Dane County District Attorney, for the prosecution

Pastor Hoffman correctly predicted that Karl's attempt to go to school while working nights at Gisholt would not work out. For the semester he pulled a C, a D, and two Fs. In January of 1968 the university readmitted him with the understanding that if he dropped out again, he would not be allowed to reapply for three years. He left anyway and went to work selling *Colliers Encyclopedias* with a new friend named David Knauss. The son of a local construction magnate, Knauss had gone hippie in a big way, playing Bob Dylan songs on his guitar and dealing as well as using marijuana. Karl was impressed with Knauss and looked to him as something of a role model, but he was losing his hair to pattern baldness, making him more bashful than ever, and the spoils of the Sexual Revolution continued to elude him. Knauss could not get over what a flop Karl was with girls.

The pair worked small Wisconsin towns from Janesville north to Stevens Point. The commission was $125 on a $300 sale. In his first week out, Karl sold three sets and began to think that he was on the road to riches. But then he decided that the books were a rip-off, and his sales fell off. In late March, he quit the encyclopedia business, borrowed $400 from the Bank of Madison, bought a 1963 Volkswagen Beetle, and covered it with flowery McCarthy for President stickers.

Eugene McCarthy, an urbane and witty U.S. senator from Minnesota, had made a strong showing against Lyndon Johnson in the New Hampshire primary. Many New Hampshirites voted against Johnson because they did not think he was fighting to win in Vietnam, but the negative vote was widely interpreted as an endorsement of McCarthy's peace plank, which called for an immediate halt to U.S. bombing of North Vietnam and a negotiated withdrawal. In Wisconsin the McCarthy campaign was run by a faculty wife named Midge Miller, whose husband Edward, also a peace activist, was a University of Wisconsin physicist whose office would be damaged in the Army Math bombing. Midge Miller had organized one of the more dramatic peace marches in Madison, in which the names of all the U.S. war dead were called out on the Capitol steps. Her call for help in electing Senator Eugene McCarthy produced a tremendous outpouring of volunteers in Madison, reviving the town-gown alliance that had been sundered by Dow Day. Support was bipartisan; it was even whispered that Governor Knowles's wife was a closet McCarthy supporter.

Karl Armstrong was one of thousands of students who went "Clean for Gene." He got a conservative haircut from one of the oldtimers at the campus barbershop on lower State Street and went to work canvassing the East Side. With Ruth and Dwight he attended a McCarthy appearance at the Dane County Coliseum in March 1968. *"Why, I felt it was a vital necessity that Eugene McCarthy be elected," he would tell the judge. "Not because I really cared that much for Eugene McCarthy, but he was the peace candidate at that time."*

———

In the last week of March Fred Harvey Harrington flew to Washington for an important meeting at the White House. The University of Wisconsin president now headed the legislative committee of the National Association of State Universities and Land Grant Colleges, the major lobbying arm of public universities in the United States. He was also a member of Lyndon Johnson's Task Force for Urban and Higher Education. For several years, the task force had been at work on a plan that President Johnson envisioned as the last cog in the turning wheel of the Great Society. The idea had come from a Johnson adviser named Eric Goldman who had devised it after a visit to the Madison campus in the summer of 1964. Johnson had bruited it in a campaign speech later that summer at the University of California at Irvine. "University extensions have solved many a problem of the American farm; isn't it time to develop extensions that will help our struggling cities?" he asked. It was the Wisconsin Idea writ large.

The meeting at the White House was to present the final draft of the Urban Grant plan to the president. As they were ushered into the Oval Office, Harrington and four other task force members found Johnson surrounded by advisers. Harrington could see at once that something was wrong. Four years earlier, when he had sat next to Johnson at a luncheon to kick off the urban-grant feasibility study, he had been impressed by the sheer size and vitality of the man. Now Johnson was so feeble that he could barely get out of his chair. His voice had lost its hearty timbre, and his handshake was limp. Paul Miller, of the Rochester Institute of Technology, made a brief presentation on behalf of the group, but Harrington could see that Johnson wasn't listening. *He's done in,* he thought. *The war has done him in.*

It was true. North Vietnam's surprise Tet Offensive in February, though militarily unsuccessful, had scored a psychological victory, spreading defeatism in the United States. On March 25, the Wise Men, a group of trusted advisers who had long supported Johnson's win-in-Vietnam policy, had advised him against further escalation. Clark Clifford, Robert McNamara's replacement as secretary of defense, had informed the president that he was recommending against a request from General William Westmoreland for an additional 206,000 troops. Members of Johnson's White House staff had advised the president to tone down a hawkish speech he was set to give on March 31. In mid-March Senator Robert Kennedy of New

York, brother of the late President John Fitzgerald Kennedy, had jumped into the Wisconsin primary and was likewise questioning the war effort. Polls indicated that Johnson could lose in Wisconsin, that he stood a good chance of becoming the first incumbent president to be defeated in a primary.

Harrington had seen Johnson at the lowest point of his career. When the educators had left, the president wrote a new ending to his March 31 address. He was calling a partial halt to the bombing of North Vietnam, he announced. He wanted peace talks to begin. And incidentally, he would not seek a second term in office.

Donald Armstrong had accompanied Dwight to only one session with Dr. O'Connor. He really couldn't see what Dwight's problems had to do with him, he told the psychologist. In the dry lexicon of the therapist, Don's refusal to cooperate "affected the prognosis negatively."

O'Connor was a West Sider. Children in his neighborhood were refusing to salute the flag at school. He had shocked his own son by offering to pay his way to Canada if he was drafted. And so he was not alarmed when Dwight began to fall under the spell of campus radicals. Since Dow Day, Dwight had been moving closer to Karl. With O'Connor's blessing, he began speaking out at East High, organizing other students, putting up posters. In March he handed out a pamphlet he had written advocating that grades be abolished and students be allowed to take whatever courses they wanted. "Hey, I'm really doing this at school," he would tell O'Connor. "Do you believe it?" O'Connor was encouraged by these "positive feelings."

At his last session with the psychologist in April 1968, Dwight spoke of Karl as a model revolutionary, a true Che Guevara. O'Connor smiled benignly on this hero worship, something not unusual between brothers. Dwight had now satisfied the terms of his parole for auto theft, and O'Connor could close out the sessions without feeling that they were a total loss. At least Dwight had found someone to look up to.

Even when she was much younger, Mira had felt a maternal protectiveness toward her brothers. On summer visits to the Tarr Valley farm where Ruth had grown up, she would get knots in her stomach worrying about how she was going to keep them away from the bull. Now, it seemed to Mira, Karl hadn't been the same since Dow Day. He had an absent look, and he wouldn't touch anything with meat in it. Karl had a good heart, she believed, but he was being misled by out-of-state agitators. She had read in the *Wisconsin State Journal* that radicals were also infiltrating the high schools, and she was afraid for Dwight.

In early May Mira invited Karl and Dwight over to see her new house in Lakeview Heights. She had selected the draperies and carpets herself. The kitchen had a built-in range and automatic dishwasher, and there was a hole in the backyard where the pool was going to go. But its most striking feature was a sunken octagonal living room with a vaulted ceiling. "Isn't it beautiful!" she exulted.

Dwight could not hide a sneaking appreciation—no Armstrong had ever lived like this—but Karl was stone faced. "You're rich," he said accusingly.

Mira was stunned; she didn't consider herself rich at all. She had just taken a job as a teacher's aide to help with the house payments. She started to protest, but Karl cut her off. "Lily-white neighborhood, living in a house with a swimming pool—how bourgeois can you get?" He pronounced the word the way they did on campus: "booge-wah."

Mira began to cry. She was hurt, but also angry that Karl would say such things in front of Dwight. "You and your revolution!" she said hotly. "The Lord says, 'Not by might, not by power, but by My spirit.' Unless you touch that inner spirit, you won't have any effect!"

Karl stormed out, dragging Dwight after him. "I just don't believe all that junk I learned in church," he shouted back.

Throughout May, the Madison campus was unsettled. President Johnson's announcement that he would not run for a second term; the coast-to-coast riots precipitated by the assassination of Martin Luther King, Jr., on April 4; and the upheavals in Paris, where students and workers had taken over the streets, and at Columbia University, where SDS had commandeered the administration building, had inspired global feelings of beleaguerment and solidarity among the young, one of those "revolutionary moments" that Harvey Goldberg talked about, in which all things seemed possible. On May 16 an SDS-led contingent occupied the Peterson Administration Building, demanding that the University of Wisconsin stop doing business with banks that had holdings in South Africa. Two nights later someone firebombed South Hall, a historic Bascom Hill building where the dean of letters and science had his offices. The following day a group called Students for Humane Institutions met at Ogg Hall, the most hivelike of the Southeast Dorms, to consider burning the entire campus. And on June 5, as students were preparing for final exams, Robert Kennedy was assassinated in Los Angeles, one more sign of an impending apocalypse.

At the beginning of the semester, Harvey Goldberg had launched his own offensive with a course called Contemporary Societies. The subject was Third World revolutions. The reading list included such books as Frantz Fanon's *Wretched of the Earth;* Barrington Moore, Jr.'s, *Social Origins of Dictatorship and Democracy;* and, of course, *Revolution in the Revolution,* Regis Debray's exegesis of the principles of Castroism. Both the readings and the lectures promoted the idea that the bloodshed of sudden, revolutionary change was preferable to the prolonged agony of corrupt social systems.

Contemporary Societies was the most popular course ever given at the University of Wisconsin. The campus political factions sat en bloc, most of them in the balcony (the "Mountain," it was called) of Ag Hall auditorium, cheering for their respective heroes and hissing the nefarious interventions of the CIA. The teaching assistants were themselves well-known radicals, moving among the flock with the dignity of apostles. Leaflets announcing rallies were passed from row to row. But when Goldberg ritualistically removed his glasses, a signal that he was about to speak, the hubbub would instantly subside and the dream weaving would begin. It happened not infrequently that spring that students went directly from Ag Hall to demonstrate in the streets.

In his letter to Harrington, William Appleman Williams had mentioned the appeal of the Debray book to students and had cautioned the president not to underestimate the new revolutionary romanticism sweeping the liberal arts campus. "It is a very powerful engine of action, and often turns basically relevant ideas and arguments into irrational *but believable* propaganda." In the months after Dow, he found his patience with his students, especially Goldberg students, increasingly strained. The New Left militants did not seem to understand that "power doesn't just roll over and play dead; power hits back." Goldberg and other young faculty zealots were playing with fire, it seemed to Williams, encouraging revolutionary hopes when there was no revolutionary situation. "You look at every fundamental change in social policy; you have to split the ruling class," he told his students. "The antiwar movement is making absolutely no effort to split the ruling class."

Williams and Goldberg had been friends since they taught together at Ohio State University. But Williams was upset with Goldberg, particularly for his taste in companions. He left it to their mutual friend George Mosse to rescue Goldberg from the loud arguments that would erupt at Goldberg's North Few Street lodgings at 3 A.M. But at dinner one night that May the two of them argued wildly. "My basic disagreement with you is that you never come forward and become publicly accountable for what you are saying," Williams complained.

"What could be more public than Agriculture Hall?" Goldberg replied wryly. "I am not whispering these things in the men's room, you know."

"Harvey, do you ever talk to them about all the violence that failed, that was counter-productive?" Williams asked.

"No," Goldberg said coldly.

"Well, that's at least as important as violence that 'accomplished' something, don't you think?"

"Violence is a fact of life," Goldberg replied.

Williams was silent. After the Second World War, when he was at the Naval Air Station in Corpus Christi, he had been beaten by local police who took exception to the help he was giving to a black voter-registration drive. The cops had brought him down to the station, thrown a blanket over him, and worked him over for nearly forty-five minutes with sand-filled rubber hoses. The beating had reopened his old war wounds, and after nine months in naval hospitals he still was not well enough to fly. The navy had let him go with an honorable discharge and a year's pay. "My experience with violence is different from yours," he told Goldberg finally. "I *know* about violence."

At the end of the semester Williams announced that he was leaving Wisconsin for a position at Oregon State University, a small school best known for its agriculture and forestry programs. Goldberg never forgave him.

Karl worked that summer at Graber's Drapery, but in early August he was fired for getting a flatbed truck loaded with a forklift stuck under the railroad overpass on South Park Street. The Democratic National Convention was set to begin in Chicago, and Karl decided to go, partly to show support for the peace candidate Gene McCarthy and partly to see Abbie Hoffman, Jerry Rubin, and their followers in the Youth International Party (Yippies), who were making their national debut.

As he would later testify, Don was very much against it. *I asked him not to go down there, principally because he was going on a shoestring type of thing, because he took a packsack and a sleeping bag along with him.... He says, "Well, all the hotels are filled. We'll just have to sleep in a park...."*

Chicago was Dow Day on a national scale. Five years later, defending himself on the witness stand, Karl would recall the experience in vivid detail:

I got into Chicago about five o'clock in the evening. I went to Lincoln Park. It was around Lincoln Park that [vigilantes] came up and asked me, said, "Are you a Yippie?" And of course I wasn't a Yippie. I didn't know what a Yippie was. But I said, "Well, this is a free country. If I want to be a Yippie, I can be a Yippie." I said, "Yah, I'm a Yippie." And they dumped me in the Chicago River.

I was soaking wet, very cold. Went into Lincoln Park, listened to people. Allen Ginsberg was there. Some priests spoke about what was going to happen that night. Mayor Richard Daley had declared that parks really didn't belong to the people, that there was a curfew and that all of these thousands of people had to leave the park. Of course, no one had any place to stay, including myself. And that night the National Guard cleared the park. People were beaten, clubbed, gassed.

I was camped at a campfire on the side of the hill with some Blackstone Rangers. We were getting off on some very, very good vibrations between us. And we were the last people to leave the park. Yards behind us were National Guardsmen with bayonets. Many of the Guardsmen were pointing their rifles at people. I actually thought they were going to shoot. They had a big truck with flood lamps lighting up the whole area. And the whole area was tear-gassed. We got out of the park.

They didn't stop there. They chased us through the streets. I saw people being chased down dead-end alleys. And I heard people being beaten and screaming. I was carrying my wet sleeping bag at the time. And they left me alone, I think because I didn't have long hair.

The next day I went to Grant Park. It was a battle scene. I guess there was about 10,000 people, 15,000 people. On all sides of us were police, National Guard. They had machine guns mounted. They had National Guardsmen planted up on top of the buildings. The same helicopters that they used in Vietnam flying overhead. And at that time I first came in contact with police provocateurs. They were dressed in these Al Capone suits. They would go marching through the crowd and take people by the collar and say, "You———." They'd shout obscenities at them. The organizers of the march were saying, "Don't do anything, don't do anything, they're trying to provoke you into a fight." And that's exactly what they were doing.

In Grant Park, we were stormed by the Chicago police. They didn't care about arresting people; they were just beating up people. It was an act of terror is what it was.

We began the march up Michigan Avenue. It was a war scene. The bridges were being held by the National Guard. They had sand bags, they had machine guns, and they were tossing tear gas indiscriminately into the crowd as it passed by.

They let us march up past the Conrad Hilton, and then they stopped us. Then they sent police into the back of the demonstration. We were kept within a square block. Then they charged between the Blackstone Hotel and the Conrad Hilton, right up through the middle of the crowd. I was in the middle because I thought that was the safe place to be and because I wasn't into acts of bravery at that time. I didn't want to get arrested. I was there just to add my number to the demonstration. And I was right there in front where the police charged.

I'm very tall, and people were looking for leadership in that situation. I said, "Well, sit down and let yourselves be arrested." People around me sat down, and we thought we were about to be arrested.

They didn't care about arrests. The two people in front of me were clubbed brutally. And at that moment I really felt like an ass. I said to myself, "Karl Armstrong, you are such a stupid person. Stupid, naive. To think that these people care about civil disobedience or anything of that sort."

It was like a very radicalizing experience. I had visions of my bones being trampled into the asphalt. People were being knocked unconscious and dragged by their hair to paddy wagons. Both men and women.

What probably saved me was the fact that I didn't have long hair. The first wave had passed over me, and I had been clubbed in the knee, but that was all. And I escaped through the two ranks of police and out to a park that bordered on the street. But all along it was as

*though I had an intuitive feeling that none of these demonstrations
would work. And from 1968 on, it was a waiting process, waiting for
other people to see the same political reality.*

Midge Miller, holding the Wisconsin delegation's McCarthy votes,
rushed into the street in front of the Hilton to try to stop the police
charge, but was able to rescue only a few of the demonstrators.
Behind her the riot squad drove a herd of panic-stricken protesters
through the plate-glass windows of the Hilton bar. Elizabeth
Boardman, who had led the Quaker mercy mission to Hanoi, was
among those arrested at the scene. Delegate Don Peterson, whose
orange "Peterson for Governor" placard would help the FBI identify the stolen van used in the Army Math bombing, stood and
denounced the "gestapo" tactics of the Chicago police and
demanded that the convention be immediately suspended and
moved to a more civilized city. He was hooted down.

At Karl's sentence hearing, Don Armstrong would recall his
son's return from Chicago.

*And when he came back, I said, "Well, how did everything go?"
He said, "First of all, Dad, I have to tell you that I lost my packsack
and all my belongings and my sleeping bag because three fellows
came along, fellows wearing blue trousers and white shirts and which
had a southern accent and came along and grabbed me and two
other fellows and threw us in the Chicago River with all our belongings." And for days he just went into a silence.*

As expected the convention nominated Vice President Hubert
Humphrey, who was wedded to the foreign policy of the Johnson
administration. The Republicans nominated Richard Nixon, whose
"peace with honor" seemed a hollow promise to partisans of the
antiwar movement. A sizable number voted for third-party candidate Dick Gregory, a black comedian and peace activist, but many
more, like Karl Armstrong, abandoned electoral politics entirely.

What took place in Chicago "shouldn't happen in a democracy,"
Karl told Ruth. Others who were there, and who would later testify
in his behalf, would recall "the talk of fascism, of how they now
understood what it must have been like in Nazi Germany, to actually see the troops on the streets, the bayonets pulled." It wasn't
America anymore, they said: It was "Amerika."

8

The Black Strike

*I brought a grenade back from Vietnam. And one day I
walked down the halls of the RAND Corporation. I looked
into the computer room, and I wanted to throw that grenade
in there.*

—ANTHONY RUSSO,
military analyst, for the defense

*Let's not have them find refuge behind a hypocritical moral-
ity that says, "My violence is justified but yours is not."*

—DOUGLAS HAAG,
Wisconsin Assistant Attorney General, for the prosecution

In the words of a song by Creedence Clearwater Revival that was
popular at the time, there was a "bad moon risin'" in the fall of
1968. SDS militants, suspecting that Madison Police Detective
George Croal, still operating undercover, was a cop, turned out the
lights at a meeting in Social Science Hall and tried to break his arm.
At a Library Mall rally, a coed pointed at Special Agent Tom
McMillen, who was dressed as a student, and shrieked, "He's not
one of us; he's wearing a wedding ring!" Incoming freshmen, who
had been watching the war on television for four years, behaved
like veteran revolutionaries, organizing their dorms into centers of

political enlightenment. In Agriculture Hall Harvey Goldberg continued teaching the social gospel to an overflow crowd. "For truly I say to you, the camel will go through the eye of the needle before the rich man shall enter the Kingdom of God," he said in his opening lecture, quoting Matthew 19.

Three thousand turned out for the first SDS "monster meeting" of the fall, filling every seat in the Union Theater. The students were all reading *Soul on Ice* by the jailed Black Panther Eldridge Cleaver and hooking thumbs in the Panther version of a fraternal secret grip. Those who had gone Clean for Gene were letting their beards grow and snapping up tattered olive green fatigues at army and navy surplus stores. The girls were removing their brassieres, had taken to wearing long, cotton peasant dresses, and had given up shaving their legs. And they had gone beyond the Pill to the hassle-free intrauterine device, or IUD.

"We in SDS don't see electoral politics as a valid way of changing America," a student admitted in an op-ed piece in the *Daily Cardinal.* Civil disobedience was also passé. The new clarion call was "resistance." On the night of October 1, someone knocked out a side window in the state headquarters of the Selective Service System, about half a mile south of campus, poured gasoline inside, and tossed in a burning bed sheet, setting off an explosion that blew out the office's plate-glass windows. On the jukebox in the Rat, students played the same Jim Morrison song over and over.

> *The old get older*
> *And the young get stronger*
> *May take a week*
> *Or it may take longer*
> *But we want the world!*
> *And we want it now!*

As William Appleman Williams had predicted, power struck back. By that fall, those accused of fomenting the Dow Day confrontation had all been hounded out of Madison. In September the gentle humanist William Sewell was replaced in the chancellor's office by Edwin Young, a labor relations expert who had helped the State Department set up non-Marxist industrial research centers in Germany after World War II. At the same time the Board of Regents cracked down on the *Daily Cardinal* for printing an obscenity (though it was inside a quote), ordering the newspaper either to pay rent of about $3,000 a year or to move its business office off campus. The newspaper's student management decided to pay the rent.

Also that fall, at the instigation of Director J. Edgar Hoover, the FBI turned its Counter-Intelligence Program (Cointelpro) against dissidents on the nation's campuses with a campaign aimed at depriving them of their scholarships. George Baxtrum, a veteran of Cointelpro campaigns against members of the Communist party and of black bag operations at the Socialist Workers' party headquarters in New York (the subject of a future lawsuit which the Bureau would settle out of court), was uneasy about using such methods against academics, all the more so because Hoover's instructions stressed the importance of using no stationery that could be traced to the bureau. Nevertheless, the Resident Agency enlisted the services of Gordon Roseleip, a conservative state senator from Darlington, as the conduit for damaging information regarding targeted students and faculty on the Madison and Milwaukee campuses.[1]

[1]A graduate student in history recently arrived from Oregon, who had been identified in a Portland newspaper as a member of the Communist party, was a typical target. The boy had become an officer in the Committee to End the War in Vietnam. On September 10, the Special Agent in Charge in Milwaukee proposed a scheme to deprive the student of his $3,300-a-year Carnegie Fellowship. The following letter, purported to be from a Vietnam veteran enrolled in history along with the Communist student, was sent to Senator Roseleip:

> The only difference between us is that [student X] is active in the Committee to End the War in Vietnam and has participated in disruptive antiwar demonstrations on the campus, while I continue to support our Government and its principles of democracy. One other difference is that [X] has been awarded over three thousand dollars per year as a graduate fellow from the Carnegie Foundation which is administered by the university while I continue to work in menial jobs to support myself.
>
> A Loyal Student

In a memo to Washington, Milwaukee's Special Agent in Charge had explained how Roseleip could make use of the anonymous letter.

> Information of this nature should give ROSELEIP some reason to accuse the Committee to End the War in Vietnam, which is a New Left organization, as being under Communist influence and should also give him an opportunity to insist that the administrators at the UW-Madison be more selective in awarding fellowships so that they are not awarded to Communist Party members.

The director replied ten days later granting authority to proceed, but urging caution.

> Your letter should be prepared on stationery that cannot be traced to the Bureau or to the Government. Assure that all necessary steps are taken to prevent the Bureau from being identified as its source.

To Special Agent Tom McMillen, the crackdown was a nightmare. Under Hoover's rules, cases had to show investigative activity every thirty to forty-five days, and McMillen now had hundreds of cases. "Where do you draw the line?" he asked Baxtrum in desperation. Baxtrum could not tell him.

One of McMillen's files concerned *Connections,* one of the new "underground newspapers" that were sprouting all over the country. It was written and edited by graduate students, preachy in a Marxist sort of way, with few readers except for a special issue on Dow Day that had sold out. McMillen did not find the paper to be much of a threat and let it slide. Along came an inspector from the Washington office on an annual visit. "Hey, you haven't done anything on this for three months," he noted. McMillen explained that he had been busy. "In Hoover's FBI, you go by the book!" the inspector screamed.

A theatrical production of *Peter Pan* staged by a student named Stuart Gordon caught the mood of the isthmus. In Gordon's interpretation, Peter Pan was a hippie, Tinker Bell was gay, Captain Hook and his pirates were police, the three Darling children were the last straight kids in America, and the voyage to Never-Never Land was an acid trip portrayed by a half-hour light show in which half a dozen nude coeds danced hypnotically to Iron Butterfly's "Inna gadda da vida." Threatened with prosecution by Dane County District Attorney James Boll, Gordon mounted the production behind locked doors in Commerce Hall. On an evening that summed up America in 1968, make-believe cops and hippies went at it on stage while real police pounded on the doors with warrants for the arrest of the producer and his nubile cast.

Dwight Armstrong's senior year at East High School ended almost as soon as it began. School administrators showed no interest in his idea for abolishing grades and required courses, and his teachers were unsympathetic to the political and personal alternatives Dwight now advocated. One day, as his chemistry teacher lectured on the harmful effects of pot and LSD, Dwight raised his hand. "Have you ever done drugs?" he asked. "What's your experience with it?"

September 12 was his final appearance in school. Karl had given him a firsthand account of what happened in Chicago, and so it was a righteous Dwight who interrupted his civics teacher, Mr. Gibson, in the middle of a discussion of the recent disorders. "You people are being softsoaped," he yelled out. "You've got to reject this; this is, this is … superficial bullshit!" He withdrew the same day. It was the last his classmates saw of him until his picture appeared in the newspapers two years later as a suspect in the Army Math bombing.

Karl did not know what to do next. He informed his former faculty adviser that he was thinking of transferring to Whitewater State University. He then wrote to John Cipperly, the dean of admissions on the Madison campus, appealing his three-year suspension. Receiving no answer, he resumed his wandering, taking a job making snowmobiles at Evinrude Motors in Milwaukee. As in Houston, he enjoyed starting from scratch in a city where he knew no one. He found a rooming house next door to a youth drop-in center on Eleventh Street and moved in with his record player and Beatles albums. He rode a bus to work and spent his weeknights in a neighborhood tavern or browsing in a nearby library. He started on the daytime shift at Evinrude, then switched to the night shift, operating a drill press, then a sand blaster, and finally a lathe. Milwaukee wasn't anything like Madison, he discovered; it was a "down" place where everybody was trying to "forget their existence." "They should have killed those hippies in Chicago," his co-workers on the assembly line were saying. The patrons of his neighborhood bar threatened to beat him up if he didn't stop playing "Hey, Jude" on the juke box. Milwaukeans were "into different things," he realized. All they talked about at Evinrude was snowmobiling. All the workers owned snowmobiles and spent their winter weekends on them, tooling around the countryside on a sort of rural pub crawl. It was almost pathetic how attached they were to their jobs, Karl thought.

In mid-October Karl's parents forwarded a letter to him from his draft board notifying him that his student deferment was canceled and that he was to report for a physical, and he took the opportunity to tender his resignation at Evinrude. Back in Madison he went straight to the Wisconsin Draft Resistance Union (WDRU) headquarters on Langdon Street to get advice about immigration to Canada, just in case he was classified 1-A. At 6 A.M. on the appointed day, he showed up at the bus depot for the ride to the induction center in Milwaukee. WDRU organizers were on the scene with handouts of a story by an ex-student named Hanley about how he made up his mind to refuse induction while on that same bus ride to Milwaukee. Karl took an armful and passed them out on the bus.

At the induction center he followed the yellow line like everyone else, but in his own mind he was resolved not to go.

"Do you ever or have you ever sleepwalked?" he was asked.

"Yes." He described his childhood sleepwalking.

"Do you sleepwalk now?"

"Yes, every several months." He was answering truthfully. He didn't know that the army didn't take sleepwalkers.

Downstairs, the sergeant informed him that he was "1-Y." He felt a wave of relief, followed immediately by gloom. He went back to his room on Eleventh Street, phoned his parents and asked them to pick up his stereo and records, as he was leaving Milwaukee. "I've been rejected," he said. "I'm not even fit to kill." He threw a few clothes into his backpack and started walking out of the city. By nightfall, he had made it to Waukesha, twenty-five miles west of Milwaukee. He got a room at the Mayflower Motel and a job washing dishes at an Italian restaurant. After two days, he collected his pay and hitched a ride to Chicago, and then began heading for Florida, where he had never been.

Even by Karl Armstrong's standards, it was a strange trip. He got rides from a redneck Vietnam veteran, a family of Georgia blacks with a George Wallace bumper sticker on their car ("If you want to stay alive in this country, you should have a Wallace sticker," they explained), a man who masturbated under a blanket while Karl drove, and a black drug dealer who invited him to join his syndicate. "You can infiltrate white society for us," the man said.

In Miami Beach he rented a room at a sleepy, roach-infested hotel with a Spanish facade and slow, circulating fans in the rooms. Miami Beach seemed to Karl to be full of men in Cadillacs looking for other men to have sex with. He quickly tired of being propositioned and went to the local employment office to look for a job. Being an experienced lathe man, he was taken on by an aerospace company in Hialeah, making stainless-steel nose cones for NASA. The other workers were Cubans, refugees from the Castro regime. Every block of Miami Beach had an anti-Castro center or banner. A Cuban department store clerk who invited Karl home to dinner informed him that her dad was strongly against the Cuban government. Karl couldn't understand it; on the Wisconsin campus, Fidel was considered a great hero. "Your father probably ripped people off," he told her.

He quit his job after a day and a half, justifying his abrupt departure with the thought that the job was "military-related." It had taken him a dozen rides to get to Florida, and it took a dozen to get back. He arrived in Madison dusty and road weary after an 80 miles-per-hour ride on a motorcycle from Janesville. He had set out with the aim of deciding what he was going to do from then on, and he had concluded that whatever he did, it would be "calm and rational." There would be no more trips—he was going to "be around in Madison."

For two weeks he secluded himself in the rec room of the Hintze Road house reading *Ramparts* and other magazines of radical outlook. He didn't leave the basement except to raid the kitchen for food. He became obsessed with the idea that he could accomplish anything if he could only visualize the goal, keeping it constantly in mind. This notion gave him a feeling of power and self-confidence, but his euphoria dissipated when he could not think of any goals.

Emerging from the rec room, he applied for a job at Badger Ordnance Works in Baraboo. The big munitions plant, which was operated for the army by the Olin Corporation, was part of the landscape of his youth. Donald would always point it out on their summer drives to the Tarr Valley, reminding Karl that Ruth's brother had died there in an explosion in the midfifties. Donald had always suspected "dirty nitro," and had even gone out to make inquiries, but had been turned away. "There wasn't enough of your uncle left to fill a five-gallon slop bucket," he would say. Thanks to the war, employment at the plant was now up to about 5,500. Pay and benefits were excellent by local standards. Quite a few Sauk County farmers had given up the plow to make rocket propellant and gunpowder for Vietnam.

But Karl was not really sure why he was applying. The plant was forty miles from Madison, and he did not have a car. He wasn't really serious about the application, yet in the back of his mind was the idea that it might be useful to know the layout of the place. In any case, he wasn't hired.

The only job he could find was selling used cars at Madison Motors on the East Side. The pay was fifty dollars every two weeks plus commissions and the use of a car. Business was slow. The salesmen whiled away the time shooting craps, playing cards, and watch-

ing one of the floor men demonstrate his karate skills in the show-
room. When a customer ventured onto the lot, the sales crew
fought over him like gulls. Karl's boss would later give the FBI a
very unfavorable account of Karl's job performance. Karl wished he
were back in school.

Mira found that she was unhappy in her new home. Her relationship with Bill had been an unequal one from the start. At East
High, he had been in the Schoep's Set; she was a nobody from the
edge of town. Now, when she felt most alone, she would sing a
Hebrew lullaby to herself. "You're lovely, you're precious," she
would hear God whisper.

She had started using alcohol to relieve her unhappiness, but she felt
bad about it, since she was trying to set an example for Dwight, who
had just lost his job at the Edgewater Hotel after trying to sell hashish
to a waitress. She had decided to try another church, to see if that
would do any good. She was going to tell Pastor Hoffman on Christmas eve, right after the midnight service, and she persuaded Karl and
Dwight to go with her. After the annual exchange of presents at the
Hintze Road house, the three of them left for church together.

The small chapel stood on a hill a few miles away. Suburbanites
filled the pews. Pastor Hoffman presided at the altar, offering
prayers for America's fighting men overseas. At the conclusion of
the service Mira took Karl and Dwight to the church lobby, where
the minister was greeting the faithful on their way out. "How nice
to see you boys," he said, turning to welcome them.

Mira blurted out her news. "I'm joining the Assembly of God."

Hoffman's momentary delight at seeing his lost sheep back in
church was replaced by dismay. The Assembly of God was a charismatic sect that practiced speaking in tongues; it was not a place for
self-respecting Lutherans. "Don't do it," he said sharply. Sotto voce,
he reminded her that Karl and Dwight still weren't out of the
woods. If she went away, it would be more difficult for him to help
them, he said.

Mira had no stomach for confrontations. As she began to falter,
Karl and Dwight stepped in and steered her toward the door.
"You'll be back," Hoffman called after her.

In January 1969, Dean Cipperly replied to Karl's appeal of his
three-year suspension, once again readmitting him on "strict proba-

tion." Karl signed up for first-year Spanish, introduction to philosophy, and a course called Social Disintegration. At the same time he hired on as a security guard with the Madison Business Protective Association, working the graveyard shift at Madison General Hospital, and rented a room in a down-at-the-heels fraternity called Phi Sigma Kappa, where he also got a "meal job" busing tables and washing pots and pans.

The Phi Sigs were the poor boys of Greek Row. They had lost their original house in the Great Depression and leased a brick-and-stucco dump a block from the Memorial Student Union. In winter arctic winds rattled the windowpanes, and clanky old steam radiators overheated the rooms. Membership was down, as it was everywhere on Greek Row, and a good third of the residents were boarders like Karl. The fraternity had long since given up its private pier and boathouse on the lake and had only one remaining draw: a cold-beer delivery system that was a marvel of make-do engineering. A thirty-five-foot hose surrounded by stovepipe and cooled by a fan delivered beer from kegs stored in a huge basement refrigerator to a tap in the main-floor party room. The bar opened every day at five P.M. For special occasions a supply of Budweiser would be laid in, but the daily drink was Pabst Blue Ribbon, known around the house as "Pabst Horse Piss." Every other week a brewery truck dumped eight half-kegs of Pabst at the back door. Even though they usually could not afford a band, Phi Sig parties were frequent and well attended.

In Karl Armstrong the Phi Sigs discovered a perfect victim for their pranks. The first time he wore his uniform home from work, they jumped him and took his gun away. Everyone in the house had a nickname, and before long Karl was dubbed "Tuffy," from the label on his imitation leather jacket. But the Phi Sigs considered him anything but tough; Karl was so "mellowed out" that some brothers wondered if he was all there.

Dwight began frequenting the fraternity shortly after Karl moved in. He made free use of the bar, which worried the house manager because Dwight was not yet eighteen. It amazed one Phi Sig that the younger Armstrong would mooch cigarettes *and* matches. One evening, according to a brother, Dwight relieved himself in a corner of the room. From then on he had his own nickname at Phi Sigma Kappa: The Social Waste.

Dwight did make one friend at the fraternity, a boarder named

Policronio De Venecia. Poli was an ingenuous twenty-three-year old from Manila, the son of a Philippine diplomat who had served his government on three continents. He was very good looking, with a seraphic smile, and seemed to think he was the greatest lover in the world. The Filippino hated work; never went to class; and—a story Dwight loved to repeat—was so "out of it" that he had once taken an exam for the wrong course. Poli opposed the Vietnam War and supported the Huk national liberation movement in his homeland. Poli also seemed to have his father's diplomatic skills: Mira, for one, took an instant liking to him because he seemed very interested in God. Before long the exotic foreigner was a regular dinner guest at her Lakeview Heights home.

On January 15 Dwight had started a new job as a lineman at Morey Airport, a small, privately owned airfield on the outskirts of Middleton, a few miles west of the city. The pay was $1.60 an hour, and, as it turned out, there was a fringe benefit: Air force ROTC cadets from the University of Wisconsin took flying lessons at the field. One of Dwight's duties was to pick up the student pilots in town and ferry them to the airport in his boss's 1963 Chevrolet Impala. Dwight befriended the young flight instructor, Mike Powers, who would take him up in the same plane used by the cadets, a twin-seater blue-and-white Cessna 150 with a top speed of 100 miles per hour. Soaring above the stark winter landscape, Dwight felt his discontents fall away like ground fog, and he would experience an unfamiliar sensation of lightness. It was about as close as he had ever come to being happy.

Chancellor Edwin Young could tell that the militants were getting impatient when they showed up in his bedroom to present a list of demands. They wanted a Black Studies Center and more black teachers and counselors and scholarship money—and they wanted it *now.* Young had the flu, and was not in the mood to argue. How did they get in? he wondered. "Well, sure, black studies," he said cautiously, "and of course we are trying to get more black teachers as fast as we can. But you know, staffing decisions require faculty and regents approval. They take some planning, some politicking."

The so-called Black Strike began the next day, February 7, 1969, when a coalition of black and white radicals formally presented the university with a list of thirteen "nonnegotiable demands." These demands included the points they had already discussed with Chan-

cellor Young, plus others that would have required changes in the
state statute and the university's charter before they could be
enacted, such as black students' control of hiring and firing and the
immediate readmission to the Madison campus of ninety-four
blacks who had been expelled by Oshkosh State University after
they allegedly shot up a fraternity house. Picket lines formed
around buildings as militants shouted "On strike, shut it down!" For
a week the strike proceeded more or less peacefully. The pickets
made it difficult for students to get to their classes, but those who
were determined could shove their way through. Ralph Hanson
admonished his UP & S employees to avoid violence.

Then, on Wednesday, February 13, roving bands led by Black Panthers from Milwaukee disrupted classes and blocked entries. When
campus and MPD forces tried to catch them, they would, in the
words of one militant, "make like steam and vaporize." The situation
came to a head in midafternoon when Patrick Korten, a leader of
Young Americans for Freedom, a conservative group derided by
activists as "Young Americans for Fascism," challenged an obstruc-
tive picket on the steps of Bascom Hall. Korten climbed the steps
wearing a black armband with the name "Hayakawa" on it, after S. I.
"Sam" Hayakawa, the conservative president of San Francisco State
College, who had his own student strike to contend with. Korten was
opposed by Peter Neufeld, a big, redheaded freshman from West
Hempstead, New York. Neufeld threw Korten down the stairs.

President Harrington was in New York on business, but he had
given Chancellor Young carte blanche to enforce Faculty Document
122. Young was convinced that the university's big mistake on Dow
Day had been an inadequate show of strength. He phoned Governor
Knowles and asked for the National Guard. A battalion, 2,100 strong,
equipped with machine guns, automatic rifles, grenade launchers, and
helicopters, deployed the next morning, establishing skirmish lines all
around the foot of Bascom Hill. As had been the case on Dow Day,
even students who were not in favor of the strike considered it an
overreaction. The protest ranks swelled instantly from 2,000 to 10,000,
and attempts to police the surging crowd resulted in predictably ugly
incidents. Detective Croal, still working the campus though not under
cover, saw a look of hatred in the eyes of the demonstrators that he
hadn't seen in months. SDS founder Tom Hayden, facing conspiracy
charges with seven others in connection with the Democratic
National Convention, addressed a crowd in the Social Science build-

ing, where he called for "more Madisons" to help San Francisco State students in their battle with President Hayakawa.

As it happened, policemen who were injured in the skirmishes were brought to the emergency room at Madison General for treatment. Only one nurse was on duty there in the evening, and when she found herself with more than she could handle, she would turn to the only available person, the night watchman—Karl Armstrong—for help. It was a "schizzy" situation, Karl told Dwight. At the end of his shift, he would change into bellbottoms before leaving the hospital so as not to be mistaken for a policeman. After a nap he would join the picket lines outside Bascom Hall. He even helped disrupt his class in Social Disintegration. Then it was back to the hospital wheeling enemy casualties down the halls. "Ohhh, you broke your fingernail, did you?" he would say mockingly. "Isn't that a shame!" He thought they were faking it for the newspapers.

Don and Ruth worried that Karl might be involved in the Black Strike. The disruption of classes, the vulgar and hostile tone of Panther rhetoric, and the sheer infantilism of "nonnegotiable demands" did not play at all well on local TV. Don could go along with peace marches that were orderly and law abiding; he could defend them in the smoke shack. He had almost joined a march once when Karl asked him to, but he didn't see anyone his own age, anyone who looked normal.

The next time Karl came home, Don came right out and asked him. "I sure as hell hope you're not involved in this black shit on campus," he said.

"So what if I am?" Karl said.

Don bristled. "You stay away from them. You stay away from them hoods. They are out to tear this country down!"

Exactly what Karl said next is unclear, but it must have infuriated Don. He ran into Karl's bedroom and came back waving the .22 he had given Karl on his fourteenth birthday and that Karl had used exactly once.

"No!" Ruth screamed. Karl began backing toward the door.

"Karl's a hippie, Mira's a religious nut," Don ranted, waving the gun. "The whole damn family's crazy!"

Karl hopped a bus back into town. It would be a while before he came home for dinner again.

9

Mifflin Street

Let's look at this man's philosophy. It is that man can act contrary to law in a violent manner when he thinks he is morally justified.

—MICHAEL ZALESKI,
Wisconsin Assistant Attorney General, for the prosecution.

People's houses were ransacked. I was teargassed. Friends of mine were beaten. And it seemed as if a war of generations had broken out.

—WILLIAM KAPLAN,
student, for the defense

In response to his forceful handling of the Black Strike, Governor Knowles received more than 2,000 letters of support, many expressing the view that the University of Wisconsin belonged not to students but to them, the taxpayers.. The conservative bloc in the state legislature took advantage of the reaction to push through bills paring back the $8 million earmarked for students from disadvantaged backgrounds, revoking the scholarships of disrupters, and establishing a committee to investigate campus subversion.

From coast to coast the student movement was becoming as iso-

lated as William Appleman Williams had feared. A mid-March
Gallup poll found that 8 out of 10 Americans favored a crackdown
on campus lawbreakers. In Wisconsin, Senate Majority Leader
Ernest Keppler threatened to fire the entire Board of Regents if it
did not take action. The regents obliged by cutting allowable out-
of-state admissions by a whopping 40 percent, the reductions to be
phased in over the next several years. A frightened Fred Harvey
Harrington came out in favor of a slate of repressive measures
offered by Governor Knowles, including an antibullhorn proposal,
banishment of students convicted of disrupting classes, prison terms
for expelled agitators caught setting foot on campus, and the dismissal of faculty members involved in disruptions. Liberal Democrats denounced the plan, saying it was really aimed at "groups we
never talk about on the floor but do in taverns, the 'kikes' of New
York and 'niggers.'" But Harrington hoped that by supporting the
Knowles slate he could avert even more draconian measures that
would, to take one example, give legislators the power to suspend
the pay of professors whose politics they disliked. Unimpressed by
such tactics, the *Daily Cardinal* demanded Harrington's resignation.
So did statehouse conservatives.

Harrington's problems were compounded in late March when
the *Cardinal* launched an investigative series by Jim Rowen called
"Profit Motive 101," which accused certain members of the Board
of Regents of profiting from university business. The regents
responded by demanding that the university dissociate itself from
the newspaper, at least by removing its titular claim to be "The
Official Student Newspaper of the University of Wisconsin."

Harrington had had to fend off attacks on the *Cardinal* before.
The paper had long been a lightning rod for conservative displeasure because its editorial staff was dominated by the "New Yorkers," who gave the paper its left-liberal tone (and much of its journalistic vitality). Jim Rowen, for example, was from Washington,
D.C., the son of a respected *Washington Post* columnist. So when a
new editorial staff was announced in the *Cardinal* on April 1, Harrington circled the names of all the Wisconsin students listed and
sent it to Robert Taylor, his vice president for public affairs, with
the question, "Can we say—and tell [Board of Regents President
Charles] Gelatt—that instate folks have one-half the jobs now?"

"We can tell him but he won't believe us," Taylor replied in a
note scrawled on the same document. "On the editorial side (rather

than the business side) there are a sufficient number of New Yorkers to keep him unhappy." In fact, the paper's new editor-in-chief,
executive editor, associate editor, page-makeup editors, sports editor, and fine arts editor were all from New York. Harrington let the
matter drop.

Karl Armstrong's roommate at Phi Sigma Kappa was a gawky,
pink-mouthed law student from northern Wisconsin named Mark
Dobberfuhl, aka Dobber. Dobberfuhl was no more successful with
girls than was Karl and so did not object when Karl began bringing
nurses over from Madison General. As it happened, Dobberfuhl
was house president that year, and his policy in regard to allowing
women upstairs was "Just don't let me see you." Karl was soon
"engaged" to a sweet and apparently very naive nurse named
Diana Palafox. Diana was not political, and Karl made no attempt
to raise her consciousness. "Diana doesn't know what a radical I
am," he confided to one of her friends.

The Phi Sig who Mark Dobberfuhl had become closest to was a
junior from River Falls, Wisconsin, named Scott Nelson, with whom
he would drink and talk the nights away. Scott was going to be a
great social reformer, Dobber a lawyer with political connections.
To Dobber's regret, Scott had moved to an apartment building on
Langdon Street at the beginning of the semester, his individualism
being offended by group living, but he still stopped by now and
then for a complimentary glass of Pabst Horse Piss.

Scott was everybody's favorite drinking buddy and a cutup, and
there were Phi Sigs who realized that they probably would have
done better in college had they never met him. Karl was wearing his
security-guard outfit when Dobber introduced them, and Scott
assumed he was conservative. He was surprised to discover during a
chance encounter in the Rat that Karl was "spiritually oriented"
and interested in ideas. Scott had started his college career on the
west side of campus, in electrical engineering, and moved east to
philosophy and history. Karl had followed a similar trajectory. Scott
had been radicalized at Dow, as had Karl. The image Scott carried
of that event, which he would produce in political discussions like a
dog-eared wallet photo, was of an MPD officer furiously clubbing a
coed as she lay on the ground, "like he was trying to pulverize her,"
he would say.

Karl had never met anyone quite like Scott. Scott was lean and intense, with straight golden hair and gray, feline eyes. His face was almost handsome but slightly off-kilter, as if it had been broken and hurriedly pieced back together. His mouth sagged at one corner, and he always looked as if he was about to utter a wisecrack— which he usually was. He despised all regulations, skipped classes routinely, and was rarely seen out of bed before noon. Scott had a classiness about him, an aura of good breeding, yet he described himself as an anarchist. He had read all the important and heavy books—*Revolution in the Revolution, One-Dimensional Man, Soul on Ice*—as well as some that Karl had never heard of—works by obscure Russian philosophers, such as Kropotkin and Bakunin, and books about the Spanish Civil War. Scott said that when it came to imperialism, the Soviet Union was just as bad as the United States. All in all, Scott was politically "very conscious," it seemed to Karl.

The ice broke up on Lake Mendota, lilacs bloomed in the University Arboretum, and the brightly painted metal tables and chairs made their annual spring appearance on the Union Terrace. Toward the end of the semester Mark Dobberfuhl nominated Karl Armstrong for membership in Phi Sigma Kappa. Where Karl was concerned, opinion among the Phi Sigs was by then divided. There were a few, Dobber and Scott among them, who liked Karl and counted him a good drinking companion. But the engineering students considered him a scofflaw who took nothing seriously, not even protesting. In any event, Dobberfuhl was a house officer, and no one had the nerve to challenge his nominee. With exaggerated formality, Dobber invited his roommate to become a Phi Sigma Kappa. To his amazement, Karl refused, explaining that he saw no reason to pay a $100 initiation fee when he already had everything he wanted from the house. Besides, he told Dobber, he already belonged to a "brotherhood."

On April 1, 1969, William Dyke rode the wave of reaction to victory in the mayoral race, benefiting as well from the fact that students under twenty-one did not yet have the vote. Dyke was a six foot six William Buckley of the backwoods; articulate but extremely conservative in his opinions. He would later run for vice president of the United States on a ticket with the southern segregationist Lester Maddox. In the meantime, Madison students gave him the nickname "Bull" Dyke.

The occasion was the Mifflin Street Block Party, scheduled for Saturday, May 3. Block parties weren't strictly legal in Madison, but they were held regularly every spring; one took place without incident in another off-campus neighborhood a week before the announced event on Mifflin Street. Nevertheless, the new mayor refused to grant a permit for the Mifflin Street affair and let it be known that a party in that location would not be tolerated. And so a confrontation was almost guaranteed.

Tom Hayden had designated Miffland one of seven "liberated zones" in the United States. It had its own countercultural dress code, mores, dietary regimen, stimulants (all of the "life drugs" plus old-fashioned alcohol and tobacco), heroes, and dialect. A nonstudent called The Whiz kept everyone's stereo working. An elderly French anarchist named John Nekkhorochef, "Nekko" for short, served as community elder. A co-op at the corner of Mifflin and Bassett streets supplied "guerrilla cookies," cigarette papers, and other necessities. Harvey Goldberg enjoyed a large following in Miffland, and the community was represented on the city council by the former history student and socialist Paul Soglin.

In defiance of Mayor Dyke, Miffland residents held their block party as planned. At about five o'clock the MPD riot squad, commanded by Inspector Herman Thomas, deployed at the intersection of Mifflin and Bassett. A Dane County unit under Sheriff Jack Leslie came in behind them and set up a new piece of riot-suppression equipment that looked like a giant zip gun, that the police called a "pepper fogger." It could spew gas out the length of a block. No one in Miffland had ever seen one, and the novel sight brought the party to life. To the beat of the Rolling Stones' "Street Fightin' Man" the crowd snake-danced up and down Mifflin, taunting the cops with a pig's head on a pike and daring them to use their new weapon. Among the hundreds looking on were Karl Armstrong and Scott Nelson.

A squad car came by warning people to clear the street; no one paid any attention; and an unearthly whine came suddenly from the intersection, rising steadily in volume. After a moment, a stream of vapor shot out of the little cannon, blanketing the entire street in fumes that sent the celebrants running. The riot squad, wearing gas masks, pursued them shouting, "Halt, you're under arrest!" But they were so slow in their protective clothing that almost anyone could outrun them.

Karl and Scott fled to a corner house on the block, the residence of Alderman Soglin, and made it inside just ahead of a Dane County officer. Someone bolted the door shut behind them. A baseball grenade exploded on the porch, releasing a cloud of tear gas. Inside, the house was like a refugee camp, packed to the attic with students. Gas was seeping in through leaky sashes, and as a result everyone was crying, but openly, in the middle of animated conversation. No one was embarrassed to be seen in tears.

Scott recognized someone in the crowd, a junior named Leo Burt. They were living in the same apartment building on upper Langdon and had a couple of philosophy courses together. Scott introduced Leo to Karl, and the future conspirators shook hands. Karl would not remember much about the encounter. As far as he knew, Burt was just another student trying to avoid being arrested for dancing in the street.

The suppression of the Mifflin Street Block Party would take three days, require hundreds of officers on overtime pay, and engulf the student community from the Southeast Dorms to fraternity row. Gas hung like heavy fog across the isthmus. Pickup loads of vigilantes from outlying communities cruised city streets, assaulting anyone with long hair. Scores of residents, including several elderly persons and a six-month-old baby, were hospitalized for injuries and breathing problems. Alderman Soglin was arrested twice while trying to intervene and given an involuntary haircut at the county jail. A former county supervisor was beaten by police as he walked home unaware of the disturbance.

Karl would recall the scene in court testimony. *I saw the political repression by the Madison Police, especially during the Mifflin Street block party, which had police roaming the streets like Gestapo, windows taped up, in unmarked cars.* Saturday night, Scott and his friend Leo retreated to the relative safety of Langdon Street, but Karl stayed on Mifflin Street late into the evening, helping drag old mattresses from the houses to feed the flames of a huge bonfire in front of the co-op and shouting "Paris lives!" WIBA's FM station, known as "Up Against the Wall FM," played Jimi Hendrix's "Star Spangled Banner," and by common impulse stereo speakers appeared in windows all along Mifflin Street. The staccato sound of electronically simulated machine-gun fire intermingled with the distant wail of sirens; the smoke of burning barricades formed a pinkish haze around the moon; and to many young residents of Miffland, Hendrix's tortured version of the national anthem seemed to be the true one, the one that expressed what America the Beautiful had become.

10

Birdbaths

*Was Karl well known in the movement? No. Was he a leader
in the movement? No. Was he a veteran of the Vietnam war?
No. Was he a scholar? No. He was dropped for grades three
times from the university, but interestingly enough, the one
course he got an "A" in was a course called "Social Disorga-
nization."*

—MICHAEL ZALESKI,
Wisconsin Assistant Attorney General, for the prosecution

*Now, my God, these things really struck us. That we were
involved in a very direct link with the war in Southeast Asia.*

—WILLIAM KAPLAN,
student, for the defense

On Tuesday, May 6, President Harrington was called before the
legislature's newly created Joint Committee to Study Disruptions to testify in regard to the university's handling of the Black
Strike and other protests. Feelings were still running high over the
Mifflin Street riot, concluded only the day before. As on Dow Day
and during the Black Strike, the lawless reactions of a few had
turned a propaganda victory into defeat, diverting attention from
the fact that a neighborhood had been attacked by the police. Not
even the *Capital Times* supported the students.

The Joint Committee to Study Disruptions was stacked with Harrington's foes, including State Senator Gordon Roseleip. Roseleip was best known as the dairy industry's great defender. For a time, he had succeeded in preventing the oleomargarine people from putting food coloring in their product to make it look like butter. Roseleip maintained that there was no comparison between the taste of butter and that of the vegetable oil-based spreads. Challenged to a blind tasting, however, he failed.

Less well known were Roseleip's efforts on behalf of Americanism. Roseleip was the statewide commander of the American Legion and had once opposed legislation making contraceptives more readily available on the grounds that it would reduce the number of poor people, thus depleting the army's primary source of conscripts. In Roseleip's lexicon, the University of Wisconsin was the "Kremlin West." He had tried to get the *Daily Cardinal* investigated by the House Un-American Activities Committee. And lately, he had been receiving a great deal of confidential information from the FBI regarding individuals targeted under the Counter-Intelligence Program. The hearings of the joint committee presented an opportunity to put this information to use. He told the *Wall Street Journal* that he hoped to show that "people with Communistic backgrounds, teachers and students, are operating at the university." He commanded the leaders of the Committee to End the War in Vietnam and of several other campus organizations to appear before the joint committee. All refused.

Harrington arrived at the statehouse at 7:30 P.M., accompanied by several aides. Heads turned as he crossed the rotunda, giving him respectful nods. It wasn't like the old days when the politicians would come running to shake his hand, but at least they didn't turn away—though he suspected it was because he had approved the use of the National Guard during the Black Strike.

The hearing was in Room 421 of the South Wing. Roseleip stared at Harrington as he walked in. The senator owned a candy store in his hometown of Darlington and looked as though he was his own best customer. He was notorious for his unguarded remarks ("Get the kikes out of Madison!") in the senate chamber. Harrington could not hide his disdain for Roseleip and all the other right-wing "oafs" on the committee.

Roseleip led off the questioning, asking Harrington about a rumor that SDS was going to hold its national convention at the university that summer. Would Harrington approve? Harrington was not expecting the question, and it threw him off balance.

"I guess I cannot now answer that question, but I would think it unlikely."

"Why?"

"We haven't had a formal application."

Roseleip exploded. "You mean to tell me, Mr. President, that you sit there and cannot disapprove something that's trying to overthrow the government of the United States?"

"I could disapprove an application," Harrington said impatiently. "That is within my power."

"Surely you're a more loyal American than that. You won't bar an organization that's causing all this trouble and costing the taxpayers...."

"Senator!" Harrington interrupted. "I am a loyal American. I have been cleared by the Department of Defense, by the Army, by the Air Force, by the Navy, by the Department of Health, Education and Welfare, by the FBI. I am entitled to inspect confidential information. I am a member of loyalty review boards. I have been cleared!"

A hush fell over the hearing room. The usually garrulous senator faltered. It had never occurred to him that Harrington might have such clearances (which, of course, were obligatory for the president of a university with dozens of military contracts). The session was being recorded, and WHA, the state-owned radio station, would play it all across Wisconsin that evening, a good, old-fashioned Cold War exchange.

Fred Harrington slept well that night, believing he had won a round with the Right. But his victory was a hollow one; in reality the conservatives had gotten what they wanted. Ralph Hanson, testifying a month earlier, had refused to sanction repression: "I think we've got enough laws," he'd said. He had frankly admitted that rigid enforcement of the law was not his "first priority in cases of mass disobedience"; rather his main concern was "preventing violence." Harrington, after revealing his security clearances, had promised to use outside force whenever necessary and had even criticized the "permissiveness" of other campuses. "We do use force. We have used force since 1967," he proclaimed. The following day, Governor Knowles signed into law several of the repressive measures that Harrington had endorsed.

The May 21, 1969, issue of the *Daily Cardinal* carried the story of the death from multiple gunshot wounds of a twenty-five-year-old San Jose man named James Rector. Rector had been in a crowd of demonstrators protesting the closing of People's Park, a vacant lot in Berkeley that the University of California administration had decided to build on, when they were fired on by Alameda County sheriff's deputies. The *Cardinal* also reported Sheriff Frank Madigan's inflammatory comment: "When you're in a war, you've got to retaliate."

In Madison later that day, the United States flag on the Library Mall was seen flying upside down, and that night, Karl Armstrong boasted to a shocked Mark Dobberfuhl that it was he who had done it. To Dobber, a Young Democrat who had actually had dreams about the president's daughter Lynda Bird Johnson, mistreating the flag was "crossing the line." "Don't put me on, man," he said. He really did not believe it.

The next night Karl returned to the fraternity house quite late. Dobber heard him moaning on the first-floor landing. "This guy's really zonked out," he thought. He helped Karl into their room and tried to calm him down. He assumed that Karl had mixed beer and pot, but Karl said no, it was something called "acid." The frightened Dobber had never seen anyone on LSD. Karl was changing, he thought. He wasn't so sure anymore that Karl was cut out to be a Greek.

The end of the school year brought a temporary cease fire on the domestic front, but the Mifflin Street Block Party riot had left permanent bad feelings. A *Capital Times* reporter accused his publisher, Miles McMillen (no relation to FBI agent Tom McMillen), of suppressing a story linking Police Chief Wilbur Emery to the John Birch Society and claiming that the attack on Miffland was planned in advance. When his charges appeared in the *Daily Cardinal,* McMillen fired the reporter. Fire Captain Ed Durkin was so upset by the assault on Miffland that he bused residents of the neighborhood to his suburban farm for a makeup party. He also bailed Alderman Soglin out of jail. Subsequently a judge found Soglin guilty of disobeying a police officer, and the city fire chief eliminated Durkin's job as head of the firemen's union.

William Appleman Williams, back in Madison to sell his house after a year at Oregon State, found the isthmus polarized, the town-gown alliance in disarray. The "radical elders" from the *Studies on the Left* days had withdrawn. Some of the better faculty members were leaving Madison for jobs at Princeton and MIT, where they didn't need a National Guard escort to get to class. Those who remained seemed dispirited. "Theory is dead," George Mosse dourly informed Williams. "We have entered a phase of mindless activity." Hans Gerth, a well-known radical professor of sociology, expressed fear over the emergent police-state atmosphere. "It's Nazi Germany all over again!" the old socialist complained. Harvey Goldberg was packing his bags for a sabbatical year in France and did not have time to see his former friend, whose move to Oregon Goldberg still regarded as a betrayal. Fred Harrington had received a "Tired President" grant from the Danforth Foundation and was preparing to leave for India. Almost everyone in a position to influence the militants was exhausted, broken, or gone, and the peace movement was turning into a children's crusade. Williams departed the city with a sense of foreboding.

Dwight Armstrong's boss at Morey Airport was a man with the unusual name of Field Morey. His father, Howard Morey, one of the original barnstormers and a trainer of World War II pilots, had in fact named him after an airfield. Morey Airport had been in the family since 1942. Howard was retired and wintered in Florida, but returned to Madison every spring, flying his own plane cross-country. Morey Airport's single strip of asphalt lay amid cornfields on the outskirts of Middleton, a mile west of Highway 12. Arriving home in May 1969, the first thing Howard Morey saw was a tall, long-haired, gat-toothed boy slouching across the tarmac toward him. The elder Morey was a stickler for appearance; after all, businessmen like Oscar "Osky" Mayer were regular airport users, as was Governor Knowles. Morey was chagrined to think that a hippie had been gassing up their $200,000 planes. "That looks like a no-good kid," he told Field. "You better tell him to clean up his act!"

Field Morey called Dwight into his office at the east end of the hangar. "Well, boy, you know you're working here, and we like your work," he said cordially. Dwight was in fact lazy and had to be told what to do, but the younger Morey was trying to be kind. Looking away, he said, "Don't like that hair of yours too much. You know, we train ROTC students out here."

"I know," Dwight said noncommittally.

As Dwight would later recount the episode, Morey's manner became confidential, and he mentioned that his father had written to the draft board of another employee recommending that in the interests of the aviation industry he be given a deferment.

"Oh yeah, tell me more," Dwight said.

"If you want to be part of the company out here ...," and he fixed his gaze on the brown shag brushing Dwight's collar bones, "we can see that you don't get sent over there to that war."

Dwight was coming along in his flight lessons with Mike Powers; he had a knack for flying, and he was almost ready to solo. It was in his interest to hang on to the job, but Dwight didn't see it that way. He hadn't registered for the draft and hadn't heard a word from his local board. How could they draft him, he wondered, when they didn't even know he existed? Besides, Oscar Mayer's son worked at the airport and he had long hair, too. Why weren't they asking him to get a haircut? Dwight ignored the request. Three weeks later, on June 7, Field Morey fired him.

In the third week of June, Madison's SDS chapter sent a delegation to Chicago for the organization's national convention. Karl Armstrong and Scott Nelson tagged along in Scott's green Volkswagen bug. They weren't SDS members—SDS did not have "members," per se—but school was out, and they had time to spare.

About 1600 delegates showed up for the event at the Chicago Coliseum. They were met by jeering Chicagoans and scowling police. Scott could not get over the hostile reactions to the Saturday parade. Hard hats ran into the street and punched and kicked the marchers. *God, they want to kill us,* Scott thought.

Security at the convention was heavy, although ironically it was people who looked "straight" who were turned away. Scott managed to bluff his way in, but Karl, who had only recently quit his job with the Madison Protective Association and still had short hair, was denied admission. He waited out front talking to disgruntled reporters from the *New York Times* and *Washington Post* who had also been excluded, while plainclothesmen on rooftops across the street took his picture.

SDS had been created in Port Huron, Michigan, in 1962 as an organization dedicated to social reform through "participatory democracy." Despite the efforts of the FBI to thwart radical influences on campus, the organization now aimed at nothing less than the overthrow of the capitalist system. One faction, the Progressive Labor party, consisting mostly of Ivy League Maoists, believed that students would make the revolution in alliance with workers. Another faction, the Revolutionary Youth Movement (RYM), contended that students would make the revolution allied with blacks. RYM also called itself "Weatherman" from the old Bob Dylan lyric, "You don't need a weatherman to know which way the wind blows." Its membership included a disproportionate number of children from wealthy families, and their slogan was Bring the War Home.

As the convention got under way, the two factions immediately accused each other of "selling out." Progressive Labor, or PL as it was called, held a numerical advantage, but RYM surprised its opponents by bringing in a contingent of Black Panthers who took over the stage and denounced PL as "racist" and "counterrevolutionary." Led by Mark Rudd, a veteran of the 1968 Columbia University takeover, and Bernardine Dohrn, a young woman from Whitefish Bay, Wisconsin, the Weatherman and Black Panthers stormed out of the meeting hall and proceeded to hold their own convention in an adjoining room.

Scott came out shaking his head. "Let's get out of here," he told Karl. "Those people are out of their gourds!"

After the convention Karl went home with Scott to Scott's parents' farm in River Falls, five hours northwest of Madison, intending to stay only a few days. The Nelson spread, with its neat two-story farmhouse, huge white dairy barn, silvery silos, ice house, and flower garden could have been a creation of Currier and Ives. A small herd of Holsteins grazed the open fields not far from the deep, swift-flowing St. Croix. The Nelsons were atypical ruralites, educated, broad-minded, and against the war. Scott's older sister, Kristin, had scandalized the mostly Norwegian community by marrying a black man. His mother, Dorothy, whom everyone called "Di," wrote poetry. His father, George, a witty and soft-spoken former military man, restored antique furniture. Meals in the big country kitchen were lavish affairs with garden vegetables, homemade butter, and ice cream and animated conversation in which one was free to criticize the government.

Di was won over by Karl and welcomed what she thought was his "calming influence" on Scott, about whom she worried sometimes. It pleased her that the two were planning to room together at Phi Sigma Kappa in the fall. When the two boys got jobs at Northstar Steel in St. Paul, forty-five minutes away, she invited Karl to stay the summer. The only thing about him that concerned Di was whether he was getting enough protein from his strict vegetarian diet.

Karl proved an appreciative houseguest who insisted on doing the dishes every night, even after a hard day's work, and who, at the end of his stay, repaid Di by buying her an automatic dishwasher. Di was stunned when Karl unpacked the gleaming appliance in her kitchen. "I really can't accept it," she said. "Yes, you can, Di. You work hard enough as it is," Karl told her.

Northstar Steel was one of the first small specialty steel mills, turning out rebar for use in reinforced concrete. The plant was huge—a half-mile long—and so hot inside that Karl and Scott had to go out in the sun where it was "only 95 degrees" to cool off. They started out as burners, using acetylene torches to cut out chunks of hot steel caught in the fast-moving rollers. Occasionally a jam would shut down the lines, but nobody hurried to restart them. The workers belonged to a union, and it seemed to Scott and Karl that all they did was complain. On coffee breaks the griping was incessant. One day Karl asked a worker why he didn't just quit, if he hated it so much.

"Why don't you?" the man replied.

Karl and Scott looked at each other. "OK. Tell the foreman I quit," Karl said.

"I quit, too," Scott said.

And with that they walked out. The foreman ran after them trying to change their minds. "You can't quit, you're the only good workers I got," he yelled.

It was late July. The Apollo 11 crew was on its way back from the first human exploration of the moon, but somehow this triumph of ingenuity and organization made little impression on Karl and Scott, who were preoccupied with a more mundane concern: Where were they going to get the money for school? George Nelson had an idea. He had a birdbath mold and suggested that the boys cast some birdbaths and try selling them door to door. Agreeing to the suggestion, they began fabricating cement birdbaths in the Nelsons' barn, lining up the finished products behind the icehouse, three dozen basins resting on ornamental pedestals.

Scott knew the perfect place to sell them—a wealthy new golf-course community called North Oaks, outside Minneapolis. In mid-August they set out for North Oaks in George Nelson's pickup, its bed weighed down with birdbaths. The news on the radio was taken up with a bizarre murder case in Los Angeles. A pregnant actress named Sharon Tate had been stabbed to death, and fork wounds had been found in her belly. Apparently, Karl and Scott were so busy talking about it that they did not see the "Private Drive—No Soliciting" sign at the entrance to North Oaks.

At the first house a young woman answered the door. She asked them to wait outside while she made a phone call. Then she told them she wasn't interested. "I don't think she liked our looks," Karl said, as they drove to the next house. They were arrested moments later and escorted directly to court, where a magistrate fined them fifty dollars apiece for violating a Green River ordinance. Scott wanted just to pay the fine and get out, but Karl stood up and started shouting. The judge said he would hold Karl in contempt if he didn't quiet down.

Scott had never seen Karl so black with anger. Looking back on the incident a few months later, he would mark it as a turning point. George Nelson, too, would regret the incident. If only he hadn't suggested birdbaths, he thought afterward, maybe the bombings would not have happened.

11

The Nitty Gritty

Karl, when he is not thinking of politics, is a very light-hearted, easy-going, gentle person, fun to be with, fun to drink with, fun to mess around with. But he was dead serious about the war in Vietnam and about America's role in the world.

—GEORGE BOGDANICH,
student, for the defense

Karl never got closer than 10,000 miles to Vietnam.

—MICHAEL ZALESKI,
Wisconsin Assistant Attorney General, for the prosecution

The University of Wisconsin campus was a less free place that fall than it had ever been. Students and faculty were now required to carry photo ID cards, bullhorns could not be used without written permission, and expelled or suspended students could not return to campus. Seventeen more such measures remained under consideration at the other end of State Street. Similar legislation had been enacted in many states and by Congress. The Board of Regents had raised out-of-state tuition by 40 percent, to almost $2,000 a year ($7,000 in today's currency), achieving through finance what the legislature had so far failed to enact—a lowering of the percentage of students from outside Wisconsin. Enrollment for the fall semester, a record 35,000 students, was nonetheless well below earlier projections.

The sedition men had a new secret weapon in Mark Baganz, a minister's son from northern Wisconsin. Baganz had done some work for the Eau Claire police department while attending the state college there, and Detective George Croal had recruited him when he transferred to the University of Wisconsin law school. Tall, with huge hands; sallow, sunken cheeks; and dead eyes under a cowl of black, straggly hair, Baganz hovered at the edges of the movement like a large bat. Officially he worked for Herman Thomas, but it was Croal who ran him. The FBI paid him twenty-five dollars per report on meetings and demonstrations he attended, sometimes more if the information was especially helpful. Croal code-named him Duroc, after a breed of hog. The detective himself went by the name Chester White. If students were going to call him a pig, Croal figured, he might as well be one.

One of Duroc's first assignments was covering the visit to campus by former Secretary of State Dean Rusk in late August. A group of 150 demonstrators shouted and jeered while Rusk spoke to a group of bankers in the Union Theater and stoned his car as he left. Duroc's report of the incident sent a ripple of alarm through the law enforcement community. Such was the paranoia in the movement, Duroc said, that demonstrators had begun to organize themselves into "affinity groups" of five or six who would talk only among themselves and look out for one another during an action. At the street level, among the rank and file, Duroc found illusions of an imminent apocalypse. A high school student told him to expect "revolution" in Madison that fall; it would start on the university campus and "spread to West High," the boy explained. A young black, whom Duroc identified as a participant in the Rusk stoning, told him that "SDS was really planning something this fall and the town would be split wide open."

"One of our informants picked up word on the mall that there are two machine guns and seven grenades in the Mifflin Street area," a nervous Inspector Herman Thomas told local agency heads at a coordination meeting in the governor's mansion on September 9. Other lawmen reported armaments of various kinds being assembled on campuses in Beloit and Milwaukee. In a confidential sum-mary for President Harrington (who had put off his departure for India to late October), Vice President Robert Taylor said the consensus was "that there will be bloodshed, probably a killing in the Madison campus area this year," and that no one had any idea how to prevent it. In fact, Taylor added with a hint of disgust, most of the two-hour meeting had been consumed by arguments over who was going to pay for riot control.

Early in that month of September 1969 Karl Armstrong and Scott Nelson moved into Room 8 on the third floor of Phi Sigma Kappa. It was a corner room with a view of the lake and of the Wisconsin Alumni Center across the street. They put one of Scott's stereo speakers in the window, and whenever an alumnus arrived, they would blast the unsuspecting visitor with a lion's roar that they had on tape. Their only attempt at decorating was a Che Guevara poster on the wall. A day or two after their arrival, the elderly North Vietnamese leader Ho Chi Minh died. Karl and Scott put a sympathy card in the mail to Hanoi.

Karl's report card for the spring semester had showed remarkable improvement: a B in Spanish, an A in Social Disintegration, and an A in philosophy. For the latter course he had written a term paper on the question of whether ends justify the means, arguing that ends and means are inextricably linked. He had once again been admitted on strict probation and signed up for a full load of philosophy courses. However, he soon found himself distracted by the demands of the movement. At a recruitment meeting in the Union he enrolled in YSA, a potentially embarrassing fact that the Young Socialists would hastily expunge from their records a year later. But the infinitely patient and lawful "base building" of the Trotskyists did not appeal to Karl, and he did not go to another meeting. Instead he threw himself into the Ken Vogel sanctuary effort. Ken Vogel, a former University of Wisconsin student and draft resister, had taken refuge in the First Congregational Church on University Avenue at the beginning of the semester. A hundred students were waiting when the FBI came to apprehend him, all wearing "Hello, My Name Is Ken Vogel" name tags. Karl had gotten his meal job back at Phi Sigma Kappa and persuaded the cook, a mountainous black woman named Teresa, to let him raid the pantry; late one night he appeared at the chapel with several shopping bags full of peanut butter sandwiches for the hungry "Ken Vogels."

The sanctuary protest lasted a week. Toward the end Karl chanced into a Madison Tenant Union (MTU) meeting in one of the church's basement conference rooms. The MTU was beginning to organize students in off-campus housing, where the baby boomers were getting their first taste of a seller's market. One of the MTU's organizers was a stocky, tense, well-spoken activist named Phil Ball. Ball was a Wisconsin native, a former high school football star, and a navy veteran who had taken part in shelling Viet Cong positions from offshore. He now considered himself a war criminal. After getting out of the navy, he had worked in the McCarthy campaign in Wisconsin and California. In August 1968 he had been having a drink in the lobby of the Chicago Hilton, watching the live coverage of the demonstration outside, when the people on TV started falling through the plate-glass window next to his table.

Ball had taken note of the tall, balding, somewhat diffident young man who had walked in on his meeting and afterward approached him about working for the MTU. Karl said he was quite impressed: He liked the idea of working with a group that was solidly issue oriented. He thought the MTU should consider expanding its focus from landlord-tenant grievances to such matters as the war, imperialism, and capitalism. Ball put him to work researching the ownership of apartment buildings around the city in preparation for a rent strike.

Leo Burt had obtained a National Defense Loan to cover his expenses for the year and was rooming on upper Langdon Street again. He stopped by Phi Sigma Kappa occasionally to see Scott, and Karl began to get to know him. Dwight also showed up frequently to visit his friend Poli. Dwight had signed up for courses at the Wisconsin School of Electronics, but had dropped out the same day. He was living with a hippie girl named Cherri Lamkin who had a room with nothing on the floor but a mattress, and he was waiting tables at the Hoffman House, a plush lakeside restaurant. Leo had a modest reserve of marijuana, and the four—Scott, Dwight, Leo, and Karl—would smoke behind the closed door of Room 8. The engineering students, recognizing the smell in the hall, began referring to the four of them as the "Damn Hippies."

Leo was now a senior, and though he had been a journalism major his first three years, like Scott and Karl he had changed to philosophy. The latter two were impressed by his grasp of ideas: Leo could take a book like Sartre's *Being and Nothingness* and go on about it for hours. He was just shy of six feet, very muscular and vain about his physique, wearing tank tops to show off his well-developed pectorals. He had a drill-sergeant's face, long and square-jawed and pitted by old acne scars. He had recently traded in his horn-rim glasses for a pair of wire rims and gotten rid of the Brylcream in his bathroom cabinet. He still wore the heavy black hightops the Marines had issued him in his ROTC days and walked like Mr. Natural, the "keep-on-truckin'" hero of Zap Comix. He was usually quiet and reserved but loved to argue, the more esoteric the subject, the better. His speech came fast, with the big-city inflections of a Philadelphian. "Yowza!" he said when he agreed, and every other word was "like." Like Karl and Scott and Dwight, he was "into his changes."

Leo had quit the University of Wisconsin crew in May after being cut from the traveling team. He still popped protein pills and worked out at the Old Red Gym, but the psychic energy that he had formerly put into rowing now went into reporting. Things were going well for him at the *Cardinal*. He had started out on the sports page, but was beginning to get political assignments. He had covered the SDS convention that summer and had turned in such a precise account of the faction fights that he had been given the SDS beat for the fall.

On Friday nights, after putting the Saturday issues to bed, Leo Burt and his *Cardinal* friends George Bogdanich and Gary Dretzka would wander over to the Nitty Gritty, a snug little blues joint in the shadow of the Southeast Dorms, to unwind. Bogdanich, a steelworker's son from Gary, Indiana, and Dretzka, from Milwaukee, were almost as big as Leo, and together the three looked more like members of a defensive backfield than like student journalists.

Steve Reiner, the paper's editor-in-chief, often joined them. Reiner, distantly related to the well-known television actor Carl Reiner, was very good looking and enormously self-assured, drove an old but well-maintained Volvo, and had a long-legged vizsla named Jude that went everywhere with him, even to *Daily Cardinal* meetings.

Despite having been forced to remove the word "official" from its subtitle, the *Cardinal* was now selling more ads and printing more pages than it had at any time in its eighty-year existence. Madison's third largest daily newspaper, it assiduously covered local politics and regularly scooped its "rivals," the *Wisconsin State Journal* and the *Capital Times.* As much as the regents hated the paper, the fact was that it more than paid its way, while its fledgling conservative rival, the *Badger Herald,* was a money loser.

Leo's drinking group could usually be found at a long, cheese-cloth-covered picnic table in front of the plywood platform that served as the Nitty Gritty's stage, listening to the music and generally having a good time. The *Cardinal*'s incipient feminist faction found this behavior obnoxious and had immediately branded them the "Male Chauvinist Pig Caucus." Judy Sanstadt, a University of Wisconsin student and Nitty Gritty waitress, was fond of the group and especially of Leo. Leo had a hundred different stories and jokes and a low, infectious laugh that was full of mischief and delight. He would read to the others from Zap Comix in the voice of a father reading to his children. Despite the Nitty Gritty's no-tipping rule, he always left change on the table. "You don't have to do that," Sanstadt told him. "I'm paid extra, you know." (She was making $1.50 an hour.) "No, you're part of the working class," Leo insisted.

Karl and Scott had let their hair grow to the point where they could no longer get into The Pub, a State Street bar catering to Greek Row, so they switched to the Nitty Gritty. Leo's friends found Karl a bit "out there." He did not say much, but he had a way of looking at them with a certain merriment in his eyes that reminded George Bogdanich of Jack Nicholson, who had just had his breakout role in *Easy Rider.* "At first it was just ordinary, friendly conversation in a tavern, and Karl seemed like a very easy-going fellow," Bogdanich would later testify. "But on the subject of politics he would be more intense, much more intense." One thing they all agreed about was that Defense Secretary Melvin Laird's "Vietnamization" plan was a ploy and that President Nixon's troop reductions (25,000 so far that year) were mere tokenism. Nixon was stepping up the air war; "Vietnamizing" was just a different way of killing.

The first SDS "monster meeting" of the fall season took place on September 18 in the Memorial Student Union's Great Hall, a third-floor ballroom fitted out in the style of the Doges Palace. Leo Burt, covering the meeting for the *Daily Cardinal,* estimated the crowd at 1,200. (Duroc, covering for the MPD and FBI, guessed 800.) Reporter's notebook in hand, Burt sat in the front row of folding chairs with the SDS heavies, including Jim Rowen and his wife Susan and David Fine, a diminutive freshman on the *Cardinal* staff who was one of the rising stars of the Madison Left. Various groups were scheduled to present their causes for the year, but the meeting's real purpose had been determined in advance by an SDS clique that called itself the Woody Guthrie Collective. This purpose was to ratify three demands as the primary objectives of the local antiwar movement: the removal from campus of the Army Mathematics Research Center, all ROTC facilities, and the Land Tenure Center, the U.S.-funded agrarian reform project in Central America that Karl Armstrong's friend Hugo Vega had worked for.

As the meeting got under way the Great Hall was abuzz with rumors that Weatherman was in town. Sure enough, after several announcements there was a tumult at the side of the hall. A dozen young men and women dressed in combat fatigues charged up waving NLF flags and threw the moderator off the stage. A bare-chested boy with long, Icelandic blond hair grabbed the microphone and pranced Mick Jagger-style at the edge of the stage while his cohorts struck fierce karate poses, daring the audience to interfere. "It's Jeff Jones! It's Weatherman!" someone cried. Shouts of "Get off the stage!" bounced off the gilded ceiling.

Jones, a member of Weatherman's Chicago collective, spoke in an unconvincing ghetto accent. "Look around this stage, what do you see up here? You don't see no motherfucking students at no motherfucking university. Everybody up here on this stage is a stone communist revolutionary!"

In response, the members of the audience simultaneously turned their chairs around and faced the other way, and Jeff Jones found himself talking to the backs of their heads. "Follow us, we're going to trash the Army Mathematics Research Center!" he announced. Chanting "Ho-Ho-Ho Chi Minh, the NLF is going to win," the Chicago contingent marched out. No one followed.

Madison SDS continued with its own agenda, ratifying what were to become known as the "Three Demands." Leo Burt's write-up was on the front page of the *Cardinal* in the morning: "Madison SDS rejects Weatherman." A new saying began to circulate on campus: "You don't need a rectal thermometer to know who the assholes are." Duroc explained the reason for the rejection in his undercover report. "He [SDS leader Alan Hunter] said that UW SDS does not want to be violent and did not want to follow policies of Chicago office." Despite a few lapses over the previous five years, the student movement in Madison remained officially committed to nonviolence.

But this admirable resolve was almost immediately challenged. In the last week of September a short, feisty Catholic priest named James Groppi marched on Madison at the head of a ragtag army of the Milwaukee poor and occupied the state assembly chamber to protest recent welfare cuts. University of Wisconsin students joined the protest, refusing to leave even when Chancellor Young came down and begged them in person. Governor Knowles finally called in the National Guard to remove them, and the city remained garrisoned for eighteen days. Meanwhile, on September 26, someone bombed the National Guard Armory at Truax Field. The method, dynamite and a timer, was suspiciously similar to that used in terrorist acts in Milwaukee, Chicago, and New York during the same period. On orders from Washington, the Stassi Shoe Store put a twenty-four-hour watch on an East Side political house occupied by the twin sisters of Howard "Howie" Machtinger, a New York Weatherman.

In the second week of October Madison SDS sent a delegation to Chicago for the Weatherman-sponsored Days of Rage gathering. Madison abstained from the notorious trashing of the city's affluent Gold Coast area by the Red People's Army, instead participating in a counterdemonstration sponsored by a new faction called Revolutionary Youth Movement II. Leo Burt, covering the event for the *Cardinal,* contrasted RYM II's "relatively peaceful action" with Weatherman's "rampage," which did thousands of dollars in damage and injured scores of policemen. "Because of the non-adventuristic, 'serving-the-people' tone of the RYM II action, the full support of the Black Panther Party was obtained," he wrote approvingly. "In addition, Fred Hampton, chairman of the Illinois Black Panthers, denounced Weatherman as 'anti-people.'"

Nevertheless, the Weatherman example was beginning to take hold. Back in Madison on October 14, a dozen SDSers, chanting "Ho, Ho, Ho Chi Minh," turned off lights and threw bags of red paint on mathematicians attending a symposium sponsored by the

Army Mathematics Research Center. University of Wisconsin students Margo Levine and Linda Stern, both of New York City, were arrested. That evening, at a party in Miffland, Duroc engaged a member of the SDS steering committee in a conversation about dynamite.

> I told him that I had had some experience with dynamite during this last summer. He asked me if I was able to obtain dynamite; what kinds; amounts; how soon, etc. He told me that he had a rather good idea of who dynamited the armory here in Madison. He mentioned no names. He continued by saying that he could see tossing a satchel of dynamite into a power plant and blacking out all of Madison. He said some things could be done only if there was tight discipline in SDS. He said this discipline might take two months to achieve.

The militants were in a volatile mood. All that was holding them back was the fact that two national antiwar protests, the National Moratorium Day and the March on Washington, lay just ahead. Madison SDS endorsed the moratorium "with reservations." On October 15, along with clergymen, mainstream politicians, Vietnam veterans, and Mothers for Peace, *Cardinal* writer Jim Rowen spoke to 15,000 at the Fieldhouse, denouncing the AMRC and calling on the community to "militantly confront the warmakers and their cohorts on this campus." Similar events, involving hundreds of thousands of Americans, took place on campuses all across the country that day.

As the doubters had predicted, the moratorium produced no results. Leo Burt caught the corrosive climate of opinion in a Staff Soapbox piece a week later. "'Cooptation,' say many radicals and cynics, is what the moratorium amounts to, nothing but a lot of 'liberal jive' and 'bourgeois reformism.'" Leo disagreed, and wrote that the radical Left should be "severely chastised" for its lackluster support of the moratorium. "It's time now that the Left get together and really work. This is a call to have 10,000 Madisonians marching on Washington on November 15."

In mid-November thirteen chartered buses left Madison for Washington, where 1 million people, the largest political assembly in U.S. history, gathered on the Capitol Mall. Karl Armstrong signed up for a seat on a bus but ended up hitchhiking. David Fine and Leo Burt also attended. President Nixon ordered 28,000 troops into the city to greet the petitioners and refused to show himself while they were in the capital.

In his "Silent Majority" speech of November 3 Nixon had tried to discourage people from coming to the demonstration, saying that he would not be influenced by clamorings in the street and that he listened only to the "silent majority." Many years later historians would discover that the march had influenced the president a great deal. It had decided him against issuing an ultimatum to Hanoi, urged on him by Henry Kissinger, to withdraw its forces from South Vietnam or face nuclear annihilation. But that was not known at the time. To Karl, David, Leo, and thousands of other participants, it looked as though the march had been a complete failure. As one defense witness would put it at Karl's sentencing, "It seemed as though people in power didn't give a damn how many people were opposed to the war and what they did about it, because the war kept going on."

12

T-16

If Karl's acts were the inevitable result of the course of history, then the question arises: Why didn't millions of others who were part of that movement take part in the same kind of acts of violence that Karl did?

—Douglas Haag,
Wisconsin Assistant Attorney General, for the prosecution

And they began to function with firebombs, and they began to function with plastic bombs, and they began to function with dynamite in lots and lots of places.

—Harvey Goldberg,
historian, for the defense

Wisconsin Dells is a resort town on the Wisconsin River about an hour north of Madison, four hours north of Chicago. Its main attraction is a winding, narrow gorge that the river has carved through the local sandstone, along the vertical banks of which enterprising locals have added a garish assortment of money-making diversions. From Memorial Day through Labor Day weekend, the Dells is a money pit for vacationing Midwesterners; the rest of the year it is a quiet little hicksville living on its summer spoils.

On the day before Thanksgiving Karl Armstrong traveled to Wisconsin Dells with Scott and several other Phi Sigs for the wedding of brother Barry Friedman. Friedman was a tall, thin chemistry student from Philadelphia who considered himself politically conscious and felt compromised by the fact that his father was a federal judge. He had bought a used Corvair convertible for his honeymoon and worried that this would make him *embourgeoisé*. He was marrying a Wisconsin Dells girl named Cathy Baker, whom he had met at the university. The ceremony was held at United Presbyterian Church, where the bride was attended by her lifelong friends Lynn Schultz and Susan Baldie. Mark Dobberfuhl served as best man.

Karl, who had just returned from the March on Washington, made a hit with Cathy's mother at the reception, serving coffee and drinks to her and all her lady friends. The bride, too, was impressed by his helpfulness. During the party Karl told Barbara Ford, the girlfriend of a Phi Sig, that he had stayed away from the violent, SDS-led confrontation at the Pentagon because he didn't want to be arrested, which struck Ford as sensible.

The bridesmaids, Lynn and Susan, were an example of the powerful bond that sometimes develops between girls who are flashy and those who are plain. Lynn was a short, bosomy Rubens type with blue eyes accented by California makeup and peroxide blonde hair that fell straight below her shoulders. She was full of fun and boy crazy, and stayed at the center of the dance floor. Susan was quiet, with a cynical sense of humor. Tall and flat chested, she had mouse-brown hair and wore glasses to correct inward-deviating eyes. She had been heavy, and though she had slimmed down, she was still unsure of herself. She sat anxiously in her folding chair, nursing a drink, desperately wishing to be like Lynn. They had gone through high school together in Wisconsin Dells, taken courses together at Madison Area Technical College, and now lived together in an apartment on Lake Monona and worked at the same company, Ray-O-Vac, as office assistants. Of the pair, Lynn had always been the lucky one, as Susan saw it. Lynn's parents, who had adopted her and raised her as their only child, doted on her and gave her everything she wanted. In high school, she had even had her own car. She was artistic and played the saxophone and never lacked for company. Lynn would never know what it was like to sit home alone on weekends.

Scott was the first one to catch Lynn's eye at the reception. Of the Phi Sigma Kappa contingent, he was the best looking and the most flamboyant. But when he showed little interest, Lynn fell in with Karl, who was bashful at first because of his receding hairline. "Premature baldness is a sign of virility," he joked. Dobberfuhl, meanwhile, took a liking to Susan. When the reception was over, the foursome returned to Madison together and went to the Nitty Gritty to get better acquainted. A few days later, they met at Lynn and Susan's apartment for a "naked dinner." Susan was consciously trying to break loose and wanted to drink and get wild like Lynn; but she felt ashamed sitting at the dinner table with no clothes on. Dobber was also uncomfortable, and the evening was not a success for either of them.

Karl and Lynn, however, enjoyed the occasion. Lynn's torso was covered by a fine tracery of coral scars from a waterskiing accident in the Gulf of Mexico, but this physical imperfection somehow added to her allure. She was a working girl and a free spirit, and she also had a car, a tan-and-white 1965 Chevrolet Impala. Karl had never met a woman who excited him as Lynn did. When he was with her, he really did feel more virile.

Susan could not understand what Lynn saw in Karl. He didn't have the beach boy look that she usually went for. He wore pants, she thought cynically; with Lynn that was sometimes enough. But Lynn found much to like about Karl. When they went out together, people said hello to him. He was gentle and funny and, despite his hair loss, rather good-looking. And from Lynn's perspective, he was also quite a big man on campus.

By the time the Groppi affair had ended and the National Guard had gone home, a phenomenon known as the Crazies had appeared in Madison. The Crazies were militants who had ceased to care about the consequences of their actions and were flirting with violence. In early November, an SDS member named Eddie Handel and several companions had charged into several university offices wearing army fatigues and carrying realistic-looking toy machine guns, scaring the secretaries. Two weeks later SDS led 300 students on a mock-Weatherman tear around campus, war-whooping and waving North Vietnamese flags but doing little damage. Duroc reported that because many students had lost interest in politics, a national phenomenon widely commented on in the media, local SDS leaders had decided on a strategy of "increasing tensions." A new SDS "Security Guard" was "training for physical confrontations," he said. The Crazies were on the rise.

Scott Nelson had not gone to a single class all semester and finally dropped out after a dream in which he showed up for a final exam and had no idea what the questions were about. "So quick it was unreal," he received a letter from his draft board ordering him to Milwaukee for his physical. Seeing that all the homosexuals were in Section B, just as in the Arlo Guthrie song, he briefly considered a false statement of sexual orientation as a way of disqualifying himself, but instead took his father's advice and enlisted in the air force.

Karl Armstrong dropped out on December 2 after a conference with his adviser in which he announced that he wanted to "broaden his understanding of societies by travel" and to work for certain "fundamental changes" in the university. At about the same time he hired on as a delivery boy and kitchen cleanup man at Gino's Restaurant and Pizzeria on State Street.

Gino Gargano was a short, hot-tempered Sicilian with a harelip and a speech impediment. He ran his restaurant like a slave galley, paying the minimum wage and cussing in the mother tongue when things went wrong. And yet his employees loved him, and no rock had ever been aimed in anger at the two fine plate-glass windows that fronted his establishment on State Street. The reason was that Gargano, in contrast to many Madison businessmen, hired long-hairs. His kitchen crew looked like the members of a commune. Karl Armstrong, who had grown a full beard that fall that made him look like Fidel Castro, fit right in.

Gargano handed Karl the keys to a four-wheel-drive Scout. There was a gas mask behind the seat in case of a riot. "The police will let you through," Gino said. "They have respect for commerce."

Meanwhile, at the Male Chauvinist Pigs table at the Nitty Gritty, the failure of the Three Demands to have an impact was much discussed. Throughout the fall the *Cardinal* had continued to publish stories about the AMRC's involvement in secret military research, alleging violations of the university's charter. Stanford and the University of Pennsylvania had chosen to dissociate from defense think tanks; why not Wisconsin? To investigate the charges against the AMRC, Chancellor Young had appointed a committee headed by Dr. Stephen Kleene, a mathematician and former acting director of the center. To no one's surprise, the committee completely exonerated the AMRC. David Siff, an English instructor who embarrassed Director J. Barkley Rosser by reading from an AMRC annual report at a faculty meeting, was promptly dismissed. Administrators of the AMRC, ROTC, and Land Tenure Center all boycotted or made only token appearances at the Wisconsin Student Association's (WSA's) hearings on the issue. Chancellor Young told SDS leader Billy Kaplan that he did not have the power to remove those institutions from the university. "Who does?" Kaplan asked. The Board of Regents, Young replied. "May we speak to them?" Kaplan asked. Young said no. "The university's refusal to even discuss these issues is another indication that proceeding through the proper channels is the surest way to receive a 'no' from established powers," the *Cardinal* commented. Karl Armstrong reached similar conclusions. *And I felt that people had to be aware that these processes are used primarily as a way to exhaust people's energies. That it's a kind of game the ruling class plays with people. That, you see, people can use the democratic processes in this country. They can petition, demonstrate, but the people that govern, the people who are in power, can ignore it.*

On Friday, December 5, Karl and Scott both wore black armbands, as did hundreds of other Madison militants. The *Cardinal*'s lead story, by Jim Rowen, explained why: Fred Hampton was dead, killed along with another Black Panther by Chicago police in a dawn raid on Hampton's apartment. Although the police insisted that they were fired upon, there were few young people in Madison who did not strongly suspect that the black revolutionary had been murdered. In its editorial on the subject the *Cardinal* recalled Hampton's words to an appreciative audience in Madison the previous May: "You can kill, jail or exile a revolutionary, but you can't kill, jail or exile the revolution." "We must mourn Fred Hampton with action," the *Cardinal* concluded. "We must eulogize him by building the vanguard of our movement into a massive unstoppable revolution."

The slaying of Fred Hampton, the jailing of Black Panthers Huey Newton and Bobby Seale, and the trial of the "Chicago Eight" on conspiracy charges stemming from the Democratic National Convention all seemed part of a pattern. "WE MUST FIGHT THIS REPRESSION. WE MUST MEET IT HEAD ON!" announced an SDS flyer.

There was going to be trouble. Duroc confirmed it in his report of a December 8 SDS meeting at which tactics for the upcoming week of demonstrations were discussed, beginning with disruptions on the second day. UP & S Chief Ralph Hanson promptly obtained a restraining order against SDS and ten of its members, and for the first three days, the campus police were able to keep a tenuous rein on the situation. The main event was to take place on Friday, December 12. "The Friday action is to be against one of the Three Demands buildings," Duroc had written. "It is to be the biggest of the week, the climax. No details have been given out."

As it happened, Duroc was unable to obtain any more details. At an SDS meeting Thursday night he was accused of spying and voted out of the organization. Plainclothesmen from Army Intelligence and the Dane County Sheriff's Office were also expelled. With their departure the authorities no longer had access to information on what was to happen next. All they had to go on was a freshly mimeographed flyer. At the top was a headline typed in capital letters. It said: THE WAR IS COMING HOME.

Friday there was a foot of new snow on the ground, the first big storm of the season. It was noon when Karl awoke, but so overcast it was still dark. Karl put on his new army surplus fatigue jacket and hurried to Bascom Hill, where a rally was in progress. The same people he had seen the night before were exhorting a crowd of 250. Karl recognized Leo Burt, in a navy blue flight jacket with an imitation fur collar, taking notes.

Chief Hanson stood by with a dozen men. They were not in riot gear, but some of them—the young ex-marine Jack Schwichtenberg, for example—carried saps, compact but effective weapons, in their pockets. Hanson was not expecting anything worse than what they had already experienced that week, affinity groups racing about trying to enter classrooms, a little window breaking if the kids could get away with it.

The group marched over Bascom Hill to the AMRC, but finding it well guarded moved on to T-16, the quonset hut used by the air force for ROTC instruction. Hanson's men raced them down Linden Drive and blocked the entrance. A tall blonde girl with a padlock on a chain took out all the windows on one side of the hut. Two other girls snuck behind the building and tried to light a Molotov cocktail, but Hanson chased them off. Karl was standing near the front entrance. Here was his old classroom, where he had tried to live out his father's fantasy of what he ought to be. Through the front windows he could see his desk. If they could get inside, they could take the legs off and use them to knock the place down. "Let's take the building!" he shouted, but nobody moved. The people behind him started throwing snowballs at the cops.

The outnumbered defenders pulled their saps and squared off with the demonstrators, daring them to fight. Schwichtenberg, who had spent three years fighting in the DMZ, balled up his sap in his fist and hit the demonstrator in front of Karl in the head. The boy went down, and Karl hastily backed away. "We'll be back!" he shouted, running after the crowd. Schwichtenberg was taken to University Hospital with a broken hand.

Karl followed the retreating SDS leaders to the corner of University and Park where several of the women split off and entered the Peterson Administration building. The larger group waited for them in front of the First Wisconsin Bank. "Hey, let's trash the bank!" Karl suggested.

A swarthy, curly-haired woman with a cigarette in her mouth regarded him with suspicion. "Who is this guy?" she asked irritably.

Someone who had noticed him at T-16 whispered, "He's a cop!" They were all staring at him.

What's wrong? Karl wondered, embarrassed. *Why don't they want to trash the bank? It's a pig institution like the others.*

At that point the party that had entered the Peterson Building came running back with armloads of documents. A dark-haired little boy with a heart-shaped face turned to Karl. "Hey, be cool, it's over," he said in a friendly, almost confidential manner. "We've got the photo IDs; we've done enough for one day."

The *Cardinal* condemned the "needless actions" of Friday as both "divided and divisive," but also criticized students for not turning out to support the protest's "clear and justifiable objectives." George Bogdanich was particularly upset. His father and his uncles all worked for U.S. Steel, and he worked in the mills himself when he was home in Gary. In a Staff Forum piece published two days before the riot, he had argued that violent and disruptive tactics played straight into the hands of Vice President Spiro Agnew. "Spiro is reaching the worker and we are not."

Bogdanich had noticed a change in the tenor of the bar talk in Madison. People who were not leaders of radical groups or long-time activists were beginning to talk about the feasibility of destroying military equipment. He had also observed a change in Karl. One night at the Nitty Gritty the Male Chauvinist Pigs were talking about Communist China and the merits of the Cultural Revolution. The conversation went on and on, and afterward Karl seemed tired of the whole discussion. There was too much talk going on and not enough being done that was effective, he said.

Karl started reading up on explosives at Memorial Library. He had always had trouble with chemistry, though, and he found the books hard to understand. One day Barry Friedman, back from his honeymoon, dropped by. His Corvair had broken down on the Interstate east of Chicago on his wedding night, and he obviously felt better about owning it. Karl had a question for him on the subject of organic chemistry. "What do you know about picric acid?" he asked.

Friedman replied that picric acid is a highly explosive chemical and asked why Karl wanted to know. "I'm the Mad Bomber," Karl said with a laugh.

A few days later Karl bantered with another brother, a chemistry major named Mark Johnson, about setting off a picric-acid bomb in Lake Mendota. Then the Phi Sigma Kappa chapter president John Norwell, aka "Biffer," saw him on the house telephone calling chemical-supply houses. Karl had a big book on explosives with him, and Biffer asked what he was up to. "I'm going to blow up the university," Karl said. Biffer laughed. Unaware that Karl had dropped out, he assumed he was working on a term paper.

Christmas came, and the campus emptied out. Scott Nelson drove home to River Falls, Lynn Schultz to the Dells. The Phi Sig cook, Teresa, took a vacation. Out-of-staters boarded the O'Hare charters in front of the Union, Leo Burt bound for Havertown, David Fine for Wilmington. The Lake Street frat house was deserted, the dorms were dark and locked, bars were empty, the campus as quiet as a winter graveyard. The sedition men, the campus administrators, and all the guardians of order breathed easier and went about their holiday shopping.

In the evenings Karl Armstrong had his job at Gino's, but otherwise his time was his own. Almost five years had passed since his one-man fast for peace in Indiana. Since then the war had consumed the lives of 40,000 Americans and of hundreds of thousands of Vietnamese. More explosives had been dropped on Vietnam than by all the powers in all theaters of World War II. *And I had a feeling that the war was going to go on forever, and that the only way that the war would stop is if people took violent means to end it.* No single incident can be said to have incited him. No defense counsel, prosecutor, or psychiatrist would ever explore with him this moment of personal crisis. In the solitude of Room 8, the arctic wind rattling his window, he worked patiently on a headband with the word REVOLUTION spelled out in colored Indian beads. *And I remember the nights before my first act of resistance, my despair over the war. I had even considered suicide. Because I didn't really want to use violence. But if I couldn't live any longer with this war, if I was going to die, I thought the best way I could die was by resisting it.*

Part III

THE WINTER

OFFENSIVE

13

Badger Ordnance Works

*Each moment that went by that some act wasn't taken to stop
the genocidal war in Southeast Asia was a wasted moment.
Patience was gone. It was a time when the hardest decisions
of our lives had to be taken.*

—MAX ELBAUM,
student, for the defense

*It is obvious Karl can't express himself without a bomb in his
hand.*

—MICHAEL ZALESKI,
Wisconsin Assistant Attorney General, for the prosecution

The twenty-seventh of December fell on a Saturday. Karl got up
late, walked to the service station on the corner of University
and Lake, filled two gallon jugs with gasoline, and hid them on the
fraternity's front porch. Then he walked up State Street to Gino's
and went to work. It was 2:30 A.M. when he returned to the fraternity. He put on extra clothes and his new beaded "Revolution"
headband. Placing the two jars of gasoline in a large grocery bag, he
set off across campus, keeping an eye out for patrols. He had recon-
noitered the target in Gino's Scout and had briefly considered carrying out the action while on a delivery, using the four-by-four to

get away. It would have given him a perfect alibi—who would suspect a pizza delivery boy? But he had decided against it, for the
Gino's logo made the truck too easy to identify.

It was a little after four in the morning when he reached the corner of Linden and Babcock. A fine, dry snow was falling, drifting
across the sidewalk in powdery rivulets, squeaking under the tread
of his lug-soled boots. Temporary Building 16 was dark and
unguarded. A narrow walk led from Babcock to the back side of
the hut, opposite the Bacteriology Building. He followed it, taking
a hammer from his belt. *I am a very non-violent person, basically.
And all the time I was wishing that there was some other way to stop
the war.* He smashed one of the rear windows, tossed the jars in, and
lit a match. The flames leaped up just as he had envisioned.

He had planned to walk calmly away, but as he reached the sidewalk of Babcock Drive, the adrenaline took hold and he accelerated toward the Lakeshore Dorms, flying past Tripp Hall, ripping
through Muir Woods, and skidding out across the frozen surface of
Lake Mendota, where he finally slowed down. Walking east along
the dark shoreline, he nearly collided with a couple coming from
the opposite direction. In the distance sirens began to wail. "I wonder what those sirens are for," he said in passing.

A few minutes past four an agriculture student named Bryce Larson was hurrying along Linden Drive on foot, worried about being
late to work at the milking parlor, when he heard glass breaking up
ahead. A moment later he saw a flickering light reflected off the
windows of Bacteriology. Larson was aware of the recent protests
against T-16 and reacted alertly, waiting at the corner of Linden and
Babcock to see whether anyone would emerge from behind the
building. Observing no one, he cautiously made his way to the rear
of T-16 and, peering in the windows, saw several small fires burning
in one of the classrooms. He took off at a run for the milking parlor,
where he called UP & S.

By the time the firemen arrived the fire had practically burned
out. A few desks had been scorched and the damage would later be
estimated at about $900. The blackened concrete floor was littered
with fragments of the two petrol bombs, which a Fire Department
investigator took as evidence. Campus cops found the set of foot-
prints that Bryce Larson had mentioned, and a big skid mark on the
sidewalk where the suspect had turned north on Babcock Drive.

Whoever it was had been moving fast, taking six-foot strides. They followed the track across Observatory Drive to Tripp Circle, losing the trail at the gatehouse entrance, where the suspect seemed to have vanished.

A little after one-thirty that Sunday afternoon, the Stassi Shoe Store put an update on the wire to Washington.

UNSUB: FIREBOMBING, ARMY ROTC BLDG., UW

There are no suspects or injuries and no indication incident inspired by New Left radical campus organizations. ROTC officials have indicated building owned by UW, however classroom tables and chairs possibly federal property.

For the moment the investigation remained in the hands of UP & S and the state fire marshal. Chief Ralph Hanson sent his best detective, Paul Radloff, to interview the students who were spending the holiday at Tripp Hall. They turned out to be mostly Hong Kong kids who were baffled by the whole thing. However, the telltale odor of marijuana smoke led Radloff to Room 304, which was occupied by a nineteen-year-old American boy named Weinberg. The student found his reveries interrupted by a policeman who was intensely interested in his whereabouts during the night.

When he got back to the fraternity house, Karl went straight to the pay phone and began calling newspapers. His first call was to someone named Dave Wagner, whom he believed to be editor of the new underground newspaper, the *Madison Kaleidoscope*. "We just hit T-16," he blurted, and hung up. Wagner had in fact recently quit the *Kaleidoscope* and taken a reporting job at the *Capital Times*, but in any case the message didn't register, and he went back to sleep.

Later in the day the new *Kaleidoscope* editor Mark Knops got a call from someone identifying himself as the "Vanguards of the Revolution." Knops had done a master's thesis on Lenin at Johns Hopkins University and recognized at once that the caller was not very sophisticated. "I think you'd better clarify the politics of the bombing," he said.

Karl went back to delivering pizzas. The year-end editions of the *Capital Times* were full of war statistics and wrap-ups on the "turbulent '60s" even though, strictly speaking, the decade would not be over for another year. Both the *Cap Times* and the *State Journal* ran the T-16 arson story on an inside page, and Karl began to consider other possible targets. One was the deep tunnels in the Baraboo Hills where Badger Ordnance Works tested its powders and propellants. He had explored them on a recent Sunday drive with Lynn Schultz, imagining himself holed up in such a spot, launching rockets at the plant. He could make the rockets himself out of aluminum tubing; all the information he needed was available in the library. But that might take a while. He reconsidered picric acid, but that, too, was complicated. He considered Army Math. *And I felt that the existence of AMRC on campus was unendurable, that the students had voted AMRC off campus. I myself had circulated the leaflets and took part in all of the demonstrations against the AMRC during the fall of '69. And we were met with almost total indifference by the university administration.* However, the center offices were three stories up and sandwiched between physics and astronomy. He did not see a way to get at it.

On the last day of 1969 another idea came to him that seemed feasible. To really work, it had to be accomplished by midnight of that same day. It had to be done on New Year's Eve.

As she had at Lakeview Lutheran, Mira had become a pillar of the Assembly of God. She had been "born again in the spirit," and with her increased self-confidence she had succeeded in giving up alcohol. But what she called The Gift eluded her. Every Sunday she answered the "altar calls," at which other members of the congregation demonstrated their virtuosity in the holy language. Mira prayed that someday she, too, would be able to speak in tongues.

Mira had made a convert of Dwight's Filipino friend Policronio De Venecia and had entered into a pact with Poli to make a Christian out of Dwight. At their insistence, in mid-December Dwight had met with Rev. Thomas Smarthout, a young minister at the Assembly of God. Mira did not find out what had happened until after Christmas, when she pressed Dwight about why he wouldn't attend the midnight service with her. Dwight said that he had taken a copy of his favorite book, a compendium of U.S.-sponsored coups in the postwar world, to the meeting. "This is *my* bible!" he had said. After reading a few pages of the fat blue paperback, Smarthout had advised Dwight that he would have to reconsider his

"Communist ideas" before Jesus could enter his heart. It had shocked Mira that a preacher would reject someone for political reasons. "Just because that man is a minister doesn't mean he's a Christian," she told Dwight.

On the afternoon of December 31, Dwight was at Mira's house watching TV. Mira was expecting him to baby-sit that evening, but around 4 P.M. Karl showed up and said he had something important to talk to him about. They walked over to Warner Park on the shore of Lake Mendota. The picnic tables and playground equipment were buried in snow. In the distance, across miles of mottled ice, the bright, white dome of the Capitol stood out against the dull gray winter sky. "You heard about the T-16 fire the other night?" Karl said. "Well, that was me."

"You're kidding!" Dwight said.

"Tonight I'm going to take out Badger Ordnance, going to hit it at midnight from the air. I need your help to get a plane."

Dwight stared at him. "No way! And besides, you don't know how to fly."

"I thought *you* might like to pilot the plane," Karl said.

"I've never flown at night," Dwight objected.

"That doesn't matter," Karl said. "If you can fly during the day, you can fly at night."

Dwight scanned the lowering sky. He could already smell the snow.

"Just get me the airplane," Karl said. "If you're not going to help, I'll do it myself."

"You'll never get the plane off the ground."

Karl remembered something Dwight had told him when he was taking lessons at Morey Airport. "You said it yourself: It's just like driving a car."

The basement floor of Phi Sigma Kappa was littered with parking meters, left there by a 250-pound varsity lineman named Saxum, who would pull them out of the sidewalk, carry them back to the house, and break them open whenever he needed change. Karl picked his way carefully through the mess, carrying the bomb components he had picked up on his way back into town. He had bought fifty pounds of ammonium nitrate from an East Side farm co-op and kerosene from a Shell Station on Troy Drive and had taken a few commercial-size Hellman's Mayonnaise jars from Gino's. He laid everything out on the long, narrow lunch counter in the basement kitchen.

The utility of ANFO—ammonium nitrate and fuel oil—as an explosive had first come to his attention the previous summer, when he and Scott Nelson had visited an uncle of Scott's in northern Minnesota. The man was a farmer and had used ANFO to open up trout and duck ponds on his land. ANFO was easy to assemble, and the price was right: Fifty pounds had come to a couple of dollars. Karl filled the mayo jars with the pearly white granules of aluminum nitrate, leaving a little room for the kerosene. The glass containers held about ten pounds each. He found a freestanding cylindrical ashtray in the TV room and filled it with the remainder. As he was finishing up, Dwight called.

"Are you still serious?" Dwight asked.

"Yeah," Karl said. He chuckled. "I've actually got my shit together."

Karl would not do anything flaky, Dwight reasoned. "All right, man," he said, "we'll try this."

Lynn Schultz and Susan Baldie arrived at the Nitty Gritty alone that evening, found a table in the middle of the room, and ordered a pitcher of beer. They sat there sizing up the young men present, looking for someone for Susan, who as usual did not have a date. Karl was supposed to have picked them up early, and Lynn was mad at him for "standing her up." Lynn was wearing a tight leather miniskirt, a dark brown suede jacket, high boots, white lipstick, and heavy mascara. She began to get looks right away.

Lynn's ability to attract men amazed Susan. Lynn kept track of her conquests, rating her dates on how good they were in bed. Her girlfriends kidded her about the number of guys she went out with: "How many are you up to now?" they would ask. "Met any five-stars lately?" One night in the Nitty Gritty they had seen a big, ponytailed hippie in chaps come in. "It can't be real," Susan whispered, with reference to his apparent endowment. "Don't you think so?" Lynn said, arching an eyebrow. She grabbed the suspect bulge as the man walked by, checking it out like an ichthyologist inspecting an unusual specimen of fish. Susan's eyes did a jitterbug behind her corrective lenses, so embarrassed she felt like crawling under the table.

Sometime between seven and eight, Karl arrived with Dwight

and introduced his brother to the two women. He took Lynn aside and asked if she would do him a favor. "Like what?" Lynn said coolly. "Give me a ride someplace," Karl said.

A moment later they returned to the table, and Lynn put her coat on. "Karl's got something going on at Badger tonight," she explained to Susan. "I have to give him a ride."

Susan's face fell as the three walked out together. A band was setting up, and she looked around helplessly at the couples nestling in for the night's entertainment. *Damn it all,* she thought, *alone again on New Year's Eve.*

Karl directed Lynn out University Avenue toward Middleton, telling her about his T-16 exploit. She could tell that he was especially proud because the ROTC headquarters was a long distance from where he lived, and he had walked out to it and back. But when he told her he wanted to bomb Badger Ordnance Works that night, Lynn was upset. It was New Year's Eve, she had a table at the Nitty Gritty, Susan was waiting there, and the Friedmans were coming around nine.

"All you have to do is drive the car," Karl said. "You don't have to go up in the plane."

Nine months later Lynn would breathlessly recount the episode for the benefit of the prosecutors. *And he told me that I was to be part of the plan and he set down exactly what I was supposed to do and that being first to take him and Dwight to Morey's Airfield in Middleton, drop them off there where they were going to steal an airplane and I was to go to Sauk City and from there I was supposed to make a telephone call to Badger Ordnance and warn the people that a bomb was going to explode in the plant in five minutes and that everyone was to evacuate so none of them would be hurt and I was then to drive to the Sauk Prairie Airport and go to the end of the airfield and place two flares, one on each side of the airfield. And then to go to a place where he designated and I was supposed to wait there for him and Dwight.* That was the plan, as Lynn would later describe it to the prosecutors.

Lynn did have a wild streak. After some consideration, she agreed to Karl's proposal.

Back in Madison the brothers dropped Lynn off at the Nitty Gritty while they went to the frat to finish making the bombs. It was 9:30 P.M. A young woman greeted them as they entered the foyer. "Hi, Crazy Man!" It was Barbara Ford, the girl Karl had spoken to about the March on Washington at Cathy Friedman's wedding. She was seated on the ratty pink sectional in the TV room watching a movie on the old black-and-white console with her boyfriend, Steve Rabideau. Rabideau, a freshman who had been a year ahead of Dwight at East, had pledged Phi Sigma Kappa that fall. A plump girl who introduced herself as Ann Mikola sat next to them.

"Hi, Crazy Girl," Karl replied. They had started addressing each other that way during the fall, when they found themselves together frequently in the TV room. Karl seemed so mellow to Ford that she had accused him of being on drugs, but he denied it. "I'm naturally high," he told her.

"What are you doing here on New Year's Eve?" Rabideau asked. He was surprised to see Dwight, who was persona non grata at the house. After a moment, Rabideau excused himself to get a bottle of whiskey he had in his room and did not return. Karl and Dwight also left, taking the back stairs to the basement. Karl retrieved the mayonnaise jars and ashtray from the pantry and placed them on the kitchen counter, added kerosene, and sealed them with tinfoil and rubber bands.

"How are you going to light them?" Dwight asked. Karl explained that ANFO would explode on impact.

When they got back to the Nitty Gritty a local rock group, the Oz, was shaking the walls with a song called "Cowboy Woman." A groupie with waist-length blonde hair and silicone-inflated breasts was gyrating in front of the stage trying to attract the band's attention. Dwight spotted Poli De Venecia in the crowd with Shankar Patel, an Indian student, and went over to talk to them. Lynn and Susan were on their feet in the center of the room with Barry and Cathy Friedman. Everyone was moving to the music.

When the number ended Barry turned to Karl and said cordially, "I see you brought the Social Waste with you." Karl managed a tight little smile. He whispered something to Lynn, and she went to get her coat. "We have to go somewhere," Karl said awkwardly. "See you later." Dwight left with them.

The abruptness of their departure left everybody wondering. "They must be going to get drugs," Susan said.

It was after 11 P.M. and snowing when they arrived at Morey Airport in the Impala, the ANFO in a cardboard box in the back seat.

The hangar was dark and deserted. Lynn pulled into the gravel parking lot and stopped next to the row of evenly spaced pines that bordered Airport Road. On the way over she and Dwight had been trying to talk Karl out of his plan. T-16 was an empty quonset hut; Badger Ordnance was a major arms plant with thousands of employees, Dwight pointed out. If they were to hit one of the fuel tanks or ammunition bunkers, it could set off a chain reaction. "Like, bombing the plant could kill enormous numbers of people. It's not a good political act," he said.

Karl dismissed the objection. "It's New Year's Eve; they're going to have a skeleton crew." Besides, he added, Lynn would make a warning call. "If somebody gets hurt, it will be like in a war." Karl seemed so calm considering the potential consequences that Dwight wondered if he really understood the gravity of the situation. *He's in some kind of mode,* Dwight thought.

Lynn departed as soon as they were out of the car, heading for Sauk City. Dwight led Karl to the service door at the back of the hangar, which was secured by a large padlock. "It doesn't seem to be on here too good," Karl said. He took the padlock in both hands and gave it a yank. The door came right off the building.

Dwight found the Cessna 150 in the dark and felt for the ignition key under the engine cowling. It was there. Another plane—a larger, newer Cessna 172—blocked the way out. Karl wondered why they didn't take it instead, but Dwight said he wouldn't know how to fly it: The 150 was the only one with which he was familiar. He opened the hangar door, and they rolled both planes out onto the snow-covered tarmac.

Dwight had the jitters. He had never soloed before, let alone flown at night. And he didn't know how to turn on the instrument panel lights. He made one more attempt to dissuade Karl, but Karl seemed to have an answer for everything. *I could justify it to myself and others by saying that the use of violence to prevent even greater violence against people is justified.*

As the brothers would later describe the takeoff to Lynn and Scott and other friends, it was like a Marx Brothers episode. With no panel lights the only way Dwight could see the ground-speed indicator was to have Karl shine a flashlight on it. But Karl had a greasy mayo jar in each arm and the ashtray between his legs. His door popped open when they were halfway down the runway, and snow came swirling into the cockpit. Dwight had to shout at Karl to hold the flashlight up.

"Can't you see I'm falling out of the plane?" Karl yelled back.

At the last possible moment the plane lurched into the air. To get his door closed, Karl put one of the mayo jars in Dwight's lap. Kerosene was leaking out at the top and running down the sides, and the cockpit stank. The Cessna's single headlight did not penetrate very far into the flurries. Dwight had not set the gyro compass, and all he had to go on for direction were his turnback indicators and altimeter.

"We're lost," he announced. He started to set the radio to 121, the emergency channel. "The control tower at Truax can talk us down."

"Don't do that!" Karl warned.

"Okay," Dwight said smoothly, "what I'll do is take the plane down gradually and try to get under this layer." As he did so, he deftly set the radio to the emergency channel without telling Karl, just in case.

They came out of the cloud over Cross Plains, a hamlet about three miles west of the city. Dwight turned the plane around. After another moment, they saw the lights of Madison, picked up Highway 12 and followed it north, staying low enough to see the car lights. It was midnight when they got to Sauk City.

Lynn was having her own problems. *I got into Sauk City to that phone booth they had told me to call from and they had given me a number and what I was supposed to say written on a piece of paper so I went to the phone booth with the intentions of making the call to warn the people and there was someone on the phone and he refused to let me use that phone even though it was important and so I wanted to find another phone booth and I stopped at another phone booth and there was a, you know, like somebody had made a sign and stuck it on the phone—"out of order."*

Flying in low over the town, Karl and Dwight saw the Impala parked next to the phone booth at the main intersection and saw Lynn get out of the car and hurriedly enter a booth. *She's making the call,* Karl thought.

Dwight began to enjoy himself. "I'll circle around and dip a wing at her," he said, as if they were out for a Saturday night cruise. Karl ordered him to stay on course.

Lynn did not see the plane go over. She went back to the phone booth. *I tried once, and I couldn't get anything and I lost a dime so I didn't know if I should waste any more time, you know, to try to find another phone booth 'cause I really didn't know where any more were located so I then went to the Sauk Prairie Airport.*

Dwight followed Highway 12 across the prairie, bumping along on the gusts. They buzzed the rooftops of Baraboo, the Ringling mansion, and Circus World. Several miles farther north Badger Ordnance came into view, looking like a small city. Dwight turned off his exterior lights and they circled overhead to get their bearings. There were several possible targets: storage bunkers; fuel tanks; the railroad siding; and the main processing plant, steaming away in the center. The bunkers were scattered. Karl decided to go for the fuel tanks.

Dwight banked for the first run, leveling off at 1,500 feet. "Take it down," Karl said. Dwight held steady. "If the plant goes up, we may as well say good-bye," he pointed out.

"Down!" Karl ordered.

Dwight took it down to 750 feet. With his free hand, Karl opened the door and began nudging the ashtray out with his foot.

"Drop," Dwight said. "Drop it! Drop it!"

Sauk Prairie Airport was nothing more than a hangar and a strip of asphalt in the middle of a corn patch north of Sauk City. There were no lights on, and it was pitch black out. *I made a wrong turn, turning in towards the farmer's barn or whatever it is and realized my mistake and backed around, went down in the driveway to the airstrip, went to the end, got out of the car. ...* Lynn was still in her miniskirt. The wind blowing in off the Baraboo Hills burned her cheeks and made her eyes water. As Karl had instructed her, she ripped the tops off the two railroad flares and knocked them together. They lit immediately, sending out a bright magenta glow. *Put one flare on the left hand side of the runway and one on the right.* She got back into the car and waited.

The ashtray fell harmlessly into a field. "Wow, really great shot, Karl," Dwight said. He banked the plane around and commenced a shallow dive. He was now so low that the plume from the plant's main stack was rising in front of them. Suddenly Karl tossed the mayo jars out the door one after the other. Dwight stared at him.

"Hey, I'm not gonna hit anything anyway," Karl said. There was no sign below that anything had exploded.

Dwight's kerosene-soaked pants were burning his thighs. He turned south and made a beeline for Sauk Prairie Airport. In the distance he could see the flares glowing in the blackness. *That Lynn is alright,* he thought.

The Cessna lowered to a few hundred feet off the plain. With the tail wind pushing him, he came down much too fast and had to pull up at the last minute. He banked into a steep turn; slowed to sixty miles per hour; and, coming in again from the north, dropped straight onto the runway, bringing the plane to a skidding stop. They jumped out, hurriedly wiped the plane for prints, and ran toward the prearranged meeting place near some stables just east of the airport.

So I got back in the car and left the airfield and went to the place where they told me to wait and I waited there a really long time and no one came and I got to think maybe this has all been some kind of a practical joke on me. I couldn't believe it was really happening so I decided to leave. I started the car and was just going around a curve on this little road and I happened to look back and two figures were running toward the car.

They were all unhappy on the drive back to Madison. Dwight's scrotum was on fire. Lynn was mad about missing the Nitty Gritty party. Karl couldn't understand why the bombs hadn't gone off. *They were disappointed that it hadn't worked until I told them that I couldn't make the phone call and at that time, you know, their attitude changed; they were actually glad then that they hadn't gone off because they didn't want people hurt.*

Lynn had hesitated to tell Karl about the flubbed phone call because she thought he might get mad at her, but he wasn't angry at all. "It's not your fault; you were just trying to keep on schedule," he said. The more he thought about it, the more he brightened. It had been a "symbolic bombing," he announced. What really mattered was the "psychological impact."

They were on University Avenue, on the long, downhill grade between Middleton and the swank, new Hilldale Shopping Mall, when the policeman pulled them over. Karl was at the wheel. For a moment, they all thought that they were going to be arrested, but as it turned out, Karl had been speeding. The officer let him off with a warning, and they continued into town.

Karl and Dwight both reeked of kerosene. Back at the fraternity house, they went upstairs to change. When they got out of the shower, they found Rick Mathieson in Room 8 sniffing the air. "What's that smell?" he asked.

Mathieson was a senior in business administration from Racine whose house name was Snakey. He wore pop-bottle specs that magnified his eyes and seemed to spend much of his time playing cards with the Crazies at the State Street Burgerville. Karl did not trust him. When he and Scott had received a note from Hanoi thanking them for their sympathy card on the death of Ho Chi Minh, Karl had told Snakey that all they had wanted was the stamps. He now explained that they had been snowmobiling. Where? With whom? Snakey wanted to know. Karl said, "I can't tell you. It was a private party, and only a few people were invited, and we don't want you to be offended that you weren't, so we can't tell you whose it was."

Karl wasn't at all convinced that Mathieson, who had spotted their Sauk County map lying on the floor with Badger Ordnance Works circled in red, had bought the story. "Rick will turn us in if he finds out," he told Dwight after Mathieson had left.

Lynn's parents had given her a case of wine for Christmas and she had planned a midnight post-function at her apartment to get rid of it. So even though it was already very late, she had Karl drive her home. Walking down to her apartment from where they parked the car, they ran into several people from the fraternity. Lynn asked them where they were going. They explained that her roommate had kicked them out. *So I asked Susan why we couldn't have the party, and she wouldn't speak to me. And so we just took the wine and went back to the fraternity house and, you know, sat around drinking wine.*

They could not find a deck of cards, so they invented a game, a sort of cross between strip poker and spin the bottle. The idea was to take turns holding an empty coke bottle upside down, using only thumb and forefinger to grip the base. "You drop it, you take something off," Karl explained. He went upstairs to get the visitor, Ann Mickola, who had gone to bed early after polishing off Steve Rabideau's bottle of whiskey. "I just want to sleep it off," she groaned. Karl dragged her downstairs in her nightgown.

Seven or eight people gathered in front of the fireplace in the party room. Karl presided in longjohns and a black, short-billed

Greek fisherman's cap, reminding Mickola of a patriarch of the Russian Revolution. Lynn curled up in his lap. Dwight lounged at the bar with his friends Poli and Shankar Patel. Snakey Mathieson poked his head in from time to time to watch. To Mickola, Karl, Dwight, and Lynn seemed to have boundless energy. *They need to get messed up,* she thought. She had no idea why.

They drank the wine and shared marijuana cigarettes. The coke bottle went around, and the clothes came off. Most of the players quickly caught on, but Dwight and Lynn were hopeless at it. *She's losing on purpose,* Dwight thought. One last time he took the bottle and held it upside down. His hand began to shake, and when he felt it slipping from his grip he suddenly flung it into the fireplace and stalked out.

It was four in the morning. Twelve hours had passed since Karl pitched his scheme to Dwight at Mira's. Events had transpired that would forever alter the lives of the participants. In a few days Professor Harvey Goldberg would be reading, in Paris, about the midnight raid on Badger Ordnance in the *International Herald Tribune.*

14

The Old Red Gym
and the Primate Lab

*Reliance on so-called "free-fire zones" meant that anything
that moved was a target within large areas of South Vietnam.
And this was probably the most indiscriminate targeting pattern ever relied upon in a war.*

—DR. RICHARD FALK,
law professor, for the defense

*He's saying, "Take the bombs out of the hands of the military
and put them in my hands." Heaven help us.*

—MICHAEL ZALESKI,
Wisconsin Assistant Attorney General, for the prosecution

Milton Zech, the manager of Sauk Prairie Airport, found the
Cessna 150 at 6 A.M. on New Year's Day, sitting in the middle
of the north–south runway with the its doors open. Two sets of
tracks led off to the east. Zech recognized the blue-and-white aircraft and called Field Morey, who, having already heard from one
of his employees that something was amiss, was about to leave for
Morey Airport. When Morey arrived, he found the service door
lying on the ground, the padlock still on it. On the opposite side of
the building, standing in the snow, was a four-seater Cessna 172.
Sure enough, the 150 was gone. The hangar doors had been closed

after the planes were rolled out, an unusual courtesy under the circumstances.

Detective Tom Kretschman of the Dane County Sheriffs arrived at 10 A.M. Whoever took the plane had to be pretty strong, Kretschman observed, because the service door had been literally ripped from its moorings, taking three sets of wood screws with it. The tracks in the snow suggested two suspects, both with big feet, and one with a slightly splay-footed walk. Morey fired up the 172 and transported Detective Kretschman to Sauk Prairie, where Sauk County deputies were already dusting the 150 for prints. Kretschman checked the fuel gauge. It was down almost ten gallons, enough for about an hour of flight, so they must have flown around for a while before landing at Sauk Prairie, he surmised. Field Morey told him that the keys had been in the 150 but were well hidden. The other plane had also had keys inside and had been first in line; somebody must have wanted the 150 specifically. The culprits evidently smoked, because the Cessna's cigarette lighter was lying on the cockpit floor, along with scattered cigarette ashes. The parties had left no car at Morey Airport, so they must have had an accomplice who dropped them off and later picked them up at Sauk Prairie. The aircraft transmitter, normally set at Channel 123.5, the flight training channel, had been turned to 121.5, for emergencies. However, Truax had reported no emergency calls during the evening. The biggest mystery was the landing. It had been a dark night, and the airport was unlit. Milt Zech pointed out power lines obstructing the approach from the north. The plane could not have missed the lines by more than a few feet, and despite a stiff tail wind had landed practically on a dime. "Nobody ever lands here from the north," Zech said. "Whoever flew that plane in here last night had to be one hell of a pilot!"

Kretschman, the Sheriff's Department counterpart of MPD Detective George Croal, had worked undercover for several years and knew the Madison Left well. This did not strike him as a political job. "Looks like a couple of kids out joyriding on New Year's Eve," he told Field Morey, "and obviously someone familiar with your operation." He asked Morey for the 150's flight log, which Morey was happy to provide. Dwight Armstrong was listed as a trainee on numerous flights with Mike Powers that spring, but there was no record of Dwight's having flown the plane by himself and certainly nothing to indicate that he was capable of expert landings at night. Morey forgot to mention that he had found the hangar doors closed that morning, so Kretschman remained ignorant of that particular fact, which might have suggested not the drunken revelries of joyriders out on a dare but the habitual behavior of a former lineman.

On New Year's Day the streets of Madison were like an ice rink. Karl and Lynn skated over to Memorial Student Union in their shoes, pausing at the Library Mall to take part in a snowball fight. At the kiosk on the ground floor of the Union, Karl bought a copy of the *Wisconsin State Journal* and paged through it as they made their way into the Rathskeller. He had called the paper during the night to tell them about the attack on Badger Ordnance, but found not a word. Instead, the front page carried the story of a break-in at the U.S. Army Reserve office on South Park. Parties unknown had tipped over filing cabinets, made off with equipment, and scrawled an illiterate statement on the wall: "Army hurt me."

The Rat was nearly deserted. Karl left Lynn at a table far in the back and disappeared for several minutes. He went to the main stairwell, where there was a bank of pay phones halfway up to the second floor. When he returned, he told Lynn that he had called the *Capital Times* and, for the second time, the *Kaleidoscope,* asking them if they were going to cover the incident. Both papers had said no. "They don't believe it happened," Karl said. "The news editor at the *Cap Times* said they'd do a story if I came in for an interview."

But that afternoon the *Capital Times* did carry an inside story about a stolen plane found at Sauk Prairie Airport. Karl called the *Kaleidoscope* once again, and Lynn noticed that he was a lot more cheerful afterward. *He told them that they should write the story up because it was really true and he had a way he could prove it now and that was to buy a* Capital Times *and to read how a plane was stolen from Morey's Airfield and that coincided with the details he had given them earlier.*

That night Lynn asked Karl if he was going to do any more bombings. "I really don't know," he said. "It depends on the need."

Dwight could tell that Ruth suspected something. When he came by for dinner that evening, she confronted him about the baby-sitting foul-up the night before. How could he stand up his sister on New

Year's Eve? And then there was the peculiar story in the *Cap Times* that day about a stolen plane. The thing that had caught her eye was that the aircraft was taken from Morey Airport, where Dwight had worked and taken flying lessons. "Did you have anything to do with this, Dwight?" she asked.

The question caught Dwight off guard, because Ruth wasn't usually that nosy. "Are you kidding? Me?" he said.

Friday morning Karl went to the Research Products Corporation office on East Washington Avenue and applied for a job manufacturing humidifiers in its assembly plant, having momentarily given up on his guerrilla career. *And I alternated between pacifism and violence. As though I was approaching it—the use of violence—and then trying to step back.* By evening his resolution had returned. Around 11 P.M. he had Lynn drive him to Copp's Department Store on the East Side. Lynn waited in the Impala while he went inside. *[He] came back out with a gallon jar of vinegar. I thought it was very unusual because he lived in a fraternity and all the cooking was done by a cook. The first thing he did with it was to empty the contents into the snow and refill the jug with gasoline.*

A little after 3 A.M. Karl had Lynn drop him off at the corner of Lake and Langdon. "Give me a few minutes," he said. It was about twenty below, forty below with the windchill factor, so cold and dry that he got a shock when he kissed Lynn good-bye. He waded through the snow with his jar of gasoline, staying in the shadows between the Alumni Center and the Old Red Gym. The big fort had a round tower on each corner with turrets at the top. Karl's objective was a tall window at ground level in the southeast tower. *I don't think I can remember even getting into a fight because I felt that the use of violence could serve no good end.* The heavy jar broke the window with its own weight and smashed on the floor inside. Karl lit a wad of newspaper, tossed it inside, and ran to where Lynn, having driven around the block, was waiting on Langdon.

The jar shattered against an interior brick wall. The gasoline ran down the wall and seeped into the dusty recesses under the floor. The fire followed, working its way laterally to the walls and climbing inside the walls to the floor above, where it found a large supply of combustible material, the hardwood surface of the multicourt basketball gym.

The Old Red Gym was on UP & S officer Norbert Sutter's route that night, along with the Wisconsin Alumni Center and Memorial

Library. He had already been through the gym earlier in the evening and had seen nothing suspicious. It wasn't until 5:24 A.M., a good two hours after the fire was set, that he saw the cherry red flames and called his dispatcher.

Six minutes later Fire Companies 1 and 4 arrived with two engines and two aerials. Shortly after, a second alarm was sounded and then a third. The first men into the building encountered a fearful sight: The floor and walls of the vast gymnasium were solid sheets of flame. By 6 A.M., eleven fire engines and seventy-two firemen were swarming over the building cutting holes in the roof to get at the fire from above.

A good part of Madison law enforcement had arrived as well. Spies worked the crowd of spectators. Army Intelligence men took down out-of-state license numbers. Campus cops found Karl's tracks; MPD officers photographed, measured, and diagrammed them. Detective Paul Radloff hurried over to Tripp Hall to check on his favorite suspect, the pot-smoking Mr. Weinberg, but found him in bed with no sign of moisture on his shoes. At 6:55 A.M. the Stassi Shoe Store alerted Washington. The Old Red Gym arson was the top of the news throughout Wisconsin that day.

Since Susan Baldie had gone home for the weekend, Karl and Lynn returned to the Lake Monona apartment and listened to the radio reports. Before long it was announced that the athletic facilities were burning; the ROTC offices in the rear were safe. *And he made a comment as to that had been a mistake, that if he had known the specific location, that's where he would have hit.*

Around noon on Saturday they drove over to Phi Sigma Kappa and invited Scott, who had just come in from River Falls, to go to lunch with them at the Union. Karl was uncertain how Scott would react, but he was anxious to reveal to him what he was now calling his "winter offensive." Scott just laughed. "Dwight can't fly a plane; he can barely drive a car," he scoffed, though Karl suspected he was actually excited by the news. The three of them walked over to the Union, stepping around the fire engines in front of the Old Red Gym. Firemen had been pumping water for nine hours, and the building had turned into an ice castle. According to the latest news the basketball courts, swimming pool, weight room, gymnastic equipment, and lockers had all been destroyed, with damage estimates ranging from $40,000 to $80,000. The gasoline bomb had cost Karl $1.08.

"I didn't mean to get it like that," he said somberly.

Scott was unsympathetic. "A lot of people are going to be pissed about the gym," he said. He himself had been looking forward to playing some basketball before going into the air force.

Karl considered that for a moment. *All my thoughts were: How am I going to end the war? Or: How am I going to help end the war?* "There's a lot more important things than going to the gym," he replied.

Lynn Schultz returned to an empty apartment, frightened by the extent of the damage to the Old Red Gym and by the furor over it. The building had been scheduled for demolition, but now the press was extolling its "historical significance," recalling all the marvelous events that it had sponsored and the ironic fact that famous socialists like Eugene Debs had spoken there. Such controversy was more than Lynn had bargained for in her relationship with Karl. When they were together, he made everything seem reasonable and right, but conviction dissipated when she was by herself. *I knew that he was against people being drafted, he was against the war, he thought that people who supported the war were wrong.* She didn't understand the "historical necessity" of violence and suspected that Karl was being influenced by others, possibly by the "SDC." (She found it hard to keep all the acronyms straight.) "SDC" was a very big, very radical organization on campus, and she was under the impression that Karl belonged to it. For all she knew, Karl was acting on "SDC" orders.

Karl called late that evening and asked her to come over to the fraternity; he needed a ride. *And I said, "All right, yeah," and I asked him where he wanted to go, and he got angry and said I was very stupid for asking a question like that over the telephone. Which, you know, naturally led me to believe something was to happen again.*

She met him in front of Gino's when he got off work at 2 A.M. He had brought her a hot sausage sandwich from the kitchen, but she said she wasn't hungry. He took the wheel and drove to an all-night gas station, where he filled a half-gallon vinegar jar and stashed it in a cardboard box. "How'd ya like a Gino's sausage sandwich?" he asked the attendant.

"Sure!" the man said, delighted by his good fortune. Gino's sausage was the best in town.

Lynn was nervous. All the reports on the radio were about sabotage. Not only had the Old Red Gym burned the night before, but someone had vandalized the Monroe Street draft-board office. Madison authorities had announced that they were increasing security at military installations. Lynn, who thought she saw a spy in every parked car they passed, could not believe how calm Karl was.

At Charter Street Karl turned left, then left again into Capitol Court. He drove slowly down the alley looking for the building that housed Selective Service headquarters for the state of Wisconsin. He had looked up the address in the phone book, 1220 Capitol Court, but neither of the two buildings on the alley bore that address. A plain white cement building on the left had no markings at all. Karl circled around the block and entered the drive again. It had to be the modern office building on the right, he decided; the white building was obviously just a warehouse of some kind. He pulled into Coyne Court, another alleyway that formed a *T* with Capitol, and parked. "Get in the driver's seat and wait for me," he told Lynn.

He walked to a point near the front of the building on its south side, broke one of the windows with his hammer, and tossed the jar of gasoline inside. A wind was blowing, and it took him several tries to get his match lit. He finally got a wad of newspaper burning, threw it into the building, ran back to the car and jumped in.

Lynn took Coyne Court toward Regent Street, a major thoroughfare, but as she accelerated, another car entered the narrow drive from Regent, momentarily blinding her with its headlights. She braked, her stomach going queasy. *It must be a cop,* Karl thought. Moments earlier, as he was trying to light the match, he had seen a man watching him from a car parked on Charter Street. He had gone right on striking matches. As Dwight would say, he was in his mode.

It had been a long night for Chester White, aka George Croal. He had started at 9 P.M., staking out the Selective Service headquarters. Another MPD plainclothesman, David Tuttle, was posted at the Spring Street side, observing the back of the building; Croal watched the front from a parking lot on Charter Street, directly across from the Wisconsin Primate Research Center. It was fifteen below out, and he kept the car running; next to him on the seat was a pad of yellow lined notepaper and a pen. According to his boss

Herman Thomas, the MPD had received word that Selective Service was going to be hit that night, and so Croal was more than usually alert.

Since his cover had been blown in the fall of 1968, the detective had been known on campus as "Red George." Harvey Goldberg was among those who suspected an element of personal vendetta in Croal's attempts to thwart the Left. Goldberg had advised Croal during his first year in the graduate school of history in 1963 and remembered him well. "The University of Wisconsin was the first non-Catholic coed school he'd gone to," he later told Bob LaBrasca, a reporter for the *Capital Times*. "At Loras College in Iowa he had been a prized scholar of 19th century social thought. He knew Marx from the point of view of the Brothers. He came here and went into the seminars and found himself verbally castrated by sharp lefties who knew their Marx chapter and verse."

Croal, a practicing Roman Catholic who had done missionary work with migrant laborers in Colorado and had studied for the priesthood, disputed this version of his legend. His political views were admittedly to the right, however. He had worked for the election of U.S. Senator Barry Goldwater, the conservative candidate for president, in 1964 and believed that Goldwater would have settled the Vietnam conflict long ago by threatening to drop a hydrogen bomb on Hanoi. He had found Harvey Goldberg to be a helpful adviser, but disagreed with his interpretation of history, especially biblical history. Croal refused to believe that Christ was a Communist; the "Eye of the Needle" in Matthew 19 referred to an actual gate in the old wall of Jerusalem, through which it was possible for a camel to pass.

Exactly what Croal saw and heard that night of January 4, 1970, will perhaps always remain a mystery. By his own account, around 3:00 A.M. he observed a car coming up Charter, a tan-and-white Impala. It slowed as it neared the middle of the block and turned left into Capitol Court. A few minutes later it came around again, and this time, Croal got the license number, writing it down on his yellow pad: K17-214. The vehicle disappeared, and the detective settled back into his seat cushions. Perhaps, as some of his colleagues suspected, he dozed off; or as he would try to explain it, his attention was completely focused on Selective Service; in any case, he was unaware of Karl Armstrong breaking a heavy thermopane window in the Primate Lab directly across the street from where he was parked. Half an hour went by. Something startled him, a puff of smoke. He walked across the street to investigate and found the Primate Lab on fire. He did not see the Impala fleeing the scene, nor did he drive his own car into the alley.

Karl could not understand why he hadn't been arrested. Instead of blocking his egress from Coyne Court, the oncoming car had veered to one side and edged by them, continuing down the alley. Lynn had pulled out onto Regent, and, in a state of near-shock, they had meandered over to Henry Vilas Park on the frozen shore of Lake Wingra. Karl was certain someone was after them and insisted she keep driving, zigzagging all over town. "This is a waste of time," Lynn said after about an hour. *And then we went back to my apartment where we turned on the radio and found out that he had bombed the Primate Lab.*

After Fire Department and other investigators had arrived, Detective Croal returned to the City-County Building and wrote up his report. It was filled with the minutiae for which he was notorious in his department.

On 4 JAN. 1970 at 3:42 AM I radioed in the report of a fire burning in the PRIMATE LAB. in the 10 blk. N. Orchard. Prior to this, I had been parked observing the SELECTIVE SERVICE CENTER, CAPITOL CT., in the parking lot across the street from the PRIMATE LAB. At approximately 3:30 AM I saw a cloud of smoke moving NORTH with the wind on ORCHARD ST. At this time I thought that smoke to have come from an auto's exhaust. I remember that the smoke cleared and I again returned my eyes to the SELECTIVE SERVICE CENTER. About 5 minutes later I saw some more smoke and at this time I saw what looked to be a fire coming from inside the PRIMATE LAB. At this I moved out of my car and walked across the street; I saw that there was indeed a fire in the LAB. I immediately returned to my car and put in the fire call. I then proceeded back to the sidewalk leading to the ORCHARD ST. entrance and at this time I observed a flash of fire ... in the nature of a muffled explosion. Also at this sidewalk position I noticed that one of the windows facing SOUTH had been broken in.

One detail was missing from the report, however: the license number of the car he'd seen in the area less than half an hour before he discovered the fire, an omission he would later attribute to "inexperience." Around 5:00 A.M. Tom McMillen called the MPD dispatcher asking for Croal, who happened to be on his way out the door. The detective took the call in the dispatcher's office. McMillen had heard about the Primate Lab and said he just wanted to touch base. "Did you notice anything unusual tonight?" he asked.

Croal looked at his yellow note pad and read the license number of the car he had seen in the alley. He wasn't positive that he'd written it down correctly, he said apologetically. McMillen thanked him and said he'd have it checked out.

The fire in the Primate Lab was quickly extinguished. Damage was slight, and there were no injuries to animals or humans, though a few researchers were working late in the building, as it turned out. Investigators, aware that Selective Service had taken the precaution of removing its nameplate from the door at 1220 Capitol Court, deduced that the Primate Lab was not the intended target.

When Karl got to work at Gino's on Sunday afternoon, his co-workers were all laughing about the bizarre incident. "Must have been a mistake," he agreed. He retreated to the Kollege Klub, a dark, smoky bar on upper State Street, where he ran into a security guard he recognized. Karl brought up the bombings. The guard said he had been inside the Selective Service Center the night before: "Yeah, there were three of us in there, and we were ready."

Karl was stunned. What if he had hit the right building? *And I felt that what I called the Winter Offensive against the Indochina War, I felt that that was enough.... I felt that ... I had risked my life enough.*

15

Reviews

This was a departure for The Cardinal *and for the campus at large. And I think the editorial shows that people were ready at this point to accept something beyond peaceful tactics to end the war.*

—Patrick McGilligan,
student, for the defense

We heard that the Daily Cardinal *didn't advocate the use of violence until the 6th of January, 1970. Well, that's very commendable. But, even so, Karl Armstrong beat them to it.*

—Douglas Haag,
Wisconsin Assistant Attorney General, for the prosecution

All day Monday, the fifth of January, the charter buses rolled up to Memorial Student Union from O'Hare. The first thing returning students noticed was the burned-out Armory. The second was a *Kaleidoscope* hawker boasting an exclusive interview with Madison's "radical saboteurs." Except for the Saturday night foul-up at the Primate Lab, the slender special edition gave brief accounts of each of the holiday incidents—including two that Karl Armstrong wasn't responsible for, the vandalizing of the Army Reserve office on South Park and of the draft-board office on Monroe Street—treating them as part of a single campaign. "In many parts of the world," the story began, "people mark the advent of the New Year by rushing into the streets at the stroke of midnight and igniting fireworks. The custom is a relic of older times, when bonfires were lit and a loud racket made to drive off evil spirits. Here in Madison, some radical activists are seeking to drive off evil spirits which are a lot more substantial, and so are the fireworks!" The message Karl had called in after T-16 was set off in a box captioned "The Terrorist Group's Statement":

> The policy of our group is to increase the level of violence against both on-campus and off-campus institutions of repression. On the campus, our activity will escalate until the university administration accedes to the demands of SDS and other student power-oriented groups. The level of violence will be raised until either these demands are met or the university physical plant is destroyed and the institution shut down.

After reading the article in the Rat, Karl hurried to his stairwell communications post and telephoned the *Daily Cardinal*. Associate Editor Peter Greenberg, a junior from Manhattan, answered. Karl identified himself as a spokesman for the "Vanguards of the Revolution" and said he'd like to clear up two things. First, he was sorry about the Primate Lab mistake; the Vanguards had nothing against monkeys.

Second, he wanted to confirm the rumors about an attempt to bomb the Badger Ordnance plant on New Year's Eve. "Badger Ordnance will be destroyed this spring, after February. We will give the employees a warning. After that they can expect explosions. We have a dozen time bombs. We will give the university about a week...."

"A week to do what?" Greenberg asked.

Karl told him that the Vanguards had issued three demands: removal of ROTC and AMRC from the campus and passage by the state legislature of a bill turning university policymaking over to the students.

"What happens if the demands aren't met?" Greenberg asked.

"There is a good possibility that the State Capitol and some of the state office buildings will be bombed," Karl said vaguely.

But he was dissatisfied with this answer. He called back an hour later as Greenberg was typing up his notes. "We urge that in January all local draft boards be burned or otherwise destroyed and that individual people should be responsible for carrying these acts out," he added.

An emergency meeting of Madison law enforcement and intelligence agencies convened at eleven-thirty that Monday morning in the City-County Building. Tom McMillen and George Baxtrum attended for the FBI, Ralph Hanson for UP & S, Frank Roberts for the office of the state fire marshal, and Detective Charles Lulling for the MPD. Dane County District Attorney James Boll and his glib young assistant Michael Zaleski, the latter just beginning his prosecutorial career, were also present. Copies of the *Kaleidoscope*'s special edition floated around the table. The fact that the paper's editors knew about a bomb attempt on Badger Ordnance before the government could even confirm it struck everyone as highly suspicious. In fact, the Sabotage Desk in Washington had advised Baxtrum that morning to consider the *Kaleidoscope* story evidence of a possible conspiracy against the military. The lawmen agreed to meet daily and to share reports until the case was solved.

Tom McMillen called the Schultz residence in Wisconsin Dells that morning, after learning from the Department of Motor Vehicles that the car Croal had spotted at the Primate Lab was registered to Lynn's parents. Lynn's mother informed him that Lynn was the primary user of the car and gave him Lynn's work number at Ray-O-Vac. The agent hadn't called Lynn, however; his orders, straight from Washington, were to check out all SDS suspects in the vicinity, and that category did not include Ray-O-Vac secretaries.[1]

Lulling had a juvenile named Tom Lutz in custody and proposed releasing the boy to act as an informant. A surly seventeen-year-old with a sparse mustache, Lutz was being held in connection with a shooting incident. He had a close relationship with the SDSers, Lulling said. "There's a good chance he could develop pertinent information."

District Attorney Boll, suppressor of the nude *Peter Pan*, sec-

---

[1]Because George Croal did not handle criminal investigations, he was not at the meeting. And since he had neglected to include the license-plate information in his report, it had not come to the attention of the MPD's point man, Detective Lulling. Thus the one solid lead in the case—the fact that a young woman had been seen cruising in the vicinity of the Primate Lab shortly before it was firebombed—did not surface.

onded the idea. "The victim in the shooting is reluctant to testify, and there's a good chance we'd have to release Lutz, anyway," he said. So the plan was agreed to, with Lulling assigned to supervise the informant.

Tuesday morning, January 6, one of the largest snowmobiling expeditions in history took place at Badger Ordnance Works. Hundreds of employees, security personnel, Sauk County sheriffs, and a U.S. military bomb squad from Savannah, Illinois, roared across the 7,500-acre grounds on sleek, motorized fiberglass sleds (more than a few of them manufactured in the Milwaukee Evinrude plant where Karl Armstrong had worked). Within an hour, three suspicious objects were found, two on the ground, half-buried in snow, and one on the roof of a fuel tank. Officials of the Olin Corporation, which operated the facility for the army, were stunned by the discovery. Badger Ordnance was one of the biggest munitions plants in the country. It had been built during World War II, situated in the lee of the Baraboo Hills, at the heart of the continent, for the same reasons that the army had chosen Wisconsin for its Math Research Center: The area was secure against enemy attack. In fact, although the compound was fenced and you needed a pass to get in, no air raid drill had ever been conducted at the plant. No one had expected an aerial assault.

Two of the containers were easily identified as mayonnaise jars, big ones of the sort used in the restaurant trade. The casing on the third, a metallic cylinder about eighteen inches long and ten inches in diameter, baffled the bomb squad; they had never seen anything like it. All three vessels contained a gooey, strong-smelling substance whose chemical composition lab tests subsequently revealed to be the common agricultural blasting mix ANFO. A night watchman told authorities that he had seen a small plane buzzing the plant with its lights off sometime after midnight on New Year's Eve. Together with the stolen plane from Morey Airport and the mysterious landing at Sauk Prairie that night, a picture began to emerge.

Wisconsin's dailies rushed into print with the story of the midnight bombers; the wire services picked it up, and small items began appearing in the nation's press. Journalists found it difficult to state the bare facts without sounding whimsical: Somewhere in the Wisconsin wilds, someone had stolen a light plane on New Year's Eve and, in the midst of a blizzard, dropped jars of fertilizer on a major munitions plant. Not since the Japanese hit California with a balloon-bomb in World War II had anyone dared attack the continental U.S. from the air.

Meanwhile in the Rathskeller students were snapping up copies of the first *Daily Cardinal* edition of the new year. The entire front page was devoted to news of the holiday rampage. Photos of scorched locker rooms in the Old Red Gym were captioned with the information that "the only rooms *not* affected were the ROTC offices." However, the *Cardinal* editorial, entitled "The End of the Road," struck a more favorable note. "All in this society are children of violence," it began. It recalled the years of effort to stop the war by peaceful means, the often-violent response to those efforts on the part of local authorities, and the recent revelations of atrocities committed by U.S. infantrymen in a Vietnamese village called My Lai. Its conclusion sent shock waves across the country:

> There are some, perhaps many in the movement who see one and only one way of renewing and strengthening the fight for change. Several of those people, whoever they are, were responsible for the firebombings of the Red Gym, the Primate Lab and the State Selective Service headquarters in the last four days. They call themselves the Vanguard of the Revolution. They are indeed. They have chosen to initiate direct action. They have chosen to show to those both in and outside of the movement that the immobile and repressive position taken by this nation can only be countered head on in the streets with bombs and guns.
>
> It is a new phenomenon on this campus, that the very men who have passed the repressive laws, called in the National Guard, summoned Dane County Sheriffs and refused to listen at all to calls for a change, are now very much against the wall, trembling not only for the safety of their institution but for their own safety as well. We can have no sympathy for them. They are receiving the inevitable product of their actions.
>
> And if acts as those committed in the last few days are needed to strike fear into the bodies of once fearless men and rid this campus once and for all of repressive and deadly ideas and institutions then so be it.

The editorial had been written by Steve Reiner, but reflected a staff "consensus" achieved through discussion. In Madison it would be remembered as the "So Be It Statement," the first endorsement of terrorism by the *Daily Cardinal* and probably the first by a college newspaper in the United States. The *New York Times* quoted it at length. The *Capital Times* responded with a front-page editorial condemning "So Be It" and offering a $1,000 reward for information leading to the bombers' arrest. The *Kaleidoscope* countered a few days later with an offer of $1,005 for the identity of anyone informing on the bombers.

If the *Kaleidoscope* was Karl's *Village Voice,* the *Cardinal* was his *New York Times. And I think that probably these two papers influenced me to a great extent as far as actually me taking, using violence.* Buoyed by the endorsements, he called the *Cardinal* again conveying fresh demands and threats. The resulting story, under the byline of Karl's friend George Bogdanich, was the lead in Wednesday's edition. What Karl wanted now was an "open forum with the university to discuss the transfer of power to the students."

> "If they [the university] don't dig this," the caller told a *Daily Cardinal* reporter, "we'll give them one day's notice before we plant bombs around the school. We have enough straights in our organization so that we can get away with it. ... We can shut this university down in a day if we want to, because we've got pretty powerful stuff."

The arrest of Timothy Slater in Memorial Library on Wednesday provided investigators with what they considered their first really viable lead. Slater, a gnomelike twenty-six-year-old activist originally from England, walked into the library wearing a green hood with holes for the eyes and mouth, carrying a black bag that appeared to have something heavy in it, and yelled, "Everybody out, this place is going to go in two minutes!" He then removed the hood and walked into the periodicals room, where he sat down to read a newspaper. He was arrested by campus police, interrogated, and arraigned on a charge of disorderly conduct. When he refused to speak, Judge William Sachtjen entered a "not guilty" plea for him. That night, the Stassi Shoe Store passed the news to Washington: "Bag Slater's possession contained clothing not volatile. All possible leads Slater's involvement as subject this investigation being considered."

Slater interested the FBI not because he had threatened to blow up the library with a bagful of notepaper and personal effects, but because someone identifying himself as Slater had called Badger Ordnance on January 2 asking about the New Year's Eve bombing, which nobody at the plant had any knowledge of at the time. Furthermore, Slater was a fugitive, wanted by the federal government for draft evasion. In 1967 Slater had sent his draft board a letter advising its members that they might be guilty of war crimes. The draft board had passed the letter and an accompanying philosophical tract, *Neither Victims nor Executioners,* to the FBI, which had set up a file on him captioned "Security Matter—Anarchist." There was more, as the Resident Agency noted in its report to Washington at the end of the week: "Slater admits working for *Kaleidoscope* newspaper and assisted in editing article describing bombings." Baxtrum and McMillen were convinced that Slater knew more than he was telling. Slater was the "break in the case," advised Robert Taylor at the university. The sedition men were closing in on the so-called Vanguards of the Revolution.

On Thursday, January 8, Fred Harvey Harrington returned from India. He and his wife had spent Christmas day on the beach in Tahiti, but whatever peace of mind he had achieved on his "Tired President" sabbatical was soon dispelled by the situation he found in Madison. That day game wardens recruited from all over Wisconsin formed a protective ring around the State Capitol, and Senate Majority Leader Ernest Keppler, a Republican from Sheboygan, announced that the wardens had orders to "shoot to kill" any would-be saboteurs. In addition, the Madison Tenant Union accused the university of complicity with speculators and slumlords, and the Teaching Assistants Association threatened to strike. Chancellor Young, ostensibly Harrington's first line of defense, seemed inclined to duck the issues. In response to the Vanguards' demand for an open forum to discuss turning over the school to the students, Young had referred them to the Wisconsin Student Association.

Robert Taylor, the university's public relations man, was a small, careful individual with a pug nose and mouse-brown hair, the unobtrusive administrator who endures long after the tigers have gone. Meeting with Harrington in the latter's office, he brought the president up to date on the arson epidemic, the letters from worried parents, the unfavorable national publicity, the renewed attempts in the legislature to abolish the campus police, and the usual threats to cut the budget. On the plus side, he informed Harrington that the FBI was close to cracking the case. The most troublesome news was that the regents had taken advantage of Harrington's absence to plot against him. "There is a sentiment among four of the regents— Ziegler, Nellen, Pellisek, and Gelatt—that you should go. They don't have all nine votes, but they could count on Gordon Walker and Walter Renk. They don't have Sandin, Pasch, or Fish."

Harrington looked out his window at the flat, white expanse of Mendota—"best view of any university president in the country," Clark Kerr, visiting from the University of California at Berkeley, had once enviously told him—and then back at Taylor, drumming an impatient tattoo on his immaculate desk. "It's Nellen, right?" he said. "Doc" James Nellen, team physician of the Green Bay Packers, was his most determined enemy on the board.

"Nellen is the leader; Pellisek is second. He shifted over."

Harrington slumped back in his chair. He had been quiet about the war, he had let Chancellor Sewell resign, he had endorsed the crackdown on troublemakers. What more did the regents want? In any case, he was not too surprised. He and Nancy had talked about his future at length while they were away. It was a war on two fronts; that was what was defeating him. No executive could function for long without his board. But he needed time, a few months to position himself nationally and to get the mess cleaned up.

"I won't resign ... yet," he told Taylor.

The Young Socialist Alliance and all the mainstream peace organizations in town condemned the bombings, as did the Wisconsin Student Association. These repudiations enabled President Harrington to assure the Board of Regents that the "vast majority" of students were "disgusted" by the bombings. However, the evening of January 8, at a meeting announced by a flyer provocatively headlined "PIECE NOW!" Madison SDS voted to support the bombings "as a blow against the day-to-day terror perpetrated around the globe by the ruling class system of American imperialism." After the *Kaleidoscope* and *Daily Cardinal* endorsements, its position was almost foreordained. As one SDSer noted, "These were revolutionary acts, and I never thought I'd see the day when the *Daily Cardinal* would be more revolutionary than SDS."

Jim Hougan, a former University of Wisconsin student reporting for the *Capital Times,* spotted the change in SDS political strategy:

> The significance of the SDS shift—from earlier deploring some acts of antimilitary vandalism as alienating a potential mass base to endorsing the sabotage—shows that the saboteurs have obviously captured at least the imagination of those students who are teetering between radical reform and "revolutionary" positions.

Meanwhile, the sedition men added the evidence of the SDS endorsement to their own suspicions and came up with the equation, *Kaleidoscope* + SDS = bombings. Washington wanted proof of the SDS connection, and they were soon able to find one when an old SDS link turned up in Mark Knops's file. In 1968 Knops had attended the SDS national convention in Boulder, and it was known that he had returned from this meeting feeling "optimistic," which was highly unusual for him. Knops had taken over the editorship of the *Kaleidoscope* in December. He was Tim Slater's boss. He had known about the bombings before the government did. *Kaleidoscope* + SDS = Mark Knops = bombings.

McMillen had closed Knops's file some time back, having "failed to establish that Knops occupies a position of leadership or has any subversive influences in his background." That now appeared to have been a mistake, and on Friday morning he and a back-up agent went to see Knops at the latter's apartment on Frances Court, a row of cheap working-class dwellings two blocks from the Southeast Dorms.

Knops received the visitors in good humor after one of his neighbors, a retired engineer named Leslie, had cussed them out for parking in his space. "I don't need to see them," he said, waving away their badges. "I know who you are. I'm not going to talk to you," he announced matter-of-factly. "Neither will any member of my staff." However, Knops couldn't resist telling them that they were mistaken in detaining Tim Slater. "He's guilty of nothing in making his telephone call to Baraboo; he was just doing his job."

As the FBI chased after a phantom SDS link, knowledge of the real conspiracy of the Armstrong brothers and Lynn Schultz filtered out into the community. Lynn confided in friends at work; her roommate, Susan, strongly suspected something; Karl, of course, told

Scott; and Dwight bragged to Policronio De Venecia about his landing at Sauk Prairie ("Just greased it on!"). Karl berated Dwight when he found out that Poli knew. "I thought we had an agreement not to tell anyone!"

"Why shouldn't I? You told Scott," Dwight replied logically.

The week following the bombings, the joke going around Phi Sigma Kappa was that the Mad Bomber who was terrorizing the city was none other than Brother Karl. As the Phi Sigs bantered about it one evening in the dining room, Mark Dobberfuhl noticed that Karl wasn't taking the teasing well. "Hey, Tuffy," he said good-naturedly, "the thing I can't understand is why'd you bomb the Red Gym?" When Karl failed to respond in his usual clownish way, Dobberfuhl began to worry that something was seriously wrong. After dinner he was working next to Scott at the triple stainless-steel sink in the basement. Scott always listened to "Inna gadda da vida" while washing dishes, off in his own world. When the song ended, Dobber confided his suspicions. He was concerned that Karl might really be involved and had decided to distance himself from him just in case, he said.

Without admitting anything, Scott affirmed Dobberfuhl's anxiety. "I'm not going near Karl," he agreed. "I'm going straight."

Karl Armstrong found himself at an impasse. He had threatened to blow up the state Capitol and the campus if various demands were not met, and had boasted of having "pretty strong stuff." But lacking any firepower, he was forced to call the *Cardinal* and announce a week's "moratorium" on bombings while he awaited the university's reaction to his demands.

Lynn hoped he was serious about the moratorium and encouraged him to extend it, to retire. But Karl was feeling pressured by the media. "Look at them, they are your children," the *Cardinal* had commented in an editorial reiterating its support for the bombers. Then, on Friday, the paper came out with an editorial praising SDS for recognizing the difference between sabotage and terror. "Where damage was done in Madison it was against property, not the property of sod walls and thatched roofs housing young women and children. But property that by its existence consolidates and furthers the cause of terror."

Karl, bowing to the expectations of his admirers, tried to break into a chemical company not more than a hundred yards from the spot where Lynn had waited for him at Sauk Prairie Airport, but, as Lynn would later confide, the effort failed. *He had a glass cutter and he thought he could do a good job but found out after getting it through one layer of glass that* [it] *was not just one layer but several layers of glass and he just gave up the idea.* Then he had Lynn drive him to Devil's Lake, explaining on the way why it was necessary to keep fighting. *All he said was that things were wrong, like the government was running things wrong, and that they should be changed. Then if you have to do it with bloodshed and everything else, it should be done, but he would hope it wouldn't come to that. But like there would just be scare tactics.*

At Devil's Lake they took the South Shore Road past the campground, winding upward through the dense scrub forest along the east side. Everything was shrouded in white, utterly silent, motionless, and eerie. *He stopped where there's a small building located at the bottom of a little like gully thing, and when he got out, he explained that four or five years back, he remembered that they were doing some dynamiting in the park and he wanted to get into this building where he believed there might still be some explosives stored....* The site was, in fact, the ruins of an old labor camp and included a big doghouse that had been used for the pets of quarry workers staying in the area. He peeked through cracks in the weathered boards. There was nothing in the ghost camp but a family of rabbits. He returned to the car empty handed, and they drove back to Madison. Lynn was relieved. Luther Allison was playing at the Nitty Gritty that night; they could go out like a normal couple.

The proprietor of the Nitty Gritty, a local TV personality known as Marshall "The Marshall" Shapiro, greeted them by name as they arrived, and Karl exchanged pleasantries with Shapiro's wife Susan, a woman of striking personal appearance who was often seen in State Street marches. The Carol Doda look-alike and other groupies were performing in a mist of pheremones in front of the stage, suburban girls looking to expand their horizons after the show. Heroin dealers lounged against the back wall waiting for customers, alongside a "wanted" poster of George Croal. Karl saw someone he knew in a booth with a girl and stopped to say hello. "This is my friend Leo," he said to Lynn. They exchanged a few words and passed on.

Karl and Lynn had been drinking at the Nitty Gritty for about an hour when a stranger sat down across from them at one of the picnic tables. The stranger introduced himself as Pete Bobo, a rock promoter working on an outdoor concert to be staged on a farm in Poynette in April. He was short and sinewy, with a full beard; dark shoulder-length hair; and a long, narrow face with predatory gray-blue eyes. A scar creased one of his eyebrows, and each of his Pop-eye forearms was decorated with a tattoo. He reminded Karl of Charles Manson, but he had an ingratiating manner. Bobo said he was originally from Buffalo, but had come to Madison from Seattle, where he owned a bar and was involved in promoting local rockers such as Jimi Hendrix before Hendrix became a star. He claimed to be the original "freak" and an associate of counterculture legends like Jerry Garcia and Ken Kesey. He was known as "Mr. Sunshine" around Kesey's Pleasant Hill, Oregon, farm because he was always handing out acid tabs. He had signed The Grateful Dead to headline the Poynette event. Bobo also mentioned the *Kaleidoscope* and dropped Mark Knops's name as a friend. After chatting a while, he invited Karl and Lynn .to a party at his place, which was right around the corner. When Karl hesitated, he added that they had "chocolate mescaline." The three of them left around midnight.

It was a second-floor walk-up on West Johnson with very little furniture, bare walls, and dingy shades covering its windows. Besides Lynn and Karl, there were only two other couples: Pete Bobo and a friend of his and two hippie-looking women, whose names they didn't get. The women offered them mescaline, pronouncing it "mes-cah-leen," and they swallowed the drug. Karl remained in the living room with the two men while Lynn went into the kitchen with the women. Tattooed on Bobo's arm was a muddy, dark blue flower with the inscription "I have loved, I have suffered, now I hate." On his ring finger was a heavy signet ring with the initials R.V.M.C. and the phrase "MDA Bomb." A biker-type, Karl figured.

The next thing he knew, he was getting ready to leave. Lynn came back into the living room, and they said good-bye. Outside he asked her if her mind had blanked out for a while. "It seemed like mine was gone for half an hour," she said. Both of them wondered if they had taken some kind of "CIA drug."

On the morning of Thursday, January 15, Detective Charles Lulling got a tip from Elliott Marannis, executive editor of the *Capital Times,* on the New Year's Eve break-in at the U.S. Army office of

South Park. With Detective Kretschman's help, Lulling rounded up five suspects, who promptly confessed to the Park Street vandalism. They were boys and girls aged fourteen to seventeen, too young to be identified by name in the papers. It looked as though the *Daily Cardinal* was right: At least some of the saboteurs were children, and Madison kids at that. Lulling was in a bad mood when he arrived at the downtown parking ramp where he was meeting daily with Tom Lutz.

The release of Lutz to act as an informant was not working out quite as the detective had hoped. He had given Lutz fifty dollars so the boy could devote himself fully to gathering information, but the returns were so poor that Lulling's suspicions were aroused. Even after a meeting with an SDS heavy at McDonald's, Lutz had nothing to report that Lulling didn't already know. "I'll give you one more day to come up with a name leading to an arrest for the bombings," he warned.

Lutz had been stalling, lying, padding his reports with commonplaces, and in fact feeding what information he could glean about the investigation to those he was supposed to be spying on. From his vantage point, Lulling was an idiot to think that he would betray his brothers. "What if I don't?" he answered.

On Friday Lynn Schultz was working at her clerical job at Ray-O-Vac headquarters on East Washington when she received a call from Tom McMillen. McMillen identified himself as an FBI agent and told her that a license plate bearing the numbers K17-214 had been seen in the Capitol Court area on the night the Primate Lab was bombed. He happened to know that this was the license of a car that she was using at the time. "So what were you doing there?" he asked her.

Lynn had already concocted a story for just such an occasion and had even rehearsed it with one of her workmates, in whom she had also confided about her involvement with Karl Armstrong in the bombings. (By that time, at least three Ray-O-Vac employees knew or suspected her role.) *I told him that I was going to my ex-fiancé's house, and that I drove by and got out. He wasn't home, which is true, I did that. And I said that I had gone back to my apartment and made the same trip again so that's why they saw my car license several times that night. And I guess they believed it.* She also gave McMillen Karl Armstrong's name. Armstrong was her current boyfriend, she told the agent, and she was intending to pick him up from work after a quick visit with her ex.

McMillen heard the flat, broad-voweled accent of a native Wis-*can*-sen-ite. Her alibi was so goofy it rang true. As for Karl Armstrong, McMillen already had the name in his SDS control file, but apparently wasn't aware of it. It was at the top of a list of people who, at a meeting on November 12, had signed up for the bus trip to Washington on the fifteenth. A few years earlier McMillen might have blue-lined the name and had an index card made on him, but by the fall of 1969, the protesters had become too numerous. About 3,000 Wisconsin students had taken part in the March on Washington.

In any case McMillen was preoccupied with other matters. That same day the Resident Agency had sent Washington a report on the latest issue of the *Kaleidoscope,* digesting its front page stories on the arrest of Timothy Slater and the recent wave of bombings.

> The article [on the bombings] went on to say, "But their significance went far beyond the acts of physical resistance themselves. The bombings were PROPAGANDA BY THE DEED, acts of resistance designed to *create* a mass movement, NOT TO SUBSTITUTE FOR IT. The act or deed functions as a catalyst, not a substitute; it smashes through the prison-like routine of everyday life, breaks through weariness and resignation, electrifying people by its spectacular nature. Repeated acts catalyze people into motion, inspire and enthuse them, break down their inhibitions, unleash their imaginations, teasingly invite emulation on a mass scale. A mass movement emerges, advancing on its own momentum, breaking down the psychological and physical barriers of the old society."
>
> It is further noted that on page 3 of this issue there was printed illustrated instructions on various ways of making a "molotov cocktail."

If the *Kaleidoscope* article "catalyzed" anyone, it was the Internal Security section of the FBI, whose senior staff recognized the ideas of the Russian Nihilist philosopher Nechayev when they saw them. With remarkable swiftness the Stassi Shoe Store received new, "urgent" instructions.

In view of the above, you should immediately intensify your investigation of this publication to identify leaders and activists in accordance with existing Bureau instructions. Ascertain if individuals affiliated with this publication are engaged in a communal-type existence and whether members of this group advocate or have a propensity for violent acts to bring about a revolution.

McMillen had learned not to quarrel with instructions from Washington, so instead of checking out Lynn Schultz's phony alibi that afternoon, he hustled up an addition to Mark Knops's file, noting the name, height, weight, complexion, hair ("long, blond reddish-colored"), and age ("22") of Knops's girlfriend. He also wrote up his interview with Lynn Schultz.

Among the hundreds of reports that McMillen had prepared in his four years of monitoring dissidents, his account of his conversation with Lynn Schultz was one of the few with any bearing on a criminal investigation. It contained the essential clue to solving the mystery of the midnight bombings: the name of the midnight bomber himself. But the crucial document never made it to the conference table at the City-County Building, where task force representatives were still meeting every other day. On orders from Washington, the Resident Agency had rescinded its agreement to share reports, a practice that was against Director Hoover's rules. Thus the one significant lead in the case would remain buried until Major Case Inspector Joe Sullivan unearthed it nine months later.

On her lunch hour, Lynn drove over to Phi Sigma Kappa and filled Karl in on the call from McMillen. She expected him to be angry or at least upset, but not even the news that the FBI had his name bothered him. "You gave them a good story," he calmly remarked.

In Karl's possession was the latest issue of the *Kaleidoscope*, with its cover story, "Everybody's Looking." "The only people who are uptight about the actions are the pigs and local ruling class . . . everyone else is digging the scene," read the unsigned piece. Inside was a takeoff on the old Uncle Sam recruiting poster: "The New Year's Gang Wants You!" Karl pointed to it and said, "That's us." He added that he wasn't sure he liked the new nomenclature.

"They might be watching you," he warned. "We're going to have to stay apart for a few months."

The implications of what he was saying were not entirely clear to Lynn. Was he dumping her?

"Take a vacation," he went on. "See your parents. Get out of Madison for a while. Try to get it out of your mind."

The Milwaukee office of the FBI had sent Madison seven men to help with the investigation. One of their tasks was to interview people who, according to the plane's log, had ever flown the stolen Cessna 150. They talked to all the ROTC cadets, as well as to more experienced pilots, but never met with Dwight Armstrong. The same team conducted a sweep of State Street looking for the source of the large mayonnaise jars used in the aerial bombing. Starting at the Memorial Union loading dock, they worked east, eventually arriving at Gino's, where Karl Armstrong was employed and where he had obtained his jars. But the jars were commonplace, they discovered. The Memorial Student Union had them; the spaghetti houses on State had them; they even found them in the basement pantry of a dumpy Lake Street fraternity where Karl Armstrong happened to be a boarder.

The brothers of Phi Sigma Kappa were amused by the stories of FBI agents inspecting the mayonnaise jars in the pantry. "They were trying to get Teresa to admit that she was making bombs!" Mark Dobberfuhl joked. Teresa, fanning herself in an overstuffed lavender chair beside the huge, eight-burner gas stove in the basement kitchen, enjoyed the attention. "Ah tol' 'em I's makin' fo' hunnert dollahs a month. What do ah need bombs fo'?" she said in her Mississippi drawl. The brothers had a good laugh about that.

Dwight came by the frat that afternoon, and while he was talking to Karl in Room 8 he said, "Don't look now, but there's a guy in the Alumni Center watching us with a pair of binoculars." Very slowly Karl turned around, in time to see whoever it was putting something in his pocket. They began to talk seriously about getting out of town.

Early Friday evening, Karl and Scott were sitting in the TV room when Snakey Mathieson walked in with someone they had never seen before. Snakey introduced the stranger as "Mike," explaining that they had met at Burgerville. The visitor's shirt, tie, pants, belt, socks, and boots were black, and he carried a black briefcase. He identified himself as a former Army Intelligence officer and smuggler who used to avail himself of the diplomatic pouch to ship drugs out of Vietnam. Karl was impressed. *This guy might make a good recruit,* he thought.

But then Mike began to ask questions. From Snakey Mike had learned that Karl had books on explosives, a subject in which he was interested. Mike didn't know who was doing the New Year's Gang bombings, but the gang's M.O. was primitive, in his opinion. Instead of firebombs they should be using explosives, and not just fertilizer. "If they had their shit together, they'd be using plastique," he said.

Scott was shaking with fright. He excused himself, hurried upstairs, and began to pack. This "Mike" had to be a provocateur, he thought. Snakey must have gone to the cops.

The Man-in-Black disturbed even Karl's unnatural calm. *Like razor blades,* he thought afterward. The episode revived his suspicions of Snakey, who had been even nosier than usual since New Year's Eve, when he had sniffed out their kerosene-soiled clothing. On the morning of the Old Red Gym fire, he had knocked on the door of Room 8 at 6 A.M. and later asked Karl why he wasn't there. Dwight had told Poli about Badger Ordnance; had Poli told Snakey, who shared a room with him?

On Saturday Dwight got himself permanently banned from Phi Sigma Kappa. It was an unusual action taken by the house elders after an older law student named Ben Proctor, who served as a kind of house mother, accused Dwight of menacing him with a butcher knife. Dwight claimed that it was all a misunderstanding, that a carload of redneck kids was after him and that he had borrowed the knife from the kitchen to defend himself. But that account did not wash with Proctor's roommate, the ex-varsity tackle Saxum, who had pitched Dwight off the front porch.

On Sunday morning Karl told Biffer that he was going on an extended skiing trip to Colorado and wanted out of his contract. He gave his parents and Mira the same story—he and Scott were driving out to Denver together. He quit his job at Gino's on the pretext that he had been shortchanged on his last paycheck. He told the *Cardinal* that because of police surveillance and the lack of supplies, the Vanguards were taking a month off. He informed Dwight and Lynn that he was going to Minneapolis to lie low with his Uncle Paul, which was his actual plan.

Scott, too, was leaving Madison, and Karl hitched a ride, fastening a pair of floppy, second-hand skis to the ski rack on Scott's Beetle and squeezing his backpack into the trunk. It was snowing when they arrived at the Nelson farm five hours later. Di had not forgotten Karl's generosity when he left at the end of the previous summer and welcomed him warmly. Karl stashed his skis in the workshop where the boys had built their birdbaths. As he was walking back to the house, he noticed their unsold inventory clustered in the snow behind the ice house like a patch of outsized toadstools, a reminder of "the System" with which he was at war. He was tired. *And I felt that what I called the Winter Offensive against the Indochina War—I felt that that was enough. You know, I felt that I had risked my life enough.*

16

The Sauk Prairie
Substation

*I used to read the New Testament daily in prison. I found that
Christ never said anything against the so-called violent revolutionaries.*

—PHILIP BERRIGAN,
activist, for the defense

*Karl Armstrong wasn't part of a movement that was driven to
violence. Karl Armstrong was violence in this town.*

—DOUGLAS HAAG,
Wisconsin Assistant Attorney General, for the prosecution

He stoled [sic] for a living" was all that Lynn Schultz knew about
Karl's Uncle Paul, but there was more to him than that. Paul
Lester Armstrong was fifty-one, with thinning gray hair, olive skin,
and fingers stained yellow by a lifetime of smoking Camel straights.
He had the high forehead and the characteristic build (six foot four,
about 250 pounds) of Armstrong men, although his face was
slightly longer than his brother Donald's and his expression craftier.
He was quiet and subdued, perhaps the result of spending half his
life in prison. He suffered from narcolepsy, acquired, he believed,
from tending an illegal still as a teenager, and had to take a four-

hour nap every afternoon. Even then, he would sometimes drop his cards in the middle of a hand of gin, dead to the world. His fingers were covered with cigarette burns, and there were telltale black scars on every piece of furniture in his house. It was terrifying to be in a car driven by Paul Armstrong. He had a wife somewhere in Alaska, a wayward daughter, and a fourteen-year-old son, Vancc, destined to play horseshoes with him in the state pen. But as long as he had a cigarette and a cup of coffee, his friends said, Paul Armstrong was alright.

He lived in a rented shanty in the shadow of grain elevators at 2828 Twelfth Avenue South, not one of Minneapolis's better addresses. It was an easy walk to Franklin Avenue, where he worked off and on at a place called Johnny's Cafe. Half the neighborhood was Native American, the rest white trash, with a sprinkling of activists, such as Russell Means of the American Indian Movement, and the former University of Wisconsin firebrand Evan Stark, who had moved there after Dow Day to start a campaign against the Honeywell Corporation, a defense contractor headquartered in Minneapolis.

A pair of men shared the house with Paul. The younger of the two, Jeff Shearer, a postman, had sunken cheeks, acne scars along his pointed jaw, and a torn pupil in one eye and limped along on his mail route like a character from *Night of the Living Dead*. The other, Malcolm "Max" Sliter, was sixty, tall, thin, with crooked teeth, and shifty eyes, and carried a loaded revolver in his waistband at the small of his back. Vance Armstrong was an occasional houseguest.

Paul Armstrong was an unlettered but likable man with a reputation for generosity, although the things he gave away rarely belonged to him. Paul was a sort of poor man's takeover artist, dismantling the industrial infrastructure and selling it off piecemeal. Just about anything metal—brass and copper fittings, wire, manhole covers—was Paul's game. He would break the material up and sell it to junkyards by the hundred weight. It was backbreaking work that sometimes kept him up all night, but Paul Armstrong wasn't tempted to get a regular job. "I never paid taxes in my life," he often boasted.

His best-known exploit was his Mafia heist, the only big score of his career. In spring 1969 he had broken into a Mob house (at least, Paul claimed it belonged to the Mob) and carried off the safe, peeling it in his basement with a hammer and chisel. It had taken him several days, but when it came to safecracking, Paul Armstrong was a patient man. Inside he had found jewelry, furs, and $93,000 in cash. "Jeff, this is what I've been waitin' for all my life," he informed his housemate. He asked Shearer to help him dispose of the furs and jewelry, which could be easily traced, he said. Shearer protested this waste, but Armstrong blithely tossed the valuables into the Mississippi. "It could mean your life," he told Shearer.

Paul Armstrong wasn't comfortable having a lot of money around. He went to Madison and gave Donald $10,000, claiming he had hit it lucky on the numbers, and stopped in Baraboo on the way back to drop another ten grand on Elsie and Charlie, an aunt and uncle who had taken Don in for a while when he was a teenager. He handed out 150 Easter baskets full of candy, $700 worth, to neighborhood kids and bought a brand-new Dodge RT for himself; a Buick Riviera for Max Sliter (who, on Franklin Avenue, was considered undeserving of such beneficence); and an old, black Cadillac hearse for his friend Frank Dunn, a man almost as big as himself who sometimes gave him a hand when there was a safe to be carried. Paul thought the hearse would be useful for "goose-hunting" excursions up north.

At the Veterans of Foreign Wars (VFW) Bingo Parlor on Franklin, one of his favorite haunts, Paul went on a binge, playing dozens of cards at once, dropping chips without thought to where they landed, losing hundreds of dollars a night. Bums clustered around him like pigeons after bread crumbs, drawn by rumors that he was handing out $500 and $1,000 bills. Like a one-man welfare agency Paul dispensed hand-outs to everyone who asked. The borrowers always promised to repay him by a certain date, but, of course, they didn't, which bothered Max. "Why do you let 'em chump you like that?" he asked. Paul shrugged it off. "Aw, I don't give a shit," he said.

With Sliter he went to Las Vegas and squandered the balance of his fortune in a matter of days. By the time Karl Armstrong arrived in January 1970, there was nothing left of the loot but the RT, the Riviera, and the hearse.

Rain was falling when Karl drove into Minneapolis. The drops froze where they landed, coating the city in ice. Telephone and power lines and tree limbs sagged and broke under the weight; schools

closed, cars skidded all over the streets, and body shops were turning down business. Snow fell for days afterward, laying down such a
thick blanket that, in the countryside, nearly all the pheasants died
and famished deer fell prey to marauding wolves. Karl weathered
the storm on Paul's sofa, which stood next to the brown enamel oil
stove in the living room. "We're all family," Paul said, introducing
him to Vance, to Paul's girlfriend Jolinda Orr, to Jeff and Max, to
the landlord Milen Walker and Walker's son Lonnie Ross Walker,
and to a coterie of young women who provided housecleaning and
other personal services to Paul in exchange for drugs.

As Karl soon discovered his uncle's place was the scene of a
modern-day adult version of *Oliver Twist* where young men and
women came and went at all hours, most of them employed in
Franklin Avenue's primary industry: theft. The thieves called themselves "boosters" and had "booster pockets" sewn into their over-
coats that were big enough to carry chainsaws. They would go off to
work every day like responsible citizens and return loaded with
goods from the Twin Cities' new shopping centers (which had not
yet caught on to the fact that they were being systematically
robbed). There were fifteen or twenty of them in the group around
Uncle Paul, each with his own specialty. "Patrolman Dan" spent his
days along the Mississippi stealing from one loading dock after
another; John Rancone, called "the Nazi" because of his swastika
tattoos, stole record albums and cigarettes; Mahfood, an Arab with
an angular, pitted face and a nasty temper, specialized in electronics. You could order anything you wanted—a new stereo system, a
camera, a portable TV or radio—and Mahfood would have it the
next afternoon.

The boosters were skilled and persistent thieves, averaging a
thousand dollars a day each in retail merchandise. They spent their
earnings on heroin, to which most of them were addicted. Paul's
companion Jolinda Orr, a homely, forty-year-old Native American
woman, was also an addict. She kept a needle hanging over the
bathtub at Paul's house and would soak in the tub for eight or nine
hours at a stretch, so blissed out that she was unaware of the water's
growing cold.

Scott Nelson, up for a visit on the assumption that Karl had given
up his criminal exploits, was shocked by Karl's surroundings. Boosters paraded in the front door with whole racks of department-store
finery. An addict fondled an empty revolver in one of the bed-

rooms, clicking off empty rounds at anyone who walked by. "This is where you come to lie low?" Scott said sarcastically. Karl admitted that he was a little nervous about the arrangement, but told Scott he saw it as a "learning experience" and a chance to study real-life "sociology." And in any case, he assured his friend, none of them knew about his other life.

Despite the incessant traffic in stolen goods and drugs, the atmosphere in the house was surprisingly calm. Unlike Donald, Paul never raised his voice, never criticized, never demanded anything. Paul and Max abstained from drugs, and Paul from liquor as well. Karl also avoided the pharmaceuticals with which the kitchen cupboards were stocked, but one day he tried methadone in liquid form and floated around for a whole afternoon. Later he confessed to Dwight that it was the best drug he'd ever had.

Being Paul Armstrong's nephew gave Karl instant entrée at Johnny's Cafe, the Sparkle, the VFW Bingo Parlor, and all the other Franklin Avenue dives, and he soon earned a reputation for benevolence in his own right, as a result of a favor rendered to Max Sliter's wife, Rickie. Most of the time Max kept his distance from Rickie, as well as from their four children, preferring to spend his nights at Paul's with a bevy of obese young women who apparently found him irresistible. (Although Sliter wasn't liked on the avenue, it was begrudgingly acknowledged that he was well endowed.) Rickie was devoted to Max, despite his open infidelities, and one day, at his behest, she pawned her wedding ring. Karl, who found Max's greed despicable, took Rickie to the pawnshop and got the ring back, putting up his own money. Rickie worshipped Karl after that, and word of his deed traveled the length of the avenue. "Just like his uncle," people began to say of him.

As Karl got to know Uncle Paul, he acquired a new perspective on his roots. Karl had never heard his grandfather Alvah Armstrong mentioned except in terms of opprobrium. In Don's portrayal Alvah was a "sleazeball" and a bigamist who had had at least four wives, including one or two he left behind in the Philippines at the end of World War I. All his adult life Alvah had hung around VFW halls acting like a veteran, Don said, when in fact Alvah had deserted near the end of the fighting to chase after a girl. Alvah was the Bad Armstrong of his generation; his brother Roy, sheriff of Valley Junction, the Good.

Uncle Paul had a more sympathetic view of Alvah. While Don was living with his grandmother Ann Rector Armstrong, Paul had been sent to live with Father Flannigan at Boy's Town in Nebraska, where he had become Flannigan's garden boy and a favorite of the famous priest. But when he reached adolescence, he had run away to look for Alvah, who, as it happened, was living nearby in Omaha. It was the heyday of Prohibition, and by then Alvah was a kingpin in the Omaha whiskey industry, running liquor to Al Capone and the Chicago Mob. Alvah found Paul a place to stay in the best establishment he could think of for a thirteen-year-old boy: a brothel. "I never slept alone," Paul liked to say.

Alvah had put Paul to work in the stills, where the sour mash made him sick and where he acquired his lifelong aversion to liquor (and perhaps, as he suspected, his narcolepsy). When Prohibition ended, the two of them returned to Wisconsin, where they made their living robbing banks, going from one town to the next, staying just ahead of the law, occasionally even getting shot at. One winter, Paul said, he and Alvah had driven down to Baraboo to visit their relatives Elsie and Charlie and found the house burned down, the family living in the chicken coop, too proud to ask for help. Paul and Alvah had gone straight into town and robbed a mercantile store; resupplied Elsie and Charlie with warm clothes, bedding, and sundries; and skipped town.

In Paul's memory, at least, Alvah was no ordinary con, but a man who redistributed wealth, taking from the haves and giving to the have-nots. And by and large, that was how Paul Armstrong himself was thought of on Franklin Avenue. The thieves he did business with knew his rule-of-thumb: "You never rob a Mom and Pop; Dayton's, McDonald's, OK."

In the first week of February Karl got a job as a lathe operator on the graveyard shift at Hobart-Federal, a small plant that made components for food slicers. His mind was elsewhere, however. Every few days the Minneapolis papers carried news of some new incident in Wisconsin: a fire in the Naval Armory in Madison, the firebombing of ROTC facilities at the University of Wisconsin–Milwaukee campus, the burning of the historic Old Main building at Whitewater State University. On February 12, after a rousing speech in the Great Hall by Chicago Eight defendants Jerry Rubin and John Froines, a demonstration of unprecedented violence, the so-called "G.E. strike," shook the isthmus.

Karl had to get back. As soon as he got off work Saturday morning, the fourteenth of February, he borrowed Frank Dunn's hearse and drove to Madison. Lynn had a surprise for him, a brand-new sporty little Fiat roadster called a Spyder, blue with black trim, with large, round amber fog lights. She was so proud of it that she had driven it out to Hintze Road to show it to Dwight.

Karl wanted to see the riot damage, so Lynn took him for a drive. Originally the "strike" had been directed against General Electric, a military contractor conducting job interviews on campus, but it had turned into a general rampage. Physical-plant employees were still at work boarding up windows in Army Math, T-16, and the Old Red Gym. Rennebohm's, the University Book Store, and Kroger's Grocery Store had also been hit, along with such unlikely targets as the Yarn Barn and No Hassel, the latter owned by Eddie Elson, a regular *Kaleidoscope* advertiser and movement sympathizer. According to the newspapers, the riot had left Madison glass companies $25,000 richer. And everywhere they had attacked, the militants had left their battle-cry spray-painted on walls and fences: "New Year's Gang—Live Like Them!"

At the Nitty Gritty Karl and Lynn ran into Policronio De Venecia, whose Jesus hair was shorn. Poli explained that he had been arrested in a demonstration on Charter Street and given an involuntary "Soglin cut" in jail.

Karl also worked in a visit with Gino, who seemed to have forgiven him for quitting, and joked that he'd had to hire two people to replace Karl. Karl remarked on the fact that Gino's plate glass was intact. Gino said that he'd been lucky; he didn't think his windows would make it through the winter.

"Don't worry, nobody's going to break your windows," Karl assured him. Something in the way he said it, "like he was somebody," made an impression on the little Sicilian. Although many more State Street windows would be broken in the months ahead, Gino's were passed over, and he would always believe that it was thanks to Karl Armstrong.

On his way back to Minneapolis Karl drove toward Sauk City and turned right, following State Highway 78 along the north bank of the Wisconsin River. He had snow-camped in the area when he was an Eagle Scout. A few miles past Prairie du Sac he came to the turnoff for the Sauk Prairie hydroelectric substation, marked by a

"Wisconsin Power & Light" sign, and took the single-lane blacktop road down to the river. The power plant was adjacent to a low, wide dam behind which was the long reservoir called Lake Wisconsin. At that time of year the dam's sluices were dry, and everything was still in its winter carapace of ice. He could see the pylons marching straight across thc snow-white plains to Badger Ordnance Works, the biggest user of the substation's output. If one could interrupt service from Wisconsin Power and Light, Karl believed, unaware of Badger's emergency generators, the war plant would be out of business.

Other than Paul, Karl told no one in Minneapolis about the New Year's Gang. But because Paul loved a good story, he could not resist telling Max and Jeff, who told friends of theirs. Even Paul's ex-wife, with whom he was not on good terms, knew about Karl's exploits. Among the boosters there were bonafide neo-Nazis who did not approve of Karl's politics, but others considered him a true champion of the people.

Karl had little idea of the impression he had made on the Franklin Avenue crowd. Ambling around Paul's kitchen calculating blast parameters in a small notebook, he soon acquired the reputation of a mathematical genius. Jeff Shearer, a regular valium user, marveled that anyone could do arithmetic *standing up*. When Karl talked about the war, it was to the boosters' ears like "soft music playing," and they would fall asleep. But Karl would shock them awake with a *pronunciamento:* "This has got to be done!" The boosters would nod, waiting to hear what he would say next. They knew that he was doing something of great importance because he kept going off to the Franklin Avenue Library, and not just to get warm. "He is getting what he needs," they would say knowingly, as though Karl were a renowned philosopher taking a sabbatical in their midst. "He has come to Minneapolis to get what he needs."

Max Sliter had spent a fair portion of his adult life in jail. He had met Paul Armstrong in Leavenworth, and they had become partners in crime. On the avenue it was said that Max was nothing but talk, that he was "the opposite" of Paul. He showed concern for others, yet even Paul knew he was insincere. But Paul chose to ignore Max's faults and to focus on his virtues. Max was good at setups; he could watch a target for months. They schemed together constantly, two aging cons who shared, if nothing else, memories of another era.

Karl did not trust Sliter, but he depended on him because Max was familiar with dynamite. After a day immersed in the *Encyclopaedia Britannica* at the Franklin Avenue Library, Karl had decided that it was TNT he would use to take out the Sauk Prairie transformers.

"What do you want with dynamite?" Max asked bluntly when Karl approached him about it.

Karl said that he had "a piece of property somewhere" and wanted to "blow some stumps."

As a con Max had a good ear for lies. Paul had told him all about the Badger Ordnance attempt, and he surmised that Karl was up to something. "You're going to get your fuckin' head blown off," he warned.

The next day Karl was on him again. "Come on, let's go!" he said in a commanding voice. "You owe me, Max."

Reflecting on those words for a moment, it occurred to Sliter that Karl was offering to forgive the debt on Rickie's ring in exchange for a ride. As one who hated to repay debts and almost never did, this struck Sliter as a bargain. They hopped into the Riviera and drove out to Rosemount, a Minneapolis suburb where Max had bought dynamite previously, only to discover that the store no longer stocked it. They were directed to another outlet in New Brighton, northeast of the city. "This is the place. Hurry up now," Max advised, when they had arrived.

Karl demurred. "I have this beard on. They might object because I look like a hippie."

"Ain't no reason for that," Max said crossly. "Come on!" They went in together, and Max asked for the twelve sticks of dynamite and four electric blasting caps that Karl wanted. The proprietor brought out thirteen sticks. It was obvious that the man had miscounted, but neither Max nor Karl corrected him. The bill came to less than five dollars.

When Karl returned to Madison a week later, his explosives riding in the back of the hearse, the *Kaleidoscope* had just come out with its own verdict on the trashing: "A beautiful military operation," the paper called it, which "saw the emergence of a real 'red army,' a hardcore fighting force of students, street people and high school

kids ... women as well as men." The paper also carried an interesting tidbit about the ongoing law-enforcement investigation: A
youth named Tom Lutz had told Mark Knops that he had been
released from jail to find the New Year's Gang and that Detective
Charles Lulling had threatened to put him "at the bottom of the
lake" if he didn't come through. According to Lutz, he'd given the
cop nothing but old information.

Karl concluded that the investigators were on the wrong track
and serenely drove about the city picking up odds and ends for his
bomb. When he had all the components, he drove over to Lynn's.
Susan Baldie had moved out in a rage, and Schultz now had the
Lake Monona apartment to herself. *It was the third weekend of
February and he came to my house and shortly after he got there, he
went back out to his uncle's car and came back with a paper bag in
which he had approximately 10 sticks of dynamite, which he brought
into my bedroom and he sat down and proceeded to tape together
these pieces of dynamite.*

Also in the bag were a rolling pin, pie tins, and a roll of wire of
the sort used in automobile ignition systems. Karl must have sensed
Lynn's disappointment that there was nothing in the bag for her.
"Spent my whole paycheck on the revolution," he said sheepishly.
He coiled a length of wire around the rolling pin and attached pie
tins to the ends to hold the wire in place. "I don't know how else to
do it," he said defensively when he noticed Lynn staring at him. "It
may look like a Mickey Mouse arrangement, but I think it'll work."

The dynamite lay strewn like pick-up-sticks where Karl had
tossed it on the bed. "Hand me the duct tape," he told Lynn. Karl
finished binding the sticks together, overlooking the strands of hair
that had somehow become entwined in the TNT.

*So this was placed in the back of my car and he explained his
intention was to go up to Sauk Prairie, the electrical power plant
that's up there near Badger Ordnance, and his intention was to go up
and try to put as much of it as he possibly could out of commission
so that Badger Ordnance would be without power.*

They went to the Nitty Gritty for something to eat, and then,
about 10 P.M., made the familiar trek out Highway 12. It had been
an exceptionally warm, sunny day, and the stalagmites of dirty snow
along the roads had shrunk. Now the temperature was rapidly
falling, and a wash of stars lit the cloudless sky. Karl entertained
Lynn with stories of Paul Armstrong and his criminal exploits, and

she was struck by how proud he was of his uncle.

It was a little after eleven when they reached the dam. A vapor lamp illuminated the transformer yard, and an orange glow came from the windows of the brick power plant next to it. Lights were also on in a caretaker's house back in the woods. Karl told Lynn to move the car back along the access road to a point where it could not be seen from the power plant and to wait. Then, from one of his sacks, he removed a used Delco twelve-volt car battery he had purchased at a Minneapolis service station and lugged it to the top of a steep, slippery bank overlooking the yard. He left it at the edge and hurried back down.

From that point on his plan began to go awry. The fence was topped by barbed wire, and he cut his hand climbing over. He placed the dynamite under a transformer, but discovered that he had left his electrical tape, which he needed to hold the caps in place, in the car. He tried folding the dynamite stick's wax paper covering over the cap to hold it in place, but his hands were bloody and numb from the cold, and he couldn't see what he was doing in the dim light of the vapor lamp. Finally he got the caps on and was about to connect them to the wire from his reel when he noticed, from his angle below a transformer, a pair of legs standing at the door of the plant. Someone was watching him. He jumped to his feet, smiling inanely. The startled employee turned and hurried inside. Karl left the unfinished bomb where it was; scrambled over the fence, cutting himself again on the barbed wire; and ran to the car, expecting Lynn to be in the driver's seat with the motor running.

I sat there for I don't know how long but I moved over on the passenger side because I was very nervous and I only had the car for about a month but in that time well, it was the first time I had learned to drive a stick shift and I knew that as scared as I was I didn't think I would be able to drive the car you know, like I should, so he came running down the hill and he came to get in the passenger's side and I was there and I don't know what he said but some word of great displeasure that I wasn't there where I was supposed to be.

Karl could hear a car coming and he hurried to the driver's side and opened the door.

And I had left the seat up too close and he couldn't get in and, by that time someone was coming down the hill.

The oncoming car passed by them, and they raced away, taking sideroads east to I-94 and hurrying back to Madison on the inter-

state. Karl was certain he had left bloody fingerprints on the dynamite and that the car had been identified.

We went back to my apartment and when we got out of the car the
first thing he did was hit me because of the fact that I hadn't done as I
was told to and he made some remark as to the effect that I didn't do
anything that he told me to and so once we walked down to the
house, I told him that I wanted no part of anything he did anymore
and that he cease calling me or seeing me and so then he picked up
his things and left.

Karl would recall the parting a little differently; in any case, it
was then that the New Year's Gang, in its original form, came to an
end.

17

Primacord

*I suppose if Karl felt firmly committed to Zero Population
Growth he'd think he was morally justified in playing King
Herod, too.*
—MICHAEL ZALESKI,
Wisconsin Assistant Attorney General, for the prosecution

*And then after all the firing was over we opened up the bus,
and there were 36 children in it. And 24 of them were dead.*
—JOHN NAVEAU,
Vietnam veteran, for the defense

The substation attempt yielded investigators many clues, but
nothing conclusive. The dynamite was DuPont Red Cross Extra
Strength, a commonplace, over-the-counter blasting agent. The hair
follicles found among the sticks could confirm the identity of a suspect, but only if a suspect were found. The same was true of the
bloody fingerprint left on a pie tin; the technology did not yet exist
to do a comparison search of all prints on record in Wisconsin. A
paper shopping bag recovered at the scene bore the words
CROWN DUPLEX and the serial number A.20.6.C. Tom
Kretschman, the county sedition man, traced it to Copp's Depart-

ment Store on Madison's East Side, where he discovered a stock of rolling pins exactly like the one found at the plant, an Ekco Ball with gold-flecked white plastic handles and ball bearings to make it work smoothly. According to store records two had been sold, at the discount price of $1.79, the week before the bombing. Kretschman requested that the manager ask his salesgirls if they remembered who had bought them. "It won't be easy," the man replied. "A lot of hippies patronize this store."

Neither the power-plant operator, who had first spotted the intruder, nor the pitman who was sent to check him out got a good look at Karl. The arriving graveyard-shift workers described Lynn's blue-and-black Spyder as a blue-and-white Triumph. On the Sunday in question the Madison Sports Car Club had held a rally in Prairie du Sac, and there had been almost three dozen sports cars in the area, several of them Triumphs, Kretschman discovered. Car Club spokesmen were indignant at the suggestion that one of their members might be implicated in a bombing.

Sauk County deputies immediately called Badger Ordnance Works to alert them to what appeared to be an attempt to cut off their external power supply. Olin Corporation increased the already-heavy patrols around the plant's perimeter. On Tuesday, the *Daily Cardinal* confirmed investigators' suspicions of the motive of the bombing:

> Mark Knops of *Madison Kaleidoscope* said that he received a phone call around 2 A.M. Monday from a spokesman for the "Vanguard of the Revolution" stating that the group had attempted to blow up the substation but were observed.
>
> Knops said the spokesman told him that the attempt was the beginning of a "second offensive" and that the organization would "retaliate for the arrest of Jim Rowen" and was in support of the TAA in its dealings with the University. The spokesman also said that there would be future attacks "even at the cost of high personal risk."
>
> Knops said the phone call was "definitely from the New Year's Gang."

After two months the New Year's Gang investigation was stalled. Pressure for a break in the case was so great that State Fire Marshal William Rossiter submitted an internal report attempting to blunt criticism of the "apparent lack of progress." He pointed to the intelligence failures, especially the paucity of information about SDS and the Black Panthers, still everyone's favorite suspects. "Some persons supposedly furnishing information turned out to be psychopaths who apparently enjoyed the sense of importance from the attention they received," he observed in an oblique reference to the unreliable Mr. Lutz. But he reserved his most biting remarks for the FBI and its refusal to share reports. "Despite this, all agencies shared their findings with the FBI," he noted with asperity.

Baxtrum maintained that the Resident Agency had nothing to share and that he was just as frustrated as was everyone else. Even with the addition of Tom Madden, a security specialist from Pittsburgh, to its staff, the Stassi Shoe Store's sedition men were each carrying upward of 150 cases, about three times what the bureau normally would have considered heavy. Equally overburdened was the Sabotage Desk in Washington, where George Menzel was opening twenty to thirty cases a day. When he had started on the job in mid-1968, Menzel had a single two-drawer filing cabinet to contend with. Now he had an entire wall of filing cabinets, all of their contents concerned with sabotage.

And yet for all the criminal activity going on, the instructions issued by Washington seemed to reflect the Hoover bureau's habitual preoccupation with politics. Go after *Cardinal* writer Jim Rowen, Washington advised. Madison obliged, opening a file under the caption "JAMES ROWEN, SECURITY MATTER—SDS." The first report anticipated White House interest in the subject of Rowen's relationship to a possible challenger to President Nixon:

> Rowen is married to the former Susan McGovern, one of the senator's four daughters. They reside in a $45-a-month one-room apartment near the Wisconsin campus. Rowen told a newsman recently he did not like being singled out as McGovern's son-in-law. "I'm a radical, a researcher, a journalist and a socialist," he said. "I'm a lot of things before I'm Senator McGovern's son-in-law. Every time I see it in print it gets me mad."

Besides monitoring Rowen, Madison agents busied themselves with the stakeout of the Machtinger twins, sisters of a Weather Underground figure. Michael Meeropol, a university student and well-known Red Diaper Baby whose parents, Julius and Ethel

Rosenberg, had been executed as Soviet spies, was a frequent visitor, increasing the FBI's interest in the house, a shabby tenement on busy East Johnson Avenue, not far from Tenney Park. The Resident Agency had even rented a room across the street. Special Agent Tom McMillen was spending so much time there that he had forgotten about following up on his interview with Lynn Schultz.

The spy Duroc, after his expulsion from SDS, had been assigned to the trial of the Chicago Eight (whose conviction had sparked riots all over the country). Upon his return to Madison, Baxtrum persuaded the MPD to reassign him to the Young Socialist Alliance, contending that it would be a good listening post even if YSA itself wasn't up to much. As for the Trot's non-violent line, it was Baxtrum's view that they were "saving it for the revolution." YSA welcomed the recruit even knowing that he had been expelled by SDS. (Like Christians, they believed that any soul could be saved.) And so Duroc began to file detailed reports on the Young Socialists, one of the few campus political groups that kept minutes of its meetings.

On Monday, March 2, Fred Harvey Harrington made the mile run to the Capitol for a meeting of the governor's education cabinet. Ever the industrious Yankee, he used the down time to answer mail, creating a small cyclone of flying paper in the back seat of his chauffeured sedan. It was often nasty stuff. "If you wonder why Wisconsin alumni are unwilling to enroll their children at Madison," a class-of-'41 alumnus complained huffily, "why the legislature passes restrictive laws, why attendance at a Founder's Day dinner, contributions to the U.W. Foundation and continuance of membership in the Alumni Association lack appeal, just take a look at the literally rotten image the university presents to its concerned and would-be faithful alumni. It's high time to clean house at Wisconsin, beginning at the very top!"

Vice President Taylor attached the contribution record of each complaining alumnus. Typical was that of a Mr. K———, class of '09:

   1962: $1,000, $350, $1,380
   1963: $160
   1964: $831
   1965: $700, $50, $1,000
   1966: $1,338

1967: 0
1968: 0
1969: 0

After Dow Day, it had been like falling off a cliff.

Warren Knowles was a moderate Republican who groomed himself like an English lord and had a voice like Liberace. That morning, he was unusually tart. The lack of clues in the firebombings was unbelievable, he told Harrington. Was the university really doing everything it could to aid the investigators?

Harrington explained that the calculated hit-and-run violence of the terrorists was harder to deal with than the organized protests of three years ago. In the university's defense he added that two students caught throwing Molotov cocktails during the Mifflin Street Block Party riot were "no longer with us."

Knowles was not satisfied. A few days later, at their monthly board meeting, the regents censured Harrington for the way troublemakers were being handled on the Madison campus and voted to hire their own prosecutor and staff to discipline the student body. Thanks to higher tuition, Regent Gelatt noted approvingly, out-of-state requests for admission were down 50 percent. Harrington retreated to his library of books on Jesus Christ. It was silly to cut out-of-state enrollments, he thought. The bright kids, the activists, the Jews, would still get in. Most likely it was the athletic program that would suffer.

Pete Bobo's real name was Peter O'Branovich. The initials R.V.M.C. on his signet ring stood for Road Vultures Motorcycle Club, a Buffalo, New York biker gang. The "MDA bomb" pictured on the ring referred to a popular new "love drug" manufactured in Miffland. His police record was like a seismic printout of his movements across the country: larceny in Erie, Pennsylvania; grand larceny in Los Angeles; car theft in Wheeling, West Virginia, and in Cleveland; disorderly conduct in San Antonio; and morals, marijuana, and firearms violations in his hometown of Buffalo. In a tavern brawl two years earlier, he had cut up a man's face with broken glass. One of his business associates considered him psychotic, and yet he had a very convincing way about him. "He is the only person I ever encountered who could sell you suicide and you would feel you got a deal," said the associate.

Bobo had invited a young Wisconsin man, Sandy Nelson, to join his promotional firm, Golden Freek Enterprises. Nelson was a product of the Green Bay State Reformatory who had been arrested for marijuana possession, cohabitation, reckless use of a firearm, and theft. The two of them had raised the $60,000 they needed to launch the Poynette festival by selling hot-dog rights and other concessions. Local authorities were none too happy about two such characters putting on a rock festival in God's Own Country.

At the end of the first week in March, the business partners found themselves in a bit of a jam. They had just been to the Stage Door to see a new buddy film, *Butch Cassidy and the Sundance Kid.* When they left the theater, Nelson found a message on his car: "Do not go home, the police are looking for you." It was from the attorney for Golden Freek Enterprises, Jack Van Metre. Nelson called Van Metre from the bar. "Get lost, stay out of sight for tonight, and contact me in the morning," Van Metre advised him. A girlfriend whom Nelson had just dumped was in the hospital suffering from an overdose of some kind of barbiturate. The cops wanted to know where she had gotten it.

While Nelson was on the phone Bobo noticed Lynn Schultz at a table. The two of them sat down with her, and Bobo introduced Sandy Nelson. "The cops are looking for us; we can't go home," Nelson said. It was all because of Poynette, they explained. Poynette was to be the first major rock festival in the Midwest, and the locals were freaked out.

Nelson struck Lynn as a nice guy. He was wearing an army field jacket just like Karl's, but had more of a party-animal aura. There was an instant chemistry between them, and he obviously needed her help. Since Susan had moved out, she had an extra bedroom. "Sure, come on over to my place," she said. As for Pete Bobo and his "CIA drug," she apparently concluded that she and Karl had been mistaken.

On Saturday, the fourteenth of March, Karl Armstrong borrowed Paul's Dodge RT, picked up Scott Nelson in River Falls, and after assuring Scott that he had no bombs in the trunk, drove to Madison for the weekend. The RT was a road monster with fat tires, racing scoops, a Hurst power train, and a 440-cubic-inch engine, the biggest street-legal machine in the United States. He opened it up on the long, straight stretch between Menomonie and Eau Claire, reaching a speed of 140 before easing off. "Could've gone 150," Scott sniffed.

It was after dark when they arrived in Madison. Karl dropped Scott off at Phi Sigma Kappa and went over to the Memorial Student Union to buy the latest issue of the *Kaleidoscope*. The front page bore the headline, "The New Year's Gang Strikes Again." The story diverted attention from the botched attempt on the power plant to the *Capital Times'* decision not to print the New Year's Gang's statement after Mark Knops had passed it to the daily's editor. "The CRAP TIMES better watch out. The gang might pay it a visit," the *Kaleidoscope* warned.

Karl had resolved to retire from the sabotage business once and for all and joked about it with Scott. "We're the gang that couldn't shoot straight," he said. But now he had second thoughts. He went over to the Nitty Gritty looking for Lynn. The great Chicago bluesman Luther Allison was back in town, and the bar was crowded. The long-anticipated strike of the Teaching Assistants Association (TAA) was set to begin on Monday, and students were celebrating the premature arrival of spring break. The strike was "a crucial step towards ending class differences," according to the *Daily Cardinal,* and anybody who was even thinking of going to class was a "scab."

Lynn saw him come in. "Oh, no, Karl Armstrong," she said to her new friend Sandy Nelson, their first night out together. Karl spotted her and shuffled over.

"Hi, Lynn," he said cheerfully, as if nothing had happened. He told Lynn he wanted her to come out into the parking lot with him because he had a few things to discuss with her. It was bitterly cold outside, the kind of mid-March weather that makes Midwesterners fall for land-in-Florida schemes. They crossed the street and stood shivering in the parking lot next to Witte Hall. *And what he wanted to know was if I wanted to do anything else and I said no and he tried to convince me why I should really see him and I should be a part of whatever he wanted to do and I told him no and I ceased wanting him to be even a friend.*

According to Lynn, Karl did not take the rejection at all well. *And at that time he said that we are the people to get the Revolution together and to keep the Revolution together and you couldn't break away from it, so we better stay quiet and you better not say anything to anybody or you're going to be in a lot of trouble.*

She was alone when she returned to the bar. "What was that all about?" Sandy Nelson asked. Lynn told him as much as she felt a new boyfriend should know.

Karl drove over to Mira's house looking for Dwight. He wanted to talk to Dwight about coming back to Minneapolis with him. Mira had been wrapping a birthday present for a nephew. Dwight was staying with Policronio De Venecia in Milwaukee; Poli had gotten a job there, she said.

Karl tried to pick a fight with her, telling her about a group "out East" (she didn't know whether he was talking about the East Coast or the Orient) that was taking drugs as part of its liturgy, and it made them "closer to God." "You should try it," he said.

Mira actually found the thought tempting. It wasn't easy living without alcohol. Bill would often thrust a drink at her after work. "C'mon, you're no fun anymore. Can't you even have a glass of wine?" She wondered what the new campus drugs were like and whether they might not help her at the altar call. "When you know that God loves you, you don't need drugs," she answered Karl, pulling herself together.

The Assembly of God service the next morning followed the charismatic formula, heavy on choir, piano, and organ. The women of the congregation dressed like fashion models, inspired by the pastor's wife, who was, in fact, a former model. Pastor Mark Carter was a man of prominent features, with a deep, powerful voice. His sermon was about Joseph, how he was sold into slavery and then became Pharoah's confidant because he could interpret dreams. The message was to make the most of your misfortune, but the words gave Mira no peace. She had lost Karl, she thought, remembering the black look in his eyes the night before. She did not answer the altar call when the service ended, but went straight outside and leaned against one of the pillars supporting the porch. She felt such a pain in her chest that she could scarcely breathe. As the congregation filed out, several women came up to see what was wrong with her.

"My brothers," she said falteringly. "They are into something. I don't know what."

The women led her back inside, and they all knelt at the rail and prayed. "Lord, save my brothers," Mira said. "God, give Karl a sign that You are real." She repeated the words over and over. "God, don't let Karl do drugs. God, show Karl Your real power."

She would recall what happened next in great detail even years afterward. She heard a voice far away, echoing as if it came from a deep well, and it was speaking a strange language. She listened even as she went on with her incantation. The voice bubbled up and down inside her, making sounds of one syllable, like baby talk. "No, God, Karl can't do drugs," she sobbed once more. Then it was like water rushing out of her mouth, *"nyet, nyet,"* and other words she had never spoken, most of which did not exist in any dictionary.

"It is the prophecy," someone next to her said. "Out of your belly will flow rivers of living water."

Pastor Carter chortled. "So! Our quiet little Lutheran is suddenly praying at the top of her lungs in the other language!"

Mira saw her daughters watching her in wide-eyed astonishment. It was then that she knew that she had received the gift of tongues. She had "become a Christian" in a sense that made her previous involvement in Lutheranism seem like belonging to a sewing circle. It was a joy beyond anything she had ever experienced.

Dwight could not think of a good reason not to go to Minneapolis. He had worn out his welcome at Hintze Road and was now sleeping on the floor of Poli's Milwaukee apartment, working for minimum wage at the fruit-packing company where Poli also had a job. "Uncle Paul only has one rule," Karl said, "anything goes!"

Dwight told Ruth he needed the family car, the Corvair, to go skiing with Karl. In Minneapolis he parked it on the street in front of 2828 Twelfth Avenue South, where it was promptly stolen. Dwight was furious because he had just installed an eight-track Craig stereo in the car. Paul told him not to worry; the car would turn up. And, in fact, two Minneapolis policemen returned the Corvair the next day. They had found it three blocks away, the radio missing. "We know who did it," one officer said. "You will press charges, won't you?"

"No," Dwight said.

The detective lost his temper. "God damn it, how do you expect us to stop this sort of thing?"

Dwight shrugged. "I don't."

Dwight adjusted easily to his new environment. With drugs in every cupboard, it was like living in a pharmacy. Opened packs of cigarettes lay on every table and chair. If he wanted to spend all day on the couch, he could, and frequently he did. His capacity to do nothing was astounding, even to heroin addicts.

Soon after his arrival he sampled something called a "Black Beauty." It contained Dexedrine, a kind of speed, and it took him higher than he had ever been.

It may have been during one such experience that he answered a knock at the door and found a pathetic-looking woman standing there with an armful of pamphlets called *The Watchtower*. She asked him if he knew anything about the Jehovah's Witnesses. Dwight invited her inside. He was interested; in fact, he wanted to know everything about the Jehovah's Witnesses. The woman could scarcely believe her luck at finding such a receptive young man. Later, after she had departed, Dwight called Mira and recapitulated the entire conversation. "What do you think?" he wanted to know.

Mira had been unhappy over Bill's reaction to her gift. Bill had backed away from her in the driveway as though she were some kind of freak and then he had thrown out all her books on religion. She had been worried, too, that Dwight's move to Minneapolis would undermine what progress she and Poli had made with him. And so his phone call came as a great relief; she had never heard Dwight discuss religion with such gusto. Earnestly she pointed out the defects in the Jehovah Witnesses's doctrine. She had been wrong about Dwight, she thought. He was doing just fine at Uncle Paul's.

On Thursday, the twenty-sixth of March, Karl's supervisor at Hobart-Federal informed him that he had not passed probation and his employment was terminated as of that day. The reasons given were "absenteeism" and that he "needed more experience on the night shift." Karl assumed the man just didn't like his beard.

The next day Karl, Dwight, Scott, and Policronio De Venecia left for New Orleans in Scott's car. It was spring break at the University of Wisconsin, and even though none of the four was currently enrolled, habit compelled them to join the thousands of students seeking temporary relief from the long winter. They got a cheap motel room in the French Quarter, made the rounds of the jazz clubs, and fooled around in the cemetery where a scene from *Easy Rider* had been filmed.

On the way back Karl pointed to refineries along the Mississippi as possible sabotage targets. It was foolish for Scott to enter the air force, as he was scheduled to do in a few days, Karl said, because the revolution had begun. He cited the fact that the Teamsters were supporting the TAA strike as proof. "Why don't you go to Canada like everybody else?" he said.

The newspapers had been full of stories about the "Camp McCoy Three," servicemen who had been arrested on a charge of sabotaging their own base in central Wisconsin. "They need people like us in the service," Scott replied. "We can fight the war from inside."

Karl didn't believe Scott. "You're copping out, man," he said.

And you're throwing your life away, Scott thought.

For Paul Armstrong the opening of fishing season meant one thing: outboard motors. Stealing them was one of his many sidelines. He enjoyed it all the more because he loved to fish and could combine business with pleasure. He had a fishing cabin upstate on Mille Lacs Lake, and often went up on opening weekend, when they were all partying. He'd take several buckets of night crawlers to peddle at Sugarbush Lake Resort in Malmo and return with some unlucky vacationer's shiny new outboard in his trunk. Now, with the hearse, he could carry several at a time. He had attached a ball hitch to the bumper in case he should come across an untended boat and trailer.

Karl was still trying to master Paul's sangfroid, and when a chance arrived to go along on one of these expeditions, he eagerly volunteered. Max Sliter and Paul's son Vance joined the party. Vance was short but heavyset, with long, curly brown hair and the beginnings of a mustache. The two roses tattooed on his right arm gave him the look of a budding biker, which he was. Karl and Dwight had met him a year or two earlier when he had visited Madison with his dad. The Armstrong men had all gone bowling together and had a great time. Later, Vance and Dwight had gone out and gotten "drunker than snot," as Vance liked to recall.

The four of them piled into the hearse and headed south on State Highway 61, scouting moorages and private docks along the Mississippi, which was still full of ice floes. Paul was looking for specific models, for which he had orders. The first ones they found were the wrong size or make. "Nah," Paul would say, with the appraising

look of a seasoned buyer, "that's not what my customers are interested in."

They continued on through Red Wing and Minnesota City. Near
the Iowa border they found what they were looking for. Paul went
to work with his bolt cutters, plucking seventy-five-horsepower out-
boards from their mounts, and they returned to Minneapolis with a
full coffin compartment.

Karl was in awe but also a little queasy. Some of the motors
weren't that new, and their owners didn't appear particularly rich.
Paul's idea of redistributive justice was more ambiguous than he
had been led to believe.

On April 11, 1970—Palm Sunday—Paul Armstrong turned fifty-
two, and all of Franklin Avenue turned up to celebrate at the
Twelfth Avenue shanty, most of them high on one thing or another.
Paul allowed himself a rare drink and promptly passed out on the
living room floor, dozing unaware while the party swirled around
him. Dwight stood watch, trying to keep people from stepping on
him.

The New Year's Gang was the talk of the party. By then, almost
everyone on Franklin Avenue had heard of the Badger Ordnance
attempt, including Lonnie Ross Walker, the son of Paul's landlord.
Lonnie Ross was a big, mean kid who did not understand campus
revolutionists. Karl made the mistake of showing him a copy of the
Kaleidoscope with "The Latest Trashing News from Champaign-
Urbana, Santa Barbara and Buffalo." An angered Lonnie Ross col-
lared Max Sliter to vent his feelings about Paul's "commie" nephews;
It was Walker's impression that Karl was actually on the staff of the
Kaleidoscope. Sliter found himself in complete agreement with
Walker. "I've done a lot of things, but I ain't no radical," he said.

Lonnie Ross sidled up to Dwight. "Got a job yet?" he asked
sneeringly. Dwight's talk about finding work in Minneapolis was the
joke of the avenue, since everybody knew that all he did was sleep
on Paul's couch. Dwight ignored the taunt. Lonnie Ross leaned
over Paul's defenseless torso and kneed him hard in the stomach.

Dwight grabbled Walker by the shoulders and threw him off.
"What the fuck are you doing?" he said.

It was what Lonnie Ross wanted. "I'm gonna bust you! I'm
gonna bust your chops!" he said, starting toward Dwight. Frank
Dunn stepped in between them. The shouting woke Paul, who got

to his feet and, seeing Walker's fists raised against Dwight, turned white. "By God, Lonnie Ross, don't you *ever* threaten my boys!" he said, his jaw quivering.

Walker squared off with him. Everyone took a step back. "Lonnie," Paul reiterated, "if you and me get into it now, you might just take me, but you'll be lookin' over your shoulder for the rest of your life." His cool, matter-of-fact delivery had its effect on Lonnie Ross, who backed off.

"Way to go, Dwight," Jeff Shearer said after Lonnie Ross had left. Dwight could scarcely believe it himself. Paul would have fought Lonnie Ross for him, he realized. He had to go outside and have a cigarette and think about that.

As Minneapolis thawed out the Armstrong brothers set out to explore the city. They discovered the beautiful old south side neighborhoods and parks, the head shops of Dinkytown, the University of Minnesota mall, and the student hangouts of the West Bank. Karl marched in Evan Stark-led demonstrations against the Honeywell Corporation and got himself arrested with a group protesting the demolition of the Red Barn, a Dinkytown establishment popular with students. Paul had to bail him out. As his funds ran low he studied the chemistry of LSD at the University of Minnesota's Walther Library, thinking that he could "raise money for the revolution" by manufacturing acid.

In the short run, however, dealing proved more practical. With stolen records, marijuana, and hashish supplied to them by Paul, the brothers commuted to Madison in the hearse, selling the goods on the Library Mall. Karl blended in with the other merchants, chatting with the Banana Man, a former East High classmate of his, who was making a small fortune with a new product, the chocolate-dipped frozen banana. "Dick-on-a-Stick, fifteen cents!" he crooned. The paranoia Karl had felt in March had evaporated. He was no longer worried about Lynn, even when he learned that she had gone to work for Pete Bobo and Golden Freek Enterprises. Jerry Garcia and the Grateful Dead had actually shown up for the Poynette Festival, which meant that Bobo was on the up-and-up.

"New Year's Gang—Live Like Them!" grafitti still covered construction fences around campus, and there were many who believed. Following the defeat of the TAA strike in court, embittered supporters vandalized the homes of department heads who had signed affidavits against striking teaching assistants. Someone skilled in the use of a high-powered rifle decommissioned the liquid nitrogen tank next to the chemistry building. Graduate students in economics stalked the cornfields south of Baraboo hoping to blow up the pylons carrying electricity to Badger Ordnance Works. Cadres of a semiclandestine SDS splinter group, the Mother Jones Revolutionary League, took rifle practice in nearby quarries, and on April 18, as a new, nationwide observance called Earth Day got under way, the league made its debut by breaking away from a rally at the Capitol and running around the square smashing windows. Before police could react, they had destroyed $100,000 in plate glass.

In a signed editorial the *Daily Cardinal*'s new editor-in-chief, a senior from Mamaroneck, New York, named Rena Steinzor, defended the Mother Jones action against criticism from YSA, arguing that it had to be understood in the broader context of actions by the New Year's Gang. By now this sort of stand in the *Cardinal* caused little surprise; just a few days earlier the paper had defended the execution of Western diplomats held hostage by Guatemalan guerrillas.

Karl had heard that there were iron mines in northern Minnesota, and where there were mining operations, he reasoned, there would be dynamite. Returning to Minneapolis, he and Dwight set off in the Corvair to see what they could find. It was dark by the time they got to Duluth at the western tip of Lake Superior. Then they were in Indian country, surrounded by reservations, forests, and lakes. It was two in the morning before they found a likely spot, the Mary Ellen Mine near Biwabik, but snow blocked the road, and they had to get out and walk the last hundred yards.

They were deep in the Vermillion Iron Range, or what was left of it. All around them were twisted mounds of earth that once had been hills. Here and there withered pine trees stood at odd angles to the ground. At the site of the dig they found a boxcar conveniently marked with signs advertising the presence of explosives. Uncle Paul's heavy-duty bolt cutters made short work of the padlock. The interior was stacked high with reels of pencil-thick, yellow cord that looked like fuse. There were thousands of feet of it. In other boxes they found heavy, collarlike objects about the size of cat-food tins. They did not know what any of the items were, but they were marked "dangerous." They took a carload back to Uncle Paul's and stashed it in the basement.

At the Franklin Library Karl learned that the fuselike material was primacord, an explosive used in mining operations to set off multiple dynamite charges in a sequence. The cat-food tins were boosters, high explosives placed at intervals along the primacord to speed up the rate of burn. In combination with dynamite, prima-cord was used in quarry mining to bring down walls of granite. It was even used in forestry. "They wrap it around a tree and then chop down the tree—it just explodes," he told Dwight. He was already thinking of the power poles to Badger Ordnance.

A day or so later Max Sliter ("Slither," Dwight called him) returned from a visit with his wife and kids. Dwight said he had something to show Max and led him down to the basement, the confetti of peeled strongboxes crunching underfoot. The explosives were lined up against a wall, covered by a sheet of plastic. Max pulled out a box. "What you got here?" he said.

"Primacord," Dwight said off-handedly, as if he had been using explosives all his life.

Max turned an unblinking yellow eye on the young Armstrong. *The kid brags a little,* he thought. Dwight was just trying to impress him because he knew Max had a record. "Where did you get this?" he inquired.

"Up there in the Iron Range, west of Duluth," Dwight said. "Brought it back yesterday in the Corvair."

"Ah," Max said. That explained why the boys had wanted to bor-row his Buick the other day. "How did you get all that in the Cor-vair?" he asked. It looked as though they had enough of it to blow the faces off Mount Rushmore.

"I had to hold my legs up," Dwight said.

"What are you going to do with it?"

Dwight hesitated. "We are going to experiment a little," he said evasively.

"Huh!" Max snorted. "You better get this stuff outta here before you blow the place up!"

Word soon got out that the Armstrong boys had stolen a "boxcar of dynamite" and stored the goods in Paul's cellar. The story received embellishment as it made its way up and down the avenue.

Paul, unaware of the cache, had almost blown up the house test firing a stolen Thompson submachine gun into the cellar, it was said. This story rang true to many people because Paul was known for his thoroughness in checking out weapons before he sold them.

It had occurred to Karl that primacord might be a good way to take out the transmission line towers between Sauk Prairie Substation and Badger Ordnance. For this reason, as well as safety considerations, he resolved to find a hiding place for the explosives closer to Madison. He was not resolved to go back into action; it was just a habit he had picked up in scouting: Be prepared.

Part IV

THE EVE OF

DESTRUCTION

18

Cambodia/Kent State

Judge, you are being called upon to make a very important determination, and that is whether or not we are still a country of laws.

— MICHAEL ZALESKI,
Wisconsin Assistant Attorney General, for the prosecution

We had seen that the people who were engaged in peaceful protest were not only just getting beaten up but they were killed.

—TOM SIMON,
student, for the defense

What struck Leo Burt's classmates most about him was his intensity. Whatever his interests were, he pursued them obsessively. He was never laid back, never paced himself. He could get As when he wanted to, but grades were not his top priority. Throughout high school and his first three years of college, rowing had been his first love and took precedence over everything else. Then it was movement politics and the *Daily Cardinal*. Ideas, too, were becoming more and more important to him.

Leo Frederick Burt was born on April 18, 1948, the second of two children born to Howard and Mary Burt. His mother died prematurely that year, and Leo was raised by his father Howard's second wife, also named Mary but called May to distinguish her from the original. Howard and May had four more children together. Howard was a mechanical engineer, another aptitude that seemed to run in the Burt family. May busied herself at home in Havertown with the children.

At one time the Burt family had been a power on the land, an Irish Catholic clan like the Kennedys of Boston, although the Kennedys were relative newcomers. The Burts had been in Philadelphia since before the Civil War and could claim both General Sherman and Cardinal O'Hara as relatives, albeit distant ones. Leo's grandfather, William P. Burt, was a founding partner in Reynolds and Company, destined to become, through years of merger and acquisition, Shearson–American Express. William P. and his wife Mary had lived on Hathaway Lane—not quite Main Line, but close. Their domain had extended over several square miles, all the way to Cobb's Creek, and abutted a famous hole on the Merion golf course. Mary Theresa Burt was an imperious woman who reminded everyone of Queen Mary, right down to the feathered toque she often wore. When William and Mary went out, it was duly reported in the society pages, unusual notice for Micks in snobbish Philadelphia. It was less unusual after William Burt, one of Leo's second cousins, became publisher of the *Mainline Times*.

William and Mary were badly hurt by the Crash of 1929, a financial setback for which Mary never forgave her husband. A long, crippling bout with Parkinson's disease took much of what was left of the fortune before it finally killed "Queen Mary" in 1967. Leo had come home for the funeral. Her estate was still worth six figures, and fifty priests attended her to the grave.

William and Mary Burt's seven children never regained the wealth and social standing that their parents had enjoyed, but for the most part they did well. Two of them, Donald and Leonard, joined the Augustinian priesthood. Donald went on to teach philosophy at Villanova, serving the university as vice president for academic affairs. It was rumored that only internal politics in his order prevented him from becoming president. Leonard quit the priesthood to marry, earning himself the epithet "black sheep of the family," which he was still called even after Pittsburg, California, where he rose to be superintendent of public schools, named a street after him. Leo's favorite aunt was a portrait artist of local renown; other Burts pursued engineering, law, poetry, and sculpture.

It meant something to be a Burt. Reunions were frequent and well attended. Burt families often vacationed together at the shore, eager to see how many people could be crammed into a beach cabin for a party (fifty or sixty was not unusual). Those were wonderful times that made a child feel the security and pride of kinship.

With so many aunts and uncles, Leo had numerous cousins of all ages. His particular cohort included his cousins Joe, David, Ricky, Mary, and Gertrude and his sister Rita, all of whom were within a year in age. Among his generation of Burts Leo hardly seemed the most likely candidate to do anything out of the ordinary. He was the most conventional, and in a family of very bright, ambitious children he did not stand out intellectually. His cousin Joe, the same age as he, earned a four-point average at Villanova while leading the antiwar movement there and then upset his uncle, the Very Reverend Donald X. Burt, by dropping out with one semester left to join the Peace Corps. No one expected Leo Burt ever to make news, unless it was in the sports pages.

Leo's family lived in a modest brick bungalow on St. Denis Lane across the street from the cemetery where Grandpa William Burt was buried. His father Howard was a taciturn man frequently away on business, and when he was home, he would go off to the shore in pursuit of Atlantic bluefish. May Burt was a sweet but somewhat absentminded woman who reminded her neighbors of Lucille Ball in "I Love Lucy." But May was a devout Catholic. The walls of her house were decorated with portraits of the Virgin Mary, and crucifixes strung with the desiccated braids of Palm Sundays past guarded every bed. Friday dinner at May's house meant creamed tuna on toast, Franco-American spaghetti or some other meatless repast. Nothing short of a communicable disease could get one of May's children out of Sunday mass. Like his older brother John, Leo attended St. Denis Elementary School followed by the all-boys Monsignor Bonner High School, serving in the altar society his senior year. He was a good but not outstanding student, scoring in the low 600s on his Scholastic Aptitude tests. Like the rest of his family, indeed, like most of Irish Philadelphia, he was a Kennedy Democrat. May doted on him. A woman of weak heart, she would not recover from the shock of the Army Math bombing and died soon after.

Leo's choice of Wisconsin over the Catholic schools closer to home raised eyebrows among his rowing friends at Monsignor Bonner. Leo figured he would have better odds of making the rowing team at a Midwestern school, they reasoned. But Wisconsin's freshman team had won the national championship in 1964, and the same crew, now competing at the varsity level, was predicted to win the 1966 national championship. (It did.) Wisconsin and the University of Washington had become the teams to beat in collegiate rowing, eclipsing the Ivy League and Catholic schools of the East. Leo was not looking to star on a losing team; he wanted to row with the best.

The secret of Wisconsin's triumph was the recruitment of big, strong boys who might be inexperienced but who promised a large capacity for work. The coaches watched for them in the registration lines, taking aside those who, like Karl Armstrong, appeared to have the right proportions. The key was height. The typical varsity rower at Wisconsin was six feet six; short ones were six feet three. What Wisconsin's coaches knew was that, other things being equal, a long body can do more work in a given amount of time than can a short one. They would never have picked Leo Burt out of the registration line; he was not even six feet.

Leo had made the freshman team anyway, one of the few in his class with any experience, let alone bragging rights to a championship. (His eight-man shell representing the Penn Athletic Club had bested the junior competition that summer at the prestigious Henley Regatta.) He impressed Randy Jablonic, the freshman coach, with his spirit and discipline. On "beer runs" in Wisconsin's 60,000-seat Camp Randall Stadium, he would run until he threw up, once completing thirty-five circuits of the stadium steps in a single workout. Varsity football players considered once around a major hardship.

Leo roomed off-campus his sophomore year with Phil Resch, Tim Mickelson, and Dan Stump, all friends from Ogg Hall, his freshman dorm. Resch and Mickelson, both from Wisconsin, were also on the rowing team, but they had been registration-line recruits. Leo was the hotshot from Philadelphia, rowing in the all-important number 8 seat, "stroke," the oarsman who sets the tempo for everyone else. Leo had infected his roommates with his passion for the sport, for the training and boat rigging, the science of it. In early spring when they were groaning from daily doubles, Leo would fire them up with glorious pictures of the rewards to come. "An oarsman must be mentally tough," he would say.

But by their second year size was beginning to tell. Resch, six feet four and 230 pounds, was so strong that his oar sometimes broke in midstroke. Mickelson was only six feet three but had perfect timing. They both moved up to varsity while Leo remained with the junior varsity.

Despite his tenuous berth Leo had stuck with the sport into his junior year. He tried to compensate for his height disadvantage by making himself stronger and fitter than anyone on the crew. He trained like a madman in the weight room, pumping iron until the arteries were popping out of his skin. His crewmates did squats with 100-pound sandbags on their shoulders; Leo used 200 pounds. But all that extra muscle interfered with his lay back, and the music went out of his stroke. Switching rowers from boat to boat, Coach Jablonic saw clearly that others made the shells fly faster. When it came time to depart for the national races on the East Coast that spring, something Leo had looked forward to for three years, he learned that he had been cut from the traveling team, and was demoted to the junior varsity "pickle boat." Tim Mickelson would never forget the look on Leo's face as he walked away from the boathouse that day.

Leo did not quit immediately, but he began to voice political sentiments among his fellow crewmen, a development that was profoundly distressing to Coach Jablonic. There had never been any place in the boathouse for politics, and Jablonic was determined to keep it that way. The annual alumni banquet was coming up. Jablonic, who had replaced the legendary Norman Sonjiu as varsity rowing coach that fall, announced that *all* crew members would get haircuts for the event, if their hair wasn't already short. "Hey, we got a lot of alums coming. They're not going to take to you guys if they think you're among the uprisers," he explained. Leo did not wear his hair long; in fact, to save the expense of going to a barbershop, he had one of his crewmates, a Sturgeon Bay boy named Richard Purinton, keep it trimmed medium length for him. But Leo had been reading Jack Scott's *The Athletic Revolution,* and it had made him aware of his rights. As it happened the boathouse walls were covered with photographs of hirsute crews from the turn of the century. He wrote to Coach Jablonic protesting the order, arguing that long hair was in the Wisconsin tradition. A notice appeared on the boathouse bulletin board: Anyone showing up at the dinner with long hair should have their locker cleared and be gone the next day. Leo cleared out.

At the *Daily Cardinal* Leo, assigned to the SDS beat, was considered part of the dominant left-wing faction, yet relatively moderate on tactical questions. During the February riots, he had taken issue with Jim Rowen about trashing, which Rowen had defended as another step higher in the revolutionary process. Leo had seen an old woman cry when a rock cracked the window of the city bus she was riding on. That wasn't right, Leo said; you could not make the revolution that way.

Leo was also among the few on the Madison campus who knew the identity of the New Year's Gang. He had suspected Karl immediately and had forced Scott Nelson to admit it before Scott left town. Where sabotage was concerned, he was on the fence. It was not until the first week of May 1970 that he made up his mind.

In a nationally televised address on the evening of April 30, President Nixon announced that a combined force of U.S. and South Vietnamese troops had entered Cambodia to root out Communist sanctuaries along the border and destroy their fabled command center. The United States had "scrupulously respected" Cambodia's neutrality in the past, he insisted, though in reality thousands of Cambodian peasants had already perished in a secret campaign of high-altitude bombardments that had been going on for a year. "There has been a great deal of discussion with regard to this decision I have made," he said. In fact, few people knew of the decision. Among those who did, Defense Secretary Melvin Laird had first urged Henry Kissinger to take the matter up with Congress, and when that failed had argued against including U.S. troops in the mission. William Watts of the National Security Council had refused a direct order from Kissinger to supervise NSC staff work on the invasion. Two other Kissinger aides, Roger Morris and Tony Lake, had resigned in protest. Secretary of State William Rogers was shown Nixon's speech only at the last moment. He had correctly predicted an uproar.

Leo Burt was in New Haven that weekend covering a protest against the arrest of Black Panther chairman Bobby Seale, accused of having ordered the murder of a New Haven Panther suspected of being a police agent. With the added incentive of free food and lodging offered by Yale's liberal president Kingman Brewster, 20,000 militants showed up, including Yippie leaders Abbie Hoffman and Jerry Rubin and several of the Chicago Eight. Rubin led the multitudes in chanting "Fuck Kingman Brewster." "As long as he's a university president, he's the enemy," Rubin said.

But it was Tom Hayden's words that most impressed Leo. "This generation will not back down," the SDS founder said with obvious emotion. "This [stopping the war] will require a crazy commitment from us, dooming us for our lives. It will necessitate a scale of commitment that neither we nor the antiwar movement has ever displayed before. It will necessitate acting, not talking, and this is probably the last speech I'm ever going to give."

By Monday students and faculty at more than 100 colleges and universities joined in a nationwide "strike" to protest the invasion. Presidents of thirty of those institutions signed a telegram to President Nixon urging him to get out of Indochina. Anger was not restricted to militant campuses like Berkeley, Columbia, and Madison: At the University of Maryland in College Park, students ransacked the Armory. In two nights of rioting at San Jose State, students drove the police off campus. Students at Hobart College in Geneva, New York, and at Kent State University in Ohio firebombed their ROTC offices, and at the latter institution they prevented firemen from putting out the blaze.

President Nixon's testy comments on the uprising were widely quoted in campus newspapers. "You know, you see these bums blowing up the campuses. I mean, storming around about this issue. Get rid of the war, there'll be another one." Governor James Rhodes of Ohio echoed those sentiments, promising to "eradicate" rioters as he called in the Ohio National Guard. On Monday a National Guard unit made good on his threat, suppressing a crowd of rock throwers with a volley from their assault rifles. Eleven protesters were seriously injured; four died.

The news from Kent State was like gasoline poured on an open fire. "If it could happen to them, it could happen to us," said a Madison militant. Nixon, besieged in the White House by busloads of enraged young people, ordered troops into the basement in the event of an attack. "The stakes are very high now," the *Cardinal* declared in a front-page editorial. "We are no longer protesting a single war but an attack on both the Southeast Asian people and the people of the United States. The issues have been reduced to one: survival." The editors concluded with a call for open rebellion. "We must strike and strike hard—into the community and on our campus to turn the tide now raging so viciously against us."

Leo had just gotten back to Madison when the news of Kent State hit. He pulled on his marine boots, grabbed his gas mask, and took off for the *Cardinal* office. Crossing the Library Mall, he ran into his former roommate Dan Stump. Stump, a physics major, was carrying an armload of books in preparation for final exams. "I can't imagine, after Kent State, that you're going on as if nothing had happened," Leo said. He had often kidded Stump about being a grind, but this time, Stump could tell, Leo really meant it.

The *Cardinal* office was in a daylight basement at 425 North Henry Mall, a block west of Bascom Hill. The editor's glassed-in cubicle was to the left as one came down the stairs. The newsroom was a clutter of green desks, Royal Standard typewriters, yellow typing paper, black-handled scissors, and bottles of LePages glue. Beyond that was the pressroom, housing a brand-new state-of-the-art offset press. A meeting to discuss coverage of the evening's expected demonstrations was under way as Leo arrived. "This place is gonna blow," Lenny Fleischer, the new editorial editor, predicted.

The new editor-in-chief, Rena Steinzor, was the granddaughter of a Russian-born garment-union activist and card-carrying Communist whose memory Steinzor held dear. Like her high school classmate Jane Kunstler, daughter of the well-known radical lawyer, William, Rena had chosen the University of Wisconsin because of its reputation as an activist campus. Steinzor was passionately engaged by the Mosse-Goldberg debate, interrupting Prof. Mosse in mid-lecture to challenge his interpretations of history. At the *Cardinal* she had allied herself with Jim Rowen. Together, during the course of the year, they had revolutionized the paper, installing "workplace democracy" and "consensus" decision making and eliminating the role of board members in the appointment of editors. Steinzor had both supporters and critics on her staff. "Rena was intimidating," an associate remembers. "She would come through the office screaming obscenities, slamming doors. She was the stereotype of an Eastern radical."

But Steinzor could also be a mother hen, and she liked Leo Burt. Even if his politics were a little soft, he could keep his cool in a riot. She assigned him to cover the rally at the Memorial Student Union that evening. And because his size made him a target, she called for someone to stay with him wherever he went. Teri Simon, a freshman and one of Steinzor's feminist protégées, raised her hand. "And don't forget to put on your gas mask," Steinzor said, knowing how much Leo hated wearing it.

That evening, in the offices of the Wisconsin Student Association on the third floor of Memorial Student Union, the WSA senate, presided over by nineteen-year-old president-elect Michael Jalliman, was debating a resolution in support of an academic strike. It passed. Outside on the flagstone terrace several thousand students had gathered. Members of the steering committee of a hastily formed "United Front" called upon the assembly to remain peaceful, but Jim Rowen stepped up the rhetoric. "We're going to fight the military on this campus and we're going to strike hard and we're going to win," he predicted. A Mother Jones spokesman galvanized the crowd to action with an offhanded, "Why don't we take a stroll over to the Math Research building?"

Burt followed the crowd to Sterling Hall with Teri Simon tagging along behind. Simon was from Milwaukee, bookish, and, like her mentor Rena Steinzor, disenchanted with male privilege. She had joined in the criticism of the Male Chauvinist Pig Caucus. But on a personal level she, too, liked Leo. He was quiet and thoughtful and struck her as more "pacifist" than the other radicals on staff. She was glad to team up with him.

Finding Sterling Hall protected by Ralph Hanson and his men, the students moved on to T-16, breaking all of its windows and setting trash on fire. When police moved in the crowd broke up into small affinity groups that raced about attacking unguarded buildings. The Land Tenure Center was set afire, along with the ROTC and draft-board offices and commercial establishments that students considered exploitative. Simon fell behind, and passing in front of Van Hise Hall, she was knocked down by a rubber bullet. By the time she got back on her feet, Leo had vanished. She wandered back to lower State Street looking for him, but was chased into a blind alley and had to hide in an apartment building.

Leo had caught a ride with *Cardinal* Associate Editor Peter Greenberg in Greenberg's 1964 Buick Special. A police car had knocked off one of the doors in a riot earlier in the year, and it was tied on with a rope. Lenny Fleischer was in the car, along with Michael Mally, the newspaper's photo editor. Mally's mouth was full of stitches and broken teeth from a beating he had received during the Earth Day riot. When the photo he had taken of a UP & S officer pointing his service revolver at a crowd of demonstrators appeared in the *Daily Cardinal*, the university had quickly agreed to pay his orthodontist's bill.

Greenberg, a graduate of the Bronx High School of Science, had a police radio in his car, but all they were hearing was references to letters in the Greek alphabet. "Something must be happening on Fraternity Row," Greenberg said. He headed back toward Langdon. As they passed the Library Mall, they saw a large crowd battling police at the foot of Bascom Hill. Gas canisters were raining down, and demonstrators were trampling each other to get inside the Union. Leo asked to be let out of the car. "I'll see you back at the *Cardinal*," he said.

It was 10:30 P.M. Dane County Sheriff Jack Leslie and his men had just arrived in elephantine vans and were beating everybody in sight. Leo hurried across the mall dodging squad cars that had jumped the curb and were chasing down demonstrators as though they were stray calves. Ahead of him sheriff's officers carried a pepper fogger into the Union and gassed the Rathskeller. Now all who had taken refuge inside were trying just as frantically to get out, including a faculty couple with an infant. Leo put on his mask and made straight for the police line in front of the building, holding his press card aloft and shouting "*Daily Cardinal*, coming through!" A pair of county cops stopped him, demanding to know where he had gotten the mask. Leo flashed his card again. "*Daily Cardinal*," he reiterated. That, he realized too late, was a mistake.

Late that night Peter Greenberg returned to the Henry Mall office with a story on the burning of Kroger's, the University Avenue supermarket accused by the *Daily Cardinal* earlier in the year of overcharging students. Someone had started a fire in the Twinkies section, and the store had gone up like a rocket. Students had snake danced around the blaze while a garage band next door played Jefferson Airplane's "Volunteers of America." The celebrants all wore complicitous grins, soon to be known as "Kroger Smiles."

The newsroom had been a battlefield nursing station all evening, with Rena Steinzor hovering like Florence Nightingale over the wounded. Teri Simon had come back with a purple bruise the size of a tulip on her back; Lenny Fleischer had badly hurt his leg scrambling over a fence; Leo Burt's head was bandaged up, his glasses held together by Scotch tape. Burt dryly inserted his experience into his story. "*Cardinal* reporter Leo Burt was beaten and had his gas mask confiscated by Dane County police who were not deterred by his press card."

After that evening *Cardinal* reporters stopped identifying themselves at demonstrations. As Leo pointed out, "You just get beaten twice as hard."

A few days later Burt ran into his former roommate Tim Mickelson on campus. Mickelson asked him about the gash between his eyes. Leo shrugged; his bike had fallen on him as he was sunbathing on Bascom Hill, he said. To Peter Greenberg, Leo seemed different after the beating. He had been an armchair radical; now he was really "pissed."

The Madison uprising quickly settled into a kind of routine. A crowd would gather on the Library Mall around noon, and then all hell would break loose. Affinity groups of four to five people, with such names as "The Motherfuckers" and "The Stone Throwers," roamed the isthmus, dodging police and attacking targets on two separate lists circulated by militants. One list included the street addresses of administrators, ROTC and Army Math faculty, and other enemies. Another gave the location of practically all scientific research sites on campus. With no fewer than fifty-five military contracts, practically all the hard sciences were tainted, and the rebellion had taken what appeared to be an antiscientific turn.

The rebels wore goggles to protect their eyes, soaked their bandannas in a mixture of baking soda and egg white (a tear-gas antidote recommended by the *Cardinal*), breathed through gauze-covered Dixie cups and constructed homemade mortars with pipe, cherry bombs, and size D flashlight batteries. The more intrepid among them blackened their faces like characters in the John Wayne movie *True Grit,* armed themselves with two-by-fours, and ambushed unwary cops in the alleys at night. Miffland barricaded itself, blocking all entry points save one for the use of the neighbor-hood. Assisted by Mother Jones cadres, residents of the Southeast Dorms blocked busy West Johnson Street with mattresses, charging out to rebuild the ramparts every time police attempted to clear it. Up Against the Wall FM broadcast riot news nonstop from the basement of Ogg Hall, relaying information gleaned from the police band. Senator Gaylord Nelson, who had received a warm reception on campus in April, was booed at the Stock Pavilion: "You are being naive! You can't change the war in the United States Senate," students jeered.

The *Cardinal* cheered the militants on. "Trash highly selective targets. Know your real enemies and do real damage," urged one editorial. Staff members joined in the action under the *Cardinal's* new motto, "Do it first, then report it." This was the revolution, many of them thought. Or as Harvey Goldberg liked to say, *Tout est possible.*

But the genie of violence, once out of the bottle, was not easily controlled. As Mark Knops had predicted in the *Kaleidoscope,* "dopers and runaways" were making the revolution alongside the students, and their targets were less selective than the *Cardinal* edi-tors might have liked. A mob broke the windows of the First Wis-consin Bank, obliging the tellers, most of them middle-aged women, to dodge stones. An elderly Jewish couple, veterans of *Kristallnacht,* had the windows broken in their State Street laundry. "Oh no, not again!" they cried.

It was enough to make Special Agent Tom McMillen's hair stand on end. This was the scenario his FBI Academy instructors had preached about. "Don't worry, they don't have much community support," his senior colleague George Baxtrum advised, but McMillen wasn't so sure. There had been reports of claymore mines and C-4 plastic explosives being trucked into Madison to serve the rebellion. Could students overthrow the United States govern-ment? To McMillen it was an open question.

From the vantage of his seventeenth-floor office Fred Harvey Har-rington watched his dream of a great university for the people dis-solving. From the upper stories of the towers he had built to house the multitudes, furniture was raining down upon passing squad cars, and undergraduates swarmed through the streets shouting out in rage. They were his kids, Harrington's Hordes. His own best students, Goldberg and Williams, had brought about their political awakening. With their long hair and impassioned faces, they resembled the portraits on the covers of Harrington's several lives of Jesus. Harrington was inclined to the view that Christ *was* a revolutionary, that Matthew 19 meant what it said. He was going to have to abandon his facade of neutrality.

On Tuesday, the day after Kent State, Harrington ended his long, self-imposed silence on the war in Vietnam. "We must get out and soon," he declared in a press statement. But it was too late. At 2:00 P.M. that afternoon, Chancellor Young, who had received phone threats at his house, requested a State of Emergency; Governor Knowles called in the National Guard, and the first troops arrived that night, setting up a machine-gun nest in front of Army Math and posting sharpshooters on neighboring buildings. Store owners on State Street boarded up their windows *before* they were hit, and out on the East Side, Oscar Mayer placed armed guards on the roof of its plant. In outlying towns the ruralites were mobilizing, oiling their shotguns and deer rifles and readying their pickups to help put down the uprising. The army intensified patrols along the perimeter of Badger Ordnance Works and declared the skies over the plant off-limits to air traffic. Madison was on the brink.

A Board of Regents' meeting was scheduled for Friday the eighth of May. On the Seventh Harrington flew to Washington, where at 3 P.M. he and Nathan Pusey of Harvard, Edward Levi of Chicago, W. Allen Wallis of Rochester, Alexander Herd of Vanderbilt, William Friday of North Carolina, Malcolm Moos of Minnesota, and Charles Hitch of the University of California at Berkeley confronted Richard Nixon with the agony of the campuses. Nixon listened to them for an hour and a half. In the end he agreed to keep Vice President Spiro Agnew silent on the subject of students and invited the university heads to select one of their number to serve in the White House for the duration of the crisis.

For a moment Harrington forgot that Nixon stood for everything he detested in U.S. foreign policy and that his administration had shelved the plan for an urban grant program in which Harrington had invested so much time and energy. Nixon's approach in the meeting had been, "OK, what can we do for you?" and "Let's get on with it," which Harrington had liked. He was finished in Madison; in fact, he had already composed his resignation speech in his head. Here was that door he needed onto the national stage, a perfect way out of Wisconsin. But how could he make his willingness known to Nixon? As he stood there chafing, someone suggested Alexander Herd, and, of course, no one contested the nomination. Herd accepted, and it was done.

The following morning, appearing on the "Today" show, Harrington denounced the invasion of Cambodia and said that campus turmoil would end only when the war ended. Later that day, in a typically well-organized, upbeat speech, he presented his resignation to the Board of Regents. The terms of the deal had already been worked out privately with key board members: a $10,000-a-year, no-strings-attached fellowship for Harrington for life. The board accepted.

In the second week of rioting the tide turned. Students found themselves being pummeled by tough young cops who looked like brothers except for their black gumshoes and the saps and mace they kept concealed until the last moment. The plainclothesmen were traveling in packs of four or five, just like the affinity groups. They were cagey, waiting until the lawbreakers were alone, away from the crowd, to arrest them. Students who were monitoring the police band in the basement of Ogg Hall figured out that the plainclothesmen were being directed by someone named Chester White, who used Greek alphabet letters in place of street names to conceal their movements. What they did not yet know was that Chester White was the former history student George Croal and that the hard-hitting plainclothesmen were "counteraffinity squads" that Croal had trained that spring.

The affinity squads resorted to operating under cover of darkness. Inspector Herman Thomas borrowed helicopters from the National Guard and hunted down the roving trashers with powerful searchlights. The insurgents assembled kites with steel wire to try to bring down the aircraft, but were unable to get the kites aloft in the still night air.

And so it went. The final blow was the "pacification" (as the MPD termed it) of Miffland by means of what Herman Thomas described as "long-range gas." The National Guard formed a ring around the neighborhood and bombarded Mifflin Street from a distance with 1.5 caliber federal gas-riot guns and Lake Erie .38 caliber grenade launchers. Inspector Thomas's men swooped in through the chemical fog, firing canisters into screen doors and windows. The barricades were taken down and an "occupation force" (again, the MPD's language) was left behind to watch over the gasping enclave.

The next day a new slogan appeared on construction fences around campus: "Where is the New Year's Gang, now that we need them?"

But the war kept going on. And in the spring of 1970 it was escalated. At that time I was in Minneapolis, was taking part in the demonstrations against the Honeywell Corporation, and of course, they had wrote up leaflets and so forth for demonstration against the Cambodian invasion. I heard that people, students at Kent State were killed. And to me that meant that the government had declared war on the students....

Karl Armstrong had spent the early days of the rebellion camped out with hundreds of students on the floor of the TV lounge in the University of Minnesota Student Union. With them he went out to demonstrations and rallies during the day, returning to catch the news from other campuses in the evening. Dwight also joined in. "This is it, we gotta bomb something," he said when they heard about Kent State, and Karl could only agree. "Let's get a shotgun and shoot out their tires!" he urged when cars began skirting a roadblock set up on campus. But in contrast to the University of Wisconsin administration, which insisted on keeping the university open no matter what, the Minnesota president voluntarily closed the University of Minnesota for a day to protest the invasion; there was little conflict between students and those who ran things and little appetite for violence on either side.

In the midst of the demonstrations Karl fell in with a group of Canadian anarchists who invited him back to their commune for a meal of brown rice and vegetables. Vegetarian food had never tasted so good, and he was attracted to one of the women in the group. The Minneapolis movement needed to get "heavier," he told her, more like Madison. The girl gave him a pained look. In a fatherly tone one of the older hippies explained the commune's belief that violence created "bad karma" and that only love could make things better. Karl toned down his rhetoric.

In mid-May he hitched a U-Haul to the Corvair and loaded it with the primacord, said his good-byes on Franklin Avenue, and headed home. In River Falls he stopped at the Nelson farm, where he added birdbaths for Ruth and Mira to his load. Scott was still in basic training at an air base in the Southwest. Di Nelson reminded Karl that his skis were in the barn, but he said he didn't need them anymore. She insisted he take his mother a flowering plant from the nursery that she and George had started. He continued south, and at Devil's Lake hid the explosives in the doghouse he had discovered that winter in the abandoned quarry. He still did not know what he was going to do with them.

Don. and Ruth Armstrong had rented out Karl's old bedroom, and he had to take the sofa bed in the basement rec room. Ruth thanked him for the gifts. She always liked having Karl at home, and she started reading the classified ads in the *Capital Times* in the hope of finding him a job. A union job with decent pay and benefits and Karl would be alright, she thought.

I had read about all of the trashing that had gone on. And I thought, I thought for sure that the university couldn't ignore the demands to remove AMRC from campus. And I got back, and I was literally stunned by the fact that the university continued to ignore demands.

His first stop in town was the campus YMCA. The United Front had its office there, across the alley from Father Arthur Lloyd's St. Francis House. He entered during the middle of the day and found only three or four people, militants he did not recognize. He had a proposal to make whereby he would become the liaison between the Madison and Minneapolis movements, which needed to be coordinated, he believed. He wanted to convey to the Madison heavies how effective nonviolence had been up north, how the movement there had gained community support and might even bring about a "bloodless revolution." But under the scrutiny of the United Front volunteers, he became tongue-tied. The activists rolled their eyes. During the past two weeks, approximately sixteen different governmental agencies had tried to place spies in their ranks; this was the most obvious one to come along in days. They laughed him out of the office.

It was the same everywhere he went. The movement was in the grip of paranoia. Scores of students had been arrested by George Croal's Greek-spouting mystery squads. It was rumored that conspiracy charges were forthcoming against members of the United Front steering committee. And in a series of interviews in the *Cardinal* an ex-CID agent had revealed that the army routinely kept tabs on peace activists. A discouraging realization came to Karl: *They think I'm a spy!*

On Friday, May 15, the *Cardinal* carried the news of the Jackson State College massacre: two dead, sixteen injured, all of them black. The newspaper immediately dispatched two reporters to Jackson, Mississippi, and according to their firsthand report published the next day, the students had been demonstrating against the disproportionate number of black college graduates being drafted and sent to Vietnam. Local police, hearing the sound of a bottle breaking and mistaking it for gunfire, had fired on the demonstrators. "The option of nonviolent protest is becoming progressively non-existent in the face of overwhelming state violence," the *Cardinal* editors commented.

Several days later the *Kaleidoscope* released its issue on the uprising. "TAKE UP THE GUN!" shouted the lead story, "TAKE IT APART!"

> No shittin'. That's where it's at now. GET A GUN AND LEARN TO USE IT! Dig it! There's no excuse not to have at least one, and to have a good hiding place for it in your pad. The Community gotta become an armed camp, an armed OUTLAWS OF AMERIKA camp!

The semester ended. Final exams were canceled for most courses, and students were given the option of taking a grade based on their midterm scores. The campus emptied; the National Guard withdrew. Mother Jones cadres went off to factory towns like Milwaukee and Racine to try to recruit the working class. Lynn Schultz quit her Ray-O-Vac job and followed Sandy Nelson and Pete Bobo to Iowa to promote another rock festival. The *Cardinal* held a staff party in Vilas Park, and Leo Burt invited Karl. Karl was aware that Leo knew about the New Year's Gang. They talked about the significance of Kent State and Jackson State. It was war, they agreed; peaceful protest was no longer an option. Karl asked Leo if he was ready to do something about it.

"Yowza," Leo said.

And it was at that time that, [I] decided that the Army Mathematics Research Center should be destroyed, that there was no possible way of removing it from campus in a peaceful means.

To be exact, it was Sunday, May 31. A thunderstorm had come

through a little after 1:00 P.M., popping a twister down south of the city before it cleared off. Dwight came down from Minneapolis, and Karl suggested a boat ride. They took Donald's old runabout and launched it at a boat ramp near Mendota State Hospital. Karl borrowed bolt cutters, vice grips, and a crow bar from Donald's workshop and stashed them under the bow. His plan was to boat over to Shorewood Hills, a nice suburb west of the university, steal some boat motors, and have Uncle Paul sell them.

It was close to 5:00 P.M. by the time they got the boat into the water. As they rounded Maple Bluff Point, they could see another storm blowing in from the south, roiling up the lake. Karl had taken mescaline before embarking and kept the thirty-five-horsepower Sea King at full throttle. The waves coming over the bow were "no problem," he assured Dwight.

By 7:00 P.M. the sky had turned green, and lightning streamed through the clouds overhead like current on a circuit board. To the south Memorial Student Union glowed beside the lake. At that moment the storm put down a bolt right behind Bascom Hill. Van Vleck, the space-age mathematics building, stood out like a marker, black against the lit-up sky. The Army Math Research Center was just below it.

Karl had slowed down to watch the light show. Dwight was amazed by how calm he was standing at the boat wheel, almost like Uncle Paul, the rain landing unnoticed on his bald dome. Dwight knew by then that Leo Burt had joined the New Year's Gang. Karl had told him about their recent attempt to firebomb the second-floor office of the Monroe Street draft board. They had borrowed a ladder from Phi Sigma Kappa and carried it all the way across campus. It didn't quite reach, so they had given up and carried it back. But that didn't matter, Karl said, because "symbolic bombings" of that sort did no good. They needed to do something that would get Nixon's attention. That's what the money from the boat motors would be used for, he now explained. For Army Math.

He slid the throttle forward. The boat leaped out into the dark.

19

"Mathematics of Death"

It is not a job shop for the Army. People at MRC do not work for the Army. They work for the university.
— R. CREIGHTON BUCK,
mathematician, for the prosecution

It works for the Army. The contract says it must work for the Army. It covers up its work for the Army. The contract says it must cover up. And this cover-up is going on at the present time.
— JOE BOWMAN,
student, for the defense

It had been a tough year for J. Barkley Rosser, Sr. In the fall the militants had splattered paint on his guests at an international symposium and attacked the center with toy machine guns. That winter they had thrown rocks at his windows on the third floor of Sterling Hall. In May they had tried to burn the place down. They had threatened his wife Annetta on the phone. They had fire-bombed the home of his neighbor, the head of air force ROTC. And they had picketed his spring symposium with signs saying SMASH ARMY MATH.

The worst had been when they tried to trip him. He was on his

way back to his office from the Wisconsin Center, where the symposium was under way, with his associate director, Steve Robinson. A
mob followed them up Bascom Hill, fifty or sixty students shouting
at once. Rosser just tried to keep moving, but they stuck their feet
in his way. Robinson, a former Green Beret with a black belt in
karate and experience in hand-to-hand combat, began to wonder if
they were going to have to fight their way out, but at that moment a
squad of Ralph Hanson's men swooped down and dispersed the
crowd.

Rosser had the confident bearing of a man who was used to getting his way. Directing the AMRC was a job that he was uniquely
well qualified to do, yet he found himself constantly under attack,
caricatured in the student press as the Dr. Strangelove of Madison.
He could not even escape the controversy within the sanctum of his
home off Nakoma Road in the heart of the West Side. His own son,
J. Barkley Rosser, Jr., an economics student at the university, was
constantly arguing with him at the dinner table, upsetting his wife
Annetta, a southern woman with no stomach for conflict. He also
faced dissension within the ranks of his staff, which included several
doves. But J. Barkley Rosser, Sr., was not to be easily swayed.

At Princeton's Institute for Advanced Study in the 1930s, Rosser
had studied under Alonzo Church, who, along with Kurt Gödel,
was engaged in pioneering work in the realm of symbolic logic. The
field had no known application then, but twenty years later it was to
provide language for computers, the first step in a historic technological leap. Ruddy, phlegmatic, with silvering sideburns and mustache and the combative temperament of his Welsh ancestors,
Rosser, like many of his colleagues, was afflicted with the arrogance
of those who possess druidic knowledge. Mathematicians were the
sorcerers of the scientific revolution. They communicated in a language that no layperson could fathom. Their esoteric formulas were
the magic powder on which modern life depended. In the twentieth
century a man could no longer brush his teeth without math, let
alone go to the moon. Even killing, the most elementary human
activity, had become math based.

The AMRC was the only army-funded think tank in the United
States. In 1969–70, Rosser presided over 28 full-time and 15 part-
time mathematicians, a support staff of 17, and a budget of $1.3 mil-
lion ($4.5 million in current dollars). He had been hired away from
Cornell, where he had been head of the math department, in 1963.

As a condition of his acceptance Rosser had successfully demanded that a powerful computing center be built, to which his mathematicians would have ready access. In the salary structure of the university at the time, only President Harrington earned more. And although it was not, as rumored, a precondition of his acceptance, Annetta Rosser, a talented violinist who had played in Einstein's informal quartet at Princeton, was made concert master of the Madison Symphony Orchestra.

Army brass was more than pleased when Rosser accepted the appointment. Not only was he one of the "Gods of Logic," a living legend whose presence in Madison would be a magnet to other established mathematicians, but he was well known in defense circles. Rosser had headed the U.S. ballistics program in World War II, trying to close the "rocket gap" with the Wehrmacht. He had contributed to the design of half a dozen of the missiles currently in use by the military, including the solid-fueled Polaris, America's first submarine-launched ICBM. He had designed the computer system for Princeton's Institute for Defense Analysis (IDA). Even the Apollo crew's recent stroll on the moon was in some measure indebted to Rosser, who had lobbied for funding the program on the grounds that though it had no scientific value, it would be a great "publicity stunt." He was on the Science Advisory Committee of the National Security Agency, a consultant to numerous think tanks, and on a first-name basis with the Joint Chiefs of Staff. No one in Wisconsin had more clout on the national level than did J. Barkley Rosser, Sr.

The idea for a mathematics think tank devoted to military problems had germinated in 1955 when the army realized that on certain questions, such as how to stop an incoming ICBM, it did not trust its own mathematicians. It required a pool of first-rate talent that it could tap into as needed. The navy had established such an institute at New York University; the army wanted one, too.

In making the case for Wisconsin, then-President E. B. Fred, a scientist with a closet full of lethal germs he was developing for the Pentagon, cited the university's long history of contributions to the military. Madison was in a good "dispersal" location, he added, well removed from conspicuous industrial and military targets. It had an active air force fighter base at Truax Field and thus would "enjoy exceptional protection" in the event of an enemy attack. As it happened, Colonel Ivan Hershner, chairman of the search committee, was looking for a site that would provide "less likelihood of interruption of operation in the event of hostilities." No one dreamed that an attack might one day come from within, from the student body.

Helen Laird, mother of the future secretary of defense and a member of the University Board of Regents, moved to approve the deal, and the Wisconsin Alumni Research Foundation (WARF) put up money for a six-story wing on Sterling Hall to house the facility. The contract required AMRC staffers to spend at least half their time on army problems, to consult with the army, to undertake technical studies on request, and to help recruit math personnel for the army. The army also expected the center to provide a place for "stimulating contact" between army and civilian mathematicians. Permanent staffers had to have security clearances, the director a top-secret rating. The director was to keep the staff focused on "highly applicable" research and "cognizant of Army mathematical problems." The agreement also stipulated that "press releases, presentations at scientific meetings, and papers should not discuss the overall Army program or the source of Army interest in the particular research area involved."

Despite Madison's amenities the first director, Rudolf Langer, had trouble recruiting top people. The contract stipulated no consulting fees, and the salaries offered weren't high enough to offset what the best mathematicians stood to lose. And many mathematicians considered the requirement of spending 50 percent of their time on army matters excessive. A period of dissension ensued. President Fred, already miffed because Langer was paid almost as much as he was, complained that raising salaries would upset the faculty pay structure and threatened to annul the whole arrangement.

Then, in 1957, the Soviets launched a satellite called Sputnik into orbit, forever changing the way earthlings thought about the heavens and stirring panic across America. In an emergency meeting with University of Wisconsin administrators, the army pleaded for an end to the bickering over AMRC. "The U.S. is in a position approximating a life and death struggle…. The program must be gotten underway for the sake of the country, regardless of the cost and regardless of university regulations and policies." The individual work requirement was dropped from the contract, replaced by a stipulation that overall, the center had to devote half its time to army problems. Salaries were raised well above faculty levels, some good people were hired, and Army Math went to work trying to catch up with the Russians.

In 1953 a group of Ann Arbor–based scientists and mathematicians had begun working on the technological aspects of brush wars, assisting the U.S. Aerial Reconnaissance Laboratory in Thailand under the code name Project Michigan. Terrain-mapping radar and infrared, seismic, and acoustical surveillance were the hot topics; in other words, tools for finding an enemy in the jungle. These were the building blocks of what would come to be known as the Electronic Battlefield used in Vietnam. A liaison between the AMRC and Project Michigan was established in 1957. In 1960 a number of AMRC permanent staffers agreed to help Project Michigan solve the difficult problem of distinguishing, electronically, between such targets as peasants armed with AK-47s and such nontargets as women, children, and water buffalo. Thus began a six-year collaboration between the two defense think tanks.

President Kennedy's secretary of defense, Robert McNamara, was fascinated by the potential of the Electronic Battlefield, and during his tenure Army Math was peppered with requests for solutions to problems of guerrilla warfare. How do you "see" the enemy at night? How do you "acquire a target" hidden by a dense canopy of foliage? What is the best shape for tires to be used on sand? How do you destroy subterranean tunnels? What are the possibilities of wiping out the enemy with artificially generated tidal waves? How can you assess "the effect of concentrated but inaccurate fire on a dispersed target"? University of Wisconsin mathematicians were fully engaged with these questions and others related to counterinsurgency warfare. They were figuring the aerosol-spread patterns of viral slurries, predicting the effects of anthrax on humans, and optimizing time-release sequences for germ bomblets. In this they were no different from mathematicians and scientists at dozens of other universities. Under Project Themis, initiated in 1961, the Pentagon had spread its largesse (hundreds of millions of dollars) and influence throughout the academic world.

Army Math went quietly about its business, coexisting peacefully with other departments and unaffected by the increasing tumult of the antiwar movement. Hardly anyone outside the center was aware of the practical applications of the math it did. Rosser, who had worked at think tanks such as the Institute for Defense Analysis, where you had to pass through two security gates to get in, insisted on keeping the doors unlocked. "Sure we do research of interest to the Army," he replied when questions first arose. "Why do you think they pay us?" But on the issue of secrecy, he fudged, insisting that all the center's work was published and available to anyone, including visiting scholars from the Soviet Bloc. As protests mounted he took the additional precaution of excising the word "Army" from the name of the institute. It was now the Mathematics Research Center. In reality it continued to devote roughly half its time to solving problems for the army.

When he wasn't publicly minimizing the military significance of Army Math's work, Rosser was privately trying to prove to the army just how well its money was being spent. The endless reports (quarterly, semiannual, and annual) that he had to write to keep the army's research and development (R & D) section happy were filled with evidence that the esoteric formulas published by the center were often inspired by and applicable to problems of the battlefield. Those reports, along with the technical abstract bulletins summarizing the AMRC's research projects, proved a gold mine for *Cardinal* reporter Jim Rowen and his faculty ally, English instructor David Siff. At a faculty meeting, Siff read aloud a 1968 annual report describing such projects as "The Probability of Survival of a Subterranean Target under Intensive Attack." The result was weeks of professorial polemics and the appointment of a university committee to investigate. The army also got after Rosser, informing him that the report on the annihilation of subterranean targets, of which he was a coauthor, violated the army's requirement that AMRC papers not disclose possible military applications. Rosser's paper "by chance" used numerical examples close to those in the army's studies, and he was obliged to have extant copies rounded up and burned. He reissued the report, basing it on the survival of anthills at which rocks are being thrown.

Rosser considered himself quite the realist in matters of public opinion. "The masses love spectacles. These don't have to make sense as long as they are big or noisy, preferably both," he had argued in behalf of a manned lunar expedition. After Rowen's opening salvo in the spring of 1969, part of the "Profit Motive 101" series, he had advised army R & D Chief Ray Hershner to hire a first-class public relations firm. "Don't get a group that sells Cadillacs," he wrote. "Get a group that has successfully promoted a new rock and roll group or something of that sort." Hershner apparently thought better of it, and Rosser tried to be his own PR man, issuing condescending white papers in which he compared Army Math to the king's shoemaker who fills an order to make shoes for the king's army, and so forth. He even accepted an invitation to speak at the Campus YMCA, where he was unpleasantly surprised by a well-prepared David Siff.

Rosser had the technical abstract bulletins that Siff and Rowen had been consulting removed from the shelves of the center's library, then made the library itself off-limits to journalists. The English Department, pressured from above, fired Siff. Rosser's secretary politely informed Rowen that he was "welcome at any time to enter the lobby of the MRC." And yet the exposés continued. Every week brought new revelations in the *Cardinal*, details of consulting trips made by permanent staffers to military bases and proving grounds, revelations of the often-deadly and top-secret applications of the center's formulas. Rowen continued to come around asking questions, until Rosser refused to see him anymore. "You can't talk to him," Rosser complained to Annetta. "He's illogical!" When the Wisconsin Student Association held hearings on the issue, he agreed to send a representative only on condition that there be no questions and declined to take part himself on the grounds that "Rowen will be there."

A university committee, appointed to investigate Rowen's accusations, issued a finding supporting Rosser's contention that the center did no classified work. This finding satisfied President Harrington and Chancellor Young, but the *Cardinal*'s editors were not persuaded. As they quickly pointed out, the committee was headed by Dr. Stephen Kleene, a mathematician and close friend of Rosser's who had served as acting director of the AMRC in 1967.

But claiming that Army Math's work was "unclassified" when the center's own contract specified that it could not reveal the military motives behind it was a cavil, like saying that work on the Manhattan Project wasn't classified because, after all, everybody knew that $E = mc^2$. It gave critics a bone to chew on, and, indeed, Siff and Rowen would not let go. When the center refused to give them a copy of its 1967 annual report, Rowen contacted the

Washington office of Senator William Proxmire, a Wisconsin Democrat known for his satirical Golden Fleece awards. Proxmire had been a supporter of President Johnson's actions in Vietnam, but now that a Republican administration was in charge, he was turning dovish, and a copy of the supposedly nonexistent report was eventually obtained. Rowen and Siff found a five-page section, pages 41 to 45, missing, apparently deleted before the report was printed. But the censor had overlooked the table of contents, according to which the missing pages dealt with Army Math's contributions to something called "Project Michigan." If the AMRC really had nothing to hide, why had it deleted a section of its annual report?

Siff and Rowen asked to see the missing pages and were rebuffed on the grounds that the material was "sensitive." However, it did not take much digging to learn that Project Michigan was the biggest military contract on a university campus in the United States. Siff called Chancellor Edwin Young on a television talk show and asked him what Project Michigan did. "Why don't you ask the University of Michigan?" Young replied.

Working through the winter, Rowen was able to piece together a fragmentary picture. One Project Michigan program in particular caught his attention. It consisted of the development of infrared detection techniques for nighttime surveillance and bombing raids against targets invisible to the eye. Several permanent members of the AMRC staff had consulted with Project Michigan on this very topic. To Rowen, the infrared-detection business rang a faint bell. Ernesto Che Guevara had been gunned down in a Bolivian jungle in October 1967. The Left had always assumed that it was a CIA hit. The mystery was, how did they find him? Fidel Castro's legendary lieutenant had survived for years in the jungle, coaching nascent guerrilla movements throughout Latin America. How was his seeming invulnerability pierced? The Project Michigan discovery suggested an answer: Che was found by infrared detection. His cigar, perhaps, or the lingering warmth of his smokeless Dien Bien Phu oven had given him away.

Rowen came out with the exposé in March, implicating the Wisconsin Alumni Research Foundation, which acted as a conduit for the army's funds and whose board included the chief executive officers of a dozen Fortune 500 companies, in a grand conspiracy with the CIA. "For the WARF trustees, who manage large enterprises with subsidiaries and branches scattered throughout the third world, the establishment of the AMRC was a sound investment, and the death of Che Guevara was a quarterly dividend," Rowen wrote.

J. Barkley Rosser, Jr., brought the subject up on Easter Sunday at his parents' home, precipitating a shouting match with his father and driving Annetta from the table in tears. He did not tell them that he had been spat upon in class because his name was Rosser.

On April 24 the *Cardinal* published Rowen's final shot at Army Math, in which he reported the army's refusal to release the Project Michigan pages on the grounds that they contained "privileged" information. Pointing out the inconsistency of such censorship with the university's open-records policy, Rowen tossed out a land mine dredged from the minutes of a May 12, 1955, meeting of the Board of Regents:

VOTED: That the regents and officers of the University of Wisconsin, with the exception of Regent Charles D. Gelatt and University President E. B. Fred, will not require, and can be effectively denied, access to top secret classified information in the conduct of business of the Army Mathematics Research Center.

It sounded awfully close to an admission that classified work did, indeed, go on at the center.

Rosser and Co. had lost the propaganda wars, at least on the east side of campus. To the militants, Army Math now stood for everything that was wrong with America. Army Math had murdered Che. Army Math was secretly assisting genocide in Vietnam. And the university not only had refused to do anything about it, but had fired a faculty member who raised questions about it. "It was clear that the Army Math Research Center had not only lied to me but had lied to the entire faculty of the English Department," David Siff would testify in Karl's defense. "The only innocents," Professor Hugh Iltis, a World War II veteran who had helped prepare documentation for the Nuremburg Tribunal, would tell the court, "were the AMRC mathematicians, many of whom are good friends of mine, who worked under the illusory premise that the only thing wrong with tainted money to support mathematical research is that there is not enough of it."

The AMRC was not alone in its troubles. The Institute of International Studies at the University of California at Berkeley had been firebombed twice that year. Harvard's Center for International Affairs had been invaded by Weatherman irregulars who punched and kicked professors and pushed one man's head through a glass door. Defense think tanks at Stanford and the University of Pennsylvania had been forced off campus. But this was small consolation to Annetta Rosser. Mrs. Rosser was fiercely proud of her husband and sensitive to slights. It irritated her when, at gatherings of faculty wives that spring, overprotective friends would introduce her simply as "Annetta." "Mrs. J. Barkley *Rosser!*" she would insist. She found herself thinking nostalgically of the old days at Princeton, of playing violin with Einstein, of dinner with Alfred North Whitehead at Harvard, of the balmy days on Iliff Street in Pacific Palisades when Barkley was designing the first computers at UCLA and their small children played every day in the sun. What had happened to America? It wasn't right that her husband, who had contributed so much to the defense of his country, was no longer safe in his own house.

At a meeting on June 19 Rosser's staff revolted. Stephen Kleene, by then dean of letters and science, had offered the center space on an upper floor of the WARF building, a towering new structure on the outskirts of the campus. The antiwar faction, including Olvi Mangasarian, Ben Noble, and Ben Rosen, urged that Rosser take Kleene up on the offer. Sterling Hall was too central, too exposed, too easy for marauding liberal arts students to get to, they argued. Compared to severing ties with the university altogether, which was what the radicals demanded, it was a modest compromise. They also wanted the center to be more open, more "academic."

Rosser had rejected such proposals several times already. He chastised his dovish colleagues, warning that they must not submit to mob rule. One of the reasons that the army had selected Wisconsin was its offer to locate the center in the heart of the campus, where it would be integrated socially as well as scientifically with the university. The WARF Building was a mile from Bascom Hill. They would feel isolated there. As for being more "open," he expressed concern about funding; they shouldn't bite the hand that was feeding them: the U.S. Army.

But Rosser was not entirely free of anxiety himself. He was leav-

ing in a few days for an extended visit to Great Britain. When he
went home, he took with him a pair of valuable antique marble
bookends, a gift from an English lord, that had been on his office
desk. It was a purely logical decision; the bookends, alone among
his office furnishings, were irreplaceable.

20

David and Leo

The killing had to be stopped, and the thing that we could do specifically in Madison, Wisconsin was to eliminate the Army Mathematics Research Center as not only symbol but real presence of death and killing and genocide in our midst. And this was the task of the day.

—MAX ELBAUM,
student, for the defense

Imagine the society we'd have if every time a person felt morally committed to a cause he could throw around one-ton bombs.

—MICHAEL ZALESKI,
Wisconsin Assistant Attorney General, for the prosecution

June passed quietly in Madison. The Guerrilla Theater Caravan tried to "keep things going" with skits on the Library Mall, but got little response from the summer student crowd. The only demonstration concerned the denial of a liquor license to the Dangle Lounge, the popular go-go bar off Capitol Square. At an "Action Conference" in Milwaukee, Rennie Davis, Dave Dellinger, and 900 other activists ratified a new movement program in which ending the war was just one of many objectives, alongside "$5,500 or fight," the welfare-rights plank. The sedition men were able to catch up on their paperwork. "Let the sixties be over," Special Agent Tom McMillen prayed.

The Stassi Shoe Store had notified Washington that it was not recommending active investigation of *Cardinal* reporter Jim Rowen at that time, "it being noted that except for one recent arrest, his anti-establishment activities have been devoted primarily to his writings." Nor had the Resident Agency found any evidence that Mark Knops, Timothy Slater, or any other members of the *Kaleidoscope* staff were involved in the New Year's bombings. On June 22 the Resident Agency asked permission to put a wiretap on the Francis Court "commune" to try to settle the matter once and for all, but Washington put the request off "until such time as institution of coverage is consistent with overall needs of Bureau." The stakeout of the Machtinger twins, though it had produced no leads, was continued.

McMillen was closing cases as fast as he could in an effort to lighten his load. The file on David Fine was one of those he hoped to get rid of. It was mostly old news: distributing antidraft leaflets during Vietnam Summer; speaking at a People Against Racism rally in Wilmington's Rodney Square; attending Delaware SDS meetings; and publishing an article in a local political journal, the *Heterodoxical Voice,* entitled, "Organizing in the High Schools or Hitting the System Where it Hurts." The file showed no activity since September 1969, when Fine had been photographed at a Black Panther rally on the Library Mall. In the interest of thoroughness, apparently, the bureau did attempt to interview David at his West Gorham Street apartment in the first week of June. David had resided there through the winter and spring with several other *Cardinal* staffers. A girl named Ann Mickola answered the door— the same Ann Mickola who had participated in Karl Armstrong's impromptu game of Coke Strip Bottle on New Year's Eve. By coincidence she had taken Fine's apartment for the summer. David and his roommates had left town, Mickola said. He had left his tennis racket in the closet and his cat Gracie (named for a singer in the Jefferson Airplane) for Mickola to take care of. On June 10 McMillen recommended that the case be closed, and two days later it was done, "as he [Fine] is not a leader in the campus protest movement and does not appear to have any current propensity for violence."

When David Fine was born in 1952, his sister Marsha, aged four, could not pronounce the word *brother.* It came out "buzza," which eventually evolved into the nickname Buzzy. As the only son, Buzzy occupied a place of distinction in the Fine family from the start. Marsha was an honors student, but David was the "genius" who knew all the colors when he was still a baby, the one who would fulfill the promise of life in America. There was no sibling rivalry; the whole family, Marsha included, pulled for David. His mother read to him every night and took him to the Academy of Music in Philadelphia to see ballet and at Christmastime to the Metropolitan Opera House in New York for "The Nutcracker." She had him studying French when he was five and made sure he got the same first-grade teacher that Marsha had had, a woman who defied the public school practicum of the day and taught phonetics. And so David became an avid reader just like his older sister and did beautifully in all his schoolwork.

Wilmington was a closed Southern town whose first family, the DuPonts, resided in baronial splendor in what was known as "Chateau Country," while the city's large population of blacks lived under Jim Crow conditions in the ghetto. In the 1950s not only schools but movie theaters and restaurants were segregated. In the hospitals black patients had their own linen, labeled "c" for colored. Black women were barred from the profession of nursing.

The Fines were opposed to racism, but when David came home from junior high school with stories of being picked on by bigger black boys, they were concerned. What would happen to him when he got to high school? "Don't let him go to P. S. (DuPont); it's going downhill," Marsha said. "David deserves better."

The Fines were scarcely wealthy. Manuel was a carpet salesman, Anne a dental hygienist, but somehow they scraped together the money to send David to the Friends Preparatory School, along with Tatnall and Tower Hill one of Wilmington's elite institutions. The beautiful stone houses of the Friends campus sat on a green, wooded hillside in the Alapocas area, about ten minutes by car from the Fine residence. David was among the first Jews admitted, and, upon entering the eighth grade, was elected class president. Class size was limited to sixteen, and everyone got to participate in athletics. David discovered a knack for tennis and competed in meets with other schools.

Manuel had been brought up in the strict Orthodox faith and had rebelled. Out of duty he accompanied his children to temple and observed the holiday rituals for Hanukkah, Passover, Rosh Hashanah, and Yom Kippur. Anne made sure David studied for his bar mitzvah, reading the Torah in Hebrew. The ceremony took place at their temple when he was thirteen. Anne would never forget how self-assured he was, "up there as cute as could be."

When David was eight, Anne had started sending him with his sister to a summer camp in the Poconos. In his thirteenth summer David announced that he wasn't returning. "I hate it," he said. Anne and Manny both worked full time. "What are you going to do all summer?" they asked. Marsha, once again, had the solution. "Why don't you send him to summer school? There's an excellent enrichment program at Exeter in New Hampshire." And so David spent the summer studying such topics as oceanography, boating on Lake Winnipesaukee, and going to Boston for Red Sox games. The next summer he participated in a similar program at Choate, which counted John Fitzgerald Kennedy among its alumni, and the following summer he attended Lawrenceville Academy in New Jersey. On top of tuition at Friends and Marsha's expenses at Boston University, the summer programs strained the family budget. But as Anne Fine said, "The children come first."

Manuel Fine loved the theater. He read *Variety* and grabbed the Arts and Leisure section of the *New York Times* every Sunday *before* reaching for the sports page. He was a friend of the manager of Wilmington's Playhouse, where Broadway shows regularly previewed, and often got free tickets. He did not belong to any left-wing groups, but he was a socialist at heart. When he was drafted in World War II, his sergeant asked, "You know why you're here?" "Yeah, we're here because the DuPont Corporation wants us here," Manuel replied. It was a story David loved to repeat. In his nervous, birdlike gestures and nasal intonation, David was "100 percent Manny," or so it seemed to Marsha. He also picked up his dad's enthusiasm for the arts and his knack for always having a ticket.

In his last summer at camp David had made the acquaintance of a young man named Will Stein, who was Marsha's camp boyfriend, a freshman at Columbia University, and a partisan of the New Left. Stein gave David history books to read and talked to him about the antiwar movement. David came home in the summer of 1965 "politically conscious."

That fall he addressed the Wilmington Antiwar Committee, a broad-based community group. "What a fabulous speech!" Ruth Kolber, a matronly committee member, told Anne Fine afterward.

David started helping Kolber, a longtime civil rights activist, on projects for the NAACP and SNCC, as well as on the grape and lettuce boycotts of the time. In the aftermath of the riot following the assassination of Martin Luther King, Jr., he assisted in the production of a documentary about the National Guard's occupation of Wilmington, and at a twenty-four-hour vigil in Rodney Square across from the Hotel DuPont, he took his turn reading the names of U.S. servicemen who had died in Vietnam. His willingness to work impressed Kolber. When he took on a job, she could count on its getting done.

Anne's friends disapproved of her laxness with David. "You allowed him to go to Washington? We wouldn't let Robby go!" But Anne supported her son, and Manuel never questioned her. In fact he would drive David downtown for demonstrations. "Where are you marching today, Buzzy?" neighbors would ask.

David had not broken any laws, but the FBI was monitoring his activities, taking note of his association with known Wilmington leftists. When David and his friend Rod Beaton, the son of one of Anne's dental patients, got themselves thrown out of a club for hawking the *Heterodoxical Voice,* a local SDS publication, an account of the incident was entered in his FBI file. After Rod took part in a demonstration against DuPont, his father, a DuPont chemical engineer and Democratic party activist, got a call from the state attorney general warning him that his son was being watched. "Has he done something illegal?" the elder Beaton asked. "If not, there's not much I can do."

At Friends David was in the top 10 percent of his class and edited the student newspaper in his junior year, the second student ever to do so. With credits from his summer programs he was able to graduate after only three years. His SAT score was in the eighty-eighth percentile (a ranking that disappointed him; he'd done better on the PSAT). But Harvard, Brandeis, and Columbia all rejected him because of his age. "You're just the sort of student we want," the Columbia recruiter told him, urging him to wait a year and reapply.

Again Marsha had the answer: "Mom, why don't you let him take a year off to travel," she said. Since he was only seventeen, he was in no danger of being drafted. But David had a better idea. He would go to Madison with Rod Beaton.

David and Rod had heard about Madison, about Williams and Goldberg and Mosse, about Miffland, even about the *Daily Cardi-*

nal. Madison was the famous Third Coast, a liberated zone. Despite the new limits on out-of-staters, the University of Wisconsin admitted both of them and even offered David a tuition scholarship, without which it would have been impractical for him to attend. In June 1969 he came to Madison for a freshman orientation program, and by the end of his visit, the campus's myriad political sects were fighting over him. He was only seventeen, so tiny he still wore children's sizes, yet he was just the sort of bright-eyed recruit they were looking for. As one movement veteran put it, "You didn't have to tell him anything; he was there already."

Jim Rowen was just about the most admirable person David Fine had ever met. He was one of the few Madison militants who could say he had won a national championship, as coxswain of the 1963 freshman eight-oar boat. Coach Jablonic had asked David, too, to try out for cox—practically begged him, in fact, because he was even smaller than Rowen. In high school Rowen had been a Democrat-for-Kennedy, but a combination of William Appleman Williams, Harvey Goldberg, and getting beat up on Dow Day had turned him into an acid-tongued disestablishmentarian who questioned not only the university's business and military ties, but even its involvement in Big Ten football. By the time David arrived Rowen was already in graduate school and a legend on the campus. He was a signer of the famous "We Won't Go" statement that had launched the draft resistance movement, the author of "Profit Motive 101," the scourge of Army Math.

David had introduced himself to Rowen at the *Cardinal*'s fall orientation meeting. "I'm interested in investigative reporting, and I hear you're the man," he had said. To Rowen, David looked about twelve years old but obviously had brains. He invited him into his workshop on power-structure research. Their paths crossed again at meetings of the Woody Guthrie Collective, an SDS clique where David was introduced to the Kaplan brothers, Susan Colson, Max Elbaum, David Siff, Kenny Mate, Michael Rosen, and other heavies. The Woody Guthries were to have a decisive influence on campus politics that year, formulating the Three Demands and emerging in the spring as the ultramilitant Mother Jones Revolutionary League. But David considered them a little old-fashioned and "Marxoid" and dropped out when they refused to accept his contributions to the *Daily Cardinal* as "mass work," a political chore required of all cadres.

Rowen was listed as a contributing editor, but he had more clout at the paper than his title indicated. He had grown a goatee and a big Afro bush that gave him a brooding appearance. Some *Cardinal* staffers were afraid of him, among them Steve Reiner, who made his editorials more left wing to try to please Rowen or to avoid conflict with him. Allied with then-news editor Rena Steinzor, Rowen had succeeded in abolishing the traditional independence of the *Cardinal* editor, making editorial decisions subject to "consensus." As it turned out, the consensus was usually what Rowen wanted it to be. Rowen, somewhat apologetically, would explain how this happened in a later interview with the Wisconsin Oral History Project:

> If people didn't agree with you, you could lash out at them and cut them to ribbons. You'd tell them that they were politically chicken-shit, that they weren't willing to take risks and that their politics weren't as good or pure as yours. The worst thing you could do was call somebody a liberal. That was the worst insult, reserved only for special occasions when you really wanted to clobber somebody. Liberalism was synonymous with weakness, a sneering term. That intimidated people. By a certain point they wouldn't argue with you anymore. We called it "gut-checking."

Rena Steinzor was Rowen's chief collaborator. "We worked as a team," Rowen would recall, and it was a team that David Fine wanted very much to be on. He would sit on top of a filing cabinet at editorial meetings and snipe at anyone who dared to contradict his idol. Walter Ezell, a pale, otherworldly, soft-spoken Christian Scientist from South Carolina, was a favorite target. "Well, we know what Walter's going to say," Rowen would say, undercutting him in advance. Ezell, both patient and determined to express his views, was frequently able to moderate the most intemperate, illogical, and unsupportable statements in a proposed editorial, but in the case of the New Year's bombings, he failed. "I know I'm in the minority," he had said politely in the January editorial meeting called to discuss the issue. "Walter is right about one thing: he's a minority of one, and we need to get on and write this editorial!" David had chimed in.

About a week after the FBI closed its file on David Fine its subject visited the Rowens at Susan's parents' home in Washington, D.C. Elinore McGovern, who had always done her own cooking, fixed beef Stroganoff. Jim and Susan had just returned from a trip to Berkeley, where they had gone to "cool out" in mid-May after hearing the rumor about impending conspiracy indictments against members of the United Front steering committee. They had broken with their Mother Jones friends when the latter, over Susan's express objections, plotted to force a Vietcong flag into her father's hands at a scheduled speaking appearance at the Field House in Madison. The senator entertained them with Senate Foreign Relations Committee reports suggesting that Pentagon figures on the results of the invasion of Cambodia were bogus; that few prisoners and hardly any arms had been taken; and, in sum, that the costly escalation had been fruitless. It was just casual talk, but David was flattered.

The following day the Rowens drove to New York to visit their friend Eliot Silberberg, the *Cardinal* fine arts editor, and they dropped David off in Wilmington. A few days later, on the third of July, Fine left home in the company of a sixteen-year-old Wilmington acquaintance named Chip in Chip's blue-and-white Volkswagen microbus. Chip wanted to go camping in Glacier National Park, but David immediately began to lobby for San Francisco, Haight-Ashbury, and Berkeley. At his insistence they stopped in Pittsburgh to visit David Minard, and since two other former housemates of David's, Cathy Hart (daughter of a well-known New York stage couple) and Susan Duckershein, were visiting, stayed over the Fourth of July riding horses with them at the Minard country home. David then directed Chip to Ann Arbor, where they visited another University of Wisconsin acquaintance, Linda Knutsen. It was the tenth of July by the time the two boys arrived in Madison.

Bill Limbach, a friend of David's from the YMCA, signed on for the trip across the plains, and around the middle of the month, they headed west on Interstate 94. David called Limbach "Kitchen" because he had found him working in the Y kitchen. A janitor's son from Racine, rangy and laconic, floundering in his university studies, Limbach called David "Fuzzy." During his one semester at the Y, David had managed to offend a number of his fellow residents. With his roommate Rod Beaton he would charge down the hall throwing body blocks and shouting "check to the boards!" The Y manager had moved them to a corner room on the top floor because David played his stereo too loudly and would sneak girls in to smoke pot. One resident was so incensed by David's outspoken political views that he joined Young Americans for Freedom just to twit him.

A few weeks into the fall semester David had decided he didn't care for the meals served at the Y and mounted a successful campaign to close the kitchen, costing Limbach and several other students their meal jobs. Then he had informed the Y management that he was leaving, offering the excuse that he was being harassed by right-wing residents. In fact, he had been in several fights. But it was also true that Rod Beaton had decided to return to Wilmington when the semester was over, and David wanted to move into a house with other *Cardinal* staffers. Despite such behavior, Limbach liked David and considered him a friend. "I didn't like the food, either," he assured David.

As the travelers neared Minneapolis David once again brought up the issue of their destination, still hoping that Chip would change his mind about going to Glacier. But Limbach sided with Chip; it was two against one, and David blew up. "Fuck you guys, I didn't come to go on some fucking camping trip to Glacier Park!" He demanded to be let out, and Chip obliged at the next interchange. As the microbus headed back onto the freeway Limbach gave him a perfunctory *V.* He was thinking of the *Cardinal* editorial about Guatemala, the one condoning the assassination of U.S. diplomats, and of David's claim that he had helped write it. "Man, you're gonna end up underground," Kitchen said.

David got back to Madison that night and went to see a girl he knew about a place to stay. She was a member of Mother Jones, and he had had thoughts about a relationship with her. But she would not even unlatch the security chain and open the door. He next tried a former girlfriend and got the cold shoulder again. He considered returning to Wilmington, but since Bill Limbach wouldn't be back for several weeks, Bill's brother Jim agreed to let David crash at their summer sublet on West Mifflin. A sign on the porch identified the house as "the Hacienda." A friend of David's had lived there, and he was familiar with the place. During the riot season its porches were like choice box seats, and the house had been gassed so many times that it had no cockroaches. David could scarcely believe his good luck: He was living rent free in one of the great political houses of Madison!

In June Leo Burt had sublet a first-floor efficiency in Iota Manor, an apartment building on upper Langdon. It was the first time that he had not gone home for the summer. He was making up an F in calculus and taking a course on contemporary China to complete his degree requirements. Karl Armstrong had moved in shortly after Memorial Day, Dwight had returned from Minneapolis, and the three of them had bought meal tickets at Tripp Commons, a baronial dining room on the second floor of the Memorial Student Union. Leo was wearing a new tank top that said "Blow Something Up!" They were all reading the best-selling revolutionary how-to by Jerry Rubin and Abbie Hoffman, called *Do It!,* which urged students to overthrow the United States government.

On the last weekend in June, Karl, Leo, and George Bogdanich drove to Iola, Wisconsin for the "People's Fair," a three-day rock festival featuring Buffy Ste. Marie singing "My country 'tis of thy people are dying." It ended with a shootout in which Michael McLaurin, later a suspect in the Army Math bombing, was wounded by biker security guards. The *Cardinal* condemned the festival in an editorial entitled "Woodstock No More," but Karl loved the "tribal feeling" and "working class" character of the 60,000 kids in attendance.

In July Karl and Dwight took off for Minneapolis to raise money. Dwight bought pot from Uncle Paul for resale to Madison dealers. Karl, Paul, and Max Sliter drove the hearse to western Nebraska to look for the marijuana that grows wild along the railroad right-aways near Grand Island, a volunteer crop left over from the days of hemp cultivation, according to Paul. The plants they found were green and immature, but they went ahead and filled the car and took the contraband to an abandoned farmhouse in Moose Lake, Minnesota, to dry. Karl returned to Madison and got a job with the Chicago and Northwestern Railroad as brakeman on the Way Freight to Elroy. Don and Ruth were delighted. The job paid $1,000 a month and offered union benefits; a man could do worse.

David, meanwhile, had landed a job delivering the *Capital Times* and had been given a column of his own in the *Daily Cardinal,* writing rock-music criticism. His first review, on July 22, was of new albums by Hot Tuna and Traffic. Hot Tuna, a blues group consisting of four of the six stars of the Jefferson Airplane, opened for the larger ensemble. David had caught their act in Toronto over spring break and again in Madison in May, on the tail end of the riots. He had also made it to their surprise jam session with Luther Allison at the Nitty Gritty that night and had played pinball with lead guitarist Jorma Kaukonen and drummer Joey Covington afterward. The column had a breezy and authoritative tone that was remarkable for an eighteen-year-old writer, an auspicious debut.

Although Leo Burt was in and out of the *Cardinal* office throughout the summer months, writing occasional op-ed pieces of an apocalyptic tenor, he seemed most concerned about getting his degree. "I gotta get these classes down or I'm screwed," he would say, rushing off to study. During the previous fall Leo had done his laundry at the Y on Saturdays and occasionally stayed for a round of Milwaukee Sheepshead (a card game similar to Skat) with David Fine and Bill Limbach, who was a crackerjack player. Leo was impressed by David's connections with East Coast heavies, such as Mark Rudd and Cathy Wilkerson, who belonged to Weatherman. On his part David thought that Leo was just "coming along" politically and certainly not as hip as one might have expected of someone from Philadelphia. All the same, he was pleased when Leo, in recognition of the fact that David was now 18, invited him to the Nitty Gritty for a beer and Gritty burgers. Although David had no idea of Leo's ulterior motives, the two of them began to get better acquainted.

It wasn't until July 26, at the Cuban Independence Day rally in Madison, that Leo found an opportunity to introduce David to Karl. Mifflin Street was decked out with Cuban flags, food booths, and a bandstand. The *Kaleidoscope* was on sale with a lengthy commemorative piece, written by alumni of the Venceremos Brigade, about the abortive raid on the Moncada Barracks in 1953 that signaled the beginning of the Cuban Revolution. "It taught the rebels that terrorism with a political purpose is good," the article concluded.

David recognized Karl at once. "I saw you at the T-16 demo," he said coolly. "You wanted to trash the bank."

Karl remembered the incident. "Yeah, man, that was me," he said. He was so open about it that David was disarmed. "No one

The East Wing of
Sterling Hall, shortly
after the bombing of
August 24, 1970.
(Skot Weidemann,
courtesy University of
Wisconsin–Madison
Division of Archives)

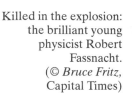

Killed in the explosion:
the brilliant young
physicist Robert
Fassnacht.
(© *Bruce Fritz,*
Capital Times)

Above: Campus police place Robert Fassnacht's remains in a waiting ambulance. (© *Bruce Fritz,* Capital Times); *Left*: A Sterling Hall clock captured the moment of the explosion.
(*Courtesy David Brown, Madison*)

Below: Where Fassnacht's lab had been, a gaping wound.
(*Del Brown, courtesy University of Wisconsin–Madison Division of Archives*)

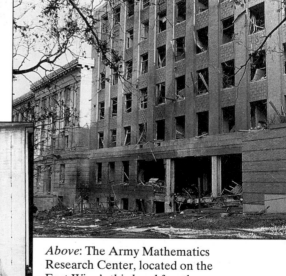

Above: The Army Mathematics Research Center, located on the East Wing's third and fourth floors, survived the explosion, but 26 other campus buildings were damaged.
(*Gary Schulz, courtesy University of Wisconsin–Madison Division of Archives*)

Left: Lorene, Karl, and Dwight with the Armstrong family dog in 1956. (*Courtesy The Armstrong Family*)

Below: Karl Armstrong at the age of twelve. (*Courtesy The Armstrong Family*)

Lorene, Ruth, and Mira Armstrong in December 1972. (*Courtesy The Armstrong Family*)

BOMB
Extra!
BOMB

VOL. 2   **MADISON**   NO. 17

INSIDE THIS ISSUE: WOMEN'S LIB

KALEIDOSCOPE

25¢
Open
war
next!

EXCLUSIVE TO KALEIDOSCOPE

The Bombers Tell Why & What Next

Exclusive statement by the bombers of the Army Math Research Center to Madison Kaleidoscope (Monday 24 August):

"Our every action is a battle cry against imperialism...Wherever death may surprise us, let it be our welcome, provided that this, our battle cry, may have reached some receptive ear and another hand may be extended to wield our weapons..." - Che Guevara

Today (24 August) the battle cry against imperialism was raised once again, as the mathematics research center of the U.S. army was struck by revolutionary cadres of the New Years Gang.

The AMRC, a think-tank of Amerikan militarism, was a fitting target for such revolutionary violence. As the major U.S. army center for solving military mathematical problems, it bears full responsibility for amerikan military genocide throughout the world. While hiding behind a facade of academic "neutrality," the AMRC plays a vital role in doing the basic research necessary for the development of heavy artillery, conventional and nuclear bombs and missiles, guns and mobile weapons, biological weapons, chemical weapons, and much more.

Its neutralist facade is exposed even by its self-proclaimed policy of operation: "To anticipate the needs of the army, and when it is able to develop or learn of new techniques to meet these needs, it should forthwith call these to the army's attention and help it find the area in which these techniques can be used."

Today's (24 August) explosion was the culmination of over a year's effort to remove AMRC's ominous presence from the Wisconsin campus. Previous efforts to even negotiate were met with indifference. Such is the response of imperialistic authority to public sentiment. Our actions, therefore, were deemed necessary, for with every passing day, the AMRC takes its toll in mutilated bodies.

We see our achievement as more than just the destruction of one building. We see it as part of a world-wide struggle to defeat amerikan imperialism, that monster which is responsible for the starvation and oppression of millions over the globe, that monster which is a direct outgrowth of corporate capitalism.

For this reason, we declare solidarity with our revolutionary brothers in Uruguay, the Tupamaros, who are struggling to loosen the U.S. military and corporate grasp on their continent. We also declare our solidarity with the San Rafael four, revolutionary black brothers who died fighting the racist court system. But more importantly, we declare our solidarity with each and every peasant, worker, student and displaced person, who, in his day-by-day existence, struggles against the oppressive conditions heaped upon him by the monster.

The Vanguard of the Revolution demands the immediate release of the Milwaukee 3, the abolition of ROTC, and the elimination of the male supremacist women's hours on the Wisconsin campus. If these demands are not met by October 30th, revolutionary measures of an intensity never before seen in this country will be taken by our cadres. Open warfare, kidnapping of important officials, and even assasination will not be ruled out. Although we have sought to prevent any physical harm to all people in the past, we cannot be responsible for the safety of pigs if our demands are not met.

Power to the People!   - Marion Delgado

Editor's Note: The detonation was supposed to occur five minutes after the phone call to the Madison Police. It exploded prematurely. The New Years Gang regrets the death of Fassnacht.

Kaleidoscope published a communiqué from the Army Math bombers, adding regrets about Fassnacht.

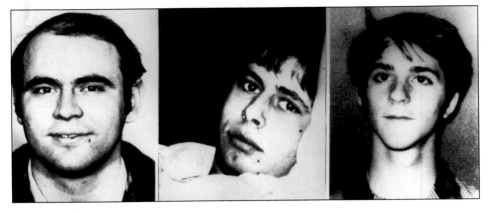

Left to right: Karl and Dwight Armstrong and David Fine, as they appeared on FBI wanted posters. (*UPI/Bettmann*)

Leo Burt's wanted poster.

Rochdale in Toronto: The "world's biggest crash pad" has since become a home for the elderly. (*Tom Bates*)

54 Langley: Karl Armstrong's last address in Toronto. (*Tom Bates*)

March 1973: *Takeover*, a new underground newspaper, hails Karl Armstrong's return to Madison.

Below: January 1976: After being apprehended in California, David Fine is released on bail in Madison. (*UPI/Bettmann*)

Karl Armstrong and David Fine at 1989 reunion of Madison radicals. (*Tom Bates*)

Karl Armstrong, proprietor of "Loose Juice": a fixture today on State Street in Madison. (*Tom Bates*)

really thought you were an agent, *really*," David said, "but people were startin' to get a little nervous."

Karl had never heard anyone talk as fast as David. "Really" came out "rilly." It was a strangely ingratiating voice, like that of an old chum who is deeply concerned about you. He admitted that trashing the bank was a dumb idea, and they laughed it off.

They were standing in front of the Hacienda, and after a while they went up to David's room and smoked some of Karl's Nebraska Green. It was "funky pot," in David's opinion, but the three of them soon were laughing and joking as if they had known each other all their lives.

On Saturday, the first of August, David and Leo attended a party at the apartment of *Cardinal* summer editor Ron Legro to celebrate the end of the summer session. David was unhappy because a hippie he had allowed to use his bathroom during the Cuban celebration had walked off with an electric razor his grandfather had given him. Miffland was degenerating, everyone agreed; druggies were pushing out the legitimate counterculturalists.

David was fascinated by Legro's new lightbox. Though it was just a psychedelic plaything, he insisted, it was politically significant because "art is *always* political." Afterward he and Leo caught a ride home with a *Cardinal* board member, who dropped them off a block from Greek Row. Leo brought up the subject of Karl. "I've known him for a while," he said. His brother and this other girl helped him, but it's basically him. Karl Armstrong is the New Year's Gang." He described going with Karl to firebomb the Monroe Street Selective Service office and discovering that their ladder was too short.

"That sounds like the New Year's Gang," David said.

David went back to work on his next column, a review of "Workingman's Dead" by the Grateful Dead. "If this beautiful LP is any indication," he wrote, "the Grateful Dead should be around forever." He was mulling over what Leo had told him about Karl Armstrong. *I thought, "This is really heavy, this is the New Year's Gang." I believed it because it didn't go against anything I had established in my mind. I had a certain amount of respect at the time. Just because here's someone who "put up" instead of "shut up." I thought it was cool that he was from Madison. I liked that—local boy who got freaked out by the war and decided to do something about it. Maybe got reached somewhat by the antiwar movement, but basically did it on his own.* Karl's East Side, working-class upbringing made him, if anything, "extra cool."

At Leo's suggestion the four of them—Karl, Leo, David, and Dwight—met the next day at an out-of-the-way pub called the Q. Fine's appearance surprised Dwight. *My God,* he thought, *he's like a little kid.*

"Something's coming up with Army Math," Leo said obliquely. David brushed aside explanations. He had read everything Jim Rowen had written on the subject. *Once it was established that [Karl] was the New Year's Gang, that he was serious about this— that's all. I just wanted to do what I had to do to bring it off, and that was that. We didn't really have any heavy political discussions. It was more like, "Hey, right on! Let's go to the bombing!"*

But timing was a problem. Karl wanted to wait until the semester break, to minimize the chance of hurting anyone. David said that his friend Rod Beaton was coming to Madison, and they were going to hitchhike to Ann Arbor that weekend to attend a blues festival. He had already arranged for a press pass to the event and planned to write it up for the *Cardinal.* Then he was going home for a few days. He wouldn't be back until the twentieth, for Eliot Silberberg's wedding. The more he thought about it, the bombing didn't really fit in to his plans.

"Think about it," Leo said. "I'll see you at the wedding."

21

Options

There is no area of science that cannot be used for harmful or illegal purposes.

—R. CREIGHTON BUCK,
mathematician, for the prosecution

It seemed to me that the university's stated policy of neutrality was clearly being violated by harboring an institution that was developing weapons of war.

—TOM SIMON,
student, for the defense

The clarity of vision Karl had experienced at the climax of the Memorial Day storm had blurred in the daunting light of successive days. Army Math was well secured. There was no obvious way to get at it without blowing up the entire building, which, as he knew, also housed physics and astronomy. He toyed with other ideas, bouncing them off Leo Burt. The primacord was still sitting in the doghouse at Devil's Lake. What about wrapping it around the Capitol rotunda and blowing the dome off? Leo advised against it; "People like the dome," he pointed out. The discussions had a bantering, fanciful quality, and often it must have seemed to Leo that Karl was joking. But then Karl would say, "Yeah, and anyway, it would take a truckload of clay packed around the primacord to direct the explosion inward."

Karl's latest proposal was to interdict the main supply route to Badger Ordnance Works by blowing up the Merrimac railroad bridge. The idea had come to him while working on the Way Freight to Elroy. The Way Freight did all the switching and spotting of cars north of Madison, dropping loads off at industries along the route. Badger was its biggest customer. Karl actually rode into the plant one day, giving security guards the peace sign from his perch high in the engine cab. The Way Freight left entire boxcars full of gunpowder and rocket fuel on a siding south of Devil's Lake while the train completed its rounds, returning to pick them up at the end of the day. It was all downhill from the siding to the trestle over Lake Wisconsin at Merrimac, a little ovr three miles away. "If you took the brakes off and unblocked the wheels, how far would the cars roll?" Karl asked a switchman. The answer was, "All the way across the river." *Unless,* Karl thought, *someone braked them to a stop in the middle of the bridge and ignited them with a stick of dynamite.*

But Leo talked him out of that scheme, too.

One afternoon Karl and Leo dropped in on Mira, and Karl introduced his new friend. Mira invited them to sit out by the pool. Karl had warned Leo not to get going on religion with Mira, but the *Capital Times* had recently carried a story on U.S. saturation bombings of Cambodia and Laos, and Leo could not resist bringing it up. "What kind of God would demand genocide?" he said. "Old women, babies blown to bits, is that what you call a 'merciful God'?"

Leo had been lifting weights all summer and looked like a Swiss mountain man in his shorts. Mira was terrified of him. *He's trying to make me look weak in front of my brother,* she thought. She went inside and leafed through her Bible, and as luck would have it the book fell open at a passage in Matthew, chapter two, that seemed pertinent. She showed it to Leo and Karl. "Satan's plan was to destroy Jesus by stamping out the whole tribe of Judah," she explained. "King Herod ordered that all Hebrew children under the age of two be killed, but an angel warned Joseph and he fled with Mary and the infant Jesus to Egypt." In other words, God, too, was against genocide.

Karl didn't like Leo's teasing Mira, so he swooped her up and spun her around to show that he was proud of her for standing her ground. His eyes were gentle and laughing again, it seemed to his sister, and for the moment, at least, she thought that she had won Karl back.

In late July, Karl told Leo he was going on a little trip to clear his mind and hitchhiked south to Chicago, following the beltline around the southern edge of the city. After a night in a barn he was heading back up Interstate 90 toward Madison when a beat-up Oldsmobile stopped for him. Inside were two brown-toothed pot-heads who said they belonged to a Jenifer Street commune in Madison. Jenifer paralleled Spaight and Williamson streets on the near East Side, a pleasant blue-collar neighborhood that was fast becoming hippiefied. Karl had recently met a dealer who said he would buy green, low-potency Midwest pot from him to cut his better, imported dope. In no time he had the potheads convinced that their fortune was to be found growing wild along the White River in Bloomfield, Indiana, where he had seen it when he was working on the survey crew in the summer of 1965. All they had to do was turn the car around and go to harvest it. But after a dust-choked night on Indiana back roads, he had to conclude that there was no longer any marijuana to be found by the White River.

Karl next persuaded the Jenifer Street boys to drive to Grand Island, Nebraska, some 500 miles away, where they would definitely find marijuana. This time, the plants were exactly where Karl said they would be, taller and more resinous now than they had been when Karl was there earlier in the summer with Paul and Max. The following afternoon Karl sold his share of the harvest for $200, negotiating the deal in the Iota Court apartment. Leo was upset; he didn't want to be involved in drug dealing.

"It's not ordinary dealing," Karl explained, "not if we use the money for the revolution."

August J. Troia, district train master for Chicago and North Western, called Karl into his office on the sixth of August after several days of his employee's unexplained absence. "A. J.," as he was known to his friends, liked Armstrong, but he had never had an employee who inspired so many complaints in so little time. It was said that Karl was a Communist and a vegetarian and that his crew was refused service at a restaurant one day because of his long hair and beard. Troia paid no attention to those stories, but he could not ignore the remarks of Roger Rheinhold, conductor on the Way Freight. "The guy is one hundred miles away!" Rheinhold said. He described an incident in which Karl had gone careening through downtown Elroy on an empty boxcar, unable to get the brake on. "He's gonna get somebody killed!"

In his office Troia addressed Karl with the directness for which he was known. "They say you're a hazard to yourself and to others," he said. "Do you not like working for the railroad?"

Karl answered with equal candor. "I am totally alienated by this kind of work," he said. "And I am constantly afraid that I am going to back into a train." In fact, standing between moving cars made him dizzy.

"Finish your engineering degree," Troia gruffly advised. "You don't belong here."

Karl suspected that Badger Ordnance was somehow behind Troia's lecture. The guards had gone berserk when he gave them the peace sign, chasing along in their jeeps and talking on their two-way radios. "You're right, it's not my bag," he said amiably, "but I'm not going back to school."

The very next day he visited Sterling Hall, accompanied by Leo and Dwight. Tacked to the East Wing entrance was a yellowing, hand-lettered sign:

> THE STUDENTS AND FACULTY
> OF THE PHYSICS DEPARTMENT
> DEPLORE THE USE OF VIOLENCE
> IN THE NAME OF PEACE.

Karl hastily opened the door and they went inside, on the lookout for cops. From the old power plant at University and Charter, he had stolen a blueprint of the vast underground network of steam tunnels that supplied heat to the campus. Karl had spotted what appeared to be a good-size shaft leading to Sterling and now wanted to find its entry portal in the basement. *I thought, first of all, if there was some way of carrying the charge into the building, say, in a briefcase. But I had seen from other bombings that such a charge would be too small, that it would not, that it would not destroy the center.* Karl had decided that Army Math should be totally destroyed, that there should be nothing left except rubble. That was the only way they could get Nixon's attention, he told the others. He proposed to carry the explosives in through a steam tunnel and plant them right under the center.

They rode the elevator to the third floor to check out the AMRC entrance. As Karl had expected, the door was locked. On the way down a physicist named James Bensinger boarded the elevator. "Well, if it isn't my old Physics TA," Karl said lamely. Five years had passed, and he could not recall Bensinger's name. Bensinger remembered him, however: Karl had been one of those students who rarely, if ever, volunteer to answer a question and had finished the year with a D. They exchanged small talk, and Bensinger got off the elevator at the first floor. Only later would it occur to him to wonder what Armstrong and his friends were doing in the building at that time.

Dwight led the way through the basement, having been there once to visit Karl's former roommate Hugo Vega, who had some sort of job with the department. If anyone stopped them, he was going to say that they were looking for Vega, but there seemed to be no one around. Deep in the maze they found what they were looking for, opened it, and looked inside. The interior of the steam tunnel was narrow and crowded with pipes. It would have been difficult to get through carrying a pipe wrench, let alone a bomb.

They retraced their steps, passing the doors to the accelerator room and the low-temperature research lab, and exited onto Lathrop Drive. Next to Lathrop Hall, a dark, tomblike building, they found a shaded expanse of lawn overlooking University Avenue and sat down. Obviously the steam tunnel was out, and they would have to find another way. "One could go in armed with the explosives," Karl said. "One could gather everyone up and get 'em out. Nobody would argue with a gun."

Leo objected. There would be witnesses; it would be risky.

"OK, OK," Karl said. He didn't like guns either, and in any case, they didn't have money for guns. *I was perplexed. I didn't know how AMRC was going to be destroyed. Because it seemed that all the alternatives had been eliminated. And one of my conspirators suggested that, well, why, why don't we just drive a vehicle up next to the building and destroy the building in that way. And like that was, ... of course, the ... logical solution.*

It was, in fact, Dwight's idea. A loading ramp stood next to the East Wing, parallel to Lathrop Drive. "Why not just put [the bomb] in a truck, drive it alongside and blow it up?"

Karl and Leo were both skeptical. What about the threat to pedestrians? To passing autos? To other buildings? To University Hospital? Karl contemplated the University of Wisconsin seal outlined in jade-and-purple flowers on the embankment in front of Lathrop Hall. *I had great hesitations ... about the destruction, about that method, because ... it was certainly not very specific to the Army Mathematics Research Center. The old Chemistry Building was there, and Birge Hall. I had had classes in those buildings, and I knew that with the bombing of AMRC that people's research was going to be destroyed.... I knew ... it was going to be a very destructive act.*

But he could not think of an alternative.

Now the time had to be chosen. Of course, the destruction of Army Mathematics Research Center was chosen as being during the semester break. Because there wouldn't be anyone, very, very few people on campus. In other words, that would be the time which there would be the minimum number of people inside the AMRC. Next thing was to determine the day and the hour. For that, the building was placed under surveillance for a period of two weeks beginning the weekend before commencement.

A momentum began to build. Karl delegated surveillance to Leo and Dwight, who hid in the bushes behind Old Chemistry, where they had a direct view of the East Wing and the loading ramp. They kept a record of everything that moved, pedestrians as well as cars, between the hours of 2 and 4 A.M. To help pass the time they would smoke marijuana, and Leo would try to explain life to Dwight. "You know," he said at one point, appraising a sliver of the lawn in his hand, "there is nothing in the world more erotic than a blade of grass." Dwight was stunned by this idea. "If we're candles, Leo's a blowtorch," he informed Karl.

Karl studied the surveillance log. Weeknights, traffic on the winding drive was surprisingly heavy:

2:30 WHITE MUSTANG COME UP LATHROP
2:33 WHITE MUSTANG COME BACK OUT OF LATHROP
2:34 RED PONTIAC UP CHARTER

2:57 P&S UP LATHROP WITH RED LIGHT FLASHING
3:46 PEDESTRIAN UP LATHROP
3:48 WHITE MUSTANG UP LATHROP/RED PONTIAC ON
CHARTER
3:50 P&S OUT OF LATHROP

But Karl thought he saw an opening. *We noticed that on the Monday morning there were no lights on in the Army Mathematics Research Center. And ... my own intuition ... told me that probably the Monday morning would be ... the more suitable time.*

In the same notebook with the Sterling Hall observations the FBI would find notes Leo had made from Jim Rowen's articles on Army Math: the $1.8 million Department of Defense contract, the center's prerogative of denying access to top-secret information to university administrators, its contributions to the Electronic Battlefield, and so forth. "I don't believe in non-violence," Leo wrote in neat, block letters, as though recanting a long-held creed.

Karl was pleased that Leo seemed to be "into" the bombing, but worried that another part of Leo was running on an old track, toward getting his degree (he had earned an A in both of his summer courses) and finding a job on a left-wing newspaper, such as the *National Guardian.* One day, in a chance encounter with *Guardian* correspondent Steve Torgoff on the Union terrace, Torgoff mentioned that the paper was against bombings. "So am I," Leo told him.

At noon on the last day of finals week Leo met a friend named Laurie Burt (no relation) on the Union terrace, and the two ordered bratwursts at the outdoor grill. Laurie was a history student who kept Leo posted on the Mosse-Goldberg debate. For three years they had been receiving each other's report cards in the mail, and they would call up and laugh about each other's grades. Now, watching the sailboats laboring in the sluggish breeze, they spoke of their plans for the fall. Leo gave no hint of being involved in anything unusual, but spoke only of his ambition to work for the *Guardian.* "I have connections there," he said, inflating the significance of his brief encounter with Torgoff.

Laurie said that she had been invited into Mosse's seminar, a coup for a woman, but that she had decided to specialize in U.S. history instead. As for the immediate future she would be joining her parents for a couple of weeks at their Thousand Islands vacation home on the St. Lawrence River.

"Well," Leo said, "if you're ever in New York, be sure to drop by."

That night in Wisconsin Dells, the motels and restaurants and arcades were full of Midwest tourists enjoying their summer vacations. Lynn Schultz's parents had gone to their card club for the evening, and she was on her way to visit her aunt and uncle. She had been home for several days, taking a break from the outdoor concert business and from her boyfriend Sandy Nelson, who was staying with his father in Springfield Corners. As she was backing her car out the driveway, an old Cadillac hearse pulled up in front of the house. Karl Armstrong.

"Where've you been all summer?" he asked in his sing-song way. Lynn tried to think of an answer that would not take several hours. The Golden Freeks had been forced out of one state after another. In Iowa the governor had shut them down in the middle of a three-day concert by cutting off food supplies and sanitation trucks. The portapotties had filled up, and the IRS had confiscated the gate receipts. They had moved to a trailer court beside a creek in Shadyside, Ohio, where Bobo had launched a new venture, billed as the "Spoon River Festival," on a 500-acre dude ranch just over the state line in Pennsylvania. The Quaker State had stopped them with an injunction claiming inadequate access roads. Still working out of Shadyside, they had started on a concert in the Pittsburgh area, but it, too, had become ensnarled in court actions. "I've been around," Lynn said coldly.

"No you haven't, you've been gone," he said, mistaking her meaning. She wasn't quite the cuddly little bunny that he remembered.

"Well, yeah," she said. "I was in Pennsylvania."

Leo had told Karl he wouldn't do the Army Math bombing without a fourth person to make a warning call. David Fine was iffy; a couple of other acquaintances Karl had approached about it had turned him down. The only other possibility he could think of was Lynn. "How long will you be home?" he asked.

A short while, she answered. *And he once again asked me if I wanted any part of anything and I told him no and I asked him what and he told me that there were some very heavy things going to hap-*

pen in Madison and that they wanted me to help and needed me to help and I should do it. I told him that I wouldn't and then I went on to ask him more specifically what he was going to do and he wouldn't tell me anything.

"Well, what are you doing right away tonight?" Lynn said. Karl said they were going up to northern Wisconsin to see if they could steal some dynamite from a quarry. That was why he had borrowed the hearse.

"I've got to go," she said. She jumped into her car and left by the back alley, but saw him a moment later at an intersection, alone at the wheel. Briefly she considered going to the police, but then she remembered that she, too, was implicated. When she got back from her aunt and uncle's, the phone rang, and it was Sandy Nelson, calling from his dad's place. "Guess who I just had a visit from," she said.

Leo liked to keep his apartment neat and had kicked Dwight out early in the summer when Dwight refused to pick up after himself. Eventually Karl, too, had moved back to Hintze Road. Every day he went jogging in nearby Warner Park, ostensibly to get in shape for the bombing, but he continued to have doubts about undertaking the task. *I still didn't want to do it. I looked for excuses not to do it.*

An excuse presented herself to him one day as he was running in Warner Park: a woman named Jan. Jan was a social worker, divorced, with two children, a "nice lady," in Karl's opinion. He had long-since overcome his shyness with women, and after speaking to her a couple of times in the park, hc invited her to go swimming. She agreed, and the next day he showed up in a red-and-white Mustang convertible with the top down. "It's my dad's," he told her, and in fact Don had bought it the year before with Uncle Paul's Mob money. They drove around Lake Monona a few times looking for a good swimming hole, but the beaches were all crowded and the water bad smelling from algae. They ended up back at her house, where they had a glass of wine. Karl liked Jan so much he began to fantasize about settling down with her, getting a regular job, helping her raise her children. But if he married her, what would he do about Army Math? It would be unfair to involve her. He would have to give it up.

Don Armstrong had grown up in what the sociologists call a "rural poverty pocket." His earliest memories were of a town called Tunnel City whose main feature was the soot-blackened entrance of a railroad tunnel that yawned over the several dozen buildings and houses like the gates of hell. The shabby settlement was surrounded by Appalachian-like hills and dreary cranberry bogs, where descendants of the Winnebagos slaved at harvest time for twenty-five cents a day. Locals said the Jesse James Gang used to hide out in Tunnel City on its northern raids. The first settlers in the region had ruined the thin topsoil by tilling too deep and bringing up sand, and as in many neglected corners of Wisconsin, the long winters and deprivation had taken their toll. Local papers were full of stories of crop failures and bankruptcies, of suspicious-looking tramps, unsolved barn burnings, disappearing livestock, suicides, outbreaks of diphtheria, kidnappings, alcoholism, shootings, blackmail, deliberately set forest fires, and incest. The demented were sent to Mendota State Hospital in Madison, where people gone crazy with the travail and loneliness of life in "God's Own Country" were bedded down and forgotten.

The difference between today's kids and people like himself who had grown up in the 1930s, Don Armstrong sometimes thought, was that they had no idea what it was like to be poor. They did not have memories like he had, of walking six miles to school along a railroad rightaway and collecting cinders for the stove on the way home. Of wading with the Indians in the cranberry bogs. Of riding the rails all over the country looking for work. Hoover Dam, Don liked to say, was really Hoover Tomb, its concrete face filled with the bodies of men who had been killed for their jobs.

The Mustang was the first new car Don had ever owned. It was *his* car; he did not allow anyone else to drive it, and Karl knew that. When Don saw it missing from the driveway, it was as if someone had stolen his baby, the only thing he had left of which he was genuinely proud. He jumped in the Corvair and drove all over the East Side looking for it, and when he found it parked out in front of a run-down house, he pulled in behind it and honked his horn.

Karl had never been with a woman as old as Jan, who was twenty-eight. He was surprised by how much more relaxed he was with her than with younger women. But just as things were getting passionate between them, he heard a loud noise outside. Somebody was honking a horn and would not stop. Karl got up, went to the window, and saw Don sitting at the curb in the Corvair. He pulled on his pants and stepped outside. Don shouted at him to bring the keys to the Mustang. Karl handed them over, and Don changed cars and drove off without another word.

Karl saw Jan peeking out the door at him. He gave her a sickly sort of grin, said good-bye, and raced home in the Corvair, screeching to a stop in front of the house. Don was still in the driveway, going over the Mustang with a chamois cloth. Karl charged him and straight-armed him in the chest, but Don outweighed him by fifty pounds, and it was like running into a telephone pole. They went into a clinch and staggered around the yard while Ruth hollered at them from the porch. Neighbors opened their venetian blinds to watch.

Suddenly the fight went out of Karl, and he gave up. The two stood there for a moment sweating and panting; Ruth was sobbing. Then Karl rushed down to the rec room, threw a few things into his backpack, and caught the bus downtown. He did not call Jan back. *And in the end I finally found that there was no use, that there was no use kidding myself any more, that it had to be done.*

22

ANFO

I recall many conversations about who would do it. The one that sticks in my mind—because to me at that time it seemed the most plausible—was the speculation that it would be a secretary that worked in Army Math, that she would carry the bomb in her lunch bag.

—PHIL BALL,
activist, for the defense

Often times in history the most grievous acts are committed by the less obvious people, who are often disturbed.

—MICHAEL ZALESKI,
Wisconsin Assistant Attorney General, for the prosecution

The semester break brought quiet to the campus. O'Hare charters carried summer visitors away, leaving the Library Mall nearly deserted. Karl dug fifteen cents out of his pocket and bought a Dick-on-a-Stick from the Banana Man, Bob Montgomery. He had recovered his composure; in fact, he was incredibly "laid back," or so it seemed to Montgomery in retrospect. He ambled over to the Memorial Student Union and found a table in the shade of the oaks growing from a raised bed on the terrace. The lake was as placid as the Sargasso Sea; the air was still, the light diffuse in the August haze; even the Hoofers fleet, rocking gently at anchor, seemed weighed down by a pervasive lethargy. He found a copy of the *Capital Times* someone had left behind and perused the front page. The Paris peace talks were stalled; air strikes continued in Cambodia and Laos. Karl turned to the local news section, where he found an interesting tidbit. Police reported the discovery of 23,000 feet of primacord stashed in a doghouse at the site of the old General Refractories quarry along South Shore Road near Devil's Lake. A Sauk County cattleman had spotted the contraband while searching for stray cows. He had called the police on August 1, and the authorities had staked out the doghouse for days hoping that whoever had stolen the material—it had been traced to the Mary Ellen Mine in Biwabik, Minnesota—would return for it.

If the investigators had been a little more patient, they might have nabbed Karl; he had been planning to go back to the quarry over the weekend. The primacord was gone, but he had never figured out how to use it. He had in any case made up his mind to use ANFO, mainly because on a budget of $200, the proceeds of his marijuana deal, it was the only thing he could afford. By now he knew that ANFO had to be ignited before it would work. He would need blasting caps, dynamite, and fuse. He asked Ruth for the Corvair, thinking it best to buy the explosives in Minneapolis. Ruth said she was going up to Tomah for the weekend to visit her parents, Alvah and Tressie Kennedy. Karl suggested dropping her off. He would pick her up on his way back.

The Kennedys lived in a white shingle house with many small rooms on 240 acres of pasture and woods in the narrow Tarr Valley, off Highway 21 outside Tomah. Alvah and Tressie were gentle people, and neither had more than a fourth-grade education. Tressie wore floral print dresses and an apron, had cornflower blue eyes, and was almost as wide as she was tall. Alvah was slender with black, snappy eyes and white hair. His cash crop was cream from his herd of Guernseys. The skim milk went to the animals, and he produced sweet butter for the family's use. Growing up on the farm, Ruth had done her share of the chores, milking cows and helping in the hay fields. She was known for her sunny disposition. Everyone had loved little Ruth.

But Alvah and Tressie were not Ruth's biological parents. Her real mother, Tressie's sister Della, had run off to Winnipeg when Ruth was only fourteen months old, and the issue of paternity was a matter for guarded speculation. Ruth had grown up believing that Tressie and Alvah were her true parents and that their children, Lola and Harley, were her blood brother and sister. It was not until she was twenty-one that she learned she was adopted.

Karl had fond memories of the Kennedy farm, where family reunions were a fourth of July ritual. When he was eleven, he got to spend the summer working in the dairy. He was given a couch to sleep on in one of the dollhouse-size bedrooms. In the morning sun flooded through his window, and he awakened to the smell of sausage and pancakes cooking on the big wood stove in the kitchen. He would remember those breakfasts, the sweet butter, the cold spring water, the redwing blackbirds stationed like sentries on the fenceposts around the farm.

The trip came off as planned, but when Karl returned from Minneapolis, he was clean shaven. Alvah Kennedy could not get over it. Alvah was a skeptical sort who did not believe everything he saw on TV. In his opinion, for example, the moon walk was bogus, a stunt contrived by Hollywood. "Just shoot the rockets up and once they're out of sight, fake the rest," he would say. He was also a conservative Republican, and Karl had learned never to argue with him. "It was just getting too hot," Karl said, explaining the missing beard. He had gotten a haircut, too, but not because he was going straight.

Nervously he walked Ruth to the car. Since the Corvair afforded few hiding places, he was forced to conceal the dynamite under the passenger seat. In the trunk, under a coat, was a pound of Uncle Paul's marijuana that Karl had taken on consignment. Ruth found the package as she moved things around to make room for her suitcase.

"What's this?" she asked, wrinkling her nose. The trunk smelled like oregano.

"I dunno, prob'ly some old weed," Karl said without conviction.

Ruth had never seen marijuana, but there was something about a quantity of strong-smelling, wilted vegetable matter in a sweaty plastic bag that aroused her suspicion. "What do you do with that?" she asked.

Karl told the truth. "I'm going to sell it," he said.

Ruth appeared somewhat relieved. At least he wasn't going to use it himself. "I don't want to see that stuff around," she said sternly.

"Don't worry, Mom, I'll take care of it," Karl said.

After dropping Ruth off, Karl drove over to Iota Court and stashed the explosives in Leo's apartment. It was Sunday, the sixteenth of August. Dwight came by, and the three of them went out cruising. On University Avenue Dwight asked Karl to stop at McDonald's and went inside to order a soft drink. Ahead of him in line was Steve Rabideau's girlfriend Barbara Ford, whom he had not seen since New Year's Eve. Barbara was in a miniskirt, and he could see why Karl liked her. "Karl's outside," he said. Ford hastened out to the parking lot. A Corvair was sitting there with a man in the driver's seat, but she did not recognize him. She had started back inside when she heard a familiar voice calling her: "Crazy Girl!" She turned around. "Crazy Man?" she said. "Why did you cut your hair?"

Karl just sat there and nodded toward the back seat. Ford noticed a young man sitting in back.

"That's Leo," Karl said. "Leo Burt."

"Hello, Leo," she said cordially.

"Hi." The passenger remained aloof.

Ford repeated her question to Karl. Why had he cut his hair and shaved his beard?

"Well, things change," he answered.

Ford walked away feeling vaguely disappointed and ran into Dwight returning to the car. He was smoking and sipping from a large paper cup. "Why did Karl shave off his beard?" she asked him.

"He wants to get in good with his father," Dwight answered smoothly. When it came to lying, Dwight had it all over Karl. It was like a gift.

A green Volkswagen bug pulled up in front of the Hintze Road house, and Scott Nelson got out. His hair was short. He was tanned and trim and, in his short-sleeved summer uniform, looking very much the part of an airman second class. He had forty days' leave and had driven down from River Falls to see Karl before heading out West on vacation, unaware that Karl was preparing a new offensive.

Don Armstrong answered the door. Karl was at Leo's, he said. Then, before Scott could escape, he launched into the tragic details of the broad-jumping accident that had ended his own air force career and from that into the arcanery of jet-engine balancing. It was midafternoon by the time Scott got away. Karl had just returned to Iota Court when he arrived. "Let's go for a ride," Karl suggested. They took the Corvair, and Karl drove over to the Truax Industrial Park bordering the marshland south of the air base. He stopped on Holmberg Street, near the headquarters of Cepek Construction and Engineering Corporation. Behind the building Scott could see a pile of concrete forms and barrels. Karl walked over to inspect them. "I'm going to be needing some barrels," he explained when he got back to the car.

"Oh yeah?" Scott said.

"Yeah. We've got heavy revolutionary activity planned."

"Oh yeah?" Scott repeated. "But why barrels?" It was his impression that the New Year's Gang had retired.

Karl did not have the nerve to ask Scott right out to join them; that would have been putting him on the spot. But Leo still insisted on a fourth, so he was testing Scott, just in case. "For the bomb, of course," he said, as if Scott already knew.

Scott left town abruptly, saying he was going out West to climb a mountain; Mount Rainier, maybe. He was not interested in joining the gang. Early that Sunday evening Karl and Leo stopped at Forest Harbor Enco Station on University. They were in identical dress blues: bell-bottom jeans, denim jackets. Karl went inside and spoke to a teenage attendant, Dennis Whipperfurth, whose father owned the station. "I have to carry some fuel oil to a cabin about twenty-five miles up north," Karl said. He pointed to one of the orange-and-silver U-Haul trailers resting on their tow bars beside the station and asked how much it would cost to rent it overnight. Whipperfurth replied, "Yes sir, that's four-ninety a day, plus a ten-dollar deposit." They went out and looked at the car to see if there would be any problem hooking the trailer to it. "A Corvair isn't the best car to pull a trailer with," the boy said politely. The trailer Karl had asked for was a good-size one, four by seven feet with a roof on it, and the attendant suggested a smaller model.

"I have to have this one," Karl said. He had already calculated the size he would need to haul half a dozen fifty-five-gallon oil drums.

Whipperfurth eyed the clamp-on hitch attached to the bumper

and shook his head. It was too small for a U-Haul, he pointed out. Karl agreed to let the attendant change the ball.

Filling out the rental agreement, he became flustered. It was the first time he had had to put his name on something connected to Army Math, and he wondered if it might somehow incriminate him. He should have brought some false ID, he realized too late. He printed his name in capital letters at the top of the form, leaving out the R in his surname, so it read "AMSTRONG." It looked ridiculous, so he squeezed a lower-case "r" in between the "A" and "M."

At 9 P.M. the boys returned to Forest Harbor Enco, picked up the trailer, and drove across town to the Truax Industrial Park, where they availed themselves of a number of Cepek Construction's empty drums. On their way back they picked up several more at an Octopus Car Wash on University Avenue, bright orange barrels used as lane dividers for entering vehicles. It was 10:30 P.M. by the time they arrived at Owens Service Station in Middleton.

The fuel-oil pump was at the west end of the station. As they removed the drums from the rear of the trailer, an attendant named Joe Reisdorf came over to help. The cash indicator on the fuel-oil pump was out of order. Employees weren't supposed to use it, but Reisdorf good-naturedly went ahead. Karl said he wanted forty-five gallons distributed evenly among the barrels.

Why two university boys needed such a large amount of fuel oil wasn't clear to Reisdorf. It couldn't be used in cars. It was mainly for heating. Farmers used it in their extra stoves when the January deep freeze set in. But this was August. The sale struck him as odd, but Reisdorf was a man who minded his own business. After a moment he had to go tend to another customer, so Karl and Leo continued filling the drums themselves, shaking them to determine how full they were. When one sprang a leak, Leo plugged the hole with a wad of gum.

Michael Martig, an off-duty employee who happened to be driving by, stopped to help, and Reisdorf came back to finish up. It took two of them to lift each barrel into the trailer. At 15.9 cents a gallon, the sale came to $7.15, which Karl paid in cash.

It was nearly midnight when Karl and Leo arrived at the staging area. Karl had found it by studying the topographical maps of Greenfield Township, just north of Devil's Lake. At the bottom of a swale on Newfield Road he turned left, following a practically invisible track through a thicket to the clearing. They unloaded the barrels and covered them with brush. In the morning Karl returned the U-Haul, reeking of fuel oil, to the Enco station. Paul Whipperfurth, the owner, was there to receive it. He refunded the deposit and cleaned the trailer out himself.

Karl had decided it would be useful to monitor police calls the night of the bombing, so Dwight called Jeff Shearer in Minneapolis and asked to borrow his radio scanner, explaining that he needed it to research a newspaper article on police brutality. Shearer knew when he was being conned, and said, "If ya lost it, ya couldn't afford to replace it."

The next day Dwight thumbed a ride to Minneapolis with a tribe of hippies on their way to Lake Minnetonka. They were packed into a big, blue rust-bucket that looked like a 1950 milk truck. The hippies were in no great hurry, and Dwight had no trouble diverting them to Uncle Paul's house, where he asked Jeff Shearer once again for the scanner, and got the same answer. Max Sliter told the hippies how to get back on the freeway. When they had left, Dwight asked Max if he knew where Dwight could get a van.

Max stared at him. "What do ya need one for?"

"Well, I want one for down in Wisconsin," Dwight said.

"I got no idea where to get a van," Max said testily. "If you want a van, you'll have to locate one yourself."

On Tuesday Dwight started angling for a ride to Madison, and Max agreed to go, claiming he had some business with Karl to take care of. A friend of his, a bartender named Vince, offered to drive them down in his Ford Thunderbird, and they all piled in. Dwight carried a blue zipper bag stuffed with marijuana from Uncle Paul. He had a smoke on the way down, enjoying the smooth T-bird ride and looking forward to having a fresh wad of cash in his pocket.

When they got to Madison, Dwight directed Sliter up Langdon to Iota Court. Max said that he had to talk to Karl alone, and sent Dwight in to get him. Karl came out and warily approached the car. He had not seen or talked to Max in over a month. He suspected that Max may have had something to do with the disappearance of the Moose Lake marijuana.

A strange scene followed in which Max tried to stiff Karl for $200, his share of the missing dope, as if Karl were the one responsible. Karl surmised that the trip to Madison was a ruse to convince

Paul that Max hadn't stolen the plants himself. However, he agreed to come up with sixty dollars, the money he owed Paul for the pound of pot he had picked up on his last trip. He went inside and got Dwight, and the four of them drove over to State Street, where Karl pointed out a basement spaghetti emporium across from Gino's and suggested that Max and his friend get something to eat there while he and Dwight found a buyer for Dwight's pot. The brothers disappeared into a head shop with the blue bag.

It was about 9:30 P.M. when they met again at a prearranged spot on State Street. The isthmus had been a steam bath all afternoon, and townspeople were cooling off in the evening air. Max and Vince were tranquilized by ravioli and beer.

"I see you got rid of the bag," Max noted with satisfaction. Karl paid him, leaving himself and Dwight without funds. Max and Vince left for Minneapolis.

Karl still was not certain how to detonate the bomb. To date he had mastered only the most primitive incendiary device, a jar of gasoline. Cognizant of the possibility that people might be in the building and would have to be warned, he knew that he could not leave the timing to chance. *I didn't really want to trust myself with any electrical devices.* But, as he was discovering, fuses could also be tricky: With ANFO, you couldn't just stick the fuse into the muck and expect it to explode.

Karl, Leo, and Dwight made a number of trips out into the countryside to test their ignition system. On the first attempt, carried out near Beaver Dam about an hour northeast of Madison, the cap went off like a cherry bomb, but neither the dynamite nor the ANFO detonated. They tried again in more familiar territory near Baraboo, and this time they were more successful, blowing the bark off a good-size oak tree and scaring a passing farmer off the road. "Looks like ANFO will do the job," Karl said.

Leo was concerned that buying ammonium nitrate and fuel oil in the quantities Karl was talking about would arouse suspicion. He thought they needed a cover story, and he favored pothole blasting since it was a common activity in the hinterlands. Without telling Karl he called the state mine safety supervisor, a man named Ed Bull, and asked what it would take to get a Wisconsin blasting license. Bull told him he would have to come in with recommendations from the Sheriff's Office and from a licensed Wisconsin blaster.

"If I have to do all that, I guess I'll have someone do the blasting for me," Leo replied, having decided to forgo the cover story.

Dwight was gassing up the Corvair at Sellers Shell on Northport Drive when Pastor Hoffman pulled him behind him. Two years had passed since the minister wrote to Dr. O'Connor in the hope that he could help the Armstrongs through their crisis. As Hoffman had predicted, Karl had dropped out of school, Dwight had given up his vocational training, and Ruth and Don's marital problems remained unresolved. The family, Hoffman believed, was as troubled as ever. "Where's your brother?" he asked Dwight.

Dwight answered that Karl had just returned from Minneapolis, where he'd been "taking courses" and "working part time." "We're studying, talking things over," he elaborated vaguely.

"What are you studying?"

"About life," Dwight replied.

"At what school?"

According to Hoffman, Dwight replied, "The school of life."

Hoffman decided to play along with him. "What course?"

"Radical thought," Dwight said.

"I'm concerned about you boys," Hoffman said, getting serious. "You know, Jesus was a revolutionary, too, but he was constructive, not destructive."

The remark struck Dwight as gratuitous. What did Hoffman know about their activities? He said nothing.

The preacher was not one to give up easily. "I'll take you out to dinner," he said. "Where d'you live?"

Dwight said he was staying with Karl at Iota Court. Hoffman was alarmed; he had seen a Cuban flag on the front porch of a house in that neighborhood. "I'll take you out to dinner after I get back from New York in eight days," he said.

"Sure," Dwight said. Eight days was an eternity. He had no idea where he'd be in eight days.

Leo's friend Jane Adamson lived in an efficiency apartment above Brown's Bookstore at the corner of State Street and Lake. She was a northern Wisconsin girl, very pretty in a pixieish way, and talkative. Her ambition was to be a TV news anchor. She and Leo had spent endless hours in the Rathskeller arguing about socialism. Occasionally they went out, but always in a group. Leo had never slept with her.

Adamson would not be able to recall later how she and Leo had ended up on her floor that day in mid-August, but there they were lying on the carpet, casually caressing and kissing each other as a zephyr off Lake Mendota wafted in through the open French doors. He had just come from a workout and smelled like soap. It did not occur to Adamson that he might be trying to seduce her. She was surprised, then, when he suddenly drew her to him and hugged her so hard that it took her breath away. She tried to disengage, but couldn't move. *He doesn't realize his own strength,* she thought.

"You don't trust me, do you?" Leo said.

"I do, Leo; I trust you a lot," she replied.

"Yeah, but not enough," he said.

"What do you mean?" she asked.

"You've really got to trust somebody to..." But Leo didn't finish the sentence. How could he ask her to trust him when in fact he was leading a double life?

Adamson shook her head. Leo was like a brother to her, and she didn't want to change that. "It's not that you aren't attractive to me," she said. "But you represent everything that is serious in life. You're not a plaything I could use and casually toss aside."

Leo hid his disappointment. "I've got to get going," he said, hurrying out. He was going to war and had no one to see him off.

Wednesday, the nineteenth. It was one in the afternoon when Karl and Leo arrived in Baraboo pulling a U-Haul trailer behind the Corvair. Karl gave Leo the scenic tour, pointing out the Ringlings' stone mansion, as well as Uncle Charley's house and the old A & W Drive-in, where his family used to stop on its way to Tomah. The Farmers Union Co-op was on Lynn Street, a long, white building with a covered loading dock. In a clean T-shirt and bell-bottoms, with his sideburns trimmed and his beard gone, Karl looked like any young farmhand stepping into the office. The proprietor, a polite, softspoken man named Ron Grotzke, was impressed by his smile.

"I work for a guy who owns a sod farm, and he needs a ton of ammonium nitrate," Karl said. "Got any bagged?"

Grotzke had to apologize for the fact that he didn't. "We had a new bagger put in this summer, and it isn't working yet."

Karl asked if he could use the phone to call another outlet, and Grotzke obliged, pointing out a list of Dane County co-ops posted in the office. Karl tried several, but there was some problem at each one. He was walking back to the car when plant manager Roger Stieve returned from his lunch break. Karl approached him and asked where they could get bagged ammonium nitrate.

"Why don't you buy bulk?" Stieve suggested.

When he thought about it, Karl didn't really have a reason not to, other than the mess it would make in the U-Haul. But that could be swept out, he rationalized. "Do you think we could get 1,500 pounds of it in the trailer?" he asked.

"It would fit in there with no trouble at all," Stieve said.

"How much would it cost for 1,500 pounds?" Karl asked.

Stieve went into the office and, after doing some arithmetic on paper, came up with a ballpark figure of forty dollars—which just happened to be the amount of cash that Karl had on him.

"Okay, we'll buy bulk," he said. Leo helped him detach the trailer and roll it over to a fertilizer bin containing a small mountain of the silvery, odorless granules. Grotzke fired up the Mustang front-end loader. A couple of buckets gave them their 1,500 pounds, but there was still room in the U-Haul. Karl asked Leo if he had any money. Leo had just cashed a check for ten dollars at Rennebohm's. Karl turned to Stieve. "Do you think we can get another 200 pounds in?"

"Plenty of room," Stieve replied. Grotzke dipped the bucket gingerly into the bin and backed up onto the metal scales in the floor. He was about fifty pounds over. Stieve started to shovel the extra off.

"Leave it, we'll take that, too," Karl said.

When the third bucket was emptied, Grotzke parked the Mustang, and he and Stieve began sweeping up the spillage. Karl and Leo started to close the doors on the trailer.

"Wait," Stieve said. He and Grotzke shoveled the remainder in, about fifteen pounds. The co-op managers prided themselves on making sure their customers got their money's worth.

When they finished, Karl was unable to close the doors, one of which seemed to be broken. Stieve left for a moment and came back with a piece of plywood about three feet long and ten inches wide. It had been used for a cement form and was covered with grit. Stieve placed the board so it would hold the trailer doors shut and went into the office to make out an invoice. Karl followed him.

"Whose name to you want on the slip?" Stieve asked.

"Do you want my name or my boss's name?" Karl replied. Stieve did not answer.

"Make it out to George Reed," Karl said.

The bill for 1,750 pounds of ammonium nitrate came to $48.97. Karl handed Stieve fifty dollars, and Stieve made change out of his pocket. Apologetically he told Karl he didn't have the three pennies.

"That's all right," Karl said.

Grotzke had come in. "There are some pennies in that desk drawer," he told Stieve. He didn't want his customer shortchanged, either.

Karl turned to go, leaving the receipt on the desk.

"Don't you want your invoice so you can be reimbursed?" Stieve asked.

"Oh, yeah," Karl said. He picked it up and shoved it into his hip pocket.

The Corvair had a new tape deck, courtesy of Mahfood in Minneapolis, and Leo popped in a tape. They drove south on Highway 12 to Devil's Lake, turned off, and followed the road along the north shore, heading for the staging area. Silver Lake, Devi-Bara, the Farm Kitchen—the local resorts had a backwoods charm, and the guests relaxing on their cabin porches that August afternoon had no reason to be suspicious of two young men in a Corvair, pulling an orange U-Haul with its doors held shut by a piece of plywood. A new song by Crosby, Stills, Nash & Young, Leo's favorite group, caught the moment with prophetic precision:

All in a dream
All in a dream
The loading had begun
Flying mother nature's silver seed
To a new home in the sun.

23

Army Math

*It wasn't just a thing of "AMRC off campus," which was a
rallying cry before, but it was more the phrase "off AMRC,"
which means get rid of AMRC.*

—TOM SIMON,
student, for the defense

*Every movement has a lunatic fringe. The people take advan-
tage of a cause to vent their own psychological hang-ups. And
this was the case here.*

— MICHAEL ZALESKI,
Wisconsin Assistant Attorney General, for the prosecution

Thursday, August 20, the day the Army Math conspiracy finally
came together, was cloudless and bright, a crisp seventy
degrees. The reception for Eliot Silberberg and his bride took place
at the groom's rooming house, a turreted Queen Anne at 947
Spaight Street. A mixed crowd of relatives and *Cardinal* friends
gathered in the backyard, which sloped down to the Lake Monona
shore, and danced to live music provided by a local bluegrass band.
Rabbi Swarsensky, who had performed the service at a West Side
synagogue, stayed only a few minutes, for, as he later explained to
the FBI, bluegrass was not his favorite musical style.

David Fine, who had just arrived from Wilmington, gave the Silberbergs a subscription to *Esquire,* a magazine he considered "semicool" and the right gift for an intellectual like Eliot. Silberberg had just received his master's degree in American literature and was leaving in a few days for a teaching job at Canisius College in Buffalo, New York. David and several friends were planning to take over his apartment, and David had already stored some of his belongings in the attic.

David's write-up of the Ann Arbor Blues Festival, which had run in one of the *Cardinal*'s last summer editions, received compliments at the party. Everyone agreed that it was the best thing he had written all year, and that he was the logical successor to Eliot Silberberg in the paper's fine arts department if he would just stay with it another year. But David's plans were uncertain. He had missed the deadline to reapply for his tuition scholarship, and with out-of-state tuition up 60 percent, his parents could not make up the difference. He said he might just hang out for a year writing for the *Cardinal* and assisting Michael Jalliman with his "social agenda." He had discussed the latter possibility with the new WSA president when they were trapped on the third floor of the Memorial Student Union during the riots over Cambodia. He planned to have another talk with Jalliman and maybe get Rena Steinzor to put in a word for him.

But then Leo took him aside. "Yeah, today's the day. There's some stuff going on right now, and we'll see what happens," he said cryptically. He excused himself to make a call and a few minutes later came hurrying back. "It's happening," he whispered. "Are you still in?" David hesitated. This really wasn't part of his plans. "It's happening soon," Leo reiterated and then, as if to reassure David, added, "We've done a lot of surveillance, man. We know a lot."

In retrospect certain things that Leo said to friends that day sounded like farewells. George Bogdanich would recall snatches of wild talk about "major personal risks" and "commitment to end the war." As the sun went down and the fireflies came out he heard Leo say, "I'm ready to take the next leap forward." It worried Bogdanich. "Hey, take it easy, guys," he wanted to say, but he let it pass.

Meanwhile the Armstrong brothers were feuding. The fight had started the night before at Nelson's Texaco on Sherman Avenue when they returned the U-Haul used to transport the ammonium nitrate to the staging area. The station owner, Mr. Nelson himself, had been present. The argument was about who would sweep out the U-Haul. The bottom of the trailer was covered with ammonium nitrate residue, and Karl had just assumed that Dwight would do it. But when he handed Dwight the broom, Dwight threw it at him, and Mr. Nelson had been obliged to clean out the trailer himself.

Dwight had also flubbed his assignment of finding a suitable vehicle. Neither he nor Karl had the know-how to hot-wire a car, and they had spent all day Thursday walking around Madison looking for an unlocked van with keys in the ignition. When the four met that evening at Leo's apartment, David immediately zeroed in on this defect in the plan. "No way this should be done, man," he snapped. "It's obvious. You don't have the van."

"It's the only time," Karl said. "We can't wait till school is back in session."

David started asking questions. "How big a blast is 1,700 pounds of nitrate going to make?"

Karl gave him the TNT equivalent. "It's 3,400 sticks of dynamite," he said.

David had edited the *Cardinal*'s off-the-wire story on the precinct-station bombing in New York a few months earlier. It was the biggest act of sabotage in the country that year and involved only fifteen sticks of dynamite. This would be more than 200 times as powerful. Was it really necessary to use that much explosive? David asked.

Karl answered truthfully. "I'm not sure. It might be only a little thing. Then again," he said, "it might be really big."

David could not believe how blasé Karl was. "Karl, if you don't know, don't do it. It's not worth it," he said. Karl did not react. "Do you know about all these other buildings? The way you're talking, you're not really sure that it's not going to cave a roof in," David pressed.

"Well, it's happening; it's all ready to go," Karl insisted. "This is the best time, and we just have to take that risk." Karl remained silent, thinking, *The kid has a serious case of motormouth. If they had to, they could do it without him.*

David nervously regarded the others. Somewhere inside him a voice was saying, *Sorry, I'm out.* But he did not have the nerve to back out. *I'm into it this far, I'm probably already a coconspirator,* he thought. *Maybe we'll get lucky and it won't be as bad as I think.*

At eleven-fifteen Thursday evening Professor Larry Travis, a University of Wisconsin computer scientist, discovered his van missing from in front of the Computing Center on West Dayton, where he had stopped by to drop something off. He went back up to his second-floor office and called the MPD. The dispatcher told him to call University Protection & Security, since the incident had taken place on campus. It was a white Ford Econoline with an orange Peterson-for-Governor bumper sticker on it, Travis told the university dispatcher when he reached him. "A student must have borrowed it to move his stuff."

Friday, August 21, was another unusually temperate day. David and Leo found a table on the nearly empty terrace, and Leo went into the Rathskeller to get something to drink. Crossing the cavernous dining area, he saw one of his old journalism school professors, Jack Holzhueter, and stopped him. He said he wanted to tell Holzhueter how much he'd enjoyed his newswriting course. He had trouble figuring out what was expected of him at first, but in the end he had found the course very useful.

Holzhueter, a thin man of severe mien, was surprised by this belated compliment from a student he hadn't seen in a while. Leo was still on crew when they had met, and the young instructor had pigeonholed him as a jock, a rather conservative one at that. The girl assigned to the seat in front of Leo had insisted on being moved. "I can't stand sitting in front of that fucking Nazi!" she had complained.

They walked out onto the terrace together, and Holzueter asked what his plans were.

"I'm going to have to go underground," Leo said matter-of-factly.

Holzhueter regarded him quizzically. "I assume you mean to escape the draft," he said.

"No," Leo replied.

"Then why?" Holzhueter asked. They faced each other on the ocher-colored flagstones.

Leo looked away. "I can't tell you," he said, sounding rather resigned.

"I think that's a terrible thing to have to do," Holzhueter said with genuine alarm. "I can't understand why you would do that."

Arriving at his table, Leo sat down. Holzhueter recognized his companion, David Fine, as one of the young *Cardinal* reporters, a good one. Leo smiled bleakly and waved him away. "You'll find out," he said.

Around two in the afternoon David left for his paper-delivery route, which a friend had taken care of in his absence. Leo ambled over to the Library Mall and sat on a concrete bench facing the fountain. Jane Adamson came by and greeted him. He stared at her; she spoke again, and when he muttered a banality, Adamson walked away. Leo had been such a good friend; she was surprised that he would drop her just because she had refused to sleep with him.

As he started up Langdon, heading back to his apartment, Leo almost immediately ran into John Lorenz, one of his former crewmates—another person who reminded him of the Leo he used to be. Lorenz was six feet six and about 240 pounds and had easily made varsity, even though he was as round shouldered as a bear. Along with Tim Mickelson, Lorenz had gone home to Havertown with Leo in the summer of 1968 to train for a shot at the Olympics. The effort was interrupted when Mickelson's mother was killed in a freak highway accident on her way to visit him. But they had had many a philosophical talk that summer on the veranda of the Penn Athletic Club boathouse. Even then, Lorenz recalled, Leo didn't think that family was that significant an influence on a person, that you could remake yourself from day to day. He asked Leo how he was doing. "Alright," Leo said, but he seemed preoccupied, not quite himself. He had to go, he explained; he had some writing to do.

The lead story in the *Capital Times,* headlined in twenty-four-point type, announced the resignation of Vice Chancellor for Administration Robert Atwell: U.W. AIDE LASHES USE OF POLICE ON CAMPUS:

"One need not defend the stupid, vicious and destructive acts of a few young people in order to be critical of the absence of any serious Administration or Regent tactic other than massive police action," Atwell stated. "They [regents and administrators] no longer view police action as a last resort but as the routine first step. Tension between students and citizenry has risen to a worse than alarming level; my own view is that much of this tension is attributable to what I believe to have been an excessive use of armed force. The escalation of violence has risen to the point where there will be bloodshed unless sensible persons can find ways to de-escalate."

David's *Capital Times* delivery bag was identifiable by its Che Guevara button. He filled it at the paper drop on Regent Street and walked his route, a ragged remnant of the Greenbush, where students lived side by side with a fast-fading population of elderly immigrants. When he was done, he walked over to Leo's to help with the communiqué. Leo was working on it at the dinette table while the Armstrong brothers kibbitzed. David read over what they had done. The political overview was rough, and he set about fine-tuning it, putting things in context:

> We declare solidarity with our revolutionary brothers in Uruguay, the Tupamaros, who are struggling to loosen the U.S. military and corporate grasp on their continent. We also declare our solidarity with the San Rafael four, revolutionary black brothers who died fighting the racist court system. But more importantly, we declare our solidarity with each and every peasant, worker, student and displaced person, who, in his day-by-day existence, struggles against the oppressive conditions heaped upon him by the monster.

In the midst of these exertions the phone rang, and Karl answered, carrying on a conversation with the caller while straining to follow an argument that had erupted over the demands and how to enforce them. Covering the receiver, he yelled, "No fucking assassinations!" When he got off the phone, he grabbed the draft and read:

> The Vanguard of the Revolution demands the immediate release of the Milwaukee 3 [blacks accused of shooting a cop], the abolition of ROTC, and the elimination of the male supremacist women's hours on the Wisconsin campus. If these demands are not met by October 30th, revolutionary measures of an intensity never before seen in this country will be taken by our cadres. Open warfare, kidnapping of important officials, and even assassination will not be ruled out.

Seeing the words on paper, he was suddenly hesitant about cutting it. For one thing they had let him keep "Vanguard of the Revolution," which he still preferred to "New Year's Gang," even if it did sound pompous. But the threats were too bloodthirsty for his taste, so he made an addition:

Although we have sought to prevent any physical harm to all people in the past, we cannot be responsible for the safety of pigs if our
demands are not met.

As Karl was making his changes on the draft, Scott Nelson
arrived unexpectedly. He'd decided against Mount Rainier, he said,
but in the morning he was leaving for the Rockies. Meanwhile he
wanted to visit Policronio De Venecia in Milwaukee and had
stopped by in the hope of getting the address from Dwight.

As he spoke, Scott became aware that he had interrupted something. The table was piled high with writing materials. He noticed
David, whom he hadn't met before. Karl was unusually tense.

"Something heavy is coming down," Karl explained. "Maybe you
ought to get out of town."

If Scott had any doubts about Karl's meaning, they evaporated
when Leo proudly handed him the draft statement to read. A
glance at the document, with its references to "revolutionary
cadres," "amerikan military genocide," and "today's explosion ..."
told Scott more than he wanted to know. He began to tremble so
violently that the others in the room wondered whether he was having a heart attack.

"This is fucked, man; this is just really fucked," he said, his voice
cracking. They all fell silent. "I've really got to be going," he said
finally. At that point Dwight announced he'd like to go along. "It's
all right by me," Scott said. The two of them piled into Scott's Volkswagen and left, but were back by late that night. Poli wasn't home,
as it happened. Scott slept on the floor and departed immediately
on Saturday morning. As he was getting into his car, Leo came up
to him.

"If I get killed," Leo said, "I would like you to explain to my parents why I have done this. Otherwise, they won't understand."

Scott took I-90 west, pushing the Beetle as fast as it would go
through the Dakota Badlands. *They're busted,* he kept thinking.
We're all busted.

Karl and Dwight had spent the night at the Hintze Road house.
They got up Saturday morning and had breakfast in the kitchen
while Don and Ruth prepared to leave for McHenry, Illinois, where
Lorene had invited them for the weekend. The Mustang incident
was not spoken of, but the feud between father and son found new

expression that morning when Donald summarily suspended Karl's Corvair privileges. Because he used the car frequently, Karl was supposed to share the payments fifty-fifty, and he was two months behind.

But Karl didn't want the Corvair for the bombing; he wanted the Mustang. "We need the Mustang to go out West," he told Ruth. "Scott's traveling in that direction, too."

Ruth pointed out that the Mustang was already half-packed, wondering how Karl could even make such a request after the fight he and Don had had. Not only could Karl not have the Mustang, she said, unless he made his payments she would not let him use the Corvair, either.

"I'm broke," Karl protested, and swore that he would apply for a job she had told him about the first thing Monday morning. Ruth carried her overnight bag out to the carport, and Karl began to panic. What if the gang was left with no car? They had things to do at the staging area that very afternoon. He followed his mother outside.

"I got to have a car this weekend," he said emphatically.

Ruth looked at him with amusement. *He has a big date,* she thought. "Alright," she told him. "You can have the Corvair, but have it back by Monday morning."

NO LIMIT ON U.S. CAMBODIA STRIKES, AIR PLAN ANNOUNCED IN SAIGON.

GUARD GETS NEW HARD-HITTING RIFLES, MORE FIRE-POWER FOR RIOTS.

The Nixon administration's final answer to the May Rebellion was implicit in the *Capital Times* headlines that weekend. It was escalating the air war over Cambodia and issuing rapid-fire M-16s to National Guard troops in case of domestic resistance. The news did nothing to dissuade Karl and Leo from their belief that Nixon was prepared to kill anyone who got in his way.

The staging area was just as they had left it: the barrels of fuel oil, the pile of ammonium nitrate in the grass, the van hidden in the brush. It was a peaceful, orderly scene, the tranquillity broken only by the white noise of insects and birds and the distant grinding of a tractor on the adjacent farm.

"Think he can see us?" Dwight asked.

"Probably," Karl said. "We can see him." He had it now, Uncle Paul's sangfroid.

"What if the guy calls the cops?" Leo interjected.

"He won't have time to go snooping around," Karl said.

Leo looked nauseated. "I can't go through with it," he said suddenly. "I am too sick."

The brothers stared at him. Leo was shivering, even though the temperature was in the seventies. Karl put his arm around him. "Nah, it's psychosomatic—you'll get over it."

Leo drained the last of a large cup of soda from the Stop 'N Go and tossed the empty container into the brush. He was resolved to do the bombing; why wasn't his body cooperating?

The brothers went to work mixing the ANFO in the barrels, the white prill turning to mush as Karl poured fuel oil over it from an empty bottle of Kraft orange juice. Dwight stuck his hand into the goo to feel the texture. It was like molasses. As it turned out, they needed only about twenty gallons of fuel oil for the ANFO. They collected the remainder in another barrel with the idea of making a giant Molotov cocktail. Karl tested the Clover Brand safety fuse he had bought in Minneapolis to verify that it burned at the advertised rate. The fuse hissed like a sparkler.

The fully loaded barrels of ANFO weighed about 500 pounds each. They were going to have to be lifted into the van by hand, but even together, Karl and Dwight were unable to do it. For Leo Burt, it was a moment of truth. Maybe this was what all his training and self-sacrifice, the 6 A.M. workouts on the lake, the boathouse squats, the beer runs in Camp Randall Stadium, the ROTC drills, had been about—not about serving in the armed forces or making varsity crew or going to the Olympics, but about this unexpected challenge. He squatted next to the barrel that Karl and Dwight had been trying to lift, testing different handholds and adjusting himself. At Quantico in the summer of 1967, he had won the squat contest, holding a sitting position, back to the wall, knees bent at right angles, longer than any other cadet. It wasn't just strength; it was a trick of the mind. With a similar trick, he overcame his nervousness and lifted the barrels into the van.

The Stassi Shoe Store was so quiet you could hear the air conditioner. Except for a visit to campus by Angela Davis in mid-July and the on-going stakeout of the Machtinger twins, there had been little to distract the sedition men from their paperwork. They had no new leads; nothing was happening on the New Year's Gang. A Volkswagen bus reportedly on its way to Madison with a cargo of explosives failed to show up. Baxtrum sent Duroc, who could no longer set foot in Miffland without attracting a pestering crowd, to Oberlin for a week-long international gathering of Young Socialists. The spy departed on August 9, just as Dwight and Leo began their surveillance of Sterling Hall. A rumor began to circulate in Miffland of "something heavy coming down," but if anyone in federal or local intelligence circles was aware of it, they did not follow up.

Duroc dutifully reported back on who from Madison had gone to Oberlin and wrote up an assessment of the "Trotskyites," as sedition men called them, that he knew would please George Baxtrum:

> These people are dedicated, intelligent, armed with cold logic, and determined to win. In the long run I consider them much more dangerous than SDS or Mother Jones.

And so there was no alert, no special patrol that Sunday night, the twenty-third of August. President Harrington and his fellow university administrators retired at a normal hour, oblivious to a threat to the campus. The National Guard was long gone. Jack Schwichtenberg, patrolling the campus in his UP & S squad car, had received no alert, and Sterling Hall, along with several other buildings on Bascom Hill, was under the protection of a single aging campus cop, Norbert Sutter.

Helen Moudry, the Armstrongs' new boarder, was a plain-looking woman in her thirties, training to be an occupational therapist at Mendota State Hospital. Dwight was amused by how anxious she seemed not to give offense to anyone in the Armstrong household. He had agreed to take her to church that evening because he felt sorry for her.

He had dropped Leo and Karl off at Iota Court on his way into town, after taking Leo to University Hospital to check on his fever. Leo was running a temperature of 101, as it turned out; the doctor had no idea why. The gang was to rendezvous at Leo's later in the evening.

Dwight took the family kitten with him and dropped Moudry off at 7:45 P.M. The woman did not notice the powdery residue of ammonium nitrate on the floor mats. Shortly after he got back to Hintze Road the Bakkens came by to pick up the camper for a trip to Colorado. Mira came inside to get the keys. She was in an enthusiastic mood, looking forward to a vacation in the Rockies. Dwight slouched after her in his big hiking boots, holding the kitten in his arms, chattering incessantly. *Gee, we'll only be gone a week,* Mira thought. *Why does he look so sad?* She lingered a moment, wondering what to do, but a blast on the horn interrupted them. "Goodbye, Dwight," she said, giving him a hug.

The New Year's Gang reconvened at Iota Court at 10 P.M. Leo was chugging aspirin, as the doctor had recommended, to lower his fever. As they had agreed earlier, they abstained from alcohol, but they passed around a joint to calm themselves. They expected to return to Leo's apartment afterward to listen to the news. Karl did not want to have to go running to Hintze Road in the midst of what he assumed would be a victory celebration, so he called home to see if he could get an extension on returning the car. Helen Moudry answered. "Are my folks home yet?" he asked.

Moudry said they weren't.

"I'm going to a party ten miles out of town," he said. "Is Mom really working tomorrow?"

Moudry said she didn't know, and Karl told her that he would call again later.

The conspirators spent the next two hours drilling one another, studying maps and charting the route into town. The plan appeared flawless. They would leave Leo's around midnight in the Corvair and drive to the staging area, where the van was loaded and ready to go. On the way back to Madison Karl would drive the van, with Dwight following in the Corvair. David was to use a phone booth at the corner of University and Park. He had called the MPD emergency number Saturday night to confirm that it worked.

"Make sure it's urgent and tell them this is happening," Karl admonished David. The latter wrote the words out on a scrap of paper, including a mention of the hospital to add the requisite note of urgency. Prosecutors would later interpret it to mean that the bombers expected casualties in the building.

They left promptly at midnight, but as they walked out the door Karl heard a voice calling his name. Several men stepped into the penumbra of light at the foot of the stairs, and the gang froze in midmarch. For a moment Karl wondered whether somebody, Lynn perhaps, had tipped off the cops, but then he recognized the interlopers. It was the Jenifer Street boys. What did they want now, at twelve o'clock on a Sunday night?

One of the hippies explained that they had harvested and dried some marijuana in the Madison area and wanted to sell some to Karl wholesale. They evidently had the contraband in the trunk of their car.

"I'm too busy tonight," Karl said.

"Aw, man, it'll only take a couple minutes. Can't we go inside and talk?" one of them whined. They were obviously anxious to unload their crop.

"I've got something to do," Karl responded sharply. "Come back tomorrow."

The conspirators were all wearing denims and dark shirts, and as they looked stone faced at their visitors, the Jenifer Street boys finally seemed to get the picture. "Heavy, man. No problem. See ya later." They backed down the steps.

The gang piled into the Corvair and went to drop off the finished communiqué at the *Kaleidoscope* office, which was next to Cecil's Sandals on Gilman. Karl slid it under the doormat, where he had left messages before, and the group drove off to the staging area for a "party," as Karl had put it, in the woods.

But as Dwight accelerated past the Hilldale Shopping Center, he discovered that the Corvair was out of gas. They were in Middleton, almost to Highway 12, by the time they found a station open. A young, clean-cut attendant approached the car. "Dwight Armstrong! Well, well," he said cordially. It was Tom Mucks, an East High acquaintance, not a bad guy, in Dwight's opinion, but definitely Schoep's Set. His father was Alumni Association Director Arlie Mucks, one of the leading critics of the protest movement in Madison. Dwight asked for two dollars' worth of gas, and they all squirmed while Mucks cheerfully cleaned the windshield.

It was 1:00 A.M. when they arrived at the staging area. Karl pulled the brush away from the van and opened the rear doors. The interior reeked of fuel oil. While the others shined flashlights on the barrels, he shoved a stick of dynamite into each drum and packed clay around it. His movements were slow and seemed to belong to some other body. *We are going ahead with this; we are going to do it,* he told himself.

He started the van and put it in gear, but it would not move. "We have no transmission," he announced.

David and Leo mouthed appropriate lamentations over this surprising circumstance. "What do we do now?" Leo asked.

Fuckin' phonies, Dwight thought, realizing they were happy about it. With a 2,000-pound bomb on board the Econoline was flat on its axles. Dwight wriggled underneath on his back and illuminated the undercarriage with his flashlight beam. As he'd suspected, the gear pin was broken and the shifter was loose. He had seen the same problem on Uncle Paul's Roadrunner. *I can fix this goddamn thing,* he thought.

But did they want him to? He had to decide. Dwight had taken a liking to the van, which had long, narrow taillights and chrome bumpers that were not standard on an Econoline. Oversize rearview mirrors added to its distinctive look. "OK," he said, taking control of the situation, "get me a piece of wire."

They were back on the western outskirts of the city by 2:30 A.M. and came in through Middleton on University Avenue, the van bottoming out and rocking like an overloaded freighter in heavy seas. Karl, with Leo beside him, slowed to about fifteen miles per hour to negotiate the hill down to Hilldale Shopping Center. Dwight, following in the Corvair with David, could not understand why Karl was driving so slowly. He pulled alongside and signaled him to speed up, advice Karl ignored. At the first opportunity he turned off University and took side streets into town, finally coming to a halt in the parking lot of the University YMCA.

It was 3:00 A.M. They were a block and a half from Sterling Hall. David knew the shortcut to Bascom Hill, and Karl sent him to reconnoiter while he and Dwight capped and fused the bomb. When he returned ten minutes later, the bomb was ready. David headed for the phone booth at University and Park. Dwight remained at the wheel of the Corvair, positioned for a quick getaway. Karl, accompanied by Leo, drove the van up Charter Street to Sterling Hall. *I used 10 feet of 40-second fuse, which was 400 seconds. And that's roughly six and a half minutes of fuse. And the plan was, of course, to drive the vehicle up to the building, light the fuse, and in the space of, well, we had even timed the length of time it would have taken to go from the vehicle, say, to University Avenue, and that was something like 40 seconds. So that left ... six minutes.* Six minutes, they estimated, was enough time for David to call in his warning and for the police to clear the building, should that be necessary. It had not occurred to them that police responding to the call might themselves be endangered.

As they turned into Lathrop Drive and started up the little rise between Sterling and Old Chemistry, Karl swore. "The place is lit up like a Christmas tree!" he said. *We had kept a last-minute surveillance on the area, but we had messed up. When I drove the truck up to the building I observed a car that was parked. I observed two bicycles. I observed a light on in the computer room. Now, that blew my mind away. Because, you know, it hadn't been reported to me.*[1]

Even as he was trying to absorb these unexpected developments Karl was maneuvering the van between a pair of steel posts to reach the loading dock and guiding it down the narrow ramp. He sidled the van up close to the building and turned off the engine. *And I didn't know if there was anyone in the building. But the light was on in the computer room. And I would have to honestly say that ... the probability was that there was someone in the computer room.*

What Karl described as the computer room was, in fact, the low-temperature laboratory. *[The van] was directly outside the laboratory that was lit up. That was, of course, the only place to place the explosive because that was right in the center of the wing that housed AMRC. And I looked from the cab into the room, and there was no one in the room from where I could see.* He looked back the way he had come. It would have been tricky backing out between the steel posts. And then, what would they do with the van?

Karl turned to Leo for a sign. Leo's fever had returned, and he was trembling all over. "It's up to you," Leo said.

In the end it was Karl. He was the Vanguard, the only one who could make it happen. Somehow, he had known that all along.

What I decided then was, I lit the fuse and got out of the truck and went up to the building and looked into the room. And I spent, I would say, about ten or fifteen seconds at the window trying to make

---

[1]In later years David Fine would steadfastly deny that he "blew his assignment" at Sterling Hall. He would not remember going to the staging area with the others. In fact, according to Fine himself, his entire involvement consisted of making the warning call.

sure that there was no one in the building. I had this key chain with a big ball on it, it was with the truck, and I was going to smash the window and warn, if there was anyone in the building, in the room.

Where was Fassnacht? According to the night watchman, Norbert Sutter, he was at his desk in the lab. Apparently Karl could not see him. *And I didn't see anyone inside that room. And so I left because … I had spent too much time as it was. That was cutting into the warning time, which was figured at … five minutes, and there was probably about five and a half minutes of fuse [left].*

They ran between Old Chemistry and Lathrop Hall to University. *And at University Avenue, why, one of the conspirators would see me and make the phone call to the Madison Police Department. Originally, we had planned to call … the Protection and Security, but we couldn't. We had phoned them up to test them at that hour, and we couldn't reach them for five minutes. So, you know, we thought that the Madison Police Department would definitely be—you know, there'd always be someone there.*

The phone booth was at the corner of University and Park. When he got there a few minutes earlier, David had put his dime in and dialed the first six digits of the MPD number, as instructed. Then he waited, the receiver tucked against his shoulder, with the seventh digit half-dialed. He was in front of the bank where he had first met Karl Armstrong. The facade was now completely bricked up, the management having tired of replacing the window glass every time there was a riot. At 3:40 A.M. he saw Leo and Karl waving as they ran across University Avenue. He let the last digit fall. A man's voice answered, "Madison Police Department." David spoke rapidly, delivering the shortest speech he had ever given:

> Okay, pigs, now listen and listen good. There's a bomb in the Army Math Research Center, University, set to go off in five minutes. Clear the building. Get everyone out. Warn the hospital. This is no bullshit, man!

He ran back to the car and jumped in next to Leo. "Let's get the hell out of here!" Karl said. Dwight put the pedal to the floor. The accident that had been waiting so long to happen was finally at hand.

Part V

OUTLAWS OF

AMERIKA

24

Devil's Lake

This is just wanton and ruthless antisocial conduct.
> —H. J. Lynch,
> Dane County District Attorney, for the prosecution

I feel that the person who did that acted out of the best of all motivations. I believe it was out of a concern for life. I believe that it was done to hinder the American government's ability to inflict harm on the people of Southeast Asia.
> —William Kaplan,
> student, for the defense

*I*t was really a weird sensation to hear the explosion. Because, I *don't know. Well, I had never heard an explosion before. It was just very, took my immediate, my immediate feeling was, well, the only thing I said right then was, "Fuck."*

Thus for the benefit of the court would Karl Armstrong describe his own reaction to the bomb blast. They were just a few blocks away, at the corner of Dayton and Park, when the shock wave hit the Corvair and lifted it off the ground. They had been planning to return to Iota Court, but it was obvious to them that the bomb had detonated prematurely, and that it was bigger than they had anticipated. Dwight turned right on Park, then right again on Spring to avoid an MPD cruiser speeding toward the campus. They fled south on Fish Hatchery Road, stopping to look back from a promontory near the Arboretum. "God, it's like an atom bomb," Dwight said. He could see debris churning in the fireball hundreds of feet in the air. "Get back in the car," Karl yelled.

Karl tuned the radio to WISM. There was no word yet on casualties. When they reached the bedroom community of Oregon, they doubled back on Highway 51, skirting the East Side. Karl turned up the volume as WISM broadcast an update. *They didn't think that anyone had been killed or injured. And I just felt, I don't know, I just felt like I had had a new lease on life.* Cries of "Oh man, yeah! All right!" came from the back seat.

They stopped for coffee and hamburgers, then continued north and west around Lake Mendota, angling toward Devil's Lake, where they considered spending the day. *And then we heard on the radio that someone had been killed. And, I don't know, that, that really destroyed me.* The news hushed everyone. Dwight, clutching the steering wheel, could hear whimpering in the back seat. *David is crying,* he thought. *He's bawling like a baby.*

But it was Leo who was in tears, hyperventilating and moaning "Jesus Christ, Jesus fucking Christ," over and over.

David was thinking. The "politics of the bombing" were vitiated, he realized. They were facing a murder rap now, and, if they were caught, hard time. "My paper route! Who'll do my paper route?" he exclaimed. "I've got to get back, man!"

Dwight could not believe it. "Your paper route? Fucking paper route? What the fuck are you talking about, man?"

But David was way ahead of him. If no one showed up to deliver his paper route that afternoon, it would look suspicious. He had to line up a substitute.

Sergeant Bob Frank and Deputy Dan Hiller, both of the Sauk County Sheriff's Department, were posted in their big maroon Pontiac wagons at the Highway 12 wayside on Sauk Hill, just south of Devil's Lake State Park, when the first white Corvair appeared, about 5:30 A.M., heading south. Why would the occupants be going back to Madison, the cops wondered, if they'd just blown up a building?

It was Monday, August 24, a time of year when Hiller and Frank were usually busy making drug busts in the campgrounds, but the Madison bombing had changed everyone's routine. In Black Earth and Mount Horeb, in Sun Prairie and Stoughton, in Cross Plains and Baraboo, in all the rural hamlets nestled in the moraine-ribbed countryside of southern Wisconsin, lawmen were on the lookout for fleeing terrorists. A Dane County patrol had spotted a "white Corvair" with several occupants careening away from campus on South Park Street less than a minute after the explosion. An APB had gone out minutes later.

Hiller and Frank had been buddies in the army and were not terribly sympathetic to campus protesters. Frank, who was married to Hiller's sister, was small, quiet, and cautious. A good salesman would need three weeks to sell him a car, Hiller liked to say. Hiller had a stonemason's build and played drums in his own combo, the Dan Hiller Band, performing for Elks and Moose Club parties and wedding dances. His repertoire included Bill Haley and Elvis but also polkas, which they loved out in Sauk County. Between the band and his graveyard shift as a deputy sheriff, he had been putting in some long nights.

The patrolmen had just heard the news about Robert Fassnacht when the Corvair went by. Frank pulled out after the car, following it up Sauk Hill while Hiller sat tight. When he got closer, Frank could see only one occupant, but he remained in pursuit. Maybe the others had been let off somewhere, he reasoned. Then, cresting the hill, he saw a second Corvair, also light colored, approaching from the south with several people in it. He called Hiller. "Looks like it might be the one," he said.

Hiller fell in behind the northbound Corvair as it passed by. A quarter of a mile up the road, just past the billboard advertising the Ski Hi Fruit Farm, the suspects turned east on Ski Hi Road, heading for Devil's Lake. Hiller followed, getting close enough to take down the license number, D-15964, Wisconsin plates. He called it in for a book check. A moment later the dispatcher called back with the information that the car was registered to Karl and Donald K. Armstrong of 606 Hintze Road in Madison. The name rang no bells.

It was ten minutes after six. The sun was just coming up, casting long shadows on the plain. The suspects turned right on South Shore Road, following it down into a woods where it was still dark; not a good place to stop, Hiller thought. Frank, meanwhile, was trying to catch up, but he had missed the Ski Hi Road turnoff and was now coming in from the north entrance to the park. As the Corvair neared some cabins along the lakeshore, Hiller radioed Frank. "I'm going to stop the car," he announced.

"I've got an uncle in Minneapolis. He's cool. We could go up there and stay with him," Karl was saying. He was just beginning to explain to David who Uncle Paul was when the Sauk County squad picked them up. "We are in deep shit," he said, watching the big maroon wagon pull out behind them. Up ahead was the turnoff to Devil's Lake. He told Dwight to take it. "We'll say we're going camping."

Dwight shook his head. "No gear."

"Say we wanted to come up early to get a campsite and go back later to get our gear." That would give them an excuse to leave, Karl thought.

In his mirror Dwight saw the deputy talking into his mike. "He's calling in the license number," he said flatly. He drove on as if nothing were wrong until he saw the lights flashing in his mirror and stopped on the shoulder. The squad car pulled in behind them and waited.

Bob Frank gunned his Pontiac through the woods. Up ahead alongside some cabins he saw Hiller's squad parked behind the Corvair. He pulled in front, boxing the suspects in. It was a windless morning, and the lake was like a mirror, reflecting the sandstone bluffs that bordered it on three sides. It was six-fifteen. Frank saw a Baraboo schoolteacher he knew casting from the bank. In his rearview mirror he could see four young men in the Corvair, clean shaven but scruffy, college types. He saw Hiller get out and approach the driver's side. They might not be just some misde-meanor fools, he thought. He grabbed his stubby .12 gauge pump and, stepping out of the car, popped a couple of shells into the chamber.

David would never forget the sound of that round slamming into place in the still morning air. *It was like amplified. You could hear it like it was a million decibels.* "Aw, shit! Aw, shit!" he cried. He could see it all. They were going to be arrested, handcuffed, jailed for murder. Even the Left would be down on them.

Hiller took ID cards and called the names in for a character check. He instructed the Sauk County dispatcher to report the information to Madison without delay, along with a description of the car. It was more of a light yellow than white, but in the dark it might well have been mistaken for white, he realized.

At Frank's suggestion Hiller brought the driver over to be interviewed by his car, where they could keep an eye on the others. The suspect was young, tall and skinny, gat toothed, with a long, pointed nose. He looked as though he hadn't had much sleep. "Where are you from?" Frank asked.

"Madison," came the confident response.

"What were you doing last night?"

"We weren't doing anything."

"Where were you?"

"At my apartment."

"What are you doing at Devil's Lake?"

"Going camping."

Hiller and Frank looked inside the Corvair. There were no sleeping bags, no tent, no camping gear of any kind.

"We're going to go back to Madison to get our stuff," the boy said. "We came out to register for a campsite first."

"The registration office doesn't open until 8 A.M.," Hiller pointed out.

"We wanted to be here early to get a good spot," the kid said smoothly. He did not seem particularly nervous. Then he said, in the octave of sincerity, "Listen, man, we got to get this car back to my mom by nine. Do you think we'll have time, after we register, to go into Madison? We'll come back in another car."

When they were done with Dwight Armstrong, they called out Leo Burt. Burt looked like he had been crying. "I just graduated from the university, and we're like having a party to celebrate. I'll be going back to Philly tomorrow," he said.

"Where were you last night?" Hiller asked.

Burt answered, "At my apartment."

Something fishy here, Hiller thought. The Armstrong kid had said the four of them spent the night at *his* apartment. They were going camping but they didn't have any gear. They were all in denim, the mufti of the student revolution. Burt even had on a pair of U.S. Marines-issue jack boots. The deputy had seen hundreds of kids dressed exactly the same way while on riot duty in Madison.

Hiller asked the one named Dwight to open the trunk, which was located in the front of the Corvair.

"I'd be glad to, but I don't have the key," Dwight said.

"Do you have the ignition key? Why don't you try that right here in front of me? I'd like to see for myself that the trunk won't open."

Dwight pulled a big key chain from his pocket and inserted one of the keys in the lock, twisting on it. It wouldn't budge. "I told you it wouldn't fit," he said petulantly.

"Do I have your permission to try it myself?" Hiller said.

"Sure," Dwight said, handing him the fistful of keys. Hiller tried every key on the chain. None worked.

At 6:39 A.M., almost three hours after the bombing, the deputies called headquarters and conferred with their supervisor, Sheriff Ralph Hearn. "I think we got the right guys," Hiller said, "but we need something to hold them on."

"Stay with them; we'll let you know as soon as we hear from Madison," Hearn said.

Frank walked back to the Corvair and told the boys that they could go get in line at the park office while the officers awaited instructions. "We'll be watching you," he added.

A station wagon from Illinois was already waiting at the gate, and Dwight pulled in behind it. Hiller and Frank parked nearby. As the officers looked on the elder Armstrong brother ambled over to a middle-aged woman who was seated on a log bench next to the park office and asked if she would hold his place in line while he took a nap.

Her name was O'Connor. She and her family had just arrived from the Chicago area and had been listening to news of the Madison bombing for the past two hours. "We all need sleep," she said cordially. "How come you rate a police escort into camp?"

He laughed and said, "Things don't look too good. We left Madison at 4:30 this morning, and they said there was a bombing or something. I'm worried about little Leo."

"You should be," O'Connor said. She thought he was referring to the driver of the Corvair, who was slouched at the wheel with a frightened, vague look. "Is he sick? Does he need a doctor?" she asked.

When he realized that she was talking about Dwight, Karl laughed again. "That one is my brother. He's not feeling too well."

O'Connor pursed her lips sympathetically.

"We're students, we have long hair. That's the only reason they stopped us," Karl went on, as if trying to win her over. Again he brought up Leo Burt. "You know, Leo is a radical," he said with a chuckle.

O'Connor said nothing. These boys were in trouble, she sensed. After a moment Karl said, "The bench you're sitting on, you know who made that? The CCC." She looked at him quizzically. "Civilian Conservation Corps. My dad was head of the crew." He pointed to the day lodge at the far end of the lake. "They built that, too."

"God, why doesn't he shut up?" Dwight wondered. He didn't see how Karl could be so cheerful.

With their five o'clock shadows the Armstrong brothers reminded Hiller of the jovial crooks in Uncle Scrooge comics. "He's pretty damn cool," he said to Frank. "It would be funny if they really did it." But then Hiller remembered Jim Jantz, a Sauk County cop who had been murdered a few years earlier. The three men who were involved in that case—Nickel, Nuttley, and Welter—had behaved the same way under questioning, "real calm, vicious, like animals," as Hiller recalled.

About 7 A.M. the Sauk County dispatcher called back with the results of the character check. The only one who appeared to have had a record was David Fine, who had been caught stealing a few sticks of butter, worth twenty-three cents, from Kroger's Supermarket in Madison the previous November. That was it, no disorderly conduct, no vandalism, no draft dodging, nothing that would indicate a political tendency. Dwight's record did not show at all, apparently falling under the protections afforded to juveniles. There was still no word from the MPD. "It's bedlam down there," the dispatcher told them. "They say they don't have anyone who can look into this right now."

Bob Frank's shift ended at seven, and he returned to headquarters in Baraboo. Karl reminded Hiller that he was supposed to return the Corvair to his mother. He and David Fine would return in another car with their camping gear, he promised.

"Okay, go ahead," Hiller said, though he had a bad feeling about it.

Hiller followed the Corvair out of the park and then turned north, heading for the sheriff's office in Baraboo. When he arrived, everybody from the night shift was still there, Frank included. They were all discussing the Devil's Lake suspects and wondering, in view of the fact that they had no hold request from Madison, what to do.

"What do you think, Dan?" Sheriff Hearn asked.

"I think they're the ones," Hiller said. "They're students. They're driving a light-colored Corvair. You don't mistake a Corvair. And their story doesn't add up. I think you should get somebody back out to the park pronto. Two of 'em are still there."

Karl and David drove into Madison, slightly bewildered to be free. It was the first time the two of them had had a chance to talk to each other. David was running the evidence through his mind like a prosecutor. "Karl, this is sort of serious," he said. "They got four names. This car, you rented the U-Haul with it. That is something that's traceable. We're at least somewhat suspicious, enough that they could go over to the place where you bought the stuff and show a picture, and there's a good chance you'll get recognized."

"We had baseball caps on," Karl said.

"Karl, come on, you're a big guy. I remembered you from a year ago down on University Avenue. You're going to get recognized."

Karl took County K around the north end of Lake Mendota and came into town on Northport Drive, avoiding the campus. He brought up Minneapolis again, hoping to calm David down. Uncle Paul's was the perfect hideout, he said soothingly. He described the Franklin Avenue scene, the boosters, the cars, Jeff and Max. David was incredulous: a bunch of cons! "You crazy son of a bitch!" he snapped. "Don't you know you can't trust these guys?" For the first time it crossed his mind that he and Leo might be better off on their own. It also occurred to him that the cops might be waiting when they got to Karl's parents' home. He suggested that they go straight to Bill Limbach's Mifflin Street apartment instead. Limbach was still out West, and David had permission to borrow his car if he needed it. But Karl insisted on going to Hintze Road. "Got to get my mom's car back."

David was beside himself. "This is no little Weatherman bombing," he yelled. "A guy's gotten killed. Do you realize what this investigation is going to be like? Anyone they're even thinking about! And they're definitely going to be thinking about us four."

"You're right," Karl said, but he had already formulated a plan. They might be able to borrow his dad's pickup with the camper on the back. A few minutes later he pulled into the driveway at 606 Hintze Road. It was eight-thirty. Don had already left for work at Gisholt. Ruth was in her white uniform, ready for another day at

Central Colony. Karl kissed her hello and introduced David as "a friend of Leo's." Ruth thanked him for returning the car and asked if they'd like some breakfast. No, they didn't have time. They had to collect their camping gear and get back to Devil's Lake.

"Could we have the camper for a day or two?" Karl asked. It was gone, Ruth said; Mira had taken it to go to Colorado. There was an awkward silence.

"Did you hear about the bombing?" Ruth asked.

"Yeah, they questioned us out at the park," Karl said.

"Don thought it was thunder," Ruth said. "Boy, was he mad when he heard it was the radicals."

"Oh yeah?" Karl asked.

"He said, 'Whoever did that should be hung!'"

The two boys hurried to the bus stop. As they stood waiting a car screeched to a stop in front of them and a man jumped out as if to apprehend them. It was Stephen Sprague, a grade-school acquaintance of Karl's, just wanting to say hello. "We got to get out of here. We got to take off!" David said.

When they reached town, David retrieved his *Capital Times* bag from Limbach's apartment and took it over to Dennis Reis's place on West Washington. Reis, a student from Green Bay who had graduated from the *Cardinal* to the *Kaleidoscope,* was still in bed with his girlfriend, listening to the news reports, when David knocked. "Denny, I got to go somewhere," David said, avoiding eye contact, and handed him the bag, the Che Guevara button still pinned to it. Reis knew the route, having delivered it while Fine was out of town. But the timing of the request and David's jittery, haggard demeanor troubled him. *David is involved,* he thought. That afternoon the *Capital Times* circulation department would receive numerous complaints of undelivered papers in the Greenbush, and all from customers of David Fine.

David was waiting at his bank when it opened at 10 A.M. In his wallet was a check for seventy dollars, all he had in his account, made out to the *Capital Times* to pay his paper bill. He crossed out the name of the newspaper and wrote "Cash," but the teller refused to honor it. He returned penniless to Limbach's apartment, where Karl was waiting for him. The car was parked behind the building. It was a 1961 Plymouth, a big green rust bucket with frayed peace symbols all over it. Limbach had left a note with the keys:

> The tire situation is sort of fucked up. Neither of the spares is any good. The one that looks all right really isn't. The rim is fucked up so under no circumstance put that rim on the car.

David tried the ignition. "Thank God!" he thought as it roared to life. Not thinking, he drove out University Avenue. Half a mile from Sterling Hall they began to see broken glass. Storefront after storefront had been damaged. As they neared the intersection of University and Charter, they saw the yellow tape, the piles of rubble. David looked toward the big plate-glass windows in the YMCA. *Trashed,* he realized, *completely blown away.*

Karl sank down in his seat and watched out of the corner of his eye. He couldn't see the East Wing, but he had a clear view of the front of Sterling and Old Chemistry and Old McArdle and Van Hise and Lathrop with their windows blown out. It was awesome, and by and large, it was the dramatic statement he had envisioned. If only no one had been hurt, he thought, it would have been a success.

From the top of the bluffs along the east side of Devil's Lake there was nothing but air to the railroad tracks several hundred feet below. The lake was named for the evil spirits that, according to legend, dwelled in those crags, causing the unwary to trip and fall to their death. Leo Burt did not give credence to such things. Sartre, in *Being and Nothingness,* had set forth the principles by which Leo now lived: You are the author of your own existence; from moment to moment, you are free to choose a new identity. Where Leo sat at the edge of the precipice, it was 300 feet straight down to the tracks of the Chicago and North Western Railroad, where, if he desired, a "life of nothingness" awaited him. In the Sartrian universe, that was proof of his freedom: He could choose death.

Dwight sat at a safer distance. "We gotta get out of the country," he said, "even if we have to hike out."

Leo said nothing. He had let Karl choose, but that, too, was a choice, one that had defined Leo in a new way. The killing of the researcher was a consequence that he would have to live with, in Sartrian terms a "coefficient of adversity" that had been there all along as a border to his freedom.

"I know my dad," Leo said quietly. "He's into Americanism. He wanted me to join the marines. He isn't going to dig this one bit."

To Dwight Leo was visibly hardening. *He's cold as fucking steel,* he thought.

It was almost noon when they saw the Plymouth pull into their campsite. They hurried down from the rocks to meet it. "They never came back," Dwight said, in answer to Karl's question about the Sauk County cops. They lost no time getting out of the park.

Karl again suggested Minneapolis. David ignored him and drove back to Madison, dropping the brothers off at Sherman Plaza, a busy East Side shopping center, while he and Leo went into town to get money and make phone calls. Karl and Dwight sat at Rennebohm's lunch counter drinking coffee and watching other customers read the newspapers. The headlines were in twenty-four-point type and could easily be read from a distance: I FOUND BOB UNDER A FOOT OF WATER. They had no money, no car, and no contacts except for Uncle Paul, and David had ruled that alternative out. "We aren't calling the shots anymore," Dwight observed sourly. The New Year's Gang was done.

David and Leo returned around 4:30 P.M. Leo had $125 in cash, money his mother had recently sent him to help him move back East. They had gotten in touch with friends on the East Coast, and the decision was made: They were going to New York. From there they would go to Canada. David guided the Plymouth smoothly onto I-94, heading for Chicago.

Leo had foreseen the possibility that he might have to go underground, that he might be cut off from his family, but that scenario had not occurred to Karl. If no one had been hurt, he had envisioned a big political trial in which he would take the fall—but not a very hard one. "We are going to have to cut all ties," he said, thinking aloud. Exile had not figured in his plans.

It was Buzzy's show now. *We were out of it, hadn't had any sleep. Pulled off the road somewhere in Chicago and picked up some papers, screaming banner headlines. We're not exactly in an upbeat mood. I was driving and falling asleep at the wheel. No one else wanted to drive. The attitude was, "You do it. If you crash, you crash."*

David smoked to stay awake, detouring north to Ann Arbor. *This guy did not have it together,* he kept thinking. He was mad at himself for allowing his awe of the New Year's Gang to cloud his judgment. He was mad at Leo for having involved him. Now he would not be able to advise Michael Jalliman on how to spend student funds. He was not going to be editor of the *Daily Cardinal.* He was so absorbed in his thoughts that he missed the turnoff to Ann Arbor and drove twenty miles out of his way.

He parked on Mary Street near his friend Linda Knutsen's place, and the four men slept in the car. In the morning he dropped the Armstrongs at the University of Michigan Student Union, while he and Leo returned to Knutsen's for breakfast and a shower. "Was it the New Year's Gang?" Knutsen asked, regarding the bombing. "I don't know anything about it," David said. "But it's a good time to get out of Madison. Everybody's paranoid—there's going to be a crackdown."

On his July visit to Ann Arbor David had stumbled upon the national headquarters of the White Panthers, which was in an old house not far from where Linda lived. He figured the White Panthers would have a network of some sort for supporting their leader, Pun Plamondon, who was wanted in connection with the bombing of a CIA recruiting office in Ann Arbor. After breakfast he and Leo went over and knocked at the door. The visit lasted about a minute; the White Panthers wanted nothing to do with the New Year's Gang.

Back at Knutsen's apartment they noticed that the license plate was falling off the Plymouth's rear bumper. David borrowed a length of twine from Linda to repair it and then drove over to the campus to pick up Karl and Dwight. What about the White Panthers? Karl wanted to know. That had been the whole reason for the detour.

"They basically said to get the fuck out of here," David replied. "They had no rap for us at all."

"What a bunch of fake revolutionaries those guys are," Karl said.

They were an easy hour's drive from the Canadian border at Windsor, and Toronto was just five hours farther up the road. But David set a course for New York. He was even angrier than he had been the night before. Not even the White Panthers supported them. "Leo, let's go, give them the fucking car," he whispered when they stopped for gas. He figured the bus was much safer. Leo hesitated, reluctant simply to dump Karl and Dwight, but David insisted. "Even though we got into it willingly, we're in hot water now. We gotta split up."

David broached the idea on the way into Toledo. Karl didn't

understand. He and Dwight had no contacts in New York; the split should have been Leo and Dwight, David and Karl. Then it dawned on him: *They think they will fare better on their own. Their friends are more likely to help two than four.* He kept silent.

They arrived at the Greyhound bus depot around seven. It was located in a sooty old building in a run-down section of Toledo. David and Leo paid $2.50 each for haircuts from a barber near the station. Karl urged Dwight to have his hair cut, too, but he refused. Leo handed Karl fifty in cash; David turned over the car keys. They agreed to meet in Times Square in seven days, by which time David and Leo would have arranged things for the trip to Canada. They embraced and gave each other thumbs-up handshakes, but it was a strained parting. They were all beginning to realize how different from one another they really were.

25

An Appointment in
Times Square

*When you travel on convoys, all along the road kids will
come out and beg for food. The game was to take a big can
like lima beans and see if you can hit one and knock them off
the road, which we were pretty successful at after a while
because we had a lot of practice.*

—SAMUEL SCHORR,
Vietnam veteran, for the defense

*Mr. Schorr, as I understand your testimony, because you
threw a couple of cans of lima beans at Vietnamese children,
Robert Fassnacht's death is justified, is that correct?*

—MICHAEL ZALESKI,
Wisconsin Assistant Attorney General, for the prosecution

It was late when Karl and Dwight got into Manhattan. A light rain
was falling. They found a place to park somewhere on the Upper
West Side and slept in the wide, comfortable seats of the Plymouth.
In the morning they picked up a copy of the *New York Times* and
read the editorial denouncing the "cowardly bomb attack on the
University of Wisconsin's Mathematics Research Center." Karl
noticed that the *Times* had dropped "Army" from the name, which
had also been the case in the *Chicago Tribune* and *Toledo Blade.*
"They're denying that it was political," he informed Dwight.

They drove downtown, parked in front of Madison Square Garden, and walked to a grocery store around the corner. Karl bought bread and peanut butter; Dwight cigarettes. As they left the store Dwight pulled a package of bologna out of a pocket. "How stupid to do that while you're buying stuff at the same time," Karl said. But when Dwight offered him a slice, he ate it.

At the corner Dwight stopped abruptly and held up his arm in warning. A New York City squad car was stopped next to the Plymouth, and an officer was looking it over. "They wouldn't already be looking for us," Karl said. Dwight was less confident, so they turned around and walked briskly away.

The Madison bombing was the talk of Franklin Avenue. "Yep, that was those Armstrong boys and their boxcar of dynamite," everyone was saying. One of the boosters had already informed on them to KSTO Radio Station's "Crimestoppers" program in the hope of collecting a reward. Paul Armstrong had been "fishing" at Milles Lacs Lake over the weekend and had just returned to Minneapolis when Karl called collect from New York City. Paul spoke bluntly: "I don't wanna know nothin'. Just tell me what you want." Karl gave him the address of a Western Union on upper Broadway and asked him to wire money. Paul said he was out of cash himself, but would borrow fifty dollars. He hung up. It was Karl and Dwight on the lam in New York, he told his son Vance, shaking his head. "Those fuckers, always up to sumpin'."

Paul's fifty dollars would not arrive until the next day. The brothers walked back uptown, stopping in front of two stone lions guarding the entrance to a museum next to a big park. They had a week's wait before them with no place to stay. Karl wanted to find an employment office and get a job.

"But we'd have to use our own names and social security numbers," Dwight objected, arguing that it would be less risky to rob someone. "What's it going to look like if we get caught?" Karl asked. Dwight stared at him and said, "I'm going to do it with or without your help."

"Then we'll have to split up. I'm not going to get busted for a lamebrain scheme like that," Karl said. They divided the remaining cash, about thirty dollars, and Karl left Dwight alone among the lions.

Karl spent the night in the broom closet of an apartment building off Washington Square. When the fifty dollars from Uncle Paul arrived the next day, he used half of it to rent a room in the Puerto Rican section of upper Broadway. The other half he spent on toiletries, a change of clothing, peanut butter, pickles, and bread. Then he presented himself to the New York State employment agency, using his real name. He interviewed at a machine shop in the South Bronx and at a warehouse in Brooklyn. The stumbling block was references. "Oh, uh ... I'll get them for you tomorrow," Karl would promise.

Through the paper-thin walls of his hotel he could hear babies crying, radios blaring, and men swearing in foreign languages. The stairwell stank of urine. His handkerchief was covered with black grime from blowing his nose. The famous New York Public Library was a disappointment. Its stacks were off-limits, and he was confined to the reading room, where he whiled away the hours looking through atlases.

He called the *Kaleidoscope*. The woman who answered was reluctant to accept a collect call from the New Year's Gang. She informed him that the paper was coming out with the communiqué the next day. "Everyone is shocked by the death," she added. "We didn't mean to kill anybody," Karl said, his voice breaking.

Dwight proved to be inept as a mugger. When it came to the moment of confrontation, he hesitated every time. *I could do it if I had a weapon,* he told himself. However, he had managed to get twenty-five dollars out of Lorene in Illinois and had discovered that, in his dirty clothes, with his long, greasy hair and forlorn look, he was a natural at panhandling. Accosting passersby in front of Nathan's Famous Hot Dogs in Times Square, he was able to make minimum wage, two dollars an hour, enough to keep himself in cigarettes and hotdogs. When a midtown businessman lectured him, Dwight responded, "OK, thanks, man. I'll take that advice to heart," and the man gave him a dollar.

He walked downtown to Christopher Street and wandered into the office of what looked like a typical alternative newspaper, asking about housing. A pleasant and articulate young man referred him to a bulletin board on the premises that had just what he was looking for, personal ads for places to stay, apartments to share, and so forth. Dwight contacted one of the listings and headed back uptown, unaware that the bulletin board was a gay dating service.

The apartment turned out to be a penthouse overlooking Central

Park. The interior had a soft white lining of dog hair provided by a number of resident samoyeds. The occupant was a mathematician who, as they got acquainted, claimed to have worked for the Army Mathematics Research Center one year and to be entirely in favor of its demolition.

"I'm kind of short on cash," Dwight told him.

"That's all right. You can stay for free," the man said. "If you need cigarette money, just say so."

Dwight moved in, marveling at the hospitality of New Yorkers. Still, he wondered why there was a peephole in the bathroom wall.

Meanwhile, in a cheap hotel at Broadway and 103rd Street, David and Leo were preparing to leave the country as fast as they could. Through his movement contacts David had obtained false IDs for both of them. On Friday morning Leo called an old friend in Philadelphia, Paul Bracken, and talked him into giving them a ride from New York to Boston that night. David arranged for himself and Leo to stay at his sister's place near Boston University. They would try to catch a ride to Canada the following morning.

The rendezvous with the Armstrongs wasn't until Wednesday of the following week, and Leo was fretting about leaving them in the lurch. "Fuck it, no way am I stickin' around here," David said. It wasn't bailing out on the Armstrongs, he argued, because "they did it to us in a different way."

The meeting with Bracken was set for 8:00 P.M. that evening at Columbia University. David and Leo spent the intervening hours polishing a second communiqué, mourning the "unnecessary death" of Robert Fassnacht, but nevertheless justifying the bombing as a "necessary task."

THE DESTRUCTION OF AMRC WAS NOT AN ISOLATED ACT BY "LUNATICS." IT WAS A CONSCIOUS ACTION TAKEN IN SOLIDARITY WITH THE VIETCONG, THE TUPAMAROS, THE CUBAN PEOPLE, AND ALL OTHER HEROIC FIGHTERS AGAINST U.S. IMPERIALISM. MAY OUR SMALL SHARE OF REVOLUTIONARY VIOLENCE AID THEM IN THEIR STRUGGLES.

Their intention was to have the communiqué published in the *Kaleidoscope* (the *Cardinal* was closed for the semester break), but for some reason—perhaps fear that it might be intercepted—they decided not to mail it directly. Who could they trust to deliver it for them? They settled on Eliot Silberberg, apparently having forgotten that he and his bride were about to leave Madison, too. They slipped the communiqué into an envelope. On the outside Leo wrote:

> ELIOT, DO NOT put fingerprints on the note inside. Wear gloves. Mail to Kaleidoscope in unfinger-printed envelope. Or else put it in some obscure place and call them to tell them where it is. Make sure they get the note (I mean, what it says) to all the media.

Then he wrote an accompanying note to Silberberg, apologizing for "all the hassle" and asking him to "please make a short call to tele company to stop the service." Presumably to assuage his guilty conscience about leaving the Armstrongs behind, Leo included Paul Bracken's number for them to call, forgetting that it would be highly unlikely for the brothers to contact Eliot Silberberg, someone they had never met, for help in eluding the authorities. And perhaps to alleviate his loneliness and anxiety, he imagined that Silberberg knew what they had done, sympathized with them, and would help them in exile.

> We (Dave & Leo) are in N.Y. with good contacts ready to head for Canada. Will get ahold of you when we get there, and when you're in Buffalo.

Leo then composed a letter to his parents:

> Dear People,
> Sorry about all this, but I called three times in the last couple days, with a busy signal greeting me.
> Monday, I got word from the *Guardian,* the paper that looks like it will hire me, to get to New York for an interview. So, I managed to get a cross-country ride with a friend in an old junker. The trip was a pain and I still have a slight fever from a virus that I picked up. I was pretty sick for awhile.
> I have to go back to Madison to get my junk together cause I really didn't have time to do it when the virus came on.
> I even saw Bracken here who was up for a few days. He's doing okay.

Did you hear about that explosion at Wisconsin? I didn't get to see it, but you could hear it far away, even when sleeping. It's a good thing I'm graduated. I might get blown up this year if I was around.

I'll be calling you when I'm back in Madison, I guess. Probably from a public phone cause I'm sure they turned off my service by now.

The job situation doesn't look that bad. If not with the *Guardian,* there are a few other openings around. Maybe even the *Capital Times* in Madison. If I have no draft worries, I should get right down to business.

I've still got enough $ so don't worry about that. I really don't even expect to have to take any more of your money at all. And I want to get those educational debts out of the way. Paying them off is the thing I worry about most.

Please save those rowing nationals clippings for me.

Will call soon,

He signed in block letters "LEO, /now: BACHELOR OF ARTS" the title surrounded by little shooting rays. On the back of the envelope he wrote "Keep that line open," as if he might call anytime. As his return address he gave "Leo the Graduate/N.Y., IN A CAR" and he added the note, "Looks like a job here."

Leo's road-not-taken had become a ruse to throw the law off his trail. He knew the FBI would be visiting his parents, and he believed his father would turn over the letter. The feds would spend a week looking for him in New York while he was making the border crossing into Canada. At a post office he bought two "First Man on the Moon" stamps, carefully tearing one off for the letter to his parents and using the other on the letter to Silberberg containing the communiqué. A few days later, under a microscope at the FBI's Washington crime lab, the edges of the two stamps would reveal a perfect match.

Paul Bracken had known Leo Burt since high school, had rowed with him on Monsignor Bonner's eight-man scull, and counted him among his closest friends. Bracken was a physics student at Columbia and politically hip. Leo had not given him any explanation for his request other than that he was "in trouble" and had to get to Canada. Bracken assumed that he was having draft problems.

He persuaded Robert Beaty, also a Monsignor Bonner graduate and oarsman, to drive, since Beaty had just bought a good used car. Beaty had shared Leo's early enthusiasm for the marines, but had stuck with it, eventually serving in Vietnam. He had just resumed his studies at St. Joseph's College, was letting his hair grow, and was thinking about joining Vietnam Veterans Against the War.

On the drive to Manhattan on the New Jersey Turnpike Bracken and Beaty speculated about Leo's possible involvement in the Madison bombing, which was still the top of the news. In high school they had called him "Leo the Commie" because he was so concerned about social issues. They had never heard him preach violence, but Bracken had seen evidence of a change in Leo in recent months. There were the tough-talking *Cardinal* editorials and Mother Jones literature he had sent, and in May he had written describing the Cambodia–Kent State riots in Madison, listing his return address as "Battle Zone/Madison, Wisconsin." Beaty agreed, but he thought the change had to do more with Leo's being dropped from varsity crew. At Christmas Leo had griped to him about Jablonic's haircut policy and how it had destroyed the crew's esprit de corps.

As they were coming into the city they heard the news of a $100,000 reward being offered by the Wisconsin Board of Regents. "If it's Leo, we'll turn him in and split the reward," they joked.

The meeting was to be at the sundial on the Columbia University quad at 8 P.M., but Bracken and Beaty were early. Leo, in dark glasses, was waiting for David on a bench at 116th Street and Broadway when he saw them get out of their car. Even at a distance they were easily recognized, both six-feet-six. Leo got up, and Bracken greeted him warmly. "You did it, right?" he joked, hoping to clear the air.

"Yeah, I lit the fuse!" Leo crowed.

They laughed with him, but a little nervously. Leo's reaction was a little *too* bluff.

Shortly after, David Fine arrived, frustrated because he had been unable to find a typewriter. Leo introduced him simply as "Dave," and the four of them walked down Broadway to the Gold Rail Bar, one of Bracken's hangouts. Leo mentioned that he and David had stopped to see the White Panthers in Ann Arbor and that they had turned out to be "nothings." "Do you know any Weathermen?" he abruptly asked Bracken.

"Not personally," the latter replied.

"Anybody in Canada?" Leo pressed.

"A few oarsmen, but no one I could ask favors of," he said uneasily. When David renewed his complaint about the seeming dearth of typewriters in New York City, Bracken volunteered to find one for him and left to see whether a friend of his who lived in the neighborhood was at home.

Leo's fever was back. He popped several aspirin into his mouth and washed them down with beer. "Clyde," he said, calling Beaty by his nickname, "Clyde, have you read Marcuse?" When Beaty admitted that he had not, Leo recommended *One-Dimensional Man* and started trying to educate Beaty about "corporate liberalism."

Beaty felt an obligation to Leo, who had wished him well when he shipped out to Vietnam and had sent letters to him in the combat zone, but he did not care for Leo's didacticism. "Look, Leo, you know how I stand on that, so don't talk to me about it," he said.

Beaty believed that if he could just get Leo back in a rowing shell, everything would be all right. "I tried to call you in Madison on the twenty-sixth," he said. "We're putting together a four-man shell at the Schuylkill Boat Club—Bracken, me, Tom Rafferty. You could be the fourth. Come on back and row with us," he pleaded.

Rafferty was another Monsignor Bonner pal and had rowed with Leo the time they won a junior first place for the Penn Athletic Club. Leo had dated the girl to whom Rafferty was now married. Leo must have been tempted, but he had chosen; rowing could no longer be part of his life. "We have to get up to Boston," he said. "Dave's sister's expecting us."

Bracken returned with his friend John Consiglio, a math student at Columbia. He had started to tell Consiglio that his Madison friends were in trouble, but Consiglio didn't want to hear it. The bombing had put everyone in a paranoid frame of mind.

They all walked back to Consiglio's place, which was on the sixth floor of a Morningside Heights tenement. The apartment doors looked as though they had been attacked with axes and were patched with sheet metal. Once inside David inserted blank social security and Selective Service cards into Consiglio's typewriter and filled them in with the names Matthew Robert James and Eugene Ronald Fieldstone. Then he asked for scissors and paste. Consiglio offered him a pair of small manicuring scissors, with which David made do. He finished the job in fifteen minutes, and the fugitives said they had to go, declining an offer of dinner. Later, Consiglio was struck by the fact that Fine was wearing a Wisconsin sweatshirt, hardly the best disguise under the circumstances, he thought.

Beaty followed Leo's directions to the hotel and parked in front of a Blimpy and Hoagie Sandwich Shop while David and Leo went inside to get their bags. "What if Leo's really in trouble?" Bracken said in a hushed voice. "Could we get in trouble for helping him?"

Before Beaty could respond David and Leo emerged with their suitcases, which they had left at the checkout desk. At that instant Bracken decided they should go ahead. The lift to Boston would be the last favor.

Marsha Fine Zimmer was a thin, nervous young woman with startling aquamarine eyes. Her husband, Bill Zimmer, had transferred from Dartmouth to woo her, and now she was working to put him through graduate school while taking graduate courses herself at night, sacrificing for him as she once had for David. It was 1:30 A.M. when Buzzy arrived at their apartment not far from Boston University. Knowing that he had flown out to Madison only ten days earlier, she was surprised to see him back on the East Coast so soon. "What are you doing here? Why aren't you in Madison?" she asked.

David told her that he and his friend Leo had left town because of the bombing; they were afraid they might be implicated because they worked for the *Cardinal,* and the *Cardinal,* of course, was a radical paper.

"*Are* you implicated?" Marsha asked. David denied it.

While David went back downstairs to get Leo, Marsha hurriedly made up beds. The following day she and her husband dropped them off at Copley Square, a hippie hangout in downtown Boston, where David said they would find a ride to Canada. She handed David a twenty-dollar bill, which was to her a week's worth of groceries. "Good luck, Buzzy," she said awkwardly. It was the last she was to see of him for six years.

On Sunday, August 30, David and Leo registered at Headquarters House, a youth hostel in Peterborough, Ontario, under the names Eugene Fieldstone and Matthew James. Leo called Paul Bracken and asked him to wire twenty-five dollars. Bracken hesitated; the trip to Boston had left him broke. He and Beaty had to hawk their class rings for gas money home. Make it out to Eugene Fieldstone and send it to a Western Union office at 175 North George Street in Petersborough, Leo urged. "OK," Bracken said, without writing down the address. He was petrified.

Sunday was Dwight's nineteenth birthday. He had moved out of the penthouse after being propositioned several times and spent the afternoon panhandling in the theater district, where the longest line was for a new Broadway musical called *Hair* which featured nudity on stage. At nightfall he bedded down on a park bench in the triangle formed by the intersection of Avenue of the Americas and Broadway. He was lying there watching field mice foraging in the yellow light when several young black men came up. "Come on man, you got money," said one, pointing a knife at him.

Dwight dug into his pocket. "I got one dime," he said sourly.

"Give it to me."

Dwight flipped it to him. "It's my birthday, man. I was going to use it for a phone call."

They merely laughed at him and walked away.

Noon, Wednesday, September 2, Times Square. Karl found Dwight in his panhandling spot in front of Nathan's. They both looked haggard. Splitting up had been a mistake, they agreed. They waited for Leo and David, watching the electronic bulletin board on the Allied Chemical Building. After a few minutes Dwight began to get edgy. "Relax," Karl told him, "we've waited a week already." Karl was so anxious not to miss the rendezvous that he had also come by the day before, just in case he had the date wrong. "They probably have it all lined out by now, contacts, money, IDs. They'll have it all arranged," he assured Dwight.

But after an hour even Karl had to admit that it looked as if they'd been stood up. "We better call home before we go anywhere," he said. "Maybe the cops aren't even looking for us." He stepped into a phone booth and called collect. Donald Armstrong accepted the charges.

"Hi, Dad," he said in a cheerful voice, as if nothing were amiss.

After establishing that Karl was calling from New York, Don bluntly informed him that the FBI was searching for him.

"For what?" Karl said.

"For the University of Wisconsin bombing."

"Dad, I didn't do that."

"Karl, if you're innocent or guilty, son, I beg of you, please turn yourself in," Don said humbly.

Karl paused. "Gosh, I don't know, Dad...." He hung up.

Moments later a news flash began to circle on the Allied Chemical Building's electronic bulletin board: FBI TO ANNOUNCE SUSPECTS IN WISCONSIN BOMBING TODAY.

The brothers ducked into the subway and rode the trains north to the end of the line. At Dyre Avenue they started walking. "David and Leo blame me for Fassnacht," Karl said. "That's why they stood us up."

In front of E. J. Korvette's, a department store at the county line, Dwight developed a cramp in his side and had to lean on Karl, and in this fashion they hobbled up the Post Road into the Pelhams, following, in reverse direction, the route that Paul Revere once took to foment rebellion against the British Empire. It was dusk when they reached Scarsdale, where trains from Grand Central Station were delivering the city's commuting executives to waiting station wagons. As the Armstrongs passed parklike estates and country clubs with pools and riding trails, the contrast with the poverty and decay of the South Bronx was such that Karl began to feel better about the bombing. He wasn't aware that these suburbs were home to many of the leaders of Madison's protest movement.

In White Plains they spent their last few nickels on Cokes and cigarettes, then settled for the night in a vacant house at the north end of the city, sitting back to back on the floor wrapped in a sheet that Karl had taken from his hotel. They fell asleep not knowing that they had been the subject of their favorite news show that night. Walter Cronkite himself, reading from a press release issued jointly by FBI Director J. Edgar Hoover and Attorney General John Mitchell, announced the indictment of four suspects in the Madison bombing on charges of sabotage, destruction of government property, and conspiracy. (Only the state of Wisconsin could bring a murder charge.) All four had been included on the FBI's "Ten Most Wanted" list—which, Cronkite noted, had been expanded to fourteen to accommodate them. Along with the Colorado bomber Cameron Bishop and black nationalists H. Rap Brown and Angela Davis (wanted in connection with the recent Marin County Courthouse shoot-out), the New Year's Gang raised to seven the suspects who were wanted for politically motivated offenses. Half the men and women on the Most Wanted list were revolutionaries.

Early Thursday morning the brothers started canvassing White Plains parking lots. After several hours of fruitless searching, they simultaneously found two unlocked autos with keys in the ignition parked across the street from each other in an industrial area at the edge of town. They took the one with the fuller gas tank, a dark blue 1968 Pontiac GTO with a 10,000 rpm Sun tachometer, five-spoke magnesium hubs, and a group of Playboy Club decals, a set of wheels much to Dwight's liking.

It was a warm, clear autumn day, the woods just beginning to turn. The Canadian border was only ten or twelve hours away. Still unaware of their "Most Wanted" status they veered east into Connecticut, thinking it safer to travel through Vermont, but then had a change of heart and crossed the Hudson into Albany, where they ran out of gas. Karl cashed in his watch for four dollars at a pawnshop a block from the State Capitol and spent it at the pump. It bought half a tank.

From Albany they followed a country road west along the Mohawk River, avoiding the New York Thruway. They had discovered a hatchet in the car, and as the gas gauge plummeted, they entertained the idea of armed robbery. Spying an isolated roadside restaurant they contemplated surprising the owner as he left with the night's receipts, but that would have involved a long wait, so they went on. A little before 6 P.M. they arrived in Little Falls, where they found a Western Union office. They drove slowly past it a number of times, checking it out. The only person inside was a fragile-looking old woman. It was a good place to rob, Dwight said, but Karl was against it, explaining, "I don't ever want to be accused of threatening an old lady with a hatchet."

At that point a police car pulled them over. "What's a couple of Wisconsin boys doin' in a New York car?" Chief Ed Manley, of the Little Falls Police Department, asked them, scrutinizing Dwight's license. He was a big man, pleasant in manner, but suspicious. The GTO had caught his eye right away, and then he had noticed Dwight's hair.

They told him they were friends of the owner, on holiday from the University of Wisconsin, and had borrowed it for the day to go to Buffalo to pick up a friend. "Who's the friend?" Manley asked. "David Fine," Karl answered.

Manley smelled a stolen car. "I'd like you to follow me in to the station," he said. "We'll have to check this out."

They trailed after him, convinced that they would be discovered. At the town's main intersection Dwight proposed turning right after the cop passed on through. The cross street led to a bridge over the Mohawk River, and then up into the hills. "I can outrun him," he said, revving the engine. The vibration shook loose the Pontiac's muffler, and it clattered to the pavement. The GTO was making so much noise now that people were staring from the sidewalks. No way, Karl said, and Dwight reluctantly followed the cop on into the station, trailing a shower of sparks.

Besides Manley there was only a single dispatcher on duty. Manley reported the license number to the state police and then called White Plains information for the owner, Gene Peternero. The number was unlisted. Meanwhile Karl and Dwight considered possible avenues of escape in case the car showed up hot. As they whispered Dwight's eye was drawn to a newspaper lying on Manley's desk. The lead story, "Suspects Named in Bombing," was illustrated with photos of all four, their names in bold type underneath. "All right if I read the paper?" he asked Manley. Without waiting for an answer he removed the newspaper from the desk.

Twenty minutes went by. At 6:45 P.M., the state police called back. Manley picked up the phone, muttered something, and hung up. "Well, I guess it all checks out. You guys can go now. I can give you a name of a place to get your car fixed."

The startled brothers walked out, taking the newspaper with them. Dwight crawled under the car and jammed the muffler back into place, and they took off, following back roads north into the Adirondacks to avoid the dragnet that they figured would await them in Buffalo, gateway to Toronto. Dwight fretted that they had only about thirty miles worth of gas in the tank, but Karl didn't seem concerned; he was completely absorbed in the story of the "Top Ten" fugitives.

The occupants of Headquarters House that evening were mostly U.S. nationals, part of the swelling cavalcade of young Americans—draft dodgers, deserters, drug dealers—looking for a haven in Canada. It didn't take the guests long to figure out that the youth hostel was being watched, and the place was buzzing with rumors of an imminent bust. A good many feared it was *they* who were about to be arrested, hence the unusual interest in a costume ball going on in town—everyone was trying to leave the building in disguise.

While the Mounties scrutinized the parade of masked men leaving by the front door, David and Leo hurriedly discarded their wallets with their IDs, useless now that they had registered with them, and exited by a rear window. They then parted company. David hitchhiked south and west, heading for the border crossing at Detroit. Leo simply disappeared. By the time the Mounties, armed with immigration warrants, came bursting into their room the next morning, they were long gone.

Civilization dropped behind quickly as the GTO rose effortlessly into the mountains. The gas gauge read empty. Except for a bowling ball, a fire extinguisher, and the hatchet, there was nothing of commercial value in the car. It was getting dark. The engine died as they crested a hill, and once again the Armstrongs appeared to be out of luck. But the car kept rolling, rounding a bend and then coasting down a long, winding grade. When the road flattened out, they saw the familiar trademark of a Shell station glowing in the distance. A cafe stood next to it, and the GTO came silently to a stop in the parking area. Inside Dwight panhandled a group of hippies in a booth, who emptied their pockets. To the fugitives the pile of cash on the table looked like a small fortune. They parlayed the bowling ball, fire extinguisher, hatchet, and spare change into a tank of gas.

Around 11:00 P.M. Officer Manley finally came across a copy of the daily paper and saw the boys' pictures on the front page. He immediately called the state police and the FBI. Another check of the Hot List brought up the GTO. It had been there for hours, in fact, but a keypunch operator had entered the license number incorrectly when Manley first called it in. New York State troopers fanned out all along Interstate 90 looking for a GTO with a loose muffler, and federal agents put every hippie house in Buffalo under surveillance. Border guards on Interstate 87 to Montreal were also alerted.

Karl and Dwight angled northeast toward Ticonderoga on Lake Champlain, then followed the lakeshore north. They ducked the freeway at Champlain, taking State Highway 11 to Mooers and an isolated country road the last few miles to the unguarded border, crossing at dawn. It wasn't until they saw a road sign in French that they even knew they were in Quebec.

The Royal Canadian Henley Course occupies the broad, protected estuary of Twelve Mile Creek where it empties into Lake Ontario at St. Catharines. The famous old 2,000-meter course, flanked by several large grandstands, a shellhouse, press center, finish tower, and "Old Boy's Clubhouse" parallels the Welland Canal, which links Ontario with Lake Erie. Ten miles away is the spectacular international tourist attraction of Niagara Falls. In the first week of September 600 oarsmen from thirty nations were gathered in St. Catharines for the world rowing championships, the third world meet since 1962. The 1970 event was of unusual interest to U.S. and Canadian authorities because they expected Leo Burt to be there. Among the things Burt had left behind in Madison, investigators had found a slip of paper mentioning the name Tim Mickelson in connection with St. Catharines. Mickelson, as the FBI soon learned, was a University of Wisconsin oarsman, the only one to make the U.S. rowing team, and a former roommate of Burt's. The bureau had asked the Royal Canadian Mounted Police to be on the lookout for the fugitive, and plainclothesmen were plentiful in St. Catharines.

Friday was a day of light workouts on the Henley Course as the national teams prepared for semifinals and finals on the weekend. The East Germans were favored. Mickelson dipped his red-white-and-blue oar in unison with seven others in his shell and pulled. *An oarsman must be mentally tough,* he reminded himself.

When he got back to Ridley College, where the team was staying, the dorm master informed him that he had had a phone call, the second one in two days. Again, the caller had declined to leave his name. Puzzled, Mickelson telephoned home to see if it had been his father, and when he learned it had not been, he became very curious. Could the caller have been Leo?

Leo's other roommate, Phil Resch, was in St. Catharines with his wife to watch the races, camped out next to Wisconsin rowing coach Randy Jablonic, who was taking pictures for the Olympics Committee. The Resches lived six blocks from Sterling Hall, and the blast had knocked framed pictures off their walls. They were all talking about it near the shellhouse when Mickelson brought up the mysterious phone calls. The group scanned the faces of the spectators picnicking on the grassy flats along the far bank, looking for Leo's Sergeant Rock features in the crowd. Mickelson was against the war; he had drawn a low number in the lottery and was giving some thought to refusing induction. He wanted to talk to Leo, to ask him what had happened. "Maybe Leo didn't really want to be involved," he speculated.

Like Leo, Resch had been an altar boy. "If Leo is involved, it's out of conviction that there is no other way to stop the war," he said, obviously moved.

Jablonic was also upset. He had seen other oarsmen through dark times—Mickelson, for example, who had quit over his mother's death, blaming himself for the freak accident that had taken her life when she tried to visit him in Havertown. With great patience Jablonic had brought him around, convincing him that his mother would have wanted him to compete. But Mickelson was his star, the best rower he had; he had not made the same effort with Leo Burt. "God, if Leo had only made varsity," he said, "this might never have happened."

The GTO rolled into Montreal under a lowering sky. Karl spent half an hour leafing through the city directory at a phone booth until he found a listing for a likely sounding organization, the American Deserters Committee. He called the number and tried to explain his situation. "Don't say anything more over the phone," the party on the other end warned. The committee office was several miles away, but Karl decided that the car was too hot to take into the city. As they set off on foot for the ADC office, it began to rain.

Karl was still thinking about Don's having spoken to them in the night, his voice, halting and distant, coming over the radio as they crossed a pass high in the Adirondacks. "Karl, Dwight, turn yourselves in, fellas. They'll find you eventually anyway. Do this for Mom and Dad, please." For a moment Karl had been on the verge of tears, but Dwight broke the spell. "Sure, Dad," he sneered. He looked at Karl. "The big dummy, to think we'd come back!"

It was far too late for Don to get involved, they agreed. As they trudged through the streets of Montreal Karl reminded Dwight of the resolution they had made during the night. "We'll cut all ties. We'll stay free as long as we can," he said.

26

Safe Houses
of the FLQ

*Doing something terrible to people who rebelled out of
important and good and social motives will not be constructive.*

—HOWARD ZINN,
historian, for the defense

Why didn't any of these scholars bother to interview Karl?
—DOUGLAS HAAG,
Wisconsin Assistant Attorney General, for the prosecution

Bernard Mergler was a *gauchiste* of the old school. He had been
brought up in a left-wing family in the Jewish Quarter of Montreal and joined the Communist party early on, staying loyal until
1956 when the Soviets invaded Budapest. With a thriving law practice representing Quebecois separatists and various people's
republics, Mergler, aged fifty-five, was a man of considerable
renown in Montreal. But when the call came that morning from the
American Deserters Committee (ADC), he didn't hesitate. Of
course, he had heard of the Madison bombing; of course, he would
come.

He met the fugitives in a tavern downstairs from the ADC office on Amherst Street. "My God, what's happened to you?" he asked. The two men were completely soaked. He sat them down in a high-backed wooden booth and ordered bowls of onion soup, sandwiches, and hot coffee. Mergler was never happier than when he was helping exiles, whether they were fleeing Mussolini's Italy or Nixon's United States. These particular fugitives, he realized at once, were totally without resources. According to the older of the pair, they had to borrow a dime from a gas station attendant to call the ADC.

Mergler was bald with a dark complexion, a dark little mustache, and a fringe of dark hair. He wore black horn-rim glasses and a dark suit and to Dwight looked very old. The first thing he wanted to know about was the car. He would have his people pick it up and take it to a "chop shop," he said; the police would never find it. When Dwight asked if that was really necessary, Mergler laughed. "You can bet they're looking for it right now." Then he questioned them about the New Year's Gang, about Army Math, and about how the bombing had been executed. "Unbelievable, unbelievable," he remarked, recalling how he had carried an injured comrade to safety when he was fighting the Falangists in Spain. In fact, he said nostalgically, he'd set a few charges himself in his day.

Mergler's loud voice made Karl uneasy, and he was certain the waitress was listening to their conversation. To Dwight the man seemed "off in a dream world." Neither brother had any idea that they were talking to the "Kunstler of Quebec."

Finally Mergler turned to the practicalities of lodging, money, and new identities. Someone from ADC would take them to a safe house. He urged them to stay out of sight. "You know you killed someone, and if you get caught, you'll be tried for murder," he said affably.

Later Dwight asked Karl if Mergler was right about his warning; the federal charges against them said nothing about murder. "He knows we didn't mean to kill Fassnacht," Karl answered. "He's just trying to scare us."

Back in Madison Major Case Inspector Joe Sullivan had the student movement on the run. To escape the grand jury inquisition, many of the heavies had fled to a remote Mendocino County commune established by Phil Stielstra, twin brother of Jonathan, the

notorious Dow Day flag cutter. "Red George" Croal and his counteraffinity squads reigned triumphant over the isthmus, and with
Fat Julie working for him, he usually had advance warning of the
militants' plans. From coast to coast activists agonized over the
moral ambiguities of the bombing. The outcome could not have
been more favorable to the sedition men if they had planned it
themselves.

But the manhunt was not going nearly so well. The bureau could
not just go charging across the border after the fugitives; it had to
ask the help of the Royal Canadian Mounted Police. Like the FBI,
the RCMP was preoccupied with threats to the social order, and
what with the separatist Fédération de la Libération de Québec
(FLQ) and the left-wing trade unions, political parties, and publishing houses that flourished in Canada, the Mounties did not have
personnel to devote to a sustained search for American fugitives.
For the tired executives of Golden Freek Enterprises the disarray
provided a golden opportunity.

The Golden Freeks were having little luck in the outdoor festival
business. One way or another, they had been shut down in three
states. "The government is making war on the youth culture," Pete
Bobo complained. Sandy Nelson had problems of his own. His
heart had stopped during the Poynette festival in April, and he had
fallen in love with the red-haired nurse who revived him. Lynn had
been a good sport about it, but it had made life complicated all the
same.

The day that Lynn Schultz turned state's evidence, Bobo and Nelson sat in Jack Van Metre's Carroll Street law office envious of her
newfound status and pondering ways that they, too, might get in
with the FBI. "They are not going to want you just because you
were involved with her," Bobo advised. They decided to base their
pitch on their knowledge of "the bombers," as they contemptuously
referred to campus radicals. Van Metre arranged an appointment at
the Stassi Shoe Store.

Bobo outlined his proposal to Baxtrum and company in a meeting in late September. He and Sandy had met Karl and would recognize him anywhere, he said. Bobo claimed also to have met
David Fine at a Mother Jones get-together in Miffland. The Golden
Freeks had dealt with the heavies in connection with the Poynette
festival. They knew Mark Knops. They had the hair and the rap to
work undercover. And they could handle themselves in a fight.

They expected no money from the bureau other than expenses; the $100,000 bounty offered by the University of Wisconsin Board of Regents was incentive enough.

Bobo's manner was smooth and businesslike, but the sedition men did not trust him. The quieter Sandy Nelson impressed them as more down to earth. Three weeks had passed since the bombing, and it was feared that at any moment the New Year's Gang would take a sugar boat to Cuba. Nixon was leaning on Hoover, and Hoover was leaning on everyone else for a break in the case. Still, Bobo and Nelson were of questionable reliability, and the agents at first declined to take them up on their offer.

But as other leads withered and Canadian authorities lost interest, the scheme looked better and better. In early October Bobo and Nelson left *en mission* for Canada in Bobo's car, a 1957 Lincoln with rear "suicide doors" that opened toward the front. Tom Madden, the new security specialist out of Pittsburgh, was to be their Madison contact. The FBI's hopes for catching the Sterling Hall bombers were now pinned on the frustrated entrepreneurs of Golden Freek Enterprises.

In Montreal September is the kindest month. The trees take on their colors, and the city bathes in the golden light of autumn. But the city's charms passed over Karl Armstrong, preoccupied as he was with thoughts of failure and a growing realization of the adverse political consequences of the bombing. It had been "objectively counterrevolutionary," he decided. Mostly he blamed himself. He really couldn't do anything right, it seemed.

The month passed in a blur of safe houses. The first was across the street from a provincial police station on whose roof helicopters landed night and day and proved not to be very safe at all. The second had only one bed, which didn't last very long under the combined weight of the Armstrong brothers.

Around the first of October they were moved to an airy, bright room on the second floor of a house on Wolfe Street, a block from Amherst. Their new landlady, a sweet old Quebecoise they addressed as Madame Gaudet, took a liking to them and even invited them to dinner. They were on the edge of the "Plateau," the old residential neighborhood in the heart of the city, where patrician graystones are interspersed with modest dwellings of the poor. Madame Gaudet's house was embellished with splendid gingerbread woodwork and fronted by an outside staircase made of iron that swooped up from the sidewalk to its second story. Lafontaine Park, with its serpentine pond, children's zoo, tennis courts, and walking paths, and the Bibliothèque Municipale on Sherbrooke Street were within easy walking distance. The side streets were busy with pedestrians and delivery boys running their orders on bikes equipped with straw baskets.

Tom Lance, the twenty-three-year-old deserter who managed the ADC office, supplied them with twenty-five dollars Canadian each week. Rent consumed half of that; the remainder they spent on a dreary diet of macaroni and tomato sauce, peanut butter and jelly, and bread. Often they were tempted to try one of the *tourtières,* the meat pies in the window of a neighborhood pâtisserie, but hesitated to spend the money. Karl nagged Dwight about his cigarette habit, which was costing too much money. "You aren't going to like it if I have to give them up," Dwight warned.

Lance, their only contact with the outside world, was an angry young man. His father, with whom he was not on good terms, was a colonel in the U.S. Marines; his education had been entirely in Jesuit schools—Brooklyn Prep, Holy Cross, Fordham. He had started out a supporter of the war in Vietnam, but had deserted in the fall of 1969 after twice being denied conscientious-objector status. Now he dreamed of returning to the States at the head of an "Army in Exile" and destroying the American power structure "by whatever means necessary."

In mid-October the city was suddenly thrown into chaos. Dwight was returning from the park when a jeep screeched to a halt on Wolfe Street and soldiers armed with automatic weapons leaped out. His knees went weak, and he put up his hands in surrender, but the men, ignoring him, burst into the house next door, where, unbeknownst to the Armstrongs, the ADC had originally been head-quartered. Karl called Bernard Mergler and informed him that Dwight had been nearly run over by the Canadian army. Mergler asked the brothers to meet him in the restaurant below his law office in downtown Montreal and quickly explained what had happened. First, the British trade minister, James Cross, had been kidnapped by two brothers named Chenier representing themselves as the "Liberation Cell." The Cheniers claimed to belong to the FLQ, but nobody knew much about them. They had made a number of demands for reforms—political, educational, managerial—which, to the surprise of the federal government in Ottawa, had generated wide sympathy in Quebec, gaining the support of the unions, the university students, and many civic groups. When the government persisted in refusing to negotiate, Pierre Laporte, the provincial labor minister, had disappeared, apparently also kidnapped. Prime Minister Pierre Elliot Trudeau had then invoked the War Measures Act. During the night, Montreal had been invaded by some 8,000 federal troops. Hundreds of people had been detained, literally dragged from their beds. "Consider yourselves lucky that they aren't looking for you," Mergler said.

Mergler apologized for the fact that he didn't have false ID for them yet; it was taking a while because people were occupied "with other things." He also wanted to set up a "new communication system" with them, to keep them from calling his office. If they had a message for him, they were to send it through Lance. "Do not call me unless it is a dire emergency," he emphasized. He gave them a little money and sent them on their way.

Mergler was just like Uncle Paul; he enjoyed everything, it seemed to Karl. But Dwight had found Mergler to be extremely tense; obviously, it had become very inconvenient for him to be dealing with Top Ten fugitives.

The October Crisis, as it would go down in history, disrupted the supply lines on which the Armstrong brothers depended. Lance suddenly dropped out of sight, and the ADC office stopped answering its phone. Federal troops armed with automatic rifles stood guard at every street corner. Toward the end of October, when Pierre Laporte's body was found in the trunk of a car, the repression intensified. The Armstrongs still had no IDs, and it became too risky for them to go out. They stopped their jaunts to the park and the library and spent the days in their room, where Karl tried to read a tattered paperback edition of *Crime and Punishment* that Lance had given him.

It was during this period that Bobo and Nelson were prowling the Plateau in search of them. The two bounty hunters had been briefed by the RCMP in Windsor, provided with street maps and the addresses of expatriate hangouts in Toronto and Montreal, and offered high-powered, untraceable semiautomatic pistols. Bobo was tempted by the guns, but Nelson refused them, remembering the bureau's warning about accepting even implied responsibility for apprehending the fugitives. Besides, they had their own protection.

They had stopped in Toronto for several days and then had driven all the way to the Province of New Brunswick, where they had stayed a week in the rain watching a Venceremos brigade that was preparing to leave for Cuba. Both the FBI and the RCMP had advised them that the fugitives would try to stow away with the group.

When they got to Montreal, the city was in an uproar over the Laporte slaying. They scouted FLQ hangouts, such as the Spanish Club, but there was no one around but police spies, who were easy to spot in their dark glasses. Following up on the advice of the Windsor Mounties, they staked out the office of the ADC, only to discover that it was closed and everyone was in hiding. Hanging out in "the Ghetto," the student neighborhood around McGill University, proved more fruitful for them; at least they were able to meet girls. Meanwhile they were running up large bills at a posh downtown hotel. Every few days Nelson called Tom Madden, whom he regarded as an "all-American guy," to ask for more money. The tab was up to around $10,000, according to Bobo, before Madden cut them off.

About the same time that Bobo and Nelson headed back to Madison, the Armstrongs decided that, no matter what the risk, they were going to have to leave the apartment. Dwight had smoked the last of his cigarettes and was having a nicotine fit; they were also out of food. The well-meaning Madame Gaudet was talking about contacting the Social Insurance Agency to come and interview them. In desperation the brothers spent a day panhandling. Dwight came back with several dollars, Karl with a maple leaf dime. "I look just as down-and-out as you," he complained. "Why won't they give me money?"

"You've just got to find the right corner," Dwight assured him.

November came and along with it, the cold. "We can't get a job; we can't collect welfare; we are going to have to rob somebody," Dwight insisted, and Karl reluctantly agreed to help him hold up a movie theater. They scraped together fourteen dollars, the proceeds of a week of panhandling, and bought a Crossman air pistol that looked like an Army .45, along with a wicked-looking knife and a couple of ski masks. They selected a dumpy neighborhood theater. With their last few dollars they paid their way in at 8 P.M. and sat through the feature, a low-budget rock documentary called *Popcorn,* twice. Afterward they made their way downstairs to the boiler room and hid under a tarp for several hours until they were sure no one was left in the building. Pulling on their ski masks, they tiptoed upstairs and discovered that the janitor was still there sweeping up. Karl pulled out the air pistol, Dwight grasped the knife, and they charged.

The man looked Turkish or perhaps Lebanese, with a gray mustache and tired eyes. He was so preoccupied with his work that he did not look up until they were upon him. *"Qu'est-ce que vous foutez là?"* he asked, or some similar question the brothers could not understand.

"Just do as we say and you won't get hurt!" Karl said, waving the air pistol. The man dropped his broom and raised his hands over his head. "No, no, that's not necessary," Karl said, suddenly embarrassed. "Put your hands down." In a polite voice Karl asked if there was anyone else around. No, they were alone. Karl ordered Dwight to check the place out, anyway, while he marched the janitor up to the lobby, sat him down, and bound his hands behind him with tape. "When does the manager get here?" he asked. The janitor explained in English that as many as half a dozen other employees would arrive before the manager, who usually didn't come in until around one in the afternoon. When Dwight returned, Karl informed him that they were going to have to bind six people.

"We don't have enough tape," Dwight said.

The janitor complained that the tape was too tight. Karl loosened it. The captive then offered them the money in his wallet, about twenty-five dollars.

"We don't rip off workers," Karl said.

Since it began to look as if they weren't going to get any money, Dwight peeked into the projection booth and suggested destroying the film, a rip-off of the counterculture in his opinion.

"Nah, let's not get into any side trips," Karl said. He put a piece of tape over the janitor's mouth and told him that they were going into the theater for a second to talk things over. Once inside they hurried down an aisle and left by a rear exit. Dwight carelessly allowed the door to slam shut, and the sound reverberated in the alley. They ran to the street and caught the subway back to Wolfe Street.

The next night they mugged two French-speaking men in

Lafontaine Park, netting fifteen dollars, one week's rent. Dwight was impressed by Karl's performance. "You really sounded vicious, man," he said.

Snow had started to fall. One day they saw Bernard Mergler on television starring in what looked like a docudrama about terrorism. The camera followed the dapper little man up the steps of an old house, into which he quickly disappeared. He emerged a moment later with several armed men, and they all piled into a car, which, according to a commentator, was "stuffed with dynamite." A squadron of police cars and motorcycles escorted Mergler's vehicle to the airport, where three of the passengers boarded a plane. It was Thursday, December 3; the footage was live, the events occurring as they watched. The funny, sentimental lawyer whose help the Armstrong brothers had taken for granted was the go-between in a deal the Canadian government had just concluded with the kidnappers of James Cross. The Chenier brothers and an accomplice were on their way to sanctuary in Cuba. The British trade commissioner was set free at the airport.

"Yep, it's old Bernie, plain as day," Dwight said. Now they understood why Mergler hadn't been in touch.

Although the hunt continued for the executioners of Pierre Laporte, the crisis eased. The brutal murder had thrown Quebecois opinion back to support for law and order. Conservatives triumphed in the Montreal municipal elections, and Pierre Trudeau's popularity soared to an all-time high. The tactics of the FLQ extremists had accomplished for him what the Madison bombing had for President Nixon. For the moment the separatists in Quebec were cowed.

With the restoration of order Lance resurfaced, and the flow of money to the fugitives resumed. Karl immediately confessed his attempts at armed robbery to the aghast Lance, who called an ADC meeting to discuss the matter. "We have to get these boys out of Montreal," he urged. "Things are hot enough without them getting caught here." Informed of the incident, Mergler agreed, and within a day or two the Armstrongs had been provided with false baptismal certificates, cash, train tickets to Toronto, and a number to call when they got there. In mid-December the broth-

ers settled accounts with their landlady and boarded the Turboliner.

Madame Gaudet, sorry to see them go, bade them farewell with,
"You boys have been such good tenants. You never make any trou-
ble." But Mergler and the staff of the ADC breathed easier. The
Armstrongs were Naomi's problem now.

27

Toronto the Good

However misguided, the bombing by Karl was a conscientious action.

—DANIEL ELLSBERG,
former Pentagon analyst, for the defense

Let's look at his act. He saw cars parked there. He saw bikes parked in the rack. He saw lights on. What did he do? He lit the fuse and walked away.

—MICHAEL ZALESKI,
Wisconsin Assistant Attorney General, for the prosecution

In Toronto's expatriate community Naomi Wall was a legend, the Mother Protector of draft dodgers and deserters in Canada. She was a small, brusque woman in her late twenties, with a macaw's beak and owlish green eyes that appeared to fill her bifocals completely. Raised in an affluent, progressive Jewish milieu in Washington, D.C., she had come to Canada in 1965 with her husband, who had a teaching appointment at the University of Toronto. In Canada, she found, the free-enterprise gospel was less dominant, churches and labor unions and farmers were more politically active, the women's movement was more socialistic, and the New Democratic party presented an electoral alternative well to the left of the Democratic party in the United States.

Working for a Canadian peace organization, she received a call one day from someone stateside who wanted to know whether draft dodgers would be extraditable in Canada. The question had not been raised before. She hung up and made inquiries and then excitedly called back. "Incredible news," she announced. "Canada has no draft; therefore, the crime of draft evasion is not extraditable!"

Shortly thereafter began a trickle that was to become a flood, the largest exodus of Americans since the War of Independence. Wall organized the Toronto Anti-Draft Programme (TADP) to help draft dodgers find jobs and housing. When all the arrangements were made, she would send them back to Detroit or Buffalo to recross the border, carrying written job offers and applications for landed-immigrant status. One Toronto publisher was hiring draft dodgers at the rate of three or four a week; if the hires had been legitimate, the company would have been larger than Random House.

Similar support groups sprang up in all the big Canadian cities. Financial support came primarily from the Canadian Council of Churches, which contributed about $1,000 a month from its own coffers and acted as a conduit for donations from the National Council of Churches in New York. A TADP publication, the *Manual for Draft-Age Immigrants to Canada,* also generated income. In fact, the two-dollar pamphlet was the largest-selling Canadian publication in the United States.

At first it was easy to get into Canada. Immigration authorities made no attempt to verify statements made on applications, and Prime Minister Trudeau, himself a former socialist and no fan of U.S. foreign policy, turned a blind eye to the influx. Exiles with money started buying land in places like Prince Edward Island, where prime farm acreage could be had at bargain prices.

By 1969 Wall was seeing 50 new immigrants a day and estimated that there were anywhere from 50,000 to 100,000 Americans in exile in Canada. (The Nixon administration put the figure at 3,000.) By this time she had divorced her professor husband and was living with a deserter in a cozy, two-story house on Lennox Avenue in the university district, which was the equivalent of Miffland for Toronto activists. The RCMP had a file on her, and Mounties occasionally dropped by the TADP office to ask, on behalf of the FBI, about one or another deserter. This was her situation in early December 1970, when Karl Armstrong arrived.

The brothers waited for her at the Varsity, a cavernous cafe on Yonge Street, after a subway ride from the train station. She appeared thirty minutes late, explained that she had another meeting to go to at once, and acted as if it were a great inconvenience to give them any time. She seemed to think they were just another pair of war resisters and was in such a hurry that Karl did not try to reveal their identities.

But Wall soon had them squared away for the night and in the next day or two arranged for them to receive a weekly allowance of twenty-five dollars. They moved every few days at first, going by the names of David Armitage and David Sprecht and using baptismal certificates to accumulate IDs. Toronto was full of exiles, refugees from any number of civil wars. The brothers stayed with a grandmotherly Ukrainian woman who had lost her husband in the Stalinist purges, with an aristocratic Italian family whose land had been stolen by Mussolini, and in a boardinghouse shared (somewhat uneasily) by Indians and Pakistanis. No one questioned the Armstrongs; they were assumed to be draft dodgers.

The city was then in transition from "Toronto the Good," a blue-nosed metropolis run by stern Scottish Presbyterians, to a more loosely governed municipality in which shops were allowed to open on Sunday. It was easy to get around on the hand-me-down streetcars that the Canadian metropolis had inherited when U.S. cities dumped their trolley systems, and the Armstrongs made use of them to search out the youth culture. The University of Toronto, adjacent to the provincial capitol, had erupted over Kent State, with bloody confrontations in front of the American Consulate, but by that fall it was quiet. North of the campus was Yorkville, a Canadian Greenwich Village, where native folk musicians such as Gordon Lightfoot, Joni Mitchell, and Kris Kristofferson often returned to play in the cafes where their careers had begun. Farther downtown Karl and Dwight located "The Hall," a kind of USO club for deserters with a housing exchange and social calendar.

But the biggest concentration of expatriates was to be found at Rochdale, aka the "Rock" or "Rat Castle," a Bloor Street skyscraper finished in raw concrete and glass, the "brutal" style favored by sixties architects. It had begun two years earlier as an experiment in alternative student housing inspired by Robert

Owen's nineteenth-century co-ops in Lancashire, England, but American exiles, possessed of that certain "drive" that Canadians so admire and fear, had turned it into the world's biggest crash pad. Visitors, of which there had been an estimated 100,000 in the previous year, were allowed to sleep in the lounges adjoining the "ashrams," or communal living halls. The only rule was, "Don't steal anything you can't use." David Fine, who had visited Rochdale over the spring break, had given it a negative review on the drive to Ann Arbor, complaining, "Even the grafitti is lousy." But Dwight, when he got to see it for himself, was pleasantly surprised. "It's far out," he assured Karl.

Karl agreed to a tour only to find that the grafitti was the least of Rochdale's disadvantages. The elevators smelled like garbage and disinfectant, pets were running loose all over the place—not only cats and dogs but turtles, rabbits, snakes, frogs, and birds—and the stairwells stank of urine and excrement. He liked the cheap movies, the braless girls in peasant dresses, and a vegetarian restaurant called Etherea, but overall the Rat Castle struck him as a trap. While he was there checking it out, the Metropolitan Toronto Police staged one of their periodic drug raids. "I can't believe you'd stay here; there's too much heat," he told Dwight.

Dwight shrugged off the objection. Sure, there was a chance he could get busted, he acknowledged, but the cops didn't really want to come in, it didn't cost him anything, and he was going to stay.

In early December Sandy Nelson rang up the Stassi Shoe Store with an urgent message for Tom Madden. Pete Bobo's old friends, the Road Vultures Motorcycle Club of Buffalo, had informed them that somebody "very big, very hot" was coming through on the "underground railroad" headed for Toronto. The place to look for them was Rochdale. The Road Vultures had connections with Rochdale building security, who were all bikers. "No guarantees, Tom, but this is what we think is happening," announced Nelson, who was getting to be as smooth a salesman as Bobo.

The Resident Agency had been embarrassed by the costly failure of the Quebec expedition. They would have to get approval from Washington this time, Madden responded coolly. A few days later he called Nelson back with the go-ahead, but warned him against any five-star hotels. No problem, Nelson said, they could stay at Rochdale for free. The bounty hunters took a plane to Toronto.

It had been bikers who had been responsible for most of the "security problems" at Rochdale—stealing drugs, raping and beating the residents, getting drunk, and riding their choppers up and down the stairwells. One of the gangs most involved in these activities was the Black Diamond Riders, a Toronto club with fraternal links to the Road Vultures. That summer Rochdale management had put the Black Diamond Riders in charge of building security, apparently on the theory that they would keep the other gangs in line. The Riders had quickly taken control of the lucrative in-house drug trade, sealing the sixth floor—the "drug floor"—with iron doors. Assigned the responsibility of keeping out "undesirables," a welcoming committee of Riders scrutinized everyone who entered the building, rejecting those who didn't look "cool." Bobo and Nelson, flashing their "R.V.M.C." signet rings like visiting bishops, were waved through.

After several days of nonstop partying they got a lead when a waitress at the Etherea Restaurant recognized Karl from a photo. He had come in once or twice, she said. The reward money now almost within their grasp, the two men extended their stay. There were nineteen floors in the building; they started searching them one by one.

Dwight Armstrong had talked his way into a room on the eleventh floor and was already earning pocket money as a drug courier, making deliveries to Yorkville. Dwight was now an imposing six feet five, his features coming into balance, his manner more confident. Bobo and Nelson were attempting to identify him by a photo that the FBI had obtained from Ruth Armstrong, which showed a chubby-cheeked five feet ten adolescent.

Karl was staying with the Italian aristocrats, and, except for an occasional meal at the Etherea, avoided Rochdale. One evening he received a long-distance call from Naomi Wall. She was in Philadelphia for her grandmother's funeral and had happened to see an item about the WISBOM manhunt in the *New York Times* and had finally realized who he was. Violence was not her thing, she said sharply. Then she asked him to get a pen and paper; she had something important to tell him.

Later that evening Karl paid Dwight an unexpected visit. Naomi had finally figured out who they were, he said, and although she was critical of the bombing, she was not going to cut them off. In fact, she was doubling their allowance. She had given Karl the address of a friend of hers who had a place where they would be more secure. They moved that night.

In both Canada and the United States, winter came on grim and gray. The Beatles had broken up; Janis Joplin and Jimi Hendrix were dead of drug overdoses. In February South Vietnamese forces invaded Laos, but there was scarcely any reaction from American campuses. A lassitude had settled over the student movement. The new decade had begun.

The state of Wisconsin had yet to bring charges against the New Year's Gang. Local authorities were still embroiled in a dispute with the FBI over access to its files, its evidence, and the minutes of the federal grand jury. In March 1971 a trio of local lawmen finally set out to solve the case on their own. At the head of the delegation was Wisconsin's Assistant Attorney General David Mebane, a tough-talking native of Toledo, stout and bald with beady eyes and a hard-boiled look. He was accompanied by Gerald "Buzz" Nichol, the new Dane County district attorney, who had defeated his Democratic opponent, a peace candidate, on the wave of antiterrorist hysteria in the fall. Bringing up the rear was Detective Charles Lulling of the MPD. The assistant attorney general was still angry over the press release Hoover had issued at the time of the Peterborough debacle, demanding that Wisconsin issue murder and arson warrants. As Mebane saw it, the state would have had no problem obtaining warrants if Hoover had been willing to give local authorities the information necessary to support the charges. For its part, the FBI continued to insist that local authorities had more than enough information on which to base a complaint.

The three lawmen had begun to reinterview friends and relatives of the suspects, traveling to Minneapolis, to Wilmington, and to Havertown, duplicating work that the FBI had already done. Lulling found Paul Armstrong at Paul's ex-wife's place, recovering from a gall bladder operation. Paul dodged his questions for hours, showing, as Lulling respectfully observed, his "life experience."

The witness that Lulling most wanted to get to was Karl's friend Scott Nelson. He was not satisfied with the FBI's accounts of its interviews with Nelson and had demanded the minutes of Nelson's grand jury testimony. U.S. Attorney John Olson had turned down his request. On the morning of March 25, Lulling, Mebane, and Nichol visited Secretary of Defense Melvin Laird at the Pentagon, hoping to get Scott Nelson returned from his air base in Spain for an interview. Fred Buzhardt, counsel to the defense secretary, advised Laird that the request would have to be supported by proof that Nelson was a "material witness," which would require FBI documents. Buzhardt arranged an audience at the U.S. Department of Justice.

It was 2:00 P.M. when the trio arrived at the Seventh Street entrance of the Internal Security annex and stopped at the reception desk. Lulling had set off an alarm entering the Pentagon that morning; he now held his coat open to offer the guard a view of his arsenal. The man covered his eyes and said, "Don't show me all that stuff."

Assistant U.S. Attorney General Robert Mardian greeted the visitors and led them to the office of Guy Goodwin, a senior attorney in the Internal Security Division. The man in charge of the federal government's voluminous WISBOM files was a Kansan with a reputation for "brass balls." He had traveled all over the country making certain that federal cases against rioters and saboteurs were vigorously prosecuted. But in David Mebane he had met his match. "The absence of extraditable charges is what allowed Burt and Fine to get away," Mebane reminded Goodwin, and demanded an interview with Scott Nelson.

First, Goodwin replied smoothly, Justice didn't want Scott Nelson brought back because of the chance that he might contradict his earlier testimony; second, Wisconsin authorities should have interviewed him when they had the chance, back in September when he was in Madison to testify. In short, the answer was no.

Mebane turned crimson, his eyes narrowed, and he leaned into Goodwin's face. "You guys have fucked us from day one! You didn't even tell us when Nelson was in town, and as for contradictions, his testimony is already full of them. We're talking about damage to twenty-six buildings. This is *state* property, it's a *state* matter, it ought to be handled by Wisconsin. Now we are going to convene our own grand jury, Mr. Goodwin, and we are going to subpoena your ass."

Robert Mardian stepped in and tried to calm Mebane, but Goodwin threw up his hands. He would leave it up to John Olson, he said disgustedly.

Spring found Karl Armstrong living in an Italian neighborhood, where he had a job delivering groceries. His room overlooked a steep, narrow, cobblestone street lined with *trattorie*. He and

Dwight had long since moved out of the safe house to which Naomi had directed them. Dwight had returned to the good life in Rochdale, panhandling in Yorkville, making drug deliveries, and selling the *Guerilla,* Toronto's underground newspaper. At the urging of their TADP supporters they had disguised themselves. Dwight had his hair curled and wore a pair of eyeglasses with French frames and safety lenses. Karl had bought a wig. The wig was too big for him, so he wore a navy blue stocking cap to hold it in place.

Karl began to visit Rochdale in the evenings for movies and dinner at the Etherea. One night, at a screening of *Yellow Submarine,* he met an attractive young woman who told him that her father owned the Toronto Maple Leafs. When the movie was over, they went to her room, and Karl tried to get her into bed. He was making some headway when his wig slipped, and he excused himself to go to the bathroom. When he reappeared without it, the girl threw him out. It was a lucky thing he was bald, he told Dwight later. "If I'd had hair under the wig, she might have been suspicious."

Karl's presence in Toronto had become an open secret in the expatriate community. At Naomi Wall's, he met TADP activists, lawyers, and university types. His softspoken, unpretentious manner, self-deprecating jokes, and evident remorse over the death and injuries he had caused combined to make a favorable impression. The issue of violence was debated, but in the end it became a personal matter. The fugitives were there, they needed help, and they were judged to be sincere. And so worries about possible repercussions were set aside and help was given.

One evening Naomi introduced Karl and Dwight to a New York filmmaker named Jay Griss, who was producing a documentary on deserters. Griss, a nervous individual with what seemed to Dwight an obsession with mammary glands, told the brothers that he was excited by the story of the New Year's Gang and proposed to make a documentary about it. Karl readily agreed, and before long he and Dwight were making regular trips downtown to be interviewed.

Occasionally somebody who had bombed a draft board would drop by The Hall. These small-time saboteurs struck Karl as nice, middle-class kids who shouldn't have become involved in violence because they didn't have the right "temperament." "The government is playing hardball, and they aren't prepared to play hardball," he would say. He began to talk about returning to action; after all, the war was still going on. One day he aired the idea of a rocket attack on the B-52 base at Plattsburg, not far from where he and Dwight had crossed into Canada. His friends discouraged him, arguing that it would only add to the already severe repression.

These people are all talk, Karl thought, but dropped the idea for the lack of money.

In April Dwight found another crash pad, smaller than the Rat Castle but no less bizarre. The "Norman Elder Museum," a gated brick townhouse in Yorkville, was owned by a wealthy adventurer, Norman Elder, whose practice it was to take in young itinerants such as Dwight. By his own estimate, 6,000 kids had stayed overnight in his home in 1969. Elder was a scion of the Toronto elite, and what he most enjoyed in life was to scandalize the staid Presbyterians among whom he had been raised. His living room was decorated with exotica collected in his travels, including a jaguar pelt and tapir skull, Amazon blow darts, an eleventh-century Chinese incense burner, a stuffed South American rhea, a camel's bladder in a case, and a Louis XIV clock. He kept a live twenty-foot python in a coffin and had a 200-pound pet pig that he walked on a leash. His girl-friend of the moment was a voluptuary who shared his desire to *épater les bourgeois.* She amazed Dwight one day by casually exposing a breast and fondling it in a busy Yorkville restaurant, enjoying the disapproving murmurs of startled Torontonians.

For Dwight's purposes, Elder's "museum" was ideally situated, halfway between Rochdale, at that moment the biggest drug-distribution center in Canada, and the busy streets of Yorkville, where he plied his various trades. He was by then one of Toronto's more successful panhandlers, a master of the "hovering" technique so effective with women. When he compared what he was doing to Karl's dreary, cautious, "make-believe life," it seemed to him that he was doing very well. At least he had interesting friends.

One of these was a Michigan boy named Robert Rainbolt. Dwight, who was still going by the name of David Sprecht, had met him shortly after he arrived in Toronto. Rainbolt resembled Dwight's cousin Vance. He was big and slovenly in appearance, his black hair cut in bangs that framed a fat, round face with red cheeks. He admitted that he was wanted in the States on various charges, and Dwight's immediate impression was that he was not to be trusted. In April they were arrested in a roundup of street people and held overnight. Dwight told the cops that he was a draft dodger, and they released him the next day without fingerprinting him. Dwight then confessed to Rainbolt who he really was and told him the whole story of the New Year's Gang. Now he would find out whether Rainbolt was a true friend. Rainbolt promised not to breathe a word.

Karl, continuing to change his address once a month, moved in with a Portuguese family who had just immigrated to Canada and considered it an honor to have an American border. He got a new job trimming trees with a pair of wise-cracking, alcoholic "Newfies" or Newfoundlanders, whose accent he could never understand. The Newfies let him borrow a car to take a driver's test, and when he passed it, they put him at the wheel of their flatbed truck. After stopping for a beer, he backed the truck into a Porsche, scraping the top of the hood. The police came to his house asking for him. Unaware that he had hit a car, Karl assumed the worst. Before going to the door, he dressed up in a coat and tie and put on his wig, which he had not worn since the night it spoiled his tryst with the sports magnate's daughter. Metropolitan Toronto police waited for him on the porch. "Are you David Armitage?" one asked. That was the name on Karl's license. Evidently, someone had seen the accident and reported it, and the truck had been traced to his employers.

"Yes," Karl said. The Portuguese family and all the neighbors were watching, astonished not only to see him being questioned by police, but to have suddenly sprouted a mop of thick, brown hair. The officers informed him that he was wanted for hit and run.

"What? I didn't know!" Karl said truthfully. His landlady and her relatives moved closer, all of them giving the policemen baleful looks.

The police appeared to be intimidated. "Well, I guess it was an honest mistake," one said, and they rather hastily departed.

Karl thanked his landlady. "Draft dodger," he said, pointing at the wig. They threw a party for him.

Karl remained with the Portuguese into June. He was preoccupied with a series of leaked Pentagon documents that the *New York Times* was publishing and that the Toronto dailies were reprinting verbatim. The documents seemed to prove that everything he had ever heard about the war in Vietnam was true.

Karl saw Dwight less frequently, sometimes only once a week. One evening Dwight showed up at his house with his friend Robert Rainbolt. After Rainbolt left, Dwight confessed to having told him everything. "We should move tonight. We should leave Toronto," Karl said. He didn't trust Rainbolt at all.

28

Busted

I'll state to the court what led to his capture. He was in the process of getting into the manufacture of drugs.

—GERALD NICHOL,
Dane County District Attorney, for the prosecution

It would be better for all of us that he not be surrendered to the United States.

—TOM HAYDEN,
activist, for the defense

Scott Nelson hated the military, but he loved being stationed in Spain. The food, the coffee, and the cognac were the best in the world, insofar as his own experience informed him, and he admired the anarchistic populace, who seemed to despise regulations as much as he did. With the help of friends in leave accounting he had contrived to spend a good part of his time off base, touring such exotic locales as Marrakesh, Malaga, and Paris and spending every weekend on the Costa Brava in the company of English girls he met at his favorite Madrid bar, the El Yeti. He collected gas coupons from less audacious servicemen, paying the base rate of eighteen cents a gallon and selling them on the black market for almost ten times that amount. With the proceeds he and another airman had rented a four-bedroom apartment with a sunken living room and a beautiful patio garden on Avenidas de Los Torros in downtown Madrid. As long as he kept his bed made and his boots shined in his room at the base, he didn't seem to have any problems. In fact, he was having the time of his life.

The summons to appear in Washington came as a shock to Scott, who had tried to put Madison and the New Year's Gang behind him. On July 16, 1971, he appeared as requested in the office of the Staff Judge Advocate at Bolling Air Force Base outside the Capitol. Also present were Madison Police Detective Charlie Lulling, Dane County District Attorney Buzz Nichol, Wisconsin Assistant Attorney General David Mebane, and Joseph Tafe, an assistant attorney general in the Subversive Activities Trial Section of the U.S. Department of Justice. The meeting had been granted after Detective Lulling threatened to fly to Madrid to interview Nelson.

By this time the Wisconsin lawmen had obtained Nelson's federal grand jury testimony, though it had taken a court order to do it, and they went through it with him line by line. Why had Karl gotten involved in revolutionary activities? Lulling asked. Was he so concerned about Vietnam? Was the war really such a hideous thing to him? Early in their friendship Karl had expressed opposition to the war, Scott replied, but as time went by he became interested in the possibility of a captaincy or vice presidency in the revolution that he was convinced was about to happen. He was building himself a niche.

Lulling pressed Scott about his relationship with Karl during this period. Scott answered that when he first arrived on the Wisconsin campus in 1967 he was a naive farm boy. The big school and city activities had swept him off his feet, and he became very much a radical himself. In 1968, however, he became disillusioned with student militants who seemed to only want to tear things down, and he started phasing himself out. As Lulling summed it up a month later in an affidavit for the Dane County grand jury, "Armstrong apparently never realized that Nelson was no longer enthralled with the revolutionary movement. He considered [Scott] to be part of it, and therefore it was like talking to your buddy in the foxhole."

A few other tidbits emerged. Lynn Schultz "was just going along for the kicks," Scott said. Karl called himself the "Mad Bomber" and told Scott that he was going to set up an explosives factory in northern Minnesota to supply arms to the movement. In fact, Scott said, Karl really seemed to believe that the revolution depended on him.

Scott was allowed to return to the good life in Madrid; the lawmen returned to Madison, where a Dane Country Grand Jury had been convened to reexamine the WISBOM witnesses. More than a hundred people were called, including service station attendants, fertilizer salesmen, and other locals whose trust the bombers had exploited. Lulling testified about the interviews he had conducted with absent witnesses, such as Scott Nelson. Since the state now had the complete WISBOM file, it was all redundant, an expensive and rather silly exercise, in the view of federal authorities, yet the appearance of Lynn Schultz on the afternoon of August 6 brought a moment of drama. Lulling had tracked her down in Monterey, California, where Sandy Nelson had taken her to recuperate from the whole ordeal. "Can you trust him, actually trust him as a person?" one of the jurors asked, referring to Karl Armstrong. "Did you approve of what he was doing?"

Lynn did not know how to explain to this middle-aged woman how old and sophisticated Karl had seemed to an eighteen-year-old from Wisconsin Dells, how proud she was to be seen with a good-looking fraternity boy at the hottest bar on campus, how gentle and compassionate he was compared to other guys she had gone out with. She answered both questions with a simple yes.

"I'm shocked," the juror said. "I can't help but say that I am shocked. I mean, did you realize what he was doing?"

Again Lynn answered yes.

"You upheld him in the name of love, you just let him go ahead and do it without calling the law or anybody?"

Before Lynn could answer, the juror began to apologize for giving her such a hard time. Lynn interrupted her. It wasn't just love for Karl that had kept her from turning him in, she confessed, but fear. "Like, if I would have to go to the police, I would have been thrown in jail, too." It was an oddly courageous performance for Schultz, who, after all, had since been romantically involved with one of the bounty hunters who was after Karl. Not once had she taken the opportunity to repudiate the Vanguard of the Revolution and his cause.

———

It was Saturday, August 2, and better-off Torontans had all gone to their summer cabins in northern Ontario to escape the heat. About 2:30 A.M., Dwight Armstrong and Robert Rainbolt were lounging in the doorway of a Yorkville cafe watching the late-night youth parade, when a girl came up and asked them if they wanted to go to Vancouver. She was looking for someone with whom to hitchhike across the country. "I only have two dollars," she explained.

Dwight looked her over. She was honey blonde and fair, with Scottish bones and deep blue eyes. She wore a white studded-leather jacket over a pop-top T-shirt, snug-fitting jeans, and a pair of Kodiak boots that came up over her calves and made her look about six feet tall. "That's okay," he said, in regard to her impecunious circumstances. He introduced himself as Stephen Scofield, his latest alias; she introduced herself as Jerardine McLoughlin, Jerry for short. She said she wanted to leave right away, but Dwight insisted on stopping by his brother's place to pick up some clothes. It was 3:30 A.M. when they knocked on Karl's door. Karl reacted grumpily. "It isn't right to leave like this," he told Dwight in her presence.

Rainbolt, as eager for adventure as Dwight, went with them as far as Wauwau, Ontario, a place so hard to get a ride from that the local hospital would round up hitchhikers and give them beds for the night. There he turned back, while Dwight and Jerry continued on to Regina, Saskatchewan, arriving in the middle of the night.

They sat in front of a truck-stop cafe under an inky sky awash with stars, surrounded by an ocean of ripe grain. Jerry gave the impression of being a rebel in her own way. She had grown up in Toronto but had never finished high school—couldn't sit still. She had starred in a film about arctic adventure and was on her second TV commercial, for bathroom tissue. But she didn't like modeling because you had to care about such matters as body weight and nails. Besides, she hated auditions and always trying to please. Commercials made her feel that she was no more than an "instrument for selling." Jerry was not only beautiful, Dwight soon realized; she was pretty cool.

At dawn Jerry got them a ride with a truck driver who was on his way to Calgary. Dwight tried being sociable in the cab, but after listening to him for a couple of hours the driver pulled off and ordered the couple into the rear of the truck. Hitchhiking was illegal, and they were entering a heavily patrolled area, he explained.

The cargo bay was piled high with boxes of musical instruments, and with the doors shut the pair was left in total darkness. The trailer had no shocks, and they had to make themselves into dead weight to ride out the bumps. After what seemed a very long time the truck stopped for gas, but the driver would not let them out. Dwight was convinced that the man had recognized him and was calling the police. "Jerry, I really have to tell you something," he said, his voice breaking. "My real name isn't Stephen, it's Dwight ... Dwight Armstrong. I'm on the Ten Most Wanted list."

McLoughlin said, "You've got to be kidding!"

"Check the post office," Dwight said. "My picture's up there." He started telling her about Army Math. "My brother, the guy you met in Toronto, was the leader. I trusted him, you know. Maybe I shouldn't have...." He broke down again.

McLoughlin found it hard to believe that such a fragile individual could be involved in, as she later put it to the police, "such an outstanding crime." "How did you feel when the bomb went off?" she said.

"I wanted to puke," he confessed.

"Were you aware of the consequences for yourself?"

"I thought so at the time, but really wasn't."

"Was anyone killed?"

Dwight told her about Fassnacht with bitterness in his voice.

"Did you know anyone was in the building?" she pressed.

"We had an idea the guard would be there," Dwight said. "I didn't want to do it when there was a chance of someone getting killed, but my brother said it had to be done then or not at all."

The driver finally let them out in Calgary, directly in front of his house. His wife was angry when she saw them get out, and Jerry theorized that the whole thing was intended to irritate the wife, part of some weird little marital spat. On their way out of the city Jerry slipped into an RCMP office to look at the wanted posters. Sure enough, there he was, though she could scarcely recognize his picture. "Armed and dangerous," it said. It also mentioned the reward. *I could make $25,000 today by turning Dwight in,* she thought.

They stuck their thumbs out for a ride to Banff. McLoughlin admitted that she didn't like being mixed up in murder. "I'm not going to turn you in," she said, "but if I'm asked, I'll tell them I know you."

Here was one of the moments Dwight lived for in his underground life, the moment when people who had found out about him revealed their true colors. They had to see him on a new "plane of consciousness," to decide between him and the law. As far as he knew, no one had ever informed on him.

McLoughlin grabbed his chin and twisted his head from side to side appraisingly. "Why don't you cut your hair, clip your eyebrows and dress as a woman?" she said cheerfully. "You'll never be caught!"

The Dane County Grand Jury considered four possible charges in the death of Robert Fassnacht: first-, second-, and third-degree murder and reckless homicide. Under the laws of Wisconsin, "Whoever causes the death of another human being with intent to kill that person or another" committed first-degree murder, punishable by life imprisonment. "Whoever causes the death of another human being by conduct imminently dangerous to another and evincing a depraved mind" was guilty of second-degree murder, punishable by a term of five to twenty-five years. For those who, "in the course of committing or attempting to commit a felony," caused "the death of another human being as a natural and probable consequence," the charge was murder in the third degree, punishable by up to fifteen years in addition to the sentence for the felony. Finally, there was reckless homicide, "reckless conduct" being defined as "an act which creates a situation of unreasonable risk and high probability of death or great bodily harm to another and which demonstrates a conscious disregard for the safety of another and a willingness to take known chances of perpetrating an injury." The punishment for reckless homicide was a fine of up to $2,500 and-or up to five years in prison.

In its summation the prosecution argued that the surveillance notebooks offered evidence of intent to kill. With the exception of three days out of the year, none of which fell in the summer, Sterling Hall was occupied seven days a week, twenty-four hours a day. Since the conspirators watched the building for at least a week, it was logical to assume they must have known it would be occupied. Considering as well the tremendous size of the bomb, the death of Robert Fassnacht was not merely the result of reckless conduct or of wanton conduct "evincing a depraved mind," nor was it a "natural and probable consequence" of the felony of arson, but was actually intended by the bombers.

The jury agreed. On September 1, 1971, the district attorney issued warrants for the arrest of the fugitives on charges of arson and murder in the first degree. And so, slightly more than a year after the bombing, the conspirators were charged with a crime for which they could be extradited from Canada.

Detective Charles Lulling had by this time become burdened with a considerable load of ill will toward the FBI. Lulling regarded Joe Sullivan, the major case inspector, as a "straight-arrow" because Joe would tell you what he thought. But since Sullivan's return to New York, Lulling had been dealing with Milwaukee SAC Ed Hayes and with Senior Resident Agent George Baxtrum, respectively a "rat" and a "snake," in Lulling's opinion.

From the start of the Army Math investigation, Lulling had sensed something wrong with the bureau 302s he was receiving: They didn't jibe with what he was hearing from agents in the field. Important facts would be missing, and some of the oversights astonished him. Special Agent Tom McMillen, for example, had gotten Karl Armstrong's name from Lynn and Dwight Armstrong's name from Field Morey and yet had not put the two together. If there was anything that displeased Lulling, it was investigators who were just going through the motions, "feebs" he called them, for "feeble." Then there were the stories planted to discredit him, such as that he had rented an army helicopter to do aerial photography of the staging area. Not true: He had rented a plane from Field Morey, and had turned his film over to the state crime lab to be developed. The next thing he knew, the FBI had it. Then of course, the bureau had obliged him to go to court to obtain the minutes of the federal grand jury. Lulling had put a hand-lettered sign on his desk with a quote he attributed to former Attorney General Ramsay Clark: "The FBI would rather see a guilty man walk free than share the credit for an arrest."

In early September, shortly after the announcement of the Dane grand jury indictments, Lulling got a tip that Dwight had been spotted in a certain College Street youth hostel in Toronto. Instead of calling Baxtrum he got in touch with Dane County Sheriff Jack Leslie, who shared his low opinion of the FBI. Leslie often hunted with Lulling at the detective's weekend place on the Wisconsin River. It did not take much to persuade him to accompany Lulling to Canada.

As the two Madison cops boarded a plane for Toronto, Dwight was fishing on the French River in northern Ontario with the filmmaker Jay Griss; a friend of Griss's named Felix Detweiler; and Detweiler's brother Fred, who was visiting from the States. Griss's Army Math project had become stalled when the Film House, a Toronto production outfit, confiscated his footage until he paid his bill. Fred was a math major at MIT, reputedly a genius. Felix, a deserter, had grown up near Munthausen, a Nazi death camp in his native Austria, he revealed. As far as he was concerned, a desk job in the U.S. Army was no different from a desk job at Munthausen. "You're still a party to genocide."

The fishing was good; even Dwight caught one, a ten-pound Northern Pike, according to his own estimate. However, the Detweiler brothers bickered like seventh graders, and when they turned in, Felix displayed himself in a red satin bikini. Alarmed by Detweiler's exhibitionism, Dwight and Griss hitchhiked back to Toronto the next day, arriving just in time to read in the *Toronto Star* of September 13 that a small posse of Wisconsin lawmen was in town looking for him.

At an urgently called meeting of Armstrong supporters at Naomi Wall's apartment, Wall chastised Dwight for living so flagrantly in the open and giving away his location. Dwight, however, knew all about "Quick Draw" Lulling, having worked with a niece of his at Hoffman House Restaurant, and considered him not much of a threat. "The description they have of me is way out of date. What chance do they have of finding me in a big city like Toronto?"

But the consensus was that Dwight had to leave; the only question was where. Algeria? Cuba? Chile? They settled on Vancouver, British Columbia. It had a big exile community just like Toronto's, coffeehouses, head shops, and an underground newspaper. Dwight quickly accustomed himself to the idea; Jerardine was in Vancouver, and they might get back together.

Karl and Naomi escorted him to the train station. Naomi provided him with the names of a number of antidraft organizers to look up once he got there. Karl gave him a Liberty silver dollar, a gift from Donald years earlier. He had carried it on all his missions, holding on to it during the most desperate moments of their flight. "Keep this. You need it more than I do," he said.

Karl took the Turboliner to Montreal to get new identification from
Bernard Mergler. He came back as "David Weller"; quit his job
with the De Leyster Company, for which he had been delivering
produce; and moved. In December he moved again, to a room at 54
Langley Avenue, on the east side of town. The house was vintage
Toronto: three stories; imitation-brick siding; a big, covered porch;
and bay windows. Karl's room was on the third floor, with a dormer
overlooking the quiet, tree-lined street. It was the eleventh place he
had stayed since coming to Toronto a year earlier.

He found a job at Toronto Gear Works, a machine shop in the East
Toronto industrial district, working the graveyard shift. It was a good
routine for a fugitive, except for the fact that the streetcar he took to
work departed from in front of the Don Jail, an ancient, grime-cov-
ered prison overlooking the Don River. Police were always coming
and going, and Karl had to wait in plain view of them. Cops never
bother a guy carrying a lunch pail, he assured himself.

In a neighborhood park he met a pleasant, auburn-haired woman
named Audrey Langlois. She was married, aged forty-five and completely "straight"—in fact, a devout Christian—but for some reason, they hit it off. He allowed her to believe that he was a draft
dodger, and, realizing how lonely he was, she offered as much com-
panionship as a married woman decently could. They went skating
together twice a week, usually at the rink in front of city hall in the
busy heart of the city. Karl exulted in the sense of immunity those
outings gave him. *I'm invisible!* he thought.

He spent Christmas day at the home of Charles "Chuck" Reuby,
exchanging gifts with his wife and kids and walking their dog, Pandi.
Reuby was an emphysemic Irish Canadian, a leprechaun of a man with
big ears, a flattened nose, mischievous blue eyes, and a Celtic sympathy
for the oppressed. His younger brothers Stan and Ralph were the owners of Toronto Gear Works, and he labored for them like any other
employee. Chuck and Karl liked to gripe about working conditions,
especially the burns they received dipping gears in a powerful cleaning
solvent. "You oughtta join the Toronto police department," he told
Karl. "You don't want to spend your life up to your elbows in Varsol!"

Hoots and jeers had been Chuck Lulling's reception upon his
return to Madison. His boss Captain Stanley Davenport, whom he

had neglected to consult about his Canada trip, disavowed the excursion and threatened disciplinary action if the detective attempted anything similar in the future. The newspapers quoted George Baxtrum to the effect that the FBI had been prepared to make arrests themselves and that Lulling and Leslie had sprung the trap. Lulling suspected that Baxtrum himself had sabotaged the mission by leaking it to the press and then making sure the Toronto papers got wind of it. "You know, there's a lot of sneaky little things that are going on, and people think that we won't know," he said the next time he saw the resident agent. "But I know, George."

Lulling was wrong about Baxtrum. The FBI *was* onto the Armstrongs; judging by internal memoranda, the bureau had traced the Naomi Wall connection as early as July, more than a month before Lulling's visit. And it was not Baxtrum who had tipped off the Toronto papers but one of the young radicals on the staff of the *Capital Times*. Lulling's accusations of sneakiness would have been better aimed at J. Edgar Hoover. The FBI director was greatly agitated over the Lulling caper and immediately inquired of Assistant U.S. Attorney General Robert Mardian whether there was any way to keep the state of Wisconsin from getting custody of the fugitives. Mardian replied that under the Webster-Ashburton Treaty, the murder charge was the only extraditable offense brought so far in the case and that "therefore the state authorities would have to institute extradition proceedings and we would have to defer to them." Hoover then issued a directive asking the U.S. State Department to seek deportation of the fugitives if they were arrested in Canada, thus allowing the federal government first crack at them.

It was late December when the authorities got their next break. Picked up for hitchhiking on his way home to Michigan for Christmas, Robert Rainbolt volunteered information about the Armstrong brothers to Ontario provincial police. After releasing him the provincial cops passed the information to the RCMP, which notified the FBI. But it was the holiday season, and by the time the bureau dispatched its agents to his parents' place near Detroit, Rainbolt had returned to Canada. Several weeks later the RCMP found him working in a Toronto record store and took him to its Sullivan Street headquarters for questioning. Rainbolt was wanted in the States for burglary of a gun store and Selective Service violations. Hoping to get all these charges dropped, he gave them the story again, complete with the aliases, David Armitage and Stephen Scofield, by which he knew the Armstrongs. These, the Mounties quickly learned, were the names of a dead person and of someone who had lost his wallet. But as for the Armstrongs, they were nowhere to be found. If Rainbolt wanted his record cleared and his reward money, he was going to have to do better, he was informed.

One cold January day Karl ran into one of his former landlords, a German. In hushed tones the man informed Karl that the police had been to his house looking for him. "I don't know what you did, David, but I thought I should tell you," he said.

"It's just traffic tickets," Karl assured him. He had picked up a number of citations while working for the De Leyster Company and he thought that might actually be the case.

Although American troop strength was down to 140,000 in Vietnam, the air war was more intense than ever, and Karl was still pondering that B-52 base he had seen just south of the Canadian border. In late January he ran into Robert Rainbolt and some friends on Yonge Street, not far from the cafe where he had first met Naomi Wall. Rainbolt introduced his associates, informing Karl that they were "into selling dope." Karl showed interest; he had been reading up on mescaline at the University of Toronto library and had compiled a list of everything he needed to synthesize it. He was also reading a paperback entitled *How to Run a Business,* from which he had deduced that what he needed for a mescaline venture was backers. He could use his drug profits for a renewed campaign of sabotage.

"Do you think I could make money selling mescaline?" he asked the dealers, who promised that he could.

"I'd like to set up a mescaline lab, but I need capital," he said.

This would be no problem; they knew somebody who could help him, a Mob connection. They could set up a meeting.

"Go ahead and set it up," he told them.

Rainbolt then insinuated that Karl ought to invite him over, since he needed a place to crash. Karl agreed, fearing that if he didn't accommodate Rainbolt, the druggie might turn him in. He did not suspect that Rainbolt had already spoken to the authorities about him. He gave Rainbolt his new alias, David Weller, and address and told him he could use the bed at night while he, Karl, was at work.

When Rainbolt arrived at 54 Langley, he immediately dunned Karl for fifty dollars. "My subsidies from the U.S. are drying up,"

Karl complained, but he gave him the money. Rainbolt left a few days later.

"Don't say anything, or you'll be in trouble," Karl warned him.

Mr. and Mrs. Kenneth Sillephant were proper Canadians who placed a premium on privacy and respected that of their boarders. Mrs. Sillephant cleaned David Weller's room and changed his linen once a week, and although she worried sometimes about her three children, whom she didn't want to be attacked by some closet pedophile living in her house, she resisted snooping. She never noticed the political orientation of Mr. Weller's personal library, the copies of the radical magazine *Ramparts,* the thick paperback edition of *The Pentagon Papers,* or *The Anarchist Cookbook.* She ignored the stack of *Playboy* magazines and averted her eyes so as not to see the pinup of a black woman over the bed. After all, Mr. Weller was a bachelor, and a man's reading preferences were his business. "Whoever rents a room is renting privacy," is how Mr. Sillephant put it to investigators afterward.

Nevertheless, they had come to know and like the quiet, soft-spoken working man who had occupied the attic apartment since December. Mrs. Sillephant was impressed by the fact that he bathed every day and paid his rent on time, qualities she found highly desirable in a tenant. He was a bit of a loner and had painted the refrigerator an odd color, red, yet they would see him playing with children in the snow and going off to skate with a proper-looking woman friend.

Late in the afternoon of February 16, 1972, a contingent of local police, led by corporals Frank Glynn and Donald Smith of the RCMP, arrived at 54 Langley Avenue with warrants for the arrest of Karleton Lewis Armstrong, aka David Roy Weller. Corporal Smith instantly recognized Kenneth Sillephant as someone he had gone to school with in the Province of New Brunswick in the early 1950s, but he had no time to enjoy this unexpected reunion. "Mrs. Sillephant and the children had best leave," he advised.

Stunned by what was happening, Kenneth Sillephant led the officers to the top floor and knocked on David Weller's door.

"Who's there?" answered a voice from inside.

"It's me, Kenny," Sillephant answered, unlocking the door with his master key. He turned and was surprised to see that the Mounties had drawn their guns. They shoved him aside and rushed into the room.

Karl had been asleep for five or six hours and was still in bed when he had heard the footsteps on the stairs.

It must be Audrey, he had thought dreamily, and was slightly baffled to hear, instead of Langlois, his landlord calling through the door.

"Come on in," he said, but even as he did so, he had a premonition because he had suddenly realized that there was more than one pair of feet on the stairs.

"Karl?" said Corporal Glynn. Four trench-coated cops stood just inside the door with their guns trained on him.

"Yeah?" he said.

Corporal Smith moved to the right side of the bed, Glynn to the left. Glynn, alone among Canadian law enforcement officials, had taken a keen interest in the WISBOM case; it was he who had discovered the Naomi Wall connection and reported it to the FBI that summer. "All right, Karl, where's Dwight?" he said, wasting no time.

"I don't know; I haven't seen him for six months," Karl answered, more or less honestly.

"We're Royal Canadian Mounted Police officers. You are being arrested on an Immigration Warrant, and also because we have reason to believe that you have been remaining in Canada by improper means," Glynn intoned. Backups entered the room, members of the Metropolitan Toronto and Ontario Provincial police forces. The bedroom, the stairwell, and the front yard were full of cops.

"I've been expecting you for some time. I knew you'd catch me sooner or later," Karl said, addressing the roomful of Canadians. He walked to his dresser and started to open the top drawer.

Glynn and Smith shouted simultaneously, "Hold it!"

"Take it easy. I haven't got a gun. I just want to get my clothes," Karl said. He put on a shirt and tie and a double-breasted Humphrey Bogart suit. Corporal Smith spotted *The Anarchist Cookbook* atop another dresser and leafed through it as Karl was getting dressed. Seeing that it was a book about making bombs and fighting guerrilla wars, he initialed it for confiscation as evidence.

Karl began to get a little giddy. "I hate this tie!" he said. "How about stopping at a men's store so I can get a new one?"

As they led him out in handcuffs Karl saw Kenneth Sillephant hovering wide-eyed at the foot of the stairs. "I'm not Dave Weller.

My name is Karl Armstrong, and I'm on the FBI's Ten Most Wanted list," he said.

Sillephant shook his hand. "Good luck," he offered.

One of the Mounties pointed out to Sillephant that Karl's wanted poster had been flashed on TV following "The FBI" show only three days earlier. "One call and you could have made $100,000," he chided.

Sillephant looked shocked. "I don't want blood money!" he said.

They stepped out onto the front porch. The street was clogged with squad cars. Karl frowned. "Where are the reporters?" The RCMP intended to stake out the house to see if any of Karl's coconspirators might show up. "We don't need publicity," Corporal Smith replied.

"I do," the prisoner said.

On the ride to the station, Karl provided the police with addititonal material for their reports. "If I had a machine gun and knew you guys were coming, I would have ambushed you. You wouldn't be alive now!" he shouted.

"How does it feel to be the oldest of the gang, the leader, and the first one caught?" Corporal Smith asked.

"Maybe it's *just* that I'm the first one caught," Karl answered but refused to elaborate.

It was 6:00 P.M. and dark by the time they reached the Sullivan Street office. The Red Star Commune was across the street, and around the block The Hall, where Karl had spent pleasant hours conversing with other American exiles. He had passed the door he was now entering dozens of times.

Inside he was photographed and positively identified by fingerprint comparison. Smith and Glynn led him upstairs to an interrogation room on the second floor. It was furnished with a desk, a bookcase, and three chairs.

"I'm going to give you the official police caution," Smith said.

"If there's any official police caution given, I don't say a word," Karl interjected. "The only way I'm going to talk to you fellows is strictly informally. I'd like to make light conversation, and you might just learn something." The Canadians made detailed notes of the discussion that followed. Karl initiated it by asking them if they would have shot him in the head if he'd resisted.

"We are happy such a course of action wasn't necessary," Glynn replied smoothly.

"You, however, told us that you would have shot us if you had the chance," Corporal Smith added.

Karl glowered. "You must appreciate that a man is entitled to his liberty, and I feel entitled to shoot anyone who tries to deprive me of it. I consider him my enemy."

"You deprived someone of his liberty permanently, didn't you?" Glynn asked opportunely.

"You mean Fassnacht?" Karl said.

"Yes."

"That's right," Karl answered, taking the bait. "But that was a tactical error, and it's something I have to live with, and during the last year-and-a-half I have judged myself for that act. I no longer feel any guilt for it. All it does now is tend to make my actions counter-revolutionary rather than revolutionary."

The Canadians pressed him about the whereabouts of other conspirators. "I will not do anything that might lead to the arrest of my revolutionary brothers," Karl announced. He preferred to talk about Sterling Hall. There was no leader, he asserted; they were all equally involved.

"What about *The Anarchist Cookbook?*" Smith asked after a moment.

"That's not a very good book," Karl said. "I've noted many errors in it."

"Then you must be the bomb expert," Smith countered. "It was you who committed the tactical error that has you all involved in a murder instead of just damage to public property."

Karl smiled. "Now you know what I meant when I said it was perhaps just that I be the first one captured. I hope that my revolutionary brothers remain free to continue their revolutionary activities."

"How can they continue their revolutionary activities?" Glynn asked.

"By merely remaining at large, they are continuing their revolutionary activities and are demonstrating that they are true, dedicated revolutionary brothers."

The Mounties were disappointed that Karl avoided referring to David and Leo by name. However, they had his admission to murder and statements suggesting his primary responsibility for the crime. Even after the city's left-wing attorneys had gotten to Karl, Toronto's chief of detectives, James Noble, had no trouble extracting an additional admission of guilt from him several days later.

Karl had always wanted to be known for his deeds. And though he had hidden in Canada, he had refused to leave Toronto when caution dictated he should have; instead, he had contemplated a new mission that would increase his risk of capture. Unlike his coconspirators, he had always been prepared for the eventuality of a show trial in which the issues of the war might be dramatized through an examination of his motives. After a year and a half in hiding, he was about to get his wish.

Part VI

JUSTICE

29

The Extradition

I feel that he does have a characterological defect.

—H. J. LYNCH,
Dane County District Attorney, for the prosecution

*Someone who was a pyromaniac would not have issued a
statement immediately after the act presenting a political
rationale for the action.*

—STAUGHTON LYND,
historian, for the defense

Until the night of February 16, when Karl Armstrong called him
from the Don Jail, Paul Copeland had known nothing about
the Army Math bombing other than what he had read in the newspapers. Karl gave him Naomi Wall's name as a reference, and after
speaking to her, he let Karl know that he would take the case.

Copeland did business out of a refurbished brick town house on
Prince Arthur Street in Yorkville. His clients included Student
Union Peace Action (Canada's largest antiwar organization), the
Toronto Anti-Draft Programme, Rochdale, and *The Guerilla*.
When it became clear to him that Armstrong might turn out to be a

major case, he contacted his former law partner Clayton Ruby to ask for help. Like himself, Ruby was young, single, and well-to-do; both men owned country homes in northern Ontario. Copeland favored leather slacks and colorful shirts when he was not in court. Ruby cut a more conservative figure, occupied a mansion in the exclusive Rosedale district, and kept a large dog for walking. He had been largely responsible for getting the Canadian border opened to deserters from the United States and had just argued successfully against the extradition of Umberto Pagan, a Puerto Rican nationalist wanted for the murder of a policeman in his native country. Ruby had split with Copeland over the issue of workplace democracy, for while he was not opposed to it in principle, he did not care for it in his own office. However, he agreed to enter the Armstrong case.

The Canadians then contacted the activist American lawyer William Kunstler in New York. As it happened, Ruby had recently defended Kunstler against a charge of battery resulting from an altercation during a speech Kunstler was giving at the University of Toronto, so Kunstler owed him a favor. Kunstler, in turn, called Los Angeles attorney Leonard Weinglass, with whom he was working on the appeal of the Chicago Eight conspiracy convictions. At the time Kunstler was also defending Father Philip Berrigan and the Harrisburg Eight, accused of, among other things, plotting to kidnap Henry Kissinger. Weinglass, meanwhile, was representing the Camp McCoy Three, a case pending from the sabotage of a central Wisconsin air base in 1969. Despite their heavy caseloads both men flew to Toronto that weekend to talk to Karl and afterward held a press conference to announce that, in accord with Karl's wishes, they would represent him if and when he was returned to the United States for trial. In the meantime they would provide attorneys Copeland and Ruby whatever assistance they could to prevent the Canadian government from turning Karl over to the American authorities.

"Why don't you arrange with the Canadians to bug his cell?" Wisconsin Assistant Attorney General David Mebane queried. It was the week after Karl's arrest, and he was sitting in attorney Guy Goodwin's office at Internal Security in Washington. "Good Guy" Goodwin he called him in private, heavy on the irony. Assistant U.S. Attorney General Robert Mardian and Dane County District

Attorney Buzz Nichol stood by trying to keep things civil between the feuding prosecutors. The federal authorities were in a dither over the involvement of Kunstler and Weinglass in the Armstrong case, and Mebane was taking the measure of his opponent's tough-mindedness. "Oh no, we wouldn't do that," Mardian declared.

Mebane shrugged. He had come to Washington to settle another matter: Who was going to get Armstrong first: Wisconsin or the federal government? In accordance with State Department instructions, the fugitive had been arrested on the old immigration warrant, setting in motion deportation proceedings. If Karl was deported, federal authorities would arrest him at the border, and he would be tried first in federal court. However, Paul Copeland had already raised a serious challenge to the deportation strategy. Even if Karl was found to be in Canada illegally, Copeland argued, the government did not have the right to dictate his destination when he left. Faced with the possibility of Karl's choosing to go to Cuba, officials of the Royal Canadian Mounted Police (RCMP) had suggested driving Karl over the Ambassador Bridge in the trunk of a car and dumping him in Detroit. It would save everybody a lot of time and expense, they argued. Mebane, however, regarded such a tactic as being fatal to the case.

But as the federal attorneys were quick to point out, because of the peculiar language of the Webster-Ashburton Treaty, there was a real chance of losing an extradition battle. "No fugitive is liable to surrender if it appears that the offence in respect of which proceedings are taken under this Act is one of a political character," it stated, without explicitly defining what it meant by "political character." When it was first drafted in 1842, its signatories probably had in mind offenses that were political per se (such as criticizing rulers and advocating free elections), not bomb throwing and assassination. Under a literal interpretation of Webster-Ashburton, even a cold-blooded killer like Lee Harvey Oswald might have escaped prosecution. If the defense could show that Karl's actions were politically inspired, it seemed, the United States might never get him out of Canada.

Underlying these issues were others that remained unarticulated, such as the ambition of both Wisconsin Attorney General Robert Warren and U.S. Attorney John Olson to run for governor of Wisconsin, the clashing egos of Mebane and Goodwin, Charlie Lulling's jealousy, and the megalomania of J. Edgar Hoover. On

March 7 a protocol was signed pledging both sides to cooperation and noninterference, but it did not put an end to intrigue. Hoover immediately set out to end-run the case, inquiring about alternatives to extradition through the U.S. Consulate in Ottawa and seeking assurances that Karl would not be released on bail, as Copeland had requested. Meanwhile Wisconsin retained a high-priced Toronto attorney, Austin Cooper, to press the extradition case in the provincial court. And so the effort to bring Karl Armstrong to justice continued on two rival fronts into the spring of 1972.

Imprisonment seemed to galvanize Karl Armstrong. Within days of his incarceration in the sterile new wing of the Don Jail, across from the bus stop where he used to wait on his way to work, he circulated a petition protesting the solitary confinement of another prisoner who was being punished for continuing to run in place in the exercise yard longer than he was allowed. As a consequence, Karl himself was placed in solitary. To protest his own treatment, Karl refused to eat the bologna sandwiches that were a staple of Don Jail cuisine. Gerald Whitehead, superintendent of the Don Jail, tried to reason with him, but Karl maintained his insistence on his "basic human right" to petition. After several weeks Whitehead moved him to what had been death row in the old wing, a grim and decrepit cell block where he was completely alone.

Even so, like the Russian anarchist Nechayev tucked away in the Peter and Paul Fortress a century earlier, Karl exerted an influence far beyond his cell. His demands were duly reported in the media, advocated in court, and discussed in the Ontario Legislature. His revolutionary proclamations were published in underground newspapers from coast to coast. "Free Karl" posters appeared on Mifflin Street; Telegraph Avenue in Berkeley; and Toronto's equivalent, Spadina Avenue. Defense committees were formed and fund-raising efforts commenced in both countries for the anticipated extradition battle.

In Madison active support for Karl came primarily from that remnant of the Left—veterans of the Mother Jones Revolutionary League, the *Daily Cardinal,* and the *Kaleidoscope*—that had supported the New Year's Gang all along. Most of these militants had never met Karl, but word of his devotion to the cause had spread. Here was a son of the working class who *believed,* and who even now, faced with life imprisonment, refused to recant. Henry Schipper, a University of Wisconsin student from Eau Claire who had performed with the Guerrilla Theatre Caravan, passionately invoked the Left's accountability in *Takeover,* one of the successor publications to the *Kaleidoscope,* a few months later:

> Without us there could have been no bombings, no Karl Armstrongs. It is now our responsibility to take care of those who took our own rhetoric perhaps a bit more seriously than we did. WE are on trial for we are Karl Armstrong. We are the process that threw him up. It is time to own up. Is Karl the shadow of a movement that died? The state says yes. They challenge us and we have to accept that challenge. If Karl goes without an uproar, it can only mean that we have gone.

In Toronto Naomi Wall and other antidraft activists organized a Karl Armstrong Defense Committee (KADC), which, coordinating with a Madison group of the same name, lined up witnesses who could testify to the political character of his acts. They envisioned a rock festival at Rochdale at which Jerry Rubin and Abbie Hoffman would speak and Bob Dylan, Phil Ochs, the Jefferson Airplane, and the Grateful Dead would perform. A flurry of letters passed back and forth between Toronto and Madison in the furtherance of these plans. A feeling of urgency, of crisis, gripped the committee members. Brother Karl was the movement: If he went down, it would all be over.

But progress was slow. The new *Cardinal* editor, Jonathan Wolman, son of the publisher of the *Wisconsin State Journal,* complained about the difficulties in a letter to Paul Copeland in March. "It is proving hard to impossible to pin down national figures in regards testifying. The Berrigans are proving impossible to reach. Abbie Hoffman has 'quit' the movement and is writing a book in the Virgin Islands. Jerry Rubin has quit politics and is into yoga." As for the rock groups mentioned for the hoped-for May concert, even politically hip entertainers considered the bombing counterproductive or counterrevolutionary or just plain wrong.

But gradually the defense began to come together. Copeland managed to reach Yale historian Staughton Lynd, with whom he was acquainted through Lynd's daughter, who attended a Toronto experimental school that Copeland's firm represented. Even though he did not approve of bombings, Lynd signed on. Naomi

Wall got through to Noam Chomsky, the MIT linguistics professor and antimilitarist; someone else reached Tom Hayden in Santa Monica.

Meanwhile the sedition men of two countries exerted themselves to determine exactly who was on the defense committees, where they got their funding, and what they were up to. Among others posing as Armstrong supporters in Madison were Pete Bobo and Sandy Nelson, recently returned from Northern Ireland, where, by their own account, they had gone on assignment for the CIA, and George Croal's promising new informant, Fat Julie. In Toronto a Canadian military intelligence officer named William Laidlau Richardson infiltrated the local defense committee, and the RCMP placed a wiretap on Paul Copeland's office phone, ostensibly for reasons unrelated to the extradition battle. Teletypes arriving at the Stassi Shoe Store blandly reported that defense committee couriers from Madison were being turned back at the Ambassador Bridge. It was getting down and dirty.

The York County Courthouse, where legal maneuvers commenced in early March, faced the American Consulate on University Avenue, halfway between the University of Toronto campus and the lakeshore business district. It was a marbled sanctuary of decorum, where judges presided in wigs, bailiffs wore long-tailed coats, and lawyers had to gown themselves before appearing at the Queen's Bench. The Armstrong case attracted a small horde of hirsute supporters to the courthouse, who were met by a phalanx of scarlet-clad Mounties. Karl's supporters defied decorum by remaining seated when the judge, a conservative named Walter Martin, entered, standing only when the prisoner was brought in and greeting him with a power-to-the-people salute. Karl reacted visibly to the crowd's adulation, returning the salutes, bestowing honorific greetings on the judge, and complaining about the hardness of his chair.

Don Armstrong attended every hearing, sometimes accompanied by Ruth, their plane fare subsidized by the KADC. The intervening months had not been easy for them. Although Ruth's co-workers at Central Colony had been supportive, many of their friends had dropped them. Don had lost his job in a major layoff at Gisholt and had been unable to find another. Ruth had been seriously injured in a car accident, and with both of them out of work, they had lost their home. Don was convinced their phone was tapped and had told the newspapers as much. The FBI, at George Baxtrum's insistence, had issued a rare formal denial.

In Don's opinion William Kunstler was a bad choice to represent Karl in Madison. "Kunstler is unpopular there," he told a reporter. He wanted the defense to appeal not to political extremists but to "average, middle-of-the-road people." Karl assured him that their logic was sound; the lawyers were going to show that the bombing was political. The *Capital Times* heralded the disagreement in bold type: "Armstrongs Split on Defense."

In court Don frantically tried to coach Karl from the sidelines, but with no more success than he had had with his son on the football field. At the second hearing Don himself took an active role, folding his arms and refusing to leave when the judge ordered the room cleared. He picketed the courthouse, complaining to reporters about "British pomp and ceremony," while Karl announced that he would not "honor" a court that did not admit his friends, insisted on being carried out of the courtroom (it required four men to lift him), and resumed his hunger strike in jail. The Ontario Supreme Court agreed with the Armstrongs, ordering the courtroom reopened to the public.

Every Wednesday on her lunch hour, Audrey Langlois took a cab to the Don Jail to visit Karl. Aside from his parents she was the one regular visitor he was permitted. She and her husband offered the Armstrongs a place to stay when they were in town and had even made their house available for meetings of his supporters. But Langlois was appalled by Karl's courtroom persona. In the presence of his supporters the modest, unassuming gentleman she knew and liked would be transformed into an almost comically vainglorious lout. Karl's defenders weren't her kind of people, she informed Mira on one of her visits. "He's just a symbol to these people; they don't care what happens to him; they're *using* him," she complained.

Mira had herself already tried to caution Karl. "He doesn't listen to me," she said.

"Or me," Audrey agreed.

On the morning of Tuesday, May 10, Ruth and Lorene joined Don in a family demonstration at the American Consulate. When they arrived, a cleaning crew was busy removing paint splashed on the building the day before to protest the mining of Haiphong harbor, North Vietnam's main port. The new escalation of the war had precipitated the biggest demonstrations since 1970, with riots and gassings in Madison reminiscent of the late sixties. Don's sign accused the United States of placing itself "above morality" in prosecuting his son while carrying on such "butchery" in Vietnam. Ruth's sign was more personal: "Does my son have to go on a hunger strike to be treated as a human being?"

A correspondent for the *Wisconsin State Journal* asked them why they believed that Karl should not be returned to Madison. Don explained that they didn't think he could get a fair trial there. "Karl is probably as gentle a person in respect to people as anyone could be, probably a lot more gentle than his father," he added.

In the competition to try Karl first, Wisconsin now held the advantage. Deportation proceedings were mired in writs and motions, and the extradition hearing was set to begin in early June. Clayton Ruby, designated to lead the defense, and Austin Cooper, the lawyer representing Wisconsin, promised an interesting match—an avowed "philosophical anarchist" worth millions versus a "hired gun" who allegedly had sold out his liberal principles long before. Darkly elegant, with a long curving nose and a sensuous mouth, Ruby exuded both sincerity and boundless self-confidence. In private he could be incredibly glib, but when he addressed the Queen's Bench, he always did so in his most respectful "little boy's voice." Cooper, a tall, balding, slightly gawky man, was one of the top criminal defense lawyers in Toronto, respected even by the cops and prosecutors whose cases he routinely succeeded in having thrown out of court. Ruby was to be assisted in court by Paul Copeland's young apprentice Bobby Kellerman and by Melvin Greenberg, a cigar-smoking movement lawyer who had been helping out from the Madison end. Backing Austin Cooper were Wisconsin's Assistant Attorney General David Mebane and Dane County District Attorney Buzz Nichol.

Ruby had won the preliminary rounds, getting the public readmitted to the courtroom and obliging Judge Martin to withdraw in favor of Harry Waisberg, a more moderate jurist whose daughter Lynn coincidentally worked for Paul Copeland. The next several rounds belonged to Cooper, who succeeded in having all the prosecution evidence, including affidavits from the Madison police and from the key witnesses, U-Haul receipts, photographs of the bomb damage, and so forth, admitted over Ruby's objections. At the same time he managed to have most of Ruby's exhibits—communiqués from the bombers, press statements by local politicians calling the bombing "political murder," etcetera—suppressed.

On June 7, 1972, as the main event got under way, York County Court was crowded with young people in blue jeans making "oink, oink" sounds at prosecutors. Naomi Wall sat in front breast-feeding her infant daughter, an affront to the dignity of the court that Judge Waisberg assiduously ignored. Detective Charles Lulling was seated with other investigators toward the back of the room. He had almost been denied entry to the courthouse because of the pistol strapped to his leg. "In Canada we don't have people running around with guns," Cooper explained.

With the words "Oyez, oyez, oyez … God save the Queen" the bailiff called the court to order. Two plainclothes policemen escorted Karl Armstrong to the glassed-in prisoner's dock. Karl was dressed in a gray double-breasted suit, his face gaunt from fasting. He smiled at the audience; saluted; and, pausing in front of the bench, addressed Judge Waisberg. "Peace be with you, your Honor, and may you serve the people well." It was Karl's standard routine, but Waisberg, unaccustomed to it, looked startled.

The first prosecution witness, Detective Charles Lulling, was in a fighting mood. All morning, Armstrong supporters from Madison had been greeting him as "Quick Draw." That annoyed him, but what really unnerved Lulling was that these militants, who regarded themselves as humanitarians, showed no concern for the rights of Karl's victims. Lulling would never forget his interview with Stephanie Fassnacht. It was a week or so after the bombing, and he wanted to check on a number of points in his investigation. He had gone to see her at her little house on East Mifflin Street, where he was greeted by her twins, two little blonde girls, who had come running up, each one grabbing a pantleg. You could not expect a man to keep his composure under those circumstances, and Lulling had lost his.

From the start the hearing was a strategic nightmare. Cooper had to try to show that Karl bombed Sterling Hall without admitting that he had political motives. Ruby, who didn't want to preempt a plea of innocence in the event that Karl was extradited, had to demonstrate that the bombing was politically motivated without admitting that Karl had done it. He began by objecting to Lulling's identification of Karl from police photos. Then he objected to Don Armstrong's being asked to identify Karl. Even Karl was frustrated by the wrangling. "If it may help I think I can identify myself as Karleton Lewes Armstrong," he said finally.

Ruby began his cross-examination of Lulling hoping to elicit certain facts from him that he had not been allowed to introduce through exhibits. He was in for a shock.

RUBY: Had the police department received any communiqué regarding the purpose of the bombing?

LULLING: No, sir.

RUBY: At any stage, did any communiqué come to your attention?

LULLING: In what way?

RUBY: Any way.

LULLING: Not to my knowledge that someone who participated in it gave me reason.

RUBY: What was the reason given by persons unknown?

LULLING: I don't recall.

With great effort, Ruby eventually extracted an admission from Lulling that he was aware of certain statements in an underground newspaper to the effect that Sterling Hall was bombed because it contained an army research center and of a letter from the fugitives.

RUBY: Do you have that letter with you?

LULLING: No, sir.

RUBY: What did the letter say about the motive of the bombing?

LULLING: It doesn't go to the motive.

RUBY: Does the letter mention the Army Mathematics Research Center?

LULLING: No, sir.

RUBY: Does it mention the New Year's Gang?

LULLING: No, sir.

RUBY: Does it mention politics in any way whatsoever?

LULLING: Not to the best of my recollection.

Ruby had never seen a cop as hard as Lulling; Lulling would not even reveal what Scott Nelson had told him about Karl's motives, claiming he didn't recall. Ruby began to lose his own composure, and went back to the matter of the communiqué. Because it had been disallowed as evidence, Lulling was his only hope of getting it into the record.

RUBY: What did the communiqué say about the reason for the bombing?

LULLING: That this was an act carried out in the tradition of the Tupamaros.

RUBY: What is Tupamaros?

LULLING: I believe this is a Spanish peasantry or some class of Spanish people that engage in revolt.

RUBY: Against the government?

LULLING: I don't know who they revolt against.

Ruby simply could not shake him, and in the end, he returned to his original line of questioning.

RUBY: Was there a concerted campaign against the Army Math Research Center?

LULLING: Not to my knowledge.

RUBY: You didn't notice any against the AMRC?

LULLING: Oh, I seen various signs about, certainly.

RUBY: Perhaps the word "concerted" threw you off. Was there a campaign?

LULLING: I wouldn't call it a campaign.

RUBY: What would you call it?

LULLING: Students letting off steam.

After a hiatus of several days the defense took its turn on June 19. The extradition battle had been bumped from the front pages by a story from Washington about a break-in at Democratic party headquarters in the Watergate apartment complex. Nonetheless, the defense lineup was noteworthy, at least to the sedition men in Madison. Nearly all of the witnesses had files. The first, Marc Levy, a twenty-two-year-old University of Wisconsin graduate in philosophy and an SDS veteran, recited the bloody history of the Madison movement from Dow Day to Army Math, then read from the mysterious "Life Above the Trees" manifesto that had come out right after the bombing: "We are not lunatics and our actions are not wanton." In his cross-examination Austin Cooper unveiled the tactic he would use with all the defense witnesses. Do you know Karle-ton Armstrong? Have you ever heard from Karleton Armstrong? When was the first time you met Karleton Armstrong? Do you know who was responsible for the bombings? Levy answered no to each question.

On Tuesday Professor Staughton Lynd, the first of the intellectual heavyweights, made his appearance. In his tailored blue suit and distinguished gray coiffeur, he looked more like a U.S. senator than a candidate for the Security Index. However, in 1965 the government had revoked his passport after he made an unauthorized visit to Hanoi with Tom Hayden. He was still bitter about it. In a lengthy presentation he compared the bombing of Army Math to John Brown's 1859 raid on Harper's Ferry (in which there were also "accidental and unintended deaths") and said that he would be very disappointed in Canada, which he considered to be America's "better conscience," if it did not find in Karl's favor. As he continued along these lines, Dan Hanley, an assistant to David Mebane, ran to a nearby library and brought back a biography of John Brown, and on cross-examination, Cooper reminded the court of the Osawatomie massacre in Kansas, in which the same John Brown had taken a group of proslavery Kansans from their beds one night and killed them.

On Wednesday it was Noam Chomsky's turn. The distinguished MIT scholar had arisen at 2 A.M. and flown to Toronto at his own expense to assist the defense. His argument was that the United States had forfeited its right to prosecute antiwar terrorists because of its own crimes in Vietnam. On Thursday Tom Hayden appeared. In his brown T-shirt and jeans, his hair pulled back in a ponytail, he looked younger than his thirty-two years. Ruby, who had met Hayden previously, reminded the court of his background as a cofounder of SDS and defendant in the Chicago Conspiracy Trial, of his books and teaching posts and time spent in Vietnam observing the conduct of the war. On the witness stand Hayden cited figures from a short-lived magazine called *Scanlan*'s on the incidence of domestic bombings as evidence of an unacknowledged guerrilla war that had taken place in the United States in the late sixties.

Rather than single out Karl Armstrong, he argued, it made more sense to view his incendiary activities in that context.

On Thursday afternoon, after Hayden's departure, Cooper ran into trouble, when the defense introduced a witness who actually knew Karl Armstrong—Phil Ball, twenty-nine, the Madison Tenant Union activist whom Karl had assisted in preparations for a rent strike in the fall of 1969. Like Hayden, Ball made no concessions to the official dress code, taking the stand in a sports shirt, hiking boots, and jeans. But he was an attractive and articulate witness and a U.S. navy veteran. "It wasn't just a local concern," he began. "We wanted to show that there were national and international reasons for our economic problems, that we were putting money into Vietnam that could be used for public housing."

Sensing Ball's strength as a witness, Cooper objected that Ball's recollections of things Karl had said to him that fall amounted to "self-serving evidence," that is, evidence about the defendant introduced through a third person, a maneuver that might be used to prevent the prosecution from cross-examining the defendant on what he had said and done.

"Your Honor, that is precisely what Mr. Cooper did in the first part of this case," Ruby countered. (Cooper had introduced evidence through affidavit, which also could not be cross-examined.)

"That is a different matter entirely. I have disposed of that, and there is no advantage for you to bring it up again," Waisberg said sharply. He sustained Cooper, and Ball had to refrain from further comments on Karl's state of mind.

June 23, 1972, the last day of testimony, fell on a Friday. Even though he was ahead on points, Austin Cooper was anxious. The ritual power salute to the accused as he entered the courtroom, which Cooper had tolerated until now, suddenly seemed unbearable. "Your Honor," he complained, "I think that I must again for the record indicate that when Mr. Armstrong came in a good 60 percent of the public attending this trial raised their fists in a clenched gesture to which Mr. Armstrong responded. I think I should record that three people sitting at the Press Table similarly raised their clenched fists when Mr. Armstrong entered the courtroom." (Correspondents representing the *Daily Cardinal* and various underground papers shared the table with the Establishment press.) Waisberg reassured Cooper that he would not be influenced by such displays.

The day before, the fired University of Wisconsin English instructor David Siff had given detailed testimony about the military work done by the AMRC, bringing up Project Michigan and the mysterious missing section from the center's 1967 annual report, as well as the embarrassing gag rule that the Board of Regents had imposed on itself in 1956. To counter that testimony, Cooper had flown in Chancellor Edwin Young, who asserted that there was no secret research going on at the University of Wisconsin "unless it was so secret that I didn't know about it."

"If there was something secret going on, would the Army tell you?" Ruby asked him on cross-examination.

"I don't think they would do it," the chancellor replied, "but if something is secret, then by definition I am not told. But I don't believe it. That is all I can say."

Cooper brought in one other last-minute witness, Professor Joe Dillinger, faculty adviser to the late Robert Fassnacht, who testified that, to his knowledge, no military work went on at the AMRC or in his own lab. In September 1970 Dillinger had given *Life* an interview in which he had guilelessly admitted that regardless of Fassnacht's dreams of maglev trains and so forth, what the federal government really wanted from the research on superconductivity was permanent target memories on armed satellites, the key to "total push-button war." Ruby, in questioning Dillinger, pressed him about it

RUBY: The work you are doing, does it have any future military application?

DILLINGER: So far as I could ascertain, no.

RUBY: Is low temperature research necessary for manned satellites?

DILLINGER: Presumably not, because the National Aeronautics and Space Administration never would support my research.

After a few more questions Ruby gave up trying to pin Dillinger down. Karl had never said that he had a political motive for destroying the low-temperature lab, anyway.

Judge Waisberg's decision came at 10 A.M. on Friday, June 30. It was a muggy morning, and the skies over Toronto were dark and threatening, as though the gods were angry but unsure who to punish first. Policemen packed the courthouse, leaving only a dozen seats for the hundred or so Armstrong supporters crowding the lobby. Squad cars loaded with riot police were parked around the entire block. As Waisberg was about to read his opinion, the overhead lights flickered out and a policeman's radio went on full blast. Naomi Wall's baby began to cry, drowning out the judge's first remarks. Waisberg said that he would reserve his verdict for the end of his statement.

It was up to Wisconsin to prove the crime apolitical, he explained, but then stressed that the defense witnesses were leftists who admittedly did not want the defendant extradited. "While some of the witnesses have credentials in their own fields, I could not accept their opinions on the issues before me. They were not impartial opinions based on reliable information. ... I find it significant that none of the witnesses, all of whom freely admitted political activity of the kind they suggest is associated with the bombings, require political asylum. That speaks eloquently for the fact that the respondent is sought for the enforcement of the criminal law in its ordinary aspect."

Karl Armstrong had sat through the hearing for the most part placidly, attentively, trying to follow Mira's advice. But as Waisberg's verdict became clear, he jumped up. "I don't think we need to listen to any more bullshit. This is bullshit, your Honour."

"Would you be seated," Waisberg said, as calmly as he could.

"If you want me out of this court, you'll have to haul me out," Karl said. He remained standing, glaring at the bench.

Austin Cooper had also sensed the decision and, in a sudden effusion of feeling, said, "I think your Honour should proceed and allow, and hopefully...."

"Allow for Canadian injustice," Karl interjected. The court erupted in bedlam, and the baby resumed its wailing.

"Mr. Cooper, you may be seated. I will continue the reasons for my judgement."

Donald Armstrong was waving with his hands, trying to get Karl to sit down, but Karl ignored him. "Those are not reasons, they are rationales!"

"I concluded that the respondent shall be committed to the Don Jail in Toronto and there remain until surrendered to the State of Wisconsin...."

"You are a pig."

"The respondent will not be surrendered until the expiration of 15 days."

"You are a pig."

"Tell Angela Davis that," someone in the audience chimed in.

Ruby was frozen in his chair. The Mounties were forming a circle around the defendant. Cooper, less surprised by Karl's outburst than were the lawyers at the defense table, rose again: "It appears that the respondent is interrupting the proceedings to the point ..."

"The proceedings are completed," Waisberg announced, jumping up. "I have made my order." He headed for a side door.

"You are a fascist pig! You are the Enemy of the People, and you are branded as such!" Karl shouted after him.

Ruth Armstrong began to weep. Donald was trying to say something, but his words were lost in the uproar. "Right on! Right on!" supporters shouted.

Outside the midday sky was black, and heavy drops of rain were beginning to splatter the pavement. A caravan of police cars began to file out of the subterranean courthouse garage. The crowd pressed in, trying to get a glimpse of the prisoner, shouting "Right on, Karl! Free all political prisoners!" Don Armstrong joined them, adding his own exhortations to the outcry. Naomi Wall and other members of the defense committee handed out leaflets announcing a rally to protest the decision that night. They had been printed in advance.

North Vietnam's emissary to Cuba, passing through Toronto that day, had declared Karl Armstrong a "hero of the Vietnamese people." Arriving at the Don Jail, however, Karl was returned to the same old narrow cell in the abandoned wing, where the guards welcomed him with a chorus of "On Wisconsin."

30

Pleadings

I'm sure there must be thousands and thousands of other veterans in this country who experienced what I experienced who with more courage would have done what Karl Armstrong did.

—RONALD CARBON,
Vietnam veteran, for the defense

And that is why out of 12,000 who were here three years ago, it has now dwindled to a hundred. Because only a hundred support acts like Mr. Armstrong's.

—MICHAEL ZALESKI,
Wisconsin Assistant Attorney General, for the prosecution

Assistant Attorney General Michael Zaleski, aged thirty-two, of medium build, was a formidable polemicist whose grating voice reminded *Daily Cardinal* editors of "Goëbels with a cold." A former Kennedy Democrat, he despised Nixon so much he had quit smoking when Nixon was elected on the theory that if Nixon could be president, anything was possible. In 1972, he had voted for George McGovern, but the Cold War had cast him in the role of an enemy of the movement. He had graduated from the University of Wisconsin Law School, a bastion of conservatism on the campus, and had gone to work for the Dane County district attorney in

1967, just in time for Dow Day. He could remember 10,000 students pelting the courthouse with rocks, audiences jeering so loudly he couldn't make himself heard to the jury, and ducking out side doors to avoid being spat upon. Zaleski had grown up poor in a Polish section of Kenosha and had put himself through college with brains and hard work. At the time of the Army Math bombing he and his wife had just redecorated their house. A few weeks after the explosion, someone had thrown a lighted kerosene lantern through his front window and burned the new carpet. The experience had confirmed him in his natural inclination, which he made no attempt to hide. Zaleski was a cop's prosecutor.

Wisconsin's Department of Justice was housed in the old Lorraine Hotel on the southwest corner of Capitol Square. Senior staff meetings took place every Wednesday morning in the conference room, and it was at one such session, on February 20, 1973, that David Mebane, now acting director, asked Zaleski to take over the Armstrong case from an assistant attorney general named Andy Somers, who had just resigned from the department. Somers had had the case for six months, and Zaleski asked him what work had been done. Somers started talking about courthouse security. He had been visiting courtrooms all over the country researching the problem and had come up with a detailed plan. "What about the trial?" Zaleski interrupted. Somers gave him a blank look.

"It's been two, three years," Zaleski pressed. "I don't even know where all the files are. This is a very mobile community, a lot of students. Where is everything? Who's going to do what?"

Somers shrugged. "There's plenty of time," he said.

"I'm going up to Canada next week for a hearing before the Canadian Supreme Court," Zaleski said testily. "If they deny the review, he's out. All we have to do is ask the Minister of Justice to sign the papers, and we're bringing him back. What the fuck are you going to do then?"

Nobody had any idea.

Appeals of the Armstrong ruling had preoccupied the Canadian judiciary for more than a year. Clayton Ruby had played a tape of David Fine's "This is no bullshit" warning call for the Federal Court of Appeal, but the panel had construed it as evidence that Armstrong did in fact know that people were in the building. Why else would the caller have said, "Clear everyone out"?

On March 5, 1973, Zaleski flew into Ottawa for the Supreme

Court decision. The city was still in winter feather, the frozen canals covered with Hans Brinkers on their way to work. If you asked Mike Zaleski, the whole extradition battle had been fought over an obviously fallacious reading of the Webster-Ashburton Treaty. "If I gunned down Jesse Jackson and I'm a Ku Klux Klanner," he would ask, "is that a political offense or murder?" The Supreme Court ultimately agreed with him, dismissing the application for review with the comment that even if Karl's crimes were politically motivated, it did not make them political crimes.

Zaleski found Minister of Justice Otto Lang in a small, cluttered office across the street. "I guess it's time this friend of yours left," Lang said, casually signing the extradition papers. Zaleski called Madison, where a plane and a small posse of lawmen were standing by, and gave the all clear.

That evening Clayton Ruby's assistant, Bobby Kellerman, visited Karl Armstrong in the Don Jail and gave him the news. Kellerman was a wiry little man with a bumpy nose, a kind expression, and a solicitous manner that belied his physical prowess. (He had been a varsity wrestler in college.) He had taken a liking to Karl personally and was unhappy about the way Karl had been treated in the Don Jail. Superintendent Whitehead had allowed Karl some company, a black American convict facing a murder charge in Kentucky. The prisoner imagined himself a jazz artist, and Whitehead had made an exception to the prohibition on musical instruments in the prison by providing him with a piccolo. The Prince of Darkness, Karl called him, but his complaints about the constant serenade to which he was exposed brought no relief.

In Kellerman's time with him Karl had never wavered in his principles and had not once been cruel or angry or impatient. Except for his courtroom outburst, which in Kellerman's view had been provoked, Karl was one of the most even-tempered, gentle people he had ever met. "It looks like it will be soon," he advised the American.

In the past month, succumbing to depression, Karl had given up the daily exercise routine he had maintained during his first year of captivity. "It will be good to move after a year in jail," he said absently.

Patrick Lucey, the Democrat who had replaced Warren Knowles in the Wisconsin governor's office in 1971, had made a state-owned plane available for the three-and-a-half-hour flight, a twin-engine craft with seating for five passengers, and the group, including Herbert Krusche of the state justice department, William Ferris and Gary Hendrickson of the Dane County Sherriffs, and MPD Det. Charles Lulling, left at 3:00 A.M. the morning of March 7 from Madison Commercial Airport. The lawmen were all in a good mood, but Detective Lulling was especially happy. "That snake, I'm gonna stick it to him!" he crowed. The reference was not to Armstrong, but to his old rival, Special Agent George Baxtrum. The detective was still angry over the fiasco of his September 1971 trip to Toronto, which he remained convinced was an FBI double cross. In escorting Armstrong back to Madison, he would have his revenge.

The plane landed at 6:30 A.M. and taxied to a remote gate of the international airport. It was a bleak, frigid dawn, and the four bundled up for the walk across the tarmac. Krusche took a final look at the extradition warrant, signed by the U.S. secretary of state, that he would be presenting to Canadian authorities. Lulling checked to see that the chambers of his pearl-handled revolvers were loaded.

Superintendent Whitehead and Detective Noble had escorted the prisoner to the airport. Jim Noble was a tall, broad-shouldered, distinguished-looking man who, in police circles, was regarded as something of a genius because of his ability to cite case law. As Krusche handcuffed the prisoner, Noble leaned over and whispered something in Karl's ear. Karl had come to like and trust Jim Noble and blanched as he listened. Lulling noticed the exchange. A moment later he pulled Noble aside. "What did you tell him?"

"I advised him not to sit next to the door," Noble said innocently.

Lulling had formed his own theory about Karl Armstrong based on the fact that Karl had been a security guard. Karl was "uniform happy"; all he wanted was attention, the detective figured, and Lulling looked forward to giving it to him all the way home. "As soon as you're in jail, why don't you give the others a call," he said once they were seated inside the plane. "Tell them how fine the jail conditions in Madison are."

Karl kept his eyes on the great Canadian city still visible through his window. He did not care for Lulling's manner or for the hardware strapped to his thick torso.

"You know, Karl, I know your mother," Lulling continued affably.

Karl fidgeted in his leg irons and cuffs. "You do? How?"

"Did she ever work at Gardner's Bakery?" Karl nodded. Lulling winked malevolently. "Well, Karl, I met her there."

For a moment Karl forgot that he was sitting next to the exit. "I doubt it, but if you did, shame on her."

In Madison, meanwhile, the isthmus was deluged with conflicting reports: "Karl Armstrong will be arriving in Milwaukee at 10:05 A.M." "Accused bomber of the Army Mathematics Research Center is expected to return to Madison at 11:40 A.M.—flight pattern unknown." In fact, David Mebane had put out disinformation about the plane's destination, and the posse landed without incident at the Rock County airport fifty miles west of the capital, the welcoming entourage composed entirely of lawmen. As they began their descent, Lulling pointed out a factory of some kind in the distance. "How many barrels to take out that plant, Karl?" The prisoner thought about it for a moment, interested, before catching himself. Lulling grinned maniacally. He hadn't forgotten the Fassnacht twins tugging on his pantlegs. Those little kids were finally going to get some justice.

Andy Somers wasn't kidding about security, Zaleski realized. When the caravan transporting Karl Armstrong arrived at the City-County Building, MPD marksmen were already standing guard along the roof. The spy Fat Julie waved greetings to Karl from a small crowd of demonstrators. The building's corridors had been stripped bare of furnishings, its locks changed, its doors reinforced; emergency buttons were installed under judges' benches; and outer entrances were placed under the implacable gaze of closed-circuit TV cameras. That afternoon Circuit Judge W. L. Jackman set bail at $450,000 cash, the largest ever in Wisconsin.

The same afternoon, at a suburban airport, 300 people waving American flags greeted Major Donald Heiliger as he arrived home after six years in a Hanoi prison camp. His release was the result of a truce signed by the United States and North Vietnam on January 27 in Paris. Veterans of Foreign Wars and American Legion Honor Guards marched in place to the blares and blasts of the Madison Grade School Band as the hometown hero stepped from the plane and embraced his parents. "The antiwar movement prolonged the Vietnam war," he told a reporter. "It provided that extra little spark of incentive for keeping the North Vietnamese going another day, another month, another year."

Karl, too, had his hometown supporters. *Takeover*'s next cover carried the banner headline, "POW RETURNS HOME," but the story was about the *capo* of the New Year's Gang, not about Major Heiliger. While incarcerated in the Don Jail Karl had received 874 write-in votes for the office of Dane County district attorney. The Youth International Party had nominated him for vice president of the United States on a ticket with Bernardine Dohrn. The Madison Area Peace Action Committee, though it had condemned the bombing, extended him an official welcome home. The *Cardinal* urged students to support him, and contributed $5,000 to his defense fund. The *Capital Times*, which had once offered a reward for his capture, now expressed sympathy, supporting a defense motion for a change of venue. Posters appeared all over town portraying him as Karl Marx. Several hundred supporters staged a nostalgic protest march up State Street. Kenny Mate, one of a coterie of sixties militants who remained in Madison, led a spin-off group in a symbolic occupation of Bascom Hall.

But most students shunned the cause. Dorm residents poured water on demonstrators passing under their windows. Angry members of the Physics Department broke up a lunchtime performance of the Armstrong Guerrilla Theatre on the Library Mall and subsequently formed the Robert Fassnacht Association to support the prosecution. State Attorney General Robert Warren warned of radicals "developing a domestic Ho Chi Minh trail." Mayor William Dyke, facing an electoral challenge from Paul Soglin, the Mifflin Street alderman, revived the bombing as a campaign issue.

Karl was locked up in a cell on the seventh floor of the City-County Building, directly beneath the office of the mayor. From his narrow window he had a view of a parking ramp across the street, where, from time to time, friends and supporters would stop and wave. He was allowed one phone call a week, one visitor a month. His visitors had to speak to him through a security window. He remained depressed, disdaining exercise and worrying his mother.

In the spring of 1973, for the first time in many years there were no major riots in Madison. There was no war to protest, no draft; the army was now all-volunteer. Though North Vietnam repeatedly violated the truce, President Nixon, because of his embroilment in a seamy domestic scandal called Watergate, lacked the political clout to back up his threats of retaliation. Eighteen-year-olds now had the vote, and in Madison they showed their muscle by boosting Paul Soglin to a narrow victory over William Dyke in the April election.

The night after the election Inspector Herman Thomas went into his office and removed all the secret intelligence files amassed by George Croal and his spy network—thousands of pages of reports—in the hope of preventing them from falling into the hands of the Soglin administration. Croal considered the files a bureaucratic exercize of little value or importance, and prided himself on the accomplishments of his squads. Nevertheless, the new police chief, a reformer named David Couper, ordered the files returned and, pledging that "in the future our intelligence gathering activities shall only be related to criminal matters," he transferred Thomas to administration, reassigned Croal to ordinary detective work, and disbanded the counteraffinity squads. Then, after having all the names that were cited blotted out, he turned the files over to the State Historical Society. After teetering from one extreme to another, Madison, like the country as a whole, was struggling to center itself.

Meanwhile, Mike Zaleski was frantically trying to put together the state's case against Karl Armstrong. A visit to Somers's office had turned up a single investigative file. Zaleski had found the supposedly secret and zealously guarded transcripts of the Dane County Grand Jury on top of a filing cabinet in the county courthouse. As he had feared, many of the key witnesses had left Madison. Lynn Schultz was somewhere in Montana, Policronio De Venecia was in Manila, and Stephanie Fassnacht was at the Bohr Institute in Stockholm. Dwight's former friend Robert Rainbolt, who had received a $12,000 advance on his reward, had spent the money on drugs and was admittedly "not all there." Scott Nelson was still in Madrid, where he had been hospitalized for acute anxiety after learning that he would be called to testify against Karl. With the help of Douglas Haag, also an assistant attorney general but not as liberal in his political convictions, Zaleski began the laborious process of finding and contacting the 100 or so people whose testimony would be crucial in the complicated case.

Like other local lawmen Zaleski had been less than overwhelmed by the FBI's cooperativeness in the early stages of the investigation, and it was with some trepidation that he approached George Baxtrum about access to the WISBOM files. But Baxtrum now appeared anxious to help and said he would pass the request on to John Olson. Olson passed it to acting FBI Director William Ruckelshaus, who passed it to Henry Peterson, an assistant U.S. attorney general. On June 14 Peterson authorized the disclosure, and Zaleski suddenly found himself in possession of a staggering load of documents.

Zaleski had seen cases in which the bureau's work had been good and others in which it had been poor. WISBOM had been a good investigation—almost too good, he thought. One curiosity that struck him immediately was that Chuck Calfee and Fred Smith, the agents who had done the lab work, could not say with scientific certainty what the bomb had consisted of. As surely as rain washes away fertilizer, the thousands of gallons of water poured on the fire had dissolved the evidence. ANFO was just a guess, but the FBI had run with it. Figuring that the bombers would have needed a truck or trailer to transport it, agents had checked the U-Haul outlets in the entire south-central part of the state, and they had located Dennis Whipperfurth, who remembered renting Karl a covered trailer. A few blocks away they had found the station with the fuel-oil pump. Then they had started calling agricultural co-ops, and again they had been lucky. Going strictly on their hunches, the agents had obtained a platt map of Greenfield Township, in which Devil's Lake is located, and walked it section by section until they came upon the staging area.

Zaleski was more than amazed; he was incredulous. Would they really have done all that gumshoe work on the strength of a *guess* that ANFO was the blasting agent? The staging area search struck him as especially speculative; Greenfield Township was a rugged area to go tramping around on the strength of a surmise. He voiced his doubts to Baxtrum. "I don't believe it. You had to have a source of information," he said.

Baxtrum insisted that Zaleski had seen everything, but as the assistant attorney general got deeper into the 302s, his perplexity deepened. Karl Armstrong came across as a loser, a nothing, and yet obviously, along with Leo Burt, he had been a ringleader. Zaleski didn't get it. What was the basis of the relationship? What was in it for Leo?

In law school Zaleski had lived in the same building, Iota Court Apartments, where Leo had stayed that summer. It wasn't the only thing he found that he had in common with the suspect. Leo had an old-fashioned, pre-Vatican II Catholic upbringing, which, as Zaleski well knew, was a disciplined religion, almost like being an Orthodox Jew. Leo had been a rower, the most rigorous sport. He had trained with the marines, the most disciplined of the armed services. Suddenly, in his senior year, he'd turned into a radical. Zaleski considered him even more culpable in the bombing than Karl because Leo was more intelligent, but he was perplexed. Brother in the navy, sister a nun, uncle a big man at Villanova—it just didn't add up. All year long, the newspapers had been full of allegations about governmental dirty tricks, about Cointelpro and a group called "The Plumbers" and mysterious break-ins. Could Leo Burt have been the Stassi Shoe Store's secret source? Was he, too, working for the government? The speculation amused Zaleski, but he didn't pursue it. That was not his job.

Zaleski was not alone in suspecting Leo Burt of being an informant. Many leftists did as well, but they were not people who knew him. Old friends like George Bogdanich and Jane Adamson who had seen him that summer and who had sensed his personal crisis had no doubt that he had acted out of conviction. However, the defense committee had its own conspiracy theory, which had its origins in a rumor that Alderman Paul Soglin had picked up at a party in Miffland not long after the bombing. The story went that the MPD had known about the bomb plot in advance, had actually followed the rocking van into town on East Johnson Avenue, and had let the bombing take place to discredit the movement. As for how the MPD knew, the explanation was simple: The tip must have come from Golden Freek Enterprises.

At this point the defense knew nothing of the bounty-hunting trips to Canada that Bobo and Nelson had made on behalf of the FBI. However, *Takeover* had published an account of their trip to Northern Ireland in 1971, ostensibly for the CIA, which had ended with the two of them in jail in Scotland on a charge of passing counterfeit currency. From Karl they knew of Lynn's connection with the two and of the mysterious "CIA drug" Bobo had given them back in January 1970. The question was, how long had the two hustlers been working for the government? And how much had Lynn told them about Karl in the spring and summer of 1970? Had Bobo and Nelson alerted the authorities, possibly in exchange for the dismissal of certain charges outstanding against them? And what about Snakey Mathieson, the Man in Black, the witness at the Primate Lab, and the man with binoculars in the Alumni Center? Was it just Karl's paranoia, or had the police been watching him all along?

Bobby Kellerman, who had come from Toronto to assist the defense, volunteered to track Lynn down. He contacted fifteen people who asked fifteen more, and before long he had an address for her in Red Lodge, Montana. The young Canadian lawyer, anxious for adventure, set off hitchhiking across the plains.

Meanwhile, attorneys Melvin Greenberg and William Kunstler barraged the court with motions—twenty-one in all—demanding to know the extent of surveillance of the defense team; the possible involvement of "White House spy squads" like those employed in Watergate and the burglary of Daniel Ellsberg's psychiatrist's office; and the "names of any and all informants, agent provocateurs, finks, stool pigeons, or any person who participated in any way at any time in any of the alleged crimes." They also asked to see the minutes of the Dane County Grand Jury and the WISBOM files to look for evidence of governmental impropriety. Finally, they petitioned Judge Jackman, who had set bail, to excuse himself from the case for reasons of prejudice.

The defense moves received enthusiastic attention in the underground press. "People intimately involved in the defense acknowledge a key to cracking the case wide open is the disclosure of the covert activities of the FBI, Army Intelligence, and CIA type operatives in Madison in 1969 and 1970," *Takeover* observed.

It was late June when Kellerman returned from Montana. He reported directly to Mel Greenberg at the latter's downtown office, and Greenberg turned up the volume on his office radio while they talked. After arriving in Red Lodge, Kellerman said, he had found Lynn in a hunting camp on top of a nearby mountain, where she was working as a cook. As soon as he introduced himself, she had become guarded and nervous. "I only have half an hour before we start dinner," she had said. The interview had been an exercise in frustration. Schultz did not want to be reminded of Karl Armstrong or the New Year's Gang, much less Sandy Nelson, with whom she had broken up when he went to Ireland. The one intriguing bit of information that Kellerman was able to get from her concerned the phone call she had received from the FBI in January 1970, during which she had given the agent Karl's name. If the feds had Karl's name in January, why hadn't they interviewed him? Kellerman wondered.

That night Greenberg's office was broken into and his files were rifled. Nothing of value was taken, not even his radio. Although other offices in the same building had been hit as well, Greenberg suspected that the break-ins at the other offices were only window dressing for a "Plumbers-type operation" and immediately requested an investigation. "If it was the government that did this, one of the major defenses that we are working on could be compromised," he said.

Greenberg's fears were not entirely unfounded, for the prosecution had been snooping on defense efforts from the start. One of the informants was Julie Maynard, who by this time was living in an FBI-underwritten apartment on State Street, a reward for having helped the bureau foil Abbie Hoffman's attempts to disrupt the 1972 Republican Convention in Miami. Pete Bobo and Sandy Nelson also infiltrated one of the defense committees.

FBI interest in the defense effort was motivated by the hope of finding clues to the whereabouts of the three remaining fugitives, who were living under different names on the West Coast. Dwight, ensconced in the Vancouver, B.C., apartment of a new girlfried, had worked as a long-shoreman for a while and was now drawing public assistance. David was employed as a clerk in a Los Angeles shipping company, took classes at Santa Monica Junior College (getting his customary good grades), attended Lakers and Kings games on a regular basis, and had even worked for the McGovern campaign stuffing envelopes. Leo likewise lived openly in another West Coast city, his whereabouts well known to the local heavies. Leo and David received financial support from acquaintances all over the country, and periodically wrote apologias for the bombing that were printed in left-wing journals and newspapers. Leo's latest letter, which had appeared in the *Daily Cardinal* in March, urged support for Karl Armstrong on the grounds that the entire student movement was on trial with him. The Bureau was so frustrated in its manhunt that it was taking out ads in magazines such as *Strength and Health* and *Muscular Development* and circulating information on Leo's acne prescription to pharmacies in various cities.

All the investigative agencies issued terse denials of Greenberg's charges. In July George Croal arrested an unstable individual who confessed to the break-in at Greenberg's office and was ordered confined to the ward for the criminally insane at Mendota State Hospital. Meanwhile, dissatisfied with the intelligence he was receiving, David Mebane had assigned one of his own men, Special Agent John Schulz of the State Justice Department, to infiltrate the KADC. He insisted on weekly updates and immediate notification of any changes in the defense posture. When the defense sent a researcher to the University Archives, Mebane dispatched Schulz to find out what documents had been copied. Schulz kept a log of Karl's long distance calls from jail, many of which were to Naomi Wall in Toronto. The desirability of a wiretap was discussed, but according to a Schulz memo of June 25, the FBI's Baxtrum nixed the idea, as he was "doubtful these calls would provide any lead as to the location of Dwight Armstrong."

In response to Greenberg's motion of prejudice, Judge Jackman withdrew from the case and was replaced by William Sachtjen, the same Bill Sachtjen who, some thirty years earlier, had worked with Ruth Armstrong at Droster's. Sachtjen hadn't forgotten the pretty and fun-loving girl from Tomah. He had kept track of Ruth's family in the way that men in public life do, picking up tidbits from his many acquaintances. He was aware that Karl had been a classmate of his daughter at Sherman Middle School and East High, he knew Pastor Hoffman, he was acquainted with Mira's husband, and he remembered once having had Mira on a jury. He knew that the family was not without its problems, but in Sachtjen's experience, few families were.

Antiwar sentiment was nothing new to Judge Sachtjen. His great-great-grandfather Tietje had come to Wisconsin to escape the incessant civil wars of mid-nineteenth-century Germany. His father, Herman, a stalwart of the Progressive party, had been an isolationist in World War II and had opposed U.S. intervention in Korea and Vietnam. Bill Sachtjen shared his father's views, but the Sachtjens were not scofflaws or rebels. Tietje had fought at Waterloo; Bill had served his country in World War II (at a desk job in Newark). The Sachtjen way to avoid military service, when avoidance was warranted, was through money and influence. Before giving up on Germany altogether, Tietje had bought his way out of the draft; political friends had helped Bill stay out of Korea. Sachtjen's son had beaten the draft by joining the National Guard, entering a hospital unit so he did not have riot duty. The judge's son-in-law had joined the reserves. Thus, in Sachtjen's view, there were lawful ways to avoid duties that went against one's conscience—including even, as a last resort, expatriation. Like his father, he expressed his own opposition to the war by voting for U.S. Representative Robert Kastenmeier and Senator Gaylord Nelson, among the most outspoken critics of the war in Congress. The idea of civil disobedience, not to mention sabotage, was completely foreign to him. As a circuit court judge, he had handled many protest cases, from Robert Cohen to Paul Soglin, and though he agreed with them about the war, he treated them without favor, reflecting the wider community's bias against the politics of confrontation. He had encountered Soglin socially after the latter had been elected to the city council. "I've seen you somewhere before," he said. "Yeah, you fined me for disorderly conduct," Soglin reminded him.

Sachtjen had a proprietary feeling about Madison, not only because of his family's long history in the area, but because, as city manager in the early fifties, he had considerably expanded its borders through annexation. He was on a first-name basis with everyone around Capitol Square and had a sense of how profoundly the bombing had affected the community.

If Greenberg had expected any sympathy from him because of his liberal views, he was quickly disabused. Sachtjen denied almost all Greenberg's motions, dismissing the allegations of governmental misconduct as pure conjecture. He refused to let the defense see either the WISBOM files or the transcript of the Dane County Grand Jury, offering to inspect the latter himself to ensure that the rights of the defendant had not been violated. In response to Greenberg's complaints about pretrial publicity, he temporarily instituted a gag order, eliciting howls of protest from the defense and derisive laughter in the Justice Department. He did give the defense permission to inspect the physical evidence—a mixed blessing, as it turned out.

On August 21 Sachtjen accompanied the defense attorneys to the federal building in Milwaukee, where a room had been set aside for the viewing. With George Baxtrum standing by watchfully, the exhibits were presented one by one: the identifying fragments of the Econoline, the stolen oil drum and homemade "Peterson for Governor" sign from the staging area, the nitrate residues from the Corvair, the U-Haul receipts, surveillance notebooks, and so forth.

The lawyers' faces grew longer as the day wore on. They were taking pictures of the photographic evidence to be introduced, and near nightfall they were shown a black-and-white blowup of Robert Fassnacht's twisted and bloodied corpse. They returned to Madison in low spirits.

Two weeks later Greenberg received a copy of Armstrong's statements that the prosecution intended to introduce, including his confessions to the Toronto police—six pages of highly inflammatory and self-incriminating remarks. And because Karl had been arrested under an immigration warrant, it would do no good to claim that he had not been properly warned of his rights. Passing Greenberg in City Hall, Judge Sachtjen asked, "Don't you want to bargain?" A few days later Greenberg met with Bobby Kellerman and Bill Kunstler to consider their options. They were all very discouraged, not only by the mountain of evidence weighing down on them, but by the lack of popular support for their client. The national press was sick of the war and had moved on to new concerns—Watergate, the Middle East, stagflation.

Bobby Kellerman wanted to fight. He had found something in the Wisconsin statutes about a common-law privilege of using force to prevent a felony. A group called Science for the People had just released a 120-page report attempting to document many of Jim Rowen's allegations about Army Math. AMRC mathematicians had been immersed in secret defense projects all along, the authors concluded, but had maintained deniability by discussing the military applications of their work off campus. Kellerman imagined that such information might sway a jury. "Mass murder is a felony," he argued enthusiastically. "If we can get all the facts out in court, show the connection between Army Math and Vietnam, Karl will be acquitted."

Kunstler had just concluded a successful defense of the Gainesville Eight, a group of servicemen arrested at the Republican National Convention in Miami, and was hopeful that the Chicago Eight convictions would be thrown out, as well. In fact, most of the government's attempts to prosecute dissidents had abjectly failed. But Kunstler was dubious about Karl's chances in a jury trial. "Zaleski is no dummy. Do you know what he is going to do?" he asked Kellerman. "First he will have the photo of the corpse passed among the jurors. Then he will put the coroner on the stand to explain exactly how Fassnacht died. For a finale he will bring on the widow Fassnacht to tell them about her husband and what he was doing there that night. Do you realize what that will be like? Karl is going to get creamed!"

Zaleski, though, had his own problems. For one thing, a trial was likely to go on for months and cost a fortune. For another, unless a deal was made, the prosecution was burdened with proving the extradition charge of first-degree murder, and that was going to be difficult. Zaleski could claim first-degree murder only by standing the evidence on its head, arguing that the warning message was intended to lure cops to their deaths, etcetera.

Zaleski decided to bluff. "We've got you by the short hairs," he told Greenberg over the phone, "but it's time to end this divisiveness. We're willing to go second, but with no deals in sentencing. With second, it's all the other charges including Sauk, everything we've got on him."

"They've brought in Kunstler; I'm not really in control," Greenberg replied. He called Zaleski back late Saturday afternoon. "It's a deal," he said, "but we want a sentencing hearing. Karl wants people to know why he did this."

"Okay, that's his right," Zaleski said. They agreed to make the announcement on September 28. Zaleski called his boss, Attorney General Bob Warren. "I just saved you fifty thousand," he said, "but Karl wants his Last Hurrah."

Paul Soglin had won the mayor's office not merely by getting out the hippie vote, but by letting Democratic party regulars run his general election campaign. With Chief Couper's help, he had brought the police department into line, but the suburbs were nervous. The return of Karl Armstrong in the midst of the contest had been a decided embarrassment. William Dyke had been able to dredge up a statement Soglin had made at the time of Karl's arrest stating that everyone who had opposed the AMRC was obligated to support the accused. Mayor Soglin still believed that Army Math had no business on campus and had said so when Science for the People announced its new study, which Soglin allowed them to do in his office. But he was wary of the defense committee and terrified of what a trial might do to the city.

On Sunday, September 23, about 500 young people gathered on Mifflin Street for the first block party in the student ghetto since

1969. Soglin had objected to the idea as vehemently as his former nemesis William Dyke once had, but relented at the last minute and issued a permit. It was a balmy afternoon. The Midwest Marijuana Growers Association had donated three pounds of pot for the occasion, and many of the celebrants were high, dancing to the music of a local dirt band. The police kept their distance.

The event was billed as the "Karl Armstrong Freedom Party." Late in the afternoon Mel Greenberg got up on the bandstand and auctioned off a cheese sandwich, Karl's uneaten jailhouse lunch, for which several intoxicated employees of the Miffland Co-op paid $100. Then cocounsel Bill Kunstler held aloft a tape recorder, smuggled from the Dane County Jail, with a message from Karl on it: "It's a beautiful day for a party—thank you, brothers and sisters, for coming."

Tom Hayden and Jane Fonda, who were in town with their infant son Troy and folk singer Holly Near to publicize the plight of Viet Cong and North Vietnamese prisoners of war who were still held by the Thieu government, had been invited to the party. But in the few months that had passed since the extradition hearing, Hayden had abandoned revolutionary rhetoric and was trying to reattach himself to the mainstream. Fluttering in the breeze over the bandstand in the 500 block of Mifflin Street that day were ten-foot banners emblazoned with the smiling images of Ho Chi Minh, Madame Binh, Salvador Allende, Che Guevara, and ... Karl Armstrong. Neither Hayden nor his wife wanted to be photographed against that backdrop, so they had secluded themselves in the home of Mayor Soglin, who had made only a perfunctory appearance himself.

The visitors ended up staying the night. After the women had gone to bed, Hayden and Soglin sat up drinking and talking shop. Hayden wanted to know every detail of Soglin's successful campaign. Around midnight Kenny Mate and Mike Fellner, both KADC members, showed up and told Hayden they wanted to talk to him before his press conference in the morning. They asked why he wasn't speaking out for Karl Armstrong. Hayden was still in blue-collar mufti and a post-Beatles shag, chain-smoking and sipping a Scotch. "Let's have it out now," he said bluntly. "You don't have the mass line, the masses can't relate to your politics. How can you wear that?" he said, pointing to the "Free Karl" T-shirt Mate was wearing. "How can you even relate to it?" He was in a fine rage.

The visitors reminded Hayden of his previous support for Karl, and for a moment he weakened. "Don't worry, in public I'll back Karl to the hilt. I can't let Jane say anything, though." The "Hanoi Jane" label had become a drag on them both.

Soglin, whose organ grinder's mustache gave him a somewhat morose appearance, had never liked the Mother Jones types who now rallied around Karl and he objected to them bullying his house guest. In his view, the strength of the movement had always consisted in the willingness of its adherents to sacrifice themselves for the cause, to go to jail, pay fines, give up careers and citizenship, and even to be beaten, as he himself had been on Dow Day. The bombing was wrong, Soglin maintained; Karl had no right to make that decision for the rest of the movement. In fact, Soglin still thought Army Math might have been a setup.

The argument lasted until 5 A.M., becoming bitter at times. "Karl just has nothing to do with what the masses will relate to," Hayden said finally, before heading off to bed.

Thursday, September 28, 1973, was the day of pleadings. About seventy-five supporters marched from campus to the City-County Building in a cold rain to show solidarity with Brother Karl. On the steps they were addressed by the new assistant to the mayor, Jim Rowen. "We were able to get six, seven, ten thousand people in past demonstrations," the speaker said plaintively. "Now we've reached this day when one person is about to take the rap for the entire movement." The Stassi Shoe Store, taking note of his return to Madison in May from Washington, where he had served as a consultant to the U.S. Senate Select Committee on Nutrition and Human Needs, advised Acting FBI Director William Ruckelshaus that Rowen "declined to put any label on his politics at the moment."

Karl had only one question for Bill Kunstler when the latter had finished explaining the advantages of pleading to second-degree murder: "How will it affect the others?" Kunstler was favorably impressed. Karl was calm when the guards brought him down to the courtroom. "Smile," he commanded Mel Greenberg. "You look like it's the end of the world." He was pleading guilty only to have the opportunity to put the war on trial, something he couldn't have done otherwise, he informed Judge Sachtjen. "I in no way regard these acts as crimes. I am not happy about the death of a human being and the injuries suffered, but I do not apologize for having taken these actions."

Judge Sachtjen promptly found him guilty of second-degree murder, four counts of arson, and the attempted bombing of the Wisconsin Power and Light substation in Prairie du Sac. Ruth threw herself on Karl, sobbing pitifully, and a U.S. marshal had to pry her off. But Karl remained strangely sanguine.

After pleading guilty to federal charges across the street in the courtroom of Judge James Doyle, Karl was returned to his cell to await the mitigation hearing. "This is exactly what I want," he told a reporter.

31

The Movement
Defends Itself

*Thank God we have an antiwar movement. Thank God we
have people who are concerned enough to dissent, to show
opposition to the war, because that may be the only difference
between the way history views us and the way it viewed Nazi
Germany.*

—ANTHONY RUSSO,
military analyst, for the defense

*The difference between Nazi Germany and our country was
that the peace movement was allowed to exist. No peace
movement could have existed in Nazi Germany or in any
other totalitarian state, your honor.*

—DOUGLAS HAAG,
Wisconsin Assistant Attorney General, for the prosecution

The sentence-mitigation hearing, in which Karl Armstrong's
lawyers would have the opportunity to argue why he should not
be punished with the legal maximum of twenty-five-years imprisonment, began on October 15, 1973, Karl's twenty-seventh birthday.
The setting was an ordinary courtroom over which Judge William
Sachtjen, still lean, his fine chiseled features intact, presided. A
hundred or so Armstrong supporters, those who had made it past
the metal detectors and the refractory clerk who was responsible
for issuing second-floor passes, filed into the room. Mike Zaleski
had to suppress a laugh; it seemed as though half of them were peo-

ple he knew, cops and FBI agents working under cover. "The times they are a-changin'," he whispered to his cocounsel, Douglas Haag.

October fifteenth was also, in an approximate sense, the anniversary of the Nazi war criminal hangings, a coincidence that was taken seriously by the defense. Over the next two weeks witnesses would remark again and again on the similarities between Nazi Germany and contemporary America, insisting that resistance, however violent, to enormous national crimes, such as the war in Vietnam, was mandated by the U.S.-sponsored Nuremberg Code. Occuring in the midst of the hearing, the "Saturday Night Massacre" in which President Nixon fired Archibald Cox, the special prosecutor investigating his alleged involvement in the Watergate scandal, seemed to underscore the defense argument that constitutional rule had broken down in America.

Sachtjen sat through the proceedings with his head cupped in his hands, benign but inscrutable. So he would remain as an earnest parade of Vietnam veterans, some of them fresh from the Gainesville Eight trial in Florida, took the stand to detail their personal experiences in Vietnam. The veterans' testimony was bitter and yet unimpeachable in its gory detail. Charles Piper, aged twenty-six, a clean-cut Madison native with four years of service in the Marine Corps, told quietly of a U.S. "Killer Team" that had rounded up villagers in suspected Viet Cong strongholds and systematically executed them. John Nouveau, aged thirty-eight, a sixteen-year veteran of the marines and the recipient of five Purple Hearts, told the story of a school bus that had strayed into his path during a firefight. He had emptied a clip into it, only to discover afterward that he had killed two dozen children. "I really enjoyed my work and I loved war," Nouveau admitted, hunched over in the witness stand to hide his tears, "but I don't like it anymore. And I don't like anyone connected with it." As Karl applauded vigorously Judge Sachtjen pounded his gavel. "It took a lot of courage to say what he said," Karl observed.

"Now Karl, I understand that," Sachtjen said, "but this is a court of law, and you will have to find other means of showing your appreciation."

Still more veterans testified—nearly a dozen in all—about atrocities they had witnessed and of their personal metamorphoses from gung-ho GIs to pacifists. Stephen Lee Hawkins, blond, hair down to his shoulders, a former high school science wizard with a top-security clearance gained during a four-year stint in the air force, described in technical language the effects of the whimsically-named weaponry deployed in Vietnam—the Pineapple Bomb, the Orange Bomb, the Mother Bomb, the Daisy Cutter, and the Puff, a sophisticated Gatling gun capable of 6,000 rounds per minute. Instead of the medals he had earned during his tour, Hawkins wore antiwar pins and a "Free Karl" button on his faded army fatigues. Bart Osborn, a graduate of Army Intelligence School with the polished manner of an executive, capped the war stories by cataloguing the deeds of the U.S. counterinsurgency program, Operation Phoenix, responsible, Osborn estimated, for the "termination" of nearly 42,000 Vietnamese civilians.

Mike Zaleski sat doodling through the testimonials. He was still angry at the defense over what he considered their "rip-off" of the student community at the Mifflin Street Block Party, raising money for a "trial" they already knew was not going to be held. "Do you know Karl Armstrong? Do you think the death of Robert Fassnacht was justified?" he asked each witness in the same, incredulous tone. But the veterans were not easily intimidated. "I can honestly say, with thousands of other antiwar veterans in this country, that with more courage I would have done what Karl Armstrong did," answered Ron Carbon, a Madison resident who had spent seventeen months in Vietnam. He was echoed by Samuel Schorr, aged twenty-six, national coordinator of Vietnam Veterans Against the War, who drew sustained applause from Karl's supporters when he told Zaleski, "I feel much more criminal than him. I killed a lot more people. I'd be glad to serve next to him in jail."

Following the veterans parade, which lasted three days, were the academic experts. Robert J. Lifton, the New York author and psychologist, described the anger of the sixties generation in "psychohistorical" terms; that is, attributing it to what was happening in Vietnam. Chandler Morse, a Professor Emeritus of economics at Cornell University, bald and dignified, with the air of a Sunday school teacher, related the findings of the Cornell Air Study, of which he was a principal author. The massive air war in Southeast Asia had amounted to "combat by proxy," he said, in which "80 percent of the casualties in North Vietnam were civilians." His testimony was corroborated by Dr. Egbert Pfeiffer, professor of zoology at the University of Montana, an angry man who spent nearly three hours on the witness stand detailing the vast ecological destruction of Vietnam, the obliteration of entire forests by herbicides, the cratering of the landscape, birth defects caused by Agent Orange, refugee camps as a way of life. All things considered, the war in Vietnam was "illegal and criminal" from the standpoint of international law and the Nuremberg Code, argued Professor Richard Falk of Princeton. Nuremberg implied that "citizens have a right, and possibly a duty, to obstruct a criminally conceived war." He went so far as to suggest that, as in Nazi Germany, U.S. businessmen and scientists who collaborated in Vietnam were indictable. As for the "warmakers" in the White House and Pentagon, "They are the ones who should be candidates for amnesty, not the defendant in this case," he said coolly.

But do you know Karl Armstrong? Zaleski asked each of them. They did not.

The verbal jousting was relieved by a showing of *Inside North Vietnam* by Felix Greene, a documentary that had been popular on campuses five years earlier and that had influenced Karl. An old man, walking with a cane, and clutching a black fedora, entered the courtroom and shook hands with Kunstler and Armstrong just as the film ended. With his halo of white hair, eighty-six-year-old former U.S. Senator Ernest Gruening of Alaska looked like the celebrated Wisconsin architect Frank Lloyd Wright. Judge Sachtjen was surprised to learn that the former senator had been publicity director of the LaFollette presidential campaign in 1924. "You probably know my father; he was active at that time, too," the judge commented. The two began to gossip about what had become of the LaFollette line, momentarily forgetting the defendant, the gallery, the lawyers, and the tragic circumstance that had brought them together.

Gruening and Senator Wayne Morse of Oregon had cast the lone votes against the Tonkin Gulf Resolution that President Johnson had used to justify his massive buildup of U.S. ground forces in Vietnam. Gruening did not blame his fellow senators. In impressive detail he told how the deception had been managed, including the fact that the resolution itself turned out to have been drafted in May, four months before the USS *Maddox* was allegedly fired upon. "In other words," Gruening said, "the United States was preparing for an episode that would justify going in there."

By this time Gruening, who had arrived in Madison with the understanding that he was to defend a draft dodger, had been enlightened as to the charges against Karl Armstrong, and he told Zaleski he preferred not to comment directly on the Sterling Hall tragedy. Yet as he reflected on the human costs of the Tonkin Gulf deception—"those 55,000 American dead, the 300,000 wounded, and the hundreds of thousands of Southeast Asians who have been murdered, killed and maimed"—his equanimity deserted him. Such a monstrous lie was "something which we must bring home to the American people," he concluded starkly, "and which so fully justifies all acts of resistance to this war in whatever form they take."

On the second Monday of the hearing the focus shifted from the war to the efforts to stop it. The testimony was reminiscent of that given in Toronto, but even more detailed. The witnesses included campus hardliners who felt compelled to stand by the East Side boy who had taken them at their word. Other speakers indicted the AMRC, citing evidence from the new Science for the People study. George Bogdanich recalled Karl's participation in the beer-fueled discussions of the Male Chauvinist Pigs Caucus. Phil Ball was allowed to tell the story of Karl's involvement in the Madison Tenant Union. Bringing up the rear were the celebrity witnesses, so scheduled to lure the media in for the conclusion of the hearing.

Daniel Ellsberg, too ill to travel, sent a tape recording. "Will we be allowed to cross-examine the tape recorder?" Zaleski asked mockingly, but Sachtjen ordered the tape to be played. "It seems clear that Karl and I were experiencing the history of the United States in the same way," said the former defense analyst and leaker of *The Pentagon Papers*. "Anything higher than a minimum sentence would be a mockery of justice." The recorded testimony was followed by a live appearance of Ellsberg's codefendant in the *Pentagon Papers* case, Anthony Russo, who had flown in during the night from California. Retracing the origins of U.S. involvement in Vietnam, Russo said that his own anger was such that he had once been tempted to blow up the RAND Corporation's computers. Historians Howard Zinn of Boston and Gabriel Kolko of Toronto underscored Russo's startling confession with their own thoughts on the history of resistance.

Philip Berrigan, bigger and more aggressive than his brother Daniel, a dropout from the priesthood, a believer in the social gospel who had gone to jail for burning draft records in Catonsville, Maryland, in May of 1968, informed Sachtjen that neither Christ nor Gandhi had opposed all violence. It wasn't the "so-called violent revolutionaries" but rather the "lukewarm" whom Christ condemned: "'So because you are neither hot nor cold I will vomit you out of my mouth.'"

Berrigan had visited Karl Armstrong in jail several weeks earlier, and like others who had met the quiet prisoner face to face, the white-haired activist had found in Karl a reflection of himself. "Why must he prove himself in what he's done and how he's lived," the witness asked plaintively, "while we ignore—what would you say—10, 12, 14 million deaths over our 24 years of involvement in Indochina? We make scapegoats of the people who have felt most deeply and most lovingly, we throw their guilt upon them and then we drive them out into the wilderness, and"—he solemnly concluded—"the wilderness is prison."

But the high point of the proceedings went largely unreported in the national media. This was the appearance of Professor Harvey Goldberg, oracle of the Third Coast, whose lectures had introduced thousands of Wisconsin students to the socialist interpretation of history. For Goldberg, the real issue in Karl's trial was not Nuremberg, but an idea going back through Lenin and Marx to Buonarroti and Babeuf, to the "Conspiracy of the Equals" of 1796, and ultimately to the "Incorruptible" Maximilian Robespierre and the Terror of 1793. Karl Armstrong and his 2,000-pound fertilizer bomb had cast a pall over the whole idea of violent revolution as a method of social change.

Goldberg looked sick, his face pinched, his complexion jaundiced, his sticklike frame more wasted than ever. Preempting Zaleski's standard line of questioning, he began by disclaiming any knowledge of Karl Armstrong and the New Year's Gang; he intended to speak only of the historical context of the bombing. Using his lecture-hall technique of parallel prepositional phrases, he evoked the glory days of the sixties. "In the ten years that I was here, I would say that it was a unique moment in our lives. That I saw an evolution of student concern, of student action, of student questioning that really was unprecedented in my own teaching career, in my own student life, and in a way I think unprecedented in the entire experience of young people in the history of the United States.

"And I talked a lot about violence," he went on. "And students had a perception that there is a lot of violence and that it is sometimes even hard to define.

"That when 12 million people suffer from malnutrition, they are being violated.

"That if black babies die three times more frequently, that that is violence.

"That if automobile manufacturers do not put in safety devices that they might, that that is violence.

"That if we pollute the atmosphere, that is violence. That there are reasons for that, there are interests involved.

"And that the path of greatest nobility is to search for the way of ending that kind of daily humiliation and violation and violence of human being to human being."

He leaned forward and rested his head in one hand, visibly burdened by the knowledge of human suffering. "You see, you see what the problem is," he said. His followers hung on his words, waiting for the spin that would make sense of all that had happened and restore the great dream of social justice. And Goldberg did not disappoint them. The violence of the movement had struck him as "very unrealistic" because it cut off communication with people the students needed to convince, he said somberly, sounding for a moment like his former friend and fellow historian, William Appleman Williams. "But when there is a sense of urgency, when people are dying in Vietnam, when they're being threatened, when you discover so much all at once—that's the problem. I tell you," he concluded, reaching out a thin hand to his listeners, "it was a traumatized generation!"

32

The Sentencing

You will answer the question that Allen Ginsberg poses so beautifully in his poem, "Howl": Must we ever plunge onward and drive our very children mad?

—WILLIAM KUNSTLER,
Attorney, for the defense

One last question: Do you feel that Daniel Ellsberg should be given three minutes or five minutes to get his butt out of that building?

—MICHAEL ZALESKI,
Wisconsin Assistant Attorney General, for the prosecution

The last day of the mitigation hearing was reserved for the Armstrongs, and for the first time in two weeks Judge Sachtjen came alive, joking with family members in an effort to put them at ease, making sure they were provided with water, and asking questions on points of interest to himself. "Who was your landlord? Do you remember that? Schlimgen, was it? The old Bringe house?" To Ruth, it was a good sign.

Donald was first to take the stand. His big chin had sagged under the weight of his misfortunes, but he was still a presence on the witness stand and spoke like a true working man. Sachtjen asked him how he and Ruth had met. "My wife worked at a store, and, incidentally, I believe, your Honor, that it was. ..."

"She worked with me, as a matter of fact," Sachtjen said, with a glance at Ruth.

"Yes, that's right."

"I was a young law student and she was a bookkeeper," the judge said. He did remember her, a pretty nineteen-year-old who had done an exceptionally good job. As Ruth had long suspected, it was he who had put dead mice in her overshoes to give her a fright, a joke he played on other shop girls as well. Even then he knew that Ruth's destiny was to get married and have children, not to be in the society pages, and it had never occurred to him to ask her out. Nevertheless, she was permanently associated in his mind with the pleasant memories of youth. "And I saw her every day for several years," he said, lost in nostalgia.

"Yes, sir," Don said humbly. He launched into the highlights of Karl's upbringing, describing the many wholesome activities that young Karl had participated in—the Boy Scouts, the Drum and Bugle Corps, the Boy's Choir. "I don't want to embarrass him, but I'd like to say that he was a very good singer."

He mentioned the family camping trips to national parks. "And I think in most respects we lived somewhat of an average type of life. I think our interests have been pretty much what is generally considered normal. We never kept any secrets from each other," he said.

Zaleski gave Haag a doubtful look; Mira's husband had told him a few things about the Armstrongs. However, he could see no advantage to the prosecution in airing the family's problems.

"But I want to get back to Karl," Don said. "Karl was much like his mother in the respect that it never took much to make him happy. In the neighborhood in which we lived out on Hintze Road, he was very popular with the younger children because he always seemed to have a way of entertaining them. I remember one particular incident. We had a dog out in the yard, and she was rather obnoxious as far as my neighbors were concerned. She did a lot of barking. I took a magazine out there one day and I gave her a pretty good whipping for it. And Karl says, 'Dad,' he says, 'You remember what you told me a long time ago?' And I said, 'What was that?' And he says, 'Well, people that don't like children and don't like dogs bear watching.'"

As he got over his nervousness Don began to pontificate as though he were at the dinner table, expanding on his religious and political convictions, discussing possible U.S. economic motives in Southeast Asia, drawing parallels between Vietnam and the Spanish Civil War. He suggested that the United States was using Vietnam as a proving ground for new weapons systems as the Germans and Italians had done in Spain.

Sachtjen began to fidget. *He's talking over his head,* the judge thought, and tried to get Don back on the subject of his family, at one point bringing up Pastor Hoffman. Sachtjen knew the Lutheran minister. "Didn't you say you later belonged to the American Lutheran ...?"

"I never belonged to the church," Donald said, cutting him off. "I felt that political views in a church, when it starts becoming a religious dogma in the respect that we should submit to a blind obedience of our political leaders, and to take and incorporate that into a religious dogma was something more than I was willing to take and accept."

Don's moralizing struck Sachtjen as insincere, but he let the matter drop, and Don continued. He and Karl agreed about the immorality of the war, he said. "I remember distinctly telling Karl, I said, 'These people that talk about obscenities and have the audacity to take and try to compare nudity or something like that, and compare it with the obscene thing that I saw in this paper when I saw the police chief of Saigon standing behind a man and [shooting him in the head], and to think that we could in any way defend this type of thing.' I was so infuriated I'd throw the paper on the doggone floor, and Karl says, 'These people are insane. They're nuts. Strictly.' I said, and this I think is very important that I tell you, I said, 'Karl, if [the] American people could for one day just experience some of this terror and bombing that's being inflicted on some of these people, I think that they could wake up.'"

He ended with the story of the time Karl had begged him to join in an antiwar march on State Street, how he had refused because he didn't want to be seen with longhairs, and how Karl had chastised him afterward for being, as Don put it, "hypothetical." "He said, 'Dad,' he says, 'You remember you told me something one time.' He said, 'If you see a wrong and you don't protest it or do something about it, you are just as guilty as those that precipitated the incident.'"

"I think that pretty much takes and sums it up," Don concluded.

Charlie Lulling had gone out into the hall to have a smoke. The first time he had interviewed Armstrong, Don had seemed like a regular guy, confused by it all, wondering what to do. "If it were my son, I'd get him the best lawyer I could," Lulling had advised him. But on his next visit something had changed. They were talking in the driveway, and all of a sudden Don had started indicting society. "Whatever happened to our adversary system?" Don had said. Lulling had walked to his car, Don right behind him, yelling, "What ever happened to our adversary system?" Lulling didn't know what Don was talking about, then or now.

When he went back inside, it was Karl's turn. Karl had not testified in Toronto. In fact, he had never given a speech in his life. When he took the stand at 11 A.M., it was the first time his supporters had heard him articulate his views in public. He had been so worried about it that he had asked a local meditationist named Allan Weinstock, aka the Swami Rama, to teach him relaxation techniques in jail. But whatever the Swami had taught him deserted him once he stepped into the box. Judge Sachtjen, the lawyers, his parents, the movement heavies, and the sedition men were now all looking expectantly at him.

George Nelson and his youngest son, Anders, Scott's younger brother, had traveled to Madison for the mitigation hearing. Scott remained at an air base in Louisiana, to which he had been transferred by mistake, where he continued to experience anxiety attacks even though the risk of having to testify against Karl had passed. Di Nelson remained at home in River Falls, but her thoughts were with Karl. One day, seated at her kitchen table, she wrote a poem that artfully expressed the anguish of those who had known and loved Karl and considered him incapable of murder:

Tangled thoughts
Fray in the whirling eddy of my mind;
They do not stem so swift a stream.
I, blind as a sky without the stars
Wonder, what is my window curtain against—
The night?
The mistral wind?
The dark laughing eyes?

Ancient beans grown
Under the lentil;
The sounds of night walk bold.
Your eyes surface above the currents of my thoughts.
I must warn you:
They are out to get you,
Alive if possible
But dead will also do.

I am damp with fear.
I wonder—
How long can you run or hide?
I wonder—how long?

She titled it "A.D. 1970, After Sterling Hall," and stuck it in a drawer.

"You don't have to take the oath," Judge Sachtjen said cordially. "You have a right to address the court in any event." Then he spoke at some length of the appeal options available to Karl. "Now, have you heard that, Karl? Do you understand what your rights are?" he said.

"Yes. If I don't make it here, I'm never going to make it," Karl answered. His voice was distant and oddly light-hearted, and he seemed on the verge of swooning.

"Karl, take your time," Sachtjen said gently. "You don't have to be nervous. You can tell the court anything that you want, anything that you desire the court to hear."

Karl had spurned his attorneys' offers to coach him, telling them that he preferred to attempt the task alone. In exile he had dreamed many times of this moment, when he would take the stand and explain why he had done what he had done. But now that the door was open, he forgot the phrases he had practiced, and all he could think about was the fact that he had killed a man.

"Well, I don't know how I found the strength to get up here," he began falteringly. "I, I thought that all the strength I ever had was used in the bombing of Army Math. And I felt that any chance of getting that strength back was destroyed when my mind was literally devastated by Mr. Fassnacht's death. And I'd have to say that the first year in exile was spent more like an invalid, trying to feel human again. Because I don't believe that Mr. Fassnacht's death can ever be justified."

Judge Sachtjen had to ask him to adjust the microphone so that he could be heard. Karl apologized in advance for rambling on, explaining that he could remember little of his life before the bombing. He had always been the engineer, leaving it to the brilliant ones to justify what he was doing, and so he began by discussing the technical aspects of the bombing, trying to explain why it was that such a large explosion had been planned, why a fuse as opposed to an electrical detonator had been chosen, how they came up with the idea of the van, and so forth. "I thought, first of all, that I could have carried, if there was some way of carrying the charge into the building, say, in a briefcase or something like that. But I had seen ... from the other bombings that had taken place that ... such a charge would be too small, that ... it would not destroy the Center."

Karl's supporters were mortified. "They should have prepared him better; he didn't rehearse," they would tell each other afterward. Again and again Karl returned to his guilt, admitting to a greater awareness of the bombing's consequences than had probably been the case. "I had had classes in those buildings, and I knew that people's research was going to be destroyed. I knew, I knew it was going to be a very destructive act." Members of the defense team cringed as he described the fatal moments before the blast, dwelling with a kind of horrified fascination on the evidence of his recklessness. "When I drove the truck up to the building I observed a car that was parked. I observed two bicycles. I observed a light on in the computer room. I observed a light on in what subsequently has been designated as Mr. Fassnacht's laboratory. Now, that blew my mind away, because, you know, it hadn't been reported to me." That was his only exculpatory remark, that an unnamed coconspirator had botched his scouting assignment. But he returned at once to his own folly. "I had a stolen vehicle filled with a ton of explosives. And there was a consideration on my part, my view of the probability of there being someone in the building. That probability was always there. It was not something I could eliminate."

After the lunch recess he told the story of his life. "We were in a constant state of terror," he said, attributing this to the threat of nuclear war. He dated his disillusionment with the United States from his arrival at the University of Wisconsin, to his discovery that science was being used "to repress the people, to maintain social control." He chronicled his conversion by the campus militants, described the influence of Dow Day and Chicago and Mifflin

Street, of the *Daily Cardinal* and the *Kaleidoscope,* of Jim Rowen's stories on Army Math. "I am a very nonviolent person," he concluded. "I don't like the use of violence. I don't feel comfortable with violence. And even when I was firebombing ROTC facilities and conducted the aerial bombing of Badger Ordnance plant, why, I felt very alienated by the violence that I was using. And all of the time I was wishing that there was some other way to stop the war."

Zaleski had been watching Sachtjen for signs of sympathy. The judge's solicitude toward the family made the prosecutor a little uneasy. If Karl were suddenly to offer a wholehearted apology— "I'm sorry for what I did; I would never do it again; it was stupid"— Sachtjen might dramatically lower the sentence, Zaleski worried. After all, who had ever heard of a second-degree murderer making a warning call?

"And I think that—I know that in my—if—in my mind ..." His voice faded out. *Uh oh, he's going to do it,* Zaleski thought, for Karl looked utterly defeated.

"If I thought there was any probability other than what I regarded as the very most remote possibility that anyone would be killed or injured, that I wouldn't have bombed the Army Mathematics Research Center; and—but I can say in good conscience, under exactly the same circumstances, in not knowing that, I would have performed ..."—he faltered again and looked at his supporters— "undertaken the same acts again to end the war."

The courtroom erupted in shouts. "Right on! Right on, Karl!"

Five, ten, fifteen.... Zaleski was counting. With every "right on" and every "yeah" from the defense table he could see Sachtjen adding years to the sentence. The wily prosecutor moved to exploit his advantage, extracting an admission from Karl on cross-examination that had no one been killed in Sterling Hall and had he not been captured, he would have continued to commit acts of sabotage. "Okay, Mr. Armstrong," he said finally, "did you send a sympathy card to the people of North Vietnam on learning of the death of Ho Chi Minh?"

"Yes, I did."

"Send one to Mrs. Fassnacht?" he snapped. He had no further questions.

"Can we have it quiet, please?" Sachtjen asked. Ruth was on the stand. Attorney Melvin Greenberg had come forward to question her.

"Are you the mother of Karl Armstrong?"

"That's correct."

"Mrs. Armstrong, is there anything which you wish to tell the court this afternoon?"

"Yes," Ruth said. "I can see that being in jail has done a lot of damage to my son. He used to have a lot of vitality. He hasn't had any exercise. His speech is very slow. He always did speak right up." She then thanked his young supporters for the candlelight march they had given Karl for his birthday two weeks earlier. "Birthdays had always been pretty special at our house.

"And Karl, we love you very much, and we always have, and we always will. You have always been a good person. And you have always loved people. You always wanted to do something for people.

"And I'm very sorry what's happened. I'm very sorry for the Fassnacht family.

"Karl, I said, has always been fond of people. Our grandchildren have always loved him. He enjoyed being with the grandchildren.

"And I guess one of the things that's been the worst for Karl is that he was very conscientious. Before he started at the university he worked at Gardner Bakery, and he saved every check so he could go to school. Never spent a cent of them.

"He's against the war in Vietnam and hated all the violence going on.

"And I can tell you that there never would have been any bombing out here at the university if people my age would have got up and done something besides letting our children do it for us. There would never have been a bombing out here.

"I guess that's all I have to say," Ruth said. She was crying.

"All right, Ruth. You step down," Sachtjen said. Ruth's few, simple remarks had moved him, and he was irritated at himself. He pointed at a longhair who was applauding. "All right, bailiff, that man in front there. Remove him. In the overalls. Get up and get out. I have told you you couldn't clap." It was the first real emotion Sachtjen had shown in two weeks. "Anybody else who claps after my admonition will be removed," he sternly added. "If you can't behave, you can't stay here."

Judgment day arrived one week later, on November 1. Several dozen supporters had camped on the steps of the courthouse all night, entertained by the San Francisco Mime Troupe. At around 6:00 A.M. a line began to form, and late-arriving reporters, including a CBS crew from New York City, competed for the limited number of press passes. "How can these people support a murderer?" one correspondent asked disbelievingly. Also in evidence were twice the usual number of uniformed police. Inside, Leonard Weinglass joined Greenberg and Kunstler at the defense table. "I think the court should note that the judge in Chicago granted a continuance today so both Mr. Kunstler and Mr. Weinglass could come down here for these proceedings," Greenberg noted. Karl was brought in, and as he had throughout the hearings, Kunstler warmly embraced him. *The kiss of death,* Zaleski thought, watching from the prosecution table.

Zaleski led off for the state, itemizing, in a rising staccato, the damages to property and people, the loss of irreplaceable research, the shattered lives. "As a result of the August 24, 1970, explosion at Sterling Hall, 26 buildings—excluding private property—were damaged. They totaled $1,369,000.

"In addition to that, there was $62,500 damage done to T-16, the Primate Lab and the Red Gym. There was total structural damage of $1,422,800.

"In addition to that, the total damage to the contents of these public buildings was $1,173,000. For a grand total of $2,596,000 [about $9 million in current dollars].

"And like I said, this is just University of Wisconsin property."

He next moved on to the human casualties. "There wasn't just one occupant of Sterling Hall, there were six. The first two, a couple of gentlemen named William Evans and Roger Whitmer, were knocked about, received cuts and bruises. The third individual was Paul Quin. He received head cuts, bruises, and was knocked unconscious. The fourth person was David Schuster. He received abrasions and a broken shoulder. The fifth person was the night watchman, Norbert Sutter. This guy's going to be disabled for the rest of his life. He has memory impairment, disc problems, partial loss of hearing and vision. He has a loss of feeling in the left side of his face and scalp. He will walk with a limp for the rest of his life.

"Then there was Dr. Fassnacht. Dr. Fassnacht was 33 years old. He was doing postdoctoral work. By all descriptions he was a brilliant young physicist. He died of internal injuries due to this explosion. His wife is now living abroad because she just can't face it around here.

"The nuclear physics department was so heavily damaged that they couldn't bring in any grad students for a year. Two nuclear physics professors dropped out of the field."

Zaleski dismissed the notion that Fassnacht had been working on something to aid the war effort. "He was working with Professor Dillinger on a problem involving electrical superconductors at temperatures near absolute zero. To carry out this work three specialized systems had to be developed and built. This took a mere 23 years to do. They had refined a number of isotopes which were unmatched in purity anywhere in the world. And all those were destroyed and are irreplaceable." He described the potential benefits of superconductivity to mankind. "Because of this bombing this work had been stymied and set back to a point that it's going to take years to make up the difference."

Zaleski reserved his sharpest barbs for the defense and its strategy of putting the war on trial. Has anyone been produced who could tell us about Karl as a person? No. Instead, these people use this as a forum. They have never heard of Karl. They bring in a guy like Dr. Lifton, a renowned psychiatrist, who testifies for Karl rather than about Karl. And that is the real tragedy of these hearings. We don't understand Mr. Armstrong. We don't know what drove him to these acts at all.

"The only source we have is Armstrong himself," Zaleski went on, "and I think his demeanor was horrible. He was so offended when someone yawned during his testimony, he called the court's attention to it. Because we should be etching every word Mr. Armstrong says in slate for future generations. Well, there are a couple of words I would like to etch in slate and show to this court. Words like, 'I am not repentant. I'd do it again.' This is the rehabilitated man that we're supposed to give a break to?"

Zaleski asked for the maximum under the plea.

Mel Greenberg opened for the defense with a meticulous review of the testimony, accentuating the words of the one witness he had who knew firsthand of Karl's political involvement. "The conversation with Phil Ball was important because Phil, remember, was on a Navy gunboat in Vietnam. And he was a witness to that gunship firing on civilians. And when Karl and Phil were talking about responsibility, Phil said, 'You know, I should have done something to stop the ship, to obstruct that. And, if I had to do it over again, I would have.'"

The last act belonged to William Kunstler, the courtroom voice of the New Left, defender of the Catonsville Nine, the Harrisburg Eight, the Gainesville Eight, the Chicago Eight, and many others who had been prosecuted for acts of opposition to the war. He was a big man with a loud, suburban New York voice and a taste for doggerel, which he would write during tedious court sessions to stay relaxed. His daughter attended the University of Wisconsin, and he had been to Madison many times both on business and for pleasure. His movements about the city were closely watched, his public utterances duly noted in FBI memos to Washington. Sometimes the surveillance worked to his advantage. At Francis Court, where he stayed overnight during the hearing in the apartment once inhabited by Mark Knops, an unwitting drunk trying to siphon gas from his car had found himself set upon by a platoon of spooks and whisked away.

Kunstler was brilliant, but his notoriety did not always help his clients, especially in small-town settings. But Kunstler had been watching Sachtjen, and knew that he was a man of some sophistication. He gave one of the most impassioned summations of his career, stressing the fact that it was children who had led the opposition to the war in Vietnam, children of the sixties—idealistic, filled with hope for a better world. And those children had been rewarded for their trouble by being first ignored and then beaten, gassed, fined, jailed, and spied upon. Now two-thirds of the population, according to the latest Gallup poll, agreed that the young had been right all along, that the war was immoral. Kunstler quoted Thomas Jefferson on slavery: "I tremble for my country when I consider that God is just." "Judge, you have to tremble for your country today. Because what you do here will really answer the question of Dr. Fassnacht's death. You have to give him a memorial, and that memorial is not the years of Karl Armstrong's life.

"I don't want to be a good American anymore, Judge. I don't want to be the equivalent of those who stood outside the neatly furnished homes and pleasant gardens of Dachau. Judge, you knew; and I knew. And we are cowards.

"As Ruth Armstrong said, 'I only wish that people my age had spoken out earlier.' Karl's father Donald said, 'I guess I was something of a hypocrite.' And then in talking about the march in which he saw his son, he said, 'I would have joined the march, but I didn't see any people my age there.'

"Judge, you weren't there, and I wasn't there. Just the young people."

Citing other judges who had ruled for the defense in controversial cases, he ended his argument with a desperate shout, "Judge, bring us home. Stop the process here. For God's sake!"

Judge Jackman had urged Sachtjen not to let Kunstler appear. The peripatetic lawyer didn't have a Wisconsin license, and the court was under no obligation to listen to him. Sachtjen had refused, arguing that he didn't wish to make an issue of Kunstler's presence. Sachtjen was impressed by Kunstler's remarks, but they did not change his mind, nor had the testimony of the star witnesses. In their closing arguments, the prosecutors had succeeded in deflating the analogy with Nazi Germany on which the defense arguments were based. American democracy might not be perfect, Zaleski and Haag had stressed, but the Bill of Rights was still in effect; the Constitution had been abused but not suspended; and eventually public opinion nationwide had forced an end to U.S. involvement in Vietnam. In the middle of the Armstrong hearing the Madison City Council had asked Congress to press impeachment charges against President Nixon for attempting to cover up the Watergate break-in. None of that would have been possible under totalitarian rule, Judge Sachtjen was persuaded, and thus Nuremberg did not apply.

Nonetheless, the raw emotion of Kunstler's final appeal had shaken him. He paused. *No, they saw the lights, they knew people were in the building, he killed a guy,* he told himself. Then he said, "Mr. Kunstler, I commend you on your ..." The words caught in his throat and he straightened up. "After careful consideration," he went on, reading from a prepared statement, "I sentence you, Karl Armstrong, to 23 years in Waupun State Prison." It was the maximum, less the time that Karl had already spent in jail.

Before the spectators could react Sachtjen was gone from the room, and a phalanx of Paul Bunyan-sized deputies had ushered Karl out. The stunned prisoner managed only a perfunctory salute as he disappeared from sight. The shock was broken by a lone voice crying from the back of the courtroom, "Long live the revolution!"

On his way out Don Armstrong punched a photographer who tried to take his picture and sent the man sprawling. Ruth charged Detective Lulling, shouting "You call that justice?" A powerfully built MPD officer named George Schiro ushered him out of her way.

A few days later Bill Sachtjen ran into Ruth in Kohl's Supermarket on the East Side. She was a good and loyal mother, he thought. She probably didn't appreciate how he had exerted himself not to let his feelings for her affect his judgment. The problem, as he saw it, was that the defense had given him practically nothing on which to base a sentence reduction, not even an apology. "Ruth, it didn't have to be this way," he started to say. But she raised her chin and turned away.

Karl was taken to Waupun State Prison, a high-walled, no-nonsense facility in central Wisconsin. It was at about the time the security doors clanged shut behind him that the reality of his sentence began to sink in. The Vietnam veteran who had said he would be proud to serve next to him in prison wasn't there. Anthony Russo, who had contemplated blowing up the RAND Corporation's computer room, had returned to Los Angeles a free man. Senator Gruening, who had said that *any* means of resistance to the war was justified, had gone back to Washington to finish his autobiography. Father Berrigan, who had said that Christ prefers zealots, was off to new missions. William Kunstler, who had called the hearing "unique and historic," would go on to his next high-profile case. His supporters had testified boldly and sincerely, but now he was alone, Karl realized; no revolutionary brotherhood could save him. As guards ushered him into the blue twilight of a cell block that seemed to go on forever, his ears began to ring, the barred cages spun around him, and he fell unconscious to the floor.

In the week following the decision Madison was hit by random window smashing, bomb threats, and the burning of police cars as Karl's supporters expressed their frustration. "A warm flame still flickers in the heart of many," *Takeover* observed hopefully. But the isthmus soon quieted down. Finally, it was over.

33

Last Rites

To condemn Karl Armstrong is to condemn an entire anguished generation.

—GABRIEL KOLKO,
historian, for the defense

I think it is unfair for the antiwar movement as a whole to bear the stigma of Mr. Armstrong and his heinous acts.

—MICHAEL ZALESKI,
Wisconsin Assistant Attorney General, for the prosecution

Mira and Lorene were driving to Toronto to visit Karl in the summer of 1972 when the subject of abuse in the Armstrong family first came up. It was Mira who initiated the conversation, very hesitantly describing the assaults that had begun when she was about eleven and that had continued until she was in high school. She had never said anything to Ruth, in part because Don had threatened her and in part because she felt so ashamed. Tearfully, Lorene confessed that she too had been victimized after Mira moved out.

Suddenly, much that had been unexplained in the lives of the

Armstrong sisters began to make sense; for example, the time Mira, ironing a dress in the basement, had fainted when Don started down the stairs. Likewise, the scratches that often appeared on Don's face while Lorene was in high school, and the permanent bruise on Lorene's tailbone, which she had passed off as the result of a fall. In fact, Lorene now confided, he had kicked her there .

The beatings, which had started when they were very young, were no secret among the children. Don didn't say "spare the rod and spoil the child," but he certainly lived by that slogan. The incidents almost always took place at night when Don was tired and Ruth was out of the house working her own shift. Usually some childish misbehavior would start Don off; then the children's pants would come down and the belt would come out. Don used the buckle end, or sometimes a knotted rope. His anger seemed to feed on itself, so that the more they screamed the harder he hit them. "Go ahead, kill me!" Mira would cry, but it never did any good. If Ruth happened to be home and tried to intervene, it only made matters worse, as Don seemed to enjoy punishing the children in front of her.

At a very early age Dwight had developed a knack for avoiding Don; from Lorene's perspective, it was she and Karl who took the brunt of his anger. Once Don threw a hairbrush at her and split her skull. Karl amazed her with the way he would take Don's punishment, both physical and verbal, without ever defending himself, just soaking it up like a sponge. Years later Don himself remarked on it in an interview with one of the underground newspapers. "Karl always was the one who could take a lot of abuse," he said. Of course, the reporter had no idea what he was talking about.

As a mother, Lorene worried that she might lapse into the same pattern of abuse in disciplining her oldest son, Willie. As a precaution, in 1973 she started a Bible study group in McHenry, and after studying the relevant passages, she and many of her friends learned to speak in tongues. When she returned to Madison for Karl's sentencing, she and Mira would pray together for a favorable result, both of them using the gift. Neither of them were asked to testify for the defense, however, and Mira, at her husband's request, did not even attend the hearings. Thus the disturbing reality of Armstrong family life had no chance to be aired.

It was not until Easter Sunday of 1975 that Mira and Lorene got up the nerve to confront their parents about it. By then Don and Ruth were living in a little house in Windsor, north of Madison. Don was very ill with lung cancer. Heavy doses of radiation had arrested the disease but had also destroyed the mylantum in his spine, with the result that he had lost feeling in his legs and, like his grandmother Ann Rector Armstrong, was obliged to walk with a cane. Even in his decrepitude, however, his daughters were still terrified of him and were counting on their husbands to protect them.

They cornered him in the kitchen after dinner, and in Ruth's hearing blurted out the whole awful story. Don reacted angrily, raising his cane to strike Lorene. Where was her protection? she wondered. Bill Bakken and her husband Tim Farr were sitting in the living room acting as though nothing was happening. Ruth, standing at the sink rinsing dishes, likewise seemed unaware of the confrontation happening right beside her.

Mira and Lorene cowered under the threatening cane, but Don didn't bring it down on them. Instead he bolted into the bathroom and locked the door. "I'll kill myself," he shouted. He got a bottle of pills out of the medicine cabinet and rattled them to prove he meant it.

"No, Dad, please don't! Daddy, I forgive you!" Mira cried, banging on the door. Lorene was sobbing. All they had wanted was to clear the air and to reconcile with him.

Don burst out of the bathroom and hurtled crablike across the living room. "That's it, I must be crazy!" he yelled on his way out the front door. He drove away and that ended the conversation for several years.

In January 1976, the FBI caught David Fine in San Rafael, California, where he had been living for about a year. No one claimed a reward, and the bureau did not reveal the source of its tip. Acquaintances suspected that David had made himself so unwelcome in the underground with his requests for money that someone in his far-flung support network had turned him in just to get rid of him.

George Baxtrum flew to San Francisco with Mark Baganz, formerly Duroc, to identify him, since the prisoner did not at first admit who he was. Baganz, who had long since abandoned undercover work, had quit the MPD after wounding an armed robber in the course of his duties, but he was glad to do a favor for an agency that had helped pay his way through college. After a night in jail, however, David obviated the need for Baganz's services when a guard asked him how he was and he said, "I'm Fine. David Fine."

By and large David had enjoyed his life of anonymity. Cut off from family, he had felt more free, in a way, than he ever had before. He didn't have to be the superachiever his parents had always expected him to be. As a fugitive he was relieved of political obligations to the movement, and so he could indulge his taste for spectator sports and music, with evenings at the Forum and the Roxy. In San Rafael he had met an attractive and rather simple girl from Petaluma with whom he thought he might even fall in love. Of course she knew nothing of Madison, nor could he ever hope to explain to her what had happened there. But he had become so used to not mentioning his involvement in the Army Math bombing that it was almost as though it had never occurred.

Returned to Madison for trial, he was released on reduced bail of $50,000 after Jim Rowen, still working in the mayor's office, offered to put him up in his own home. Harvey Goldberg invited him to speak to his class and drafted a fund-raising letter that brought in so much money that David was able to hire Jim Shellow, the top criminal defense lawyer in the state. Shellow got him off with seven years in exchange for a plea of guilty to murder in the third degree.

Dwight was apprehended the following spring in a Toronto cafe. He had slipped into San Francisco two years earlier and had lived in Polk Gulch for a while with a couple of hippie girlfriends, selling trinkets on Fisherman's Wharf and celebrating the fall of Saigon with thousands of Bay Area progressives. He had even been arrested for shoplifting in San Diego, but the police had let him go. He was so tired of living underground that he had in effect given up hiding. Prosecutors refused to go below second degree with Dwight but offered him the same sentence that David had received in exchange for waiving his right to an extradition hearing. Dwight quickly agreed, and in view of the light sentences for David and Dwight, the FBI removed Leo Burt from its Most Wanted list.

David's supporters had revived the old theory of the government's foreknowledge and had even brought in Sandra Sutherland, a left-wing private eye from Oakland, California, to try to prove it. Sutherland was good at her work, but her efforts were of no help to Fine. Several years later a dogged member of the defense committee, David Newman, incorporated some of her findings into an article in the investigative monthly *Mother Jones*. (The magazine had nothing to do with the former Madison group of that name.) Newman documented that both Pete Bobo and Sandy Nelson had had their records cleared in recognition of "services rendered to the Madison police department," but Newman had no evidence that such services had been rendered before the Army Math bombing. Bobo and Nelson denied any involvement with the police before the Sterling Hall blast, though they admitted having worked subsequently for both George Croal and the FBI.

Newman also trotted out Paul Soglin's old claim about the MPD following the van into town on East Johnson. The originator of the story was a janitor named Donald Wheeler, who was interviewed by FBI agents Robert Stauffer and Robert Dean on September 9, 1970. Wheeler had given the following account:

He stated that on August 24, 1970, he got up at approximately 1:00 A.M. and ate breakfast. Inasmuch as he was sick, he made several trips to the bathroom and his normal departure time for work was therefore delayed. He did depart from his residence at approximately 2:00 A.M. on that date, driving his 1970 Pontiac GTO. He stated that as he was approximately one-half mile past Commercial Avenue on Packers Avenue, he observed a light-colored automobile with two round tail lights on each side of the rear of the vehicle. This vehicle was in the left lane as he approached it and was parallel to a late model van-type truck. Both the van and the automobile were traveling at approximately 10 to 20 miles per hour, side by side for a distance of about two blocks. As the vehicles approached the railroad tracks near the County Garage on East Johnson Street, the automobile passed the van and cut in front and was then directly in front of the van. At this point WHEELER passed the van and as he was going over the railroad tracks, the driver of the van made a sudden swerve to the left and almost collided with the front of WHEELER'S automobile.

WHEELER described the van as light in color and being a late model. He commented that there were windows on both sides of the van but he could not see through the side windows as something dark was blocking his view. He could, however, look through the front side windows of the van and observed the driver, who was a white male, under 30, and appeared to have hair which was high on his head and somewhat bushy.

The story was consistent with known facts except for one detail: Karl had not come in on East Johnson, but on University Avenue, his customary route. Apparently the Wheeler story had circulated unchallenged in police circles, picking up embellishments along the way, until Alderman Soglin overheard the plausible but untrue version at a party.

Karl Armstrong understood the appeal of the foreknowledge theory to his old friends in the movement; they wanted to be relieved of the burden of Fassnacht. And there were enough unexplained spooks flitting at the edges of the story—the car at the Primate Lab, the spy in the Alumni Center, Snakey Mathieson, the Man in Black—to keep the mystery alive. Had he been only a pawn in a game he did not understand? Karl didn't know, but in the end it was not all that important to him. He had done the bombing himself; no one had put him up to it. He had thought that he was acting out the "consensus of the community." He did not believe that Leo was an agent. Army Math was his doing. Whether or not the government knew something, he was the one who had to bear the responsibility.

Naomi Wall, the former TADP leader, married Karl to improve his chances of a sentence reduction. Karl was in solitary at the time as a result of his involvement in a protest for better conditions for inmates and was restrained by leg irons during the exchange of vows. As a favor to Ruth, Judge Sachtjen left it to another circuit court judge to rule on the matter, and nine years were knocked off Karl's sentence.

Karl's federal sentence, set by the liberal Judge James Doyle, was only ten years, running concurrently, so he was soon up for parole. Responding to a tearful in-person appeal from Ruth, the Madison City Council endorsed his early release, as did the *Capital Times*. Congressman Robert Kastenmeier, citing the shift in national mood, pushed for approval from the U.S. Parole Board, and on January 31, 1980, the former Vanguard of the Revolution walked free. David Fine, who had become the tennis champion of his low-security federal pen, was already out of jail, and Dwight soon would be as well.

Except for an enclave of aging hippies and activists on the near East Side, the Madison Karl returned to had, like the country as a

whole, left the sixties behind, plunging into a new era of material-
ism and the pursuit of self-interest. Jim Rowen, shipwrecked politically by his support for a newspaper strike, had been denied the
office vacated by Paul Soglin in 1979. The University of Wisconsin,
now merged with the Milwaukee, Green Bay, and Racine branches,
had become a quieter, more conventional place, much like any
other Big Ten campus. Fraternity houses no longer had to take in
boarders to meet expenses, football games at Camp Randall Stadium were once again de rigueur, coeds wore bras and skirts that
went all the way below the knee. The underground newspapers
were gone, the unreconstructed *Daily Cardinal* a slender curiosity
with no more influence than *The Watchtower*. The Mifflin Street
Block Party had become a harmless annual event, complete with
souvenir booths and commemorative T-shirts. Marshall Shapiro
had long since turned the Nitty Gritty into a fern bar, etched glass
and brass replacing the Chicago blues. The New York–Madison
connection had withered, as had attendance at Harvey Goldberg's
lectures. "How can you still believe in socialism?" his longtime
friend and rival Professor Mosse asked him on the Union Terrace
one afternoon. "The earth is young," Goldberg replied.

Karl and Naomi had agreed to get divorced when he was
released, but genuine affection had developed between them and
instead they rented a small house on Spaight Street and moved in
together. Dwight, after spending several months in a halfway house,
came to stay with them at the end of the summer, sharing a room
with Naomi's son David. Dwight sensed at once that Karl and
Naomi were under a strain. Naomi missed her friends and causes;
her daughter Elizabeth, now eight years old, missed her father, an
American deserter who still lived in Toronto. In prison Karl had
spent much of his free time designing windmills that he thought
would solve the energy problems of the Third World, but he did not
know how to market his ideas now that he was free. Bobby Golden,
a cofounder of the Mifflin Street Co-op, gave him a job in his thriving produce business, and after a day of breaking down pallets and
delivering groceries he was often too tired to talk.

Naomi could understand Karl's taciturnity, but she could never
accustom herself to Donald's chauvinism. Even bedridden, missing
one lung and a third of the other, he remained a tyrant. Naomi
admired Mira, but found her evangelism wearing. Ruth was a saint,
but for Naomi a somewhat distant one. As for Dwight, Naomi had

never liked him. The Armstrongs had an enviable closeness, but she was beginning to wonder whether she could ever really be part of the family.

A documentary about Madison in the sixties, *The War at Home,* which had begun as a project of the Karl Armstrong Defense Committee, had been nominated for an Academy Award, and at the invitation of its producer, Glen Silber, Karl flew to Los Angeles in March to attend the event. With Silber and the film's editors, Barry Brown and Chuck France, he arrived in a limousine and paraded past the grandstand in his rented tux. There was a lot of screaming, and when they got into the lobby, he discovered that Tom Hayden and Jane Fonda were right behind them. Silber introduced them. "Yeah, sure, I testified for you in Toronto," Hayden recalled. Fonda made him promise to call her office about film rights to his story.

Karl was amazed by how small Jane Fonda was. He phoned her office as soon as he got back to Madison, but he was unable to get through to her or to anyone in authority. He did not call back. *The War at Home* did not win an Oscar.

Lung cancer had devastated Donald. He was skin and bones, in constant pain, addicted to morphine. Ruth supported him, fed him, cleaned him. "How do you do it?" Karl asked her after trying to fill in for a weekend. "I'm just used to it," Ruth said. Karl strongly supported her when she decided it was time to put Don in a nursing home. "I won't go, I'll die!" Don protested when, in the summer of 1980, she finally moved him out. To punish her he started smoking again.

Don reconciled with both Karl and Dwight before the summer was over. "It's my fault," he told them with regard to the bombing. "You did it because of the way I brought you up." Karl accepted his apology. "It's almost as if it were his bombing," he commented at the time. "He knows that I extracted my ideals—that decision— fom his life." With Mira and Lorene it was not so easy. Ruth never mentioned the Easter Sunday episode except to sigh sometimes and say, "I wish Donald hadn't been so hard on the girls." The whole matter had been swept back under the rug, but Don remained suspicious of Mira. "You've come to torment me!" he shouted, wagging his finger at her when she dropped in to see him in his new quarters. Mira ran back to her car, crying "I hate him! I hate him!"

Eventually Don learned to put up with the girls' visits, even to tolerate their Jesus talk. He opened up to them, went over his entire life, going back to when he was five and living in Tunnel City. He could still remember Ann Rector Armstrong complaining to friends in his presence about what a burden he was. Donald was God's punishment of her for having raised a gangster like Alvah, she told everyone in town. And then there were the beatings. Ann Rector was crippled by arthritis, but she could still deliver a smarting blow with her cane. It was for his own good, she had told him. If she didn't beat the devil out of him, he would end up like Alvah.

His daughters saw him in a new light now. When he punished them, he had always said it was for their own good, just as Ann Rector had said to him. And when he had raised his cane to beat them that Easter Sunday of 1975, he had only been acting out a role for which he had been programmed years ago.

October 15 was Karl's thirty-fourth birthday, and Naomi threw a party for him, inviting relatives and a few of his longtime supporters. Acting on a presentiment, Mira skipped the party to be with Donald. Reverend Sam Hunt, the former pastor of the East Madison Baptist Church, met her at the nursing home. Hunt was fifty-one, a native Oklahoman who had preserved his sweet country accent even after twenty years in Madison. Mira had met him through an interdenominational charismatic group called Women Aglow, of which he was an adviser. Hunt had acquired the gift of tongues himself, and his belief in it had, over the past year, cost him both his job and his marriage. "There is no war like a holy war," he liked to say.

Donald was in a morphine-induced trance when they arrived. Hunt and Mira prayed together for him to regain his lucidity, considering it no use trying to save him unless he was in possession of his faculties. At Mira's urging, Hunt anointed him with sanctified oil. Don woke up.

"Mike?" he said softly, using her old nickname, his voice like a rustle of dry leaves. He signaled her to come closer. "Mike, everything I've ever feared has happened," he rasped. She took his hand. It was cold, the skin dry.

"Donald, do you want to receive Jesus as your Savior?" Pastor Hunt asked.

"Yes sir!" he said. Don raised a hand heavenward, and to Mira it seemed that he was placing his hand in God's. She ran to the

kitchen and borrowed cranberry juice and crackers for communion. When she returned, Hunt took her aside.

"Mira, you've been hanging on to him. You are the one who is keeping him alive. You have to let go."

They knelt at the bedside and prayed that all cords be cut. Mira felt the room whirling around her and was afraid for a moment that she was going to pass out, but suddenly Donald went to sleep. To Mira, he looked like a baby, the stress gone from his face. Pastor Hunt helped her to her feet.

"Good-bye, Dad," she said softly.

Two hours later the call came that he was gone. Mira was over-joyed. Donald had been such a heavy, melancholic spirit; he had lived his life in a prison worse than Karl's, she knew. Now he was free, and she was sure that she would see him again one day.

Ruth called Karl with the news. "He waited until you got out of prison," she added pointedly. For Donald, that was love.

Ruth's father, Alvah Kennedy, came down from Tarr Valley for the funeral. Paul Armstrong bestirred himself from his South Min-neapolis haunts to attend also. Mira caught her breath when she saw him, he looked so much like Donald. The memorial service was held at Ryan's Funeral Home on Sherman Avenue, in the heart of the old East Side, and reflected Mira's influence. One of her confi-dantes, a charismatic like herself, sang a song composed for the occasion, "words courtesy of the Lord," as she explained it. The family's longtime friend and spiritual adviser, Pastor Kenneth Hoff-man, presented a reading. Sam Hunt gave the eulogy.

The family was separated in the usual way from the main body of mourners, and Hunt was struck by the way the audience was divided. On one side were Mira's friends, charismatics, carefully groomed, aglow with the love of God. On the other were associates of the Armstrong brothers, less optimistic-looking, battered veterans of a failed revolution. The remarkable thing was that they were all the same age. They had come through the sixties on separate and yet oddly parallel paths, both groups seeking some kind of renewal, some greater meaning in life. Freaks and Jesus Freaks—were they really so different? Hunt told them of Donald's deathbed conver-sion and expressed the hope that they would all allow the Lord to come into their lives. He concluded with an anonymous verse of a sort to give comfort to the family:

Child of My love, fear not the unknown morrow
Dread not the new demand life makes of thee.
Thy ignorance doth hold no cause for sorrow,
Since what thou knowest not is known to me.

At this point, Dwight fled to the parking lot, where he sat on the bumper of Paul's van and cried. He could not believe in God because no decent Supreme Being would have created a world of such great imperfections as this. He lit a cigarette.

Paul came around the corner of the van, a little choked up himself. They both smoked for a while in silence. Finally Dwight asked about the Franklin Avenue scene, about the price of pot; and what had become of the old Cadillac hearse. They were still talking when the service ended, and everyone left for the reception at Lakeview American Lutheran Church.

Karl had detested the service. It was just the sort of evangelicalism that Don always hated, and it had featured nothing personal, nothing really about Donald Armstrong. But Mira was ecstatic over what she considered to have been the "miracle" of Don's last hours. Don had never actually apologized, but she believed that God had seen through his hard exterior to his tender heart and had forgiven him. *"God, You are so good!"* she thought.

At his own request Donald Armstrong's remains were cremated. His ashes were taken to the Tunnel City cemetery along with a small, featureless stone marker to be placed next to the grave of Don's firstborn, Lorena. Dwight could not attend, and so the interment party consisted only of Ruth, Mira, Karl, Lorene, Paul, Alvah Kennedy, and Reverend Hunt. It was a cold, clear day, and a blustery wind herded fallen leaves among the tombs. The graveyard population had grown considerably since the winter day in 1940 when Don and Ruth had buried their infant daughter. There were new headstones bedecked with ribbons and medallions commemorating service in more recent conflicts: World War II, Korea, Vietnam. No generation had escaped. But that day, at least, the guns of nearby Camp McCoy were quiet.

Karl placed the marker in the ground, and they formed a shivering circle around it. Hunt read from 1st Corinthians, Chapter 15, verses 50 to 58, those phrases—"Oh death, where is thy sting?"—that offer the fundamental bargain of religion, that the consciousness of the faithful, the powers of thought and cherished memories, will not perish with the body but will live forever.

The ashes were contained in a disposable blue plastic urn. The plan was for Hunt to toss them in the air and let the wind scatter them, but it did not go as expected. The bones had not been properly ground, and fragments flew out and tumbled across the grounds. Hunt did not know what to do; he had never done a scattering before. They were all too embarrassed to comment, so they acted as though nothing had happened and went home.

In the spring, as soon as the snowcover melted, Karl and Mira returned to Tunnel City equipped with gardening tools. By then Naomi had left Karl and returned to Toronto, and he was accompanied by a new friend, Fran, an aging flower child with straight blond hair and sky-blue eyes, whose father was an air force officer.

It was a fine day. Don's bones lay where they had fallen, protected through the long winter by a heavy snowpack. Fran was disgusted by the sight. "How could you leave him that way?" she asked. They did not have a headstone for Don, so Karl just dug a hole next to Lorena's grave while Mira carefully raked the fragments together. They did not have anything to put the bones in, so they used their hands to scoop them into the hole. Karl filled it in with dirt and packed it hard.

Fran walked back to the car, anxious to get going, and Karl followed. Mira went walking under the trees, carrying her paperback bible. According to family records, Ann Rector was buried somewhere in the cemetery, but Mira could not find her headstone. At Grandma Tessie's tomb she paused, reflecting on the tragedies that had befallen her family. In years to come she would find a kind of rueful solace in the words of Exodus 20, Chapter V:

> ... For I the Lord thy God am a jealous God, visiting the iniquity of the fathers upon the children unto the third and fourth generation of them that hate me....

"It can end," Mira vowed. "It is going to stop with my generation. I will be a Christian and teach my children about God."

At the height of the Cambodia/Kent State upheaval, a group of *Daily Cardinal* editors and reporters covering the riots had found themselves in front of Chadbourne Hall, a dormitory at the corner of University and Park, where they spotted a parked motorcycle and, nearby, a soda machine with a box of empties beside it. "Let's get Rennie's," one of them suggested, referring to the Rennebohm's Pharmacy across the street. They filled a bottle with gasoline siphoned from the motorcycle's tank, tore a handkercheif in half for a wick, and started toward the building. At the last moment, they spotted a policeman on the roof, spun about, and buried the Molotov cocktail in a vacant lot across from Sellery Hall, where presumably it still lies. They did not have the nerve to do what Karl Armstrong had done at the Primate Lab, to go ahead and throw a bomb even when he knew, or believed, that he was being watched.

Karl had something that the young middle-class members of his fan club lacked. For example, as some of his followers suggested at his mitigation hearing, he had the courage of his convictions. But anything else that may have been buried in Karl's psyche was not brought up for discussion. The defense team, preoccupied as it was by ideological concerns, did not pursue a psychological profile of its client. The Wisconsin press, though it voted Sterling Hall the "story of the decade," never inquired into Armstrong family history. Nor were the Armstrong sisters anxious to go public with revelations of family dysfunction; like many abused children, they continued to love and protect the memory of the abusive parent.

Karl himself was the chief protector. At Waupun State Prison, he refused to participate in group therapy. The resident psychiatrist, Dr. Richard Arnesen, considered him one of the "best-defended" individuals he had ever encountered and later estimated that at least fifty hours of one-on-one therapy would be needed to get to the bottom of his problems. In his mitigation testimony, however, Karl had let drop a couple of clues, vividly recalling the clubs of Dow Day and Chicago and how, from the day he was beaten in front of the Chicago Hilton, he was just biding his time. Describing the bombings, he spoke of how detached he felt from his violent acts, as though it were not he, Karl, who was doing them, but someone else. Who was that other Karl whose sudden black angry looks would sometimes frighten Mira and alarm his friend Scott Nelson? Perhaps it really wasn't the gentle Karl most people knew who stalked Sterling Hall in the summer of 1970, but another Armstrong, Karl's great-grandmother Ann Rector, her anger transmitted through three generations of domestic violence, raising her cane in righteous fury and bringing it down with a mighty thud.

Whatever demons may have possessed Karl at the time, his actions cannot be explained by them alone. The sleepwalker had to be awakened, his repressed anger summoned forth and given sanction. That summons came from a peace movement frustrated by the failure of nonviolent protest to end a devastating and misguided war. The rationale was provided by naive converts to the Marxist doctrine of class war, idealistic students driven to cynical despair by the brutal actions of fearful and confused authorities. In his testimony, Karl acknowledged his intellectual debt when he referred to the "historical necessity of . . ." The phrase stuck in his throat, but no one among his defenders, least of all Harvey Goldberg, could ·have doubted what he was going to say. Karl really had taken them at their word, and the word was violence.

The proponents of violence, whether of the right or left, whether in the White House or in the editorial offices of the *Daily Cardinal*, were always few in number but clever in their invocation of realism. In reality, however, violence was counterproductive wherever it was employed as an instrument of policy. Though based on the most advanced mathematical formulas, the mayhem of the Electrical Battlefield only succeeded in driving the conservative Vietnamese peasantry into the Communist camp. On the home front, the use of blunt force against student protesters drove them straight into the arms of the Marxists, undermining the efforts of liberal intellectuals like George Mosse to keep things in perspective. The resort to violent and confrontational tactics by young people in the grip of millenarian fevers scared away supporters in the adult community, brought the dismissal of sympathetic and visionary administrators such as Fred Harvey Harrington, caused progressive educational programs for minorities and urban areas to be shelved, and precipitated a withdrawal of taxpayer and alumni support from which public universities in the United States have yet to fully recover. Least realistic of all was it to batter an already battered child named Karl Armstrong.

Shortly after he reburied his father Karl received a letter from the author James Michener. It was postmarked St. Michaels, Maryland, May 12, 1981. As Michener had authored a book (nonfiction) on Kent State, Karl had written to him asking his opinion about the Army Math bombing and its impact. At the time of the Wisconsin blast, Michener replied, he was in Kent, Ohio, researching the book on the May shooting incident. He was struck by the cessation of bombings, the new restraint shown by the police, and especially by the changed attitudes of the young following the Wisconsin event.

> What I had foreseen did occur: Americans did, *en masse,* back off from the great confrontation. The bombings and the excesses on both sides did diminish. In the years that followed, I often commented on this when people tried to make Kent State the watershed. It prepared the way, but the revulsion following the Wisconsin incident was the true watershed, at least from my point of view—and I was studying nothing else.

Karl was not sure how to interpret the letter. He put it in his box of memorabilia, along with his old scouting badges and his clips from the *Kaleidoscope* and the *Daily Cardinal,* and went back to work. With the help of a few friends, he bought a vending business called "Loose Juice" and began selling smoothies from a sort of gypsy wagon on lower State Street, next to the Library Mall. He found an apartment on Francis Court, the one formerly occupied by *Kaleidoscope* editor Mark Knops. According to his roommate Phil Ball, the former tenant union activist, he still sometimes walked in his sleep and suffered night terrors in which he threw chairs at a tall, menacing figure in the corner of his bedroom. But in time he was accepted back into his community.

Most of those who had been involved in the movement found similarly peaceful ways to work within the system. Like Paul Soglin and Tom Hayden, they learned how to get elected, how to lobby, how to use the legal system to obtain their ends. They founded New Age magazines and newspapers and film production companies, environmental law firms, social investment houses, community banks, organic food co-ops, health maintenance organizations, recycling companies, windmill farms, alternative schools, and restaurants featuring a more inventive and healthful American cuisine. They showed the business world that employee ownership could work, formed advocacy groups for the poor, for women, minorities, homosexuals, political prisoners, tropical rain forests, whales, baby seals, and the elusive spotted owl. On public policy boards and commissions they pressed for clean air and water, energy conservation, urban growth limits, the preservation of natural areas, the development of bike paths, improved social services and mass transit, and equal opportunity for all. Even within the limits of a national agenda set by conservatives (the Reagan Administration numbered many of those Young Americans for Freedom once dismissed by militants as "fascists"), their influence on American life was immense and ever increasing.

The bombing had not killed the movement but only changed it, cured it of that romantic revolutionism that went back through Marx and Lenin and Babeuf and Buonarroti to Robespierre the Incorruptible and the Terror of 1793. It had demonstrated anew what an inexact science violence is as an instrument of social change, what terrible and unexpected side effects it has. And so, in the end, although the person of Karl Armstrong had aroused considerable sympathy on the Left, his actions had not sparked the revolution that he had hoped for. Instead they had brought about a renewal of the peace movement's original commitment to nonviolence. That renewal was to be Robert Fassnacht's memorial, and, as James Michener so deftly noted, Karl Armstrong's unwitting contribution to his times.

Postscript

Stephanie Fassnacht never remarried. She is employed today as a computer programmer with the Institute for Poverty Research in Madison. Her son Christopher, after graduating from Harvard University in physics and serving in the Peace Corps, now works for the Harvard-Smithsonian Institute of Astrophysics in Cambridge, Massachusetts. Heidi and Karin recently graduated from the University of Wisconsin in geology and forestry, respectively. Professor Heinz Barschall, who returned to finish out his teaching career on the Madison campus, had the opportunity to teach Heidi. "She was clearly the best student in the class," he said.

Fred Harvey Harrington, after a stint with the Ford Foundation in India, returned with his wife, Nancy, to Madison, where he is at work on his memoirs.

Professor George Mosse retired in 1988 but still accepts invitations to lecture at universities throughout the world. In his last years of active teaching he was often heard to say that, in spite of everything, he missed the students of the sixties.

Professor William Appleman Williams died of cancer in Newport, Oregon, in 1990. "With passionate argument and complex analysis, he championed self-determination for all people," the New York Times *noted in its obituary.*

After a bout with liver cancer, Harvey Goldberg passed away in 1987. His executors discovered a stock portfolio that the secretive professor had managed himself. He had died a millionaire.

Jim Rowen, still married to Susan McGovern, is an investigative reporter for the Milwaukee Journal.

Scott Nelson, whose anxiety attacks relating to Karl Armstrong continued for several years after the sentencing, eventually settled down to raise a family in his home town of River Falls, where he owns a swimming pool and spa business.

Mark Knops, married and the father of two, recently received a law degree from Arizona State University in Tempe.

Lynn Schultz, married for the second time, resides quietly in a small town outside Madison, shunning all inquiries about her past.

Paul Armstrong, arrested in a sting operation in Minneapolis in 1981, died on a prison operating table in 1986.

Mira, Lorene, Karl and Dwight Armstrong, all divorced, and their mother Ruth all reside in the Madison area, where they remain a tight-knit family. Dwight, after serving three years in Indiana State Prison for drug manufacturing, now works in the produce business and shares an apartment with Karl, who still sells fruit juice from his stand next to Memorial Library. On the twentieth anniversary of the Mifflin Street block party in 1989, he stunned a reunion of sixties radicals, including mayor re-elect Paul Soglin, by apologizing for the bombing.

David Fine, after earning a law degree from the University of Oregon, was denied admission to the Oregon Bar, in part on the strength of testimony from Special Agent (retired) George Baxtrum suggesting that David was still covering up aspects of his involvement in the Army Math bombing. Fine now works as a paralegal with a Portland firm specializing in patent law.

Leo Burt was never found.

Index